Heroes and Legends: The Most Influential Characters of Literature

Thomas A. Shippey, Ph.D.

THE
GREAT
COURSES

PUBLISHED BY:

THE GREAT COURSES
Corporate Headquarters
4840 Westfields Boulevard, Suite 500
Chantilly, Virginia 20151-2299
Phone: 1-800-832-2412
Fax: 703-378-3819
www.thegreatcourses.com

Thomas A. Shippey, Ph.D.

Professor Emeritus
Saint Louis University

Professor Thomas A. Shippey is Professor Emeritus at Saint Louis University. He holds B.A., M.A., and Ph.D. degrees from the University of Cambridge. Professor Shippey began teaching at the University of Birmingham in England and became a Tutorial Fellow of St. John's College, Oxford, and University Lecturer in English at the same university. He subsequently held the Chair of English Language and Medieval Literature at the University of Leeds before moving to the Walter J. Ong, S.J., Chair of Humanities at Saint Louis University. He has been a Visiting Professor at Harvard University and The University of Texas at Austin.

Professor Shippey has published more than 100 articles, mostly in the fields of Old and Middle English language and literature but also on Old French, Old Norse, and comparative medieval literature. He also has taken a long-standing interest in modern fantasy and science fiction, collaborating with the science fiction author Harry Harrison on three novels and coauthoring three more with him. Professor Shippey is a regular reviewer for *The Wall Street Journal* on both medieval and modern topics and writes for several other journals, including *The Times Literary Supplement* and the *London Review of Books*. In recent years, he was President of the International Society for the Study of Medievalism. He is now a member of the Editorial Board for the series National Cultivation of Culture and a contributor to the *Encyclopedia of Romantic Nationalism in Europe*. He is, however, probably best known for his three books on J.R.R. Tolkien. He was an adviser on pronunciation for Peter Jackson's three *Lord of the Rings* movies and figures prominently on the backup DVDs of all three.

Professor Shippey has given invited lectures and keynote speeches at conferences in at least 25 states, Washington DC, and more than 10 countries in Europe. Former students of his are professors at a number of major universities and colleges in Europe and America. Often replayed on television is his appearance in *The Story of English*, hosted by Robert McCrum and Robert MacNeil, in which he conducted a dialogue in Old English and Old Norse to show how misunderstandings could arise in a bilingual culture. He recently cotaught an innovative online course on philology through Tolkien for the Mythgard Institute and is working on a book on Old Germanic poetry generally, provisionally entitled *How the Heroes Talk*.

Professor Shippey's books include *The Road to Middle-earth: How J.R.R. Tolkien Created a New Mythology*; *Beowulf: The Critical Heritage* (with Andreas Haarder); *J.R.R. Tolkien: Author of the Century*; and his edited collection *The Shadow-Walkers: Jacob Grimm's Mythology of the Monstrous*. The last two of these won Mythopoeic Society Scholarship Awards in 2001 and 2008, respectively. He also received a Distinguished Scholarship Award in 1996 from the International Association for the Fantastic in the Arts. ∎

Table of Contents

Table of Contents

Table of Contents

Disclaimer

In this guidebook, the spelling of character names in literature from antiquity and the Middle Ages may vary according to particular sources used by the professor.

Heroes and Legends:
The Most Influential Characters of Literature

Scope:

Storytelling, and the creation of heroes and heroines to tell stories about, is the most universal human art form. Over the millennia of human history, millions of tales, novels, romances, and epics have been written and published, and many more must have been told in the far longer millennia of prehistory. The vast majority vanished without a trace once their immediate purpose had been served—forgotten, discarded, out of print.

A small number survive and become classics. Of that small number, an even smaller number does more than survive: They inspire imitations, sequels, remakes, and responses. It is the heroes and heroines—and sometimes the villains—of these super-survivors who have created and continue to create our imaginative world. "Don't the great tales never end?" asks the hobbit Sam Gamgee in J.R.R. Tolkien's *The Lord of the Rings*. Sam has good reason to see that the answer is: No, they don't.

This course considers a selection of the men and women—and, in one case, monsters—who are at the heart of the "great tales." Their history spans 3,000 years, from the epics of Homer to the latest publishing and multimedia sensations, such as Harry Potter. The characters in them have given words to the language, such as "odyssey" or "quixotic." They have powerfully affected political history, as in the case of Harriet Beecher Stowe's Uncle Tom, who brought forward, perhaps even enabled, the abolition of slavery. No one can be sure what effect the grim warning of George Orwell's *Nineteen Eighty-four* had on generations of politicians, but the word "Orwellian" remains very much alive in our political rhetoric. We do know that Ian Fleming's James Bond story *From Russia with Love* was one of John F. Kennedy's favorite books. Great-tale heroes have also created whole genres of fiction, as Sherlock Holmes did for the detective story and Dracula did for vampires. Sometimes they have revived them, as Tolkien's hobbits and heroes did for epic fantasy, now once again popular in the mass market. Many characters have become literally iconic—images that everyone recognizes—such as James Fenimore Cooper's Deerslayer, the American rifleman, or Robin Hood with his bow, both of them embodying the same spirit of freedom in the greenwood though hundreds of years and thousands of miles apart. Generations of women have had their resolve strengthened not to submit to domination and abuse by the (very different) presentations of female courage and independence in Chaucer's Wife of Bath, Jane Austen's Elizabeth Bennet, and Alice Walker's Celie.

Heroic continuity, however, is only one part of this course's thematic structure. Although some things seem to be universal, such as our admiration for courage, even heroes and heroines are affected by changing cultural values and, in their turn, contribute to those changes. The tale of Arthur's queen Guinevere would have been impossible without the medieval cult of romantic love, which would have seemed alien and unreasonable to earlier heroes, such as Odysseus or Beowulf. Not only would the story of Robinson Crusoe have been physically impossible before the European age of discovery, but Robinson's very thought processes are those of the new age of capitalism. Both Orwell's Winston Smith and Fleming's James Bond are products of the Cold War era, the one expressing fear; the other, defiance of the new specter of totalitarianism, imposed from within or without. Tolkien's hobbits clearly represent the spirit of the citizen armies of the two World Wars, their essentially peaceful nature exceeded only by their determination to do their duty.

By studying these characters, the super-successes of literature, you will come to understand the secrets of super-success: the new idea, yes, but also the old ideas and images reshaped, sometimes coming back after all memory of them seems to have faded. You will also sense the great currents of historical and cultural change to which the authors have reacted and that their characters embody and express. Most of all, the "great tales" offer an insight into the human heart, in all its variety and complexity, that nothing else can provide. ■

Frodo Baggins—A Reluctant Hero
Lecture 1

W hy do some fictional characters hold our attention, not just for a few days or months but for decades, even generations? In this course, we'll look at some of literature's most compelling heroes and legends—characters as diverse as Beowulf and Elizabeth Bennet—to try to understand what it is about them that captures our imagination. Why did the adventures of Odysseus enthrall the ancient Greeks, and why have they continued to captivate readers to the present day? What made Sherlock Holmes a celebrity in Victorian England, and why does he continue to be a bankable hero in 21st-century Hollywood? In this course, we'll meet many heroes, heroines, and villains that will help us answer these questions.

A Pivotal Moment for Frodo and Sam

- A pivotal moment in *The Lord of the Rings* comes near the end of the second volume of the trilogy, when Frodo Baggins and his companion Sam have gone off on their own to try to carry out their mission. That mission is to get to the heart of Mordor, the land of the Dark Lord, and there, to throw the Ring of Power into the fires of the Cracks of Doom. This is the only way to destroy it and, thus, break Sauron's power forever.

- The two companions know they're facing thousands of goblins and trolls and the Dark Lord himself, and there's another threat they don't know about: Shelob, the giant spider, who guards the secret entrance to Mordor. Even if they get past her and through all the Dark Lord's inner defenses, even if they manage to destroy the Ring, they don't have a plan for how to get back. It's a suicide mission.

- Frodo and Sam pause to rest and begin to talk about legends and old adventures. Sam remarks that the two are in a legend now and speculates that one day, someone may write a book about them, making Frodo "the famousest of the hobbits." In response, Frodo laughs, believing that the idea of himself as a hero in a book is genuinely funny.

- Nothing like laughter has been heard in the ruined land on the outskirts of Mordor for thousands of years. In such a place, Frodo's laughter is a kind of exorcism. It dispels the gloom and defeatism that are among the chief weapons of the Dark Lord.

- Shortly afterward, Sam and Frodo go to sleep, with their minds at rest. It's an undramatic moment, but it sheds light on the question of what makes some characters unforgettable and some stories, such as *The Lord of the Rings*, so successful: Nothing has the same charm as the completely unexpected—unless it's the unexpected that we've been unknowingly anticipating.

Unexpected Heroes
- There are likely many secrets to the unparalleled success of Tolkien's work, but among them must be the hobbits Bilbo and Frodo. Can hobbits—small, dedicedly unwarlike creatures without strength or courage—be heroes? Although they are certainly unexpected heroes, they seem to be the kind of heroes that readers were waiting for—without knowing they were waiting. What caused that situation?

- Literary talent and inspiration are, of course, among the requirements for lasting success in the world of fiction. But an author's responses to events and changing cultural values are also among those requirements. Further, writers don't just respond to changing cultural values, but they also help to shape them.

- In Tolkien's case, he was responding, in part, to the two World Wars. Two of Tolkien's three closest friends died in World War I, and perhaps even more significant than their deaths was the way in which they died: without romance or glory and without ever seeing the men who killed them. This impersonal element led to a paradox.
  ○ On the one hand, more and more people were being required to behave heroically; on the other hand, after all those impersonal

Much of Tolkien's world is medieval—full of knights and dragons—but it's also contemporary in the picture it gives of the nature of true heroism.

and mechanical deaths, it was no longer possible to believe in the traditional images of heroism, brave charges, and gallant stands.

○ This dominant mood was expressed in a post-1918 war memoir by the novelist Robert Graves: *Good-Bye to All That*.

• After 1918, traditional heroism seemed to be impossible. The most common reaction was cynicism, as with Graves, but what those who were not cynics were waiting for—whether they knew it or not—was an image of a new style of heroism that they could believe in and not feel cynical about. That's what Tolkien provided with the hobbits.

Bilbo: A New Heroic Style
• In the early stages of Tolkien's novel *The Hobbit*, Bilbo is anything but a hero compared with the fierce dwarves. In fact, Bilbo does the worst thing a creature can do in the old heroic world: He loses

self-control. When Thorin tries to recruit him for an expedition to kill the dragon Smaug, Bilbo shrieks and falls down, "shaking like a jelly." Right from the start, on an old heroic scale of 1 to 10, Bilbo is a 0. But throughout the book, he rises steadily up the scale, with perhaps five main turning points.

o In chapter 5, when Bilbo becomes separated from the dwarves as they try to make their escape from the goblins, he comes to a goblin tunnel. He draws his elvish blade, finds it comforting, and goes on to meet the strange creature Gollum, win a riddle-contest with him, and make his own escape.

o Bilbo takes another step at the start of chapter 6. He has just made up his mind that it is "his duty," having escaped from the tunnels, to go back and look for the dwarves when he overhears the dwarves deciding to leave him in the tunnels. At this moment, Bilbo, for the first time, is definitely ahead of the dwarves when it comes to courage.

o More clearly marked is the moment in chapter 8 when Bilbo wakes up to find himself being attacked by a giant spider and manages to kill it. He feels "a different person," enough of an old-style hero by this time to give his sword a name, Sting.

o But Bilbo's peak of courage comes in chapter 12 when he conquers his own fear and goes down the tunnel to the cave of Smaug to steal the cup.

o The final step up the heroic scale for Bilbo comes when he creeps away from the dwarves and hands over the priceless Arkenstone jewel to Bard and the Elvenking for them to use as a bargaining point against the dwarves. This is courage of a different kind because it could be seen as dishonorable, even treacherous.

• Bilbo's heroism is different from traditional saga–style heroism in important ways. First, none of his five main turning points (except the last, to some extent) is recognized by the outside world. They all take place when Bilbo is alone, and most of them when he is in the dark. His courage is shown in conquering his own fear. Further, Bilbo's decision concerning the Arkenstone represents moral courage—doing what many would call wrong and accepting the risk of blame. Both styles of courage seem especially relevant to the modern world.

Frodo's Heroism

- Frodo, too, starts off fairly low on the scale of heroism. When Gandalf first explains to him about the Ring and the danger it creates, his response is: "I wish it need not have happened in my time." For those of Tolkien's generation, that phrase was reminiscent of Neville Chamberlain's claim that the agreement he made with Hitler in 1938 had brought "peace in our time." The words "in our time" or "in my time" were associated with appeasement and shirking one's duty.

- Like Bilbo, Frodo improves slowly. His first real step up the scale comes at the end of the Council of Elrond. None of the leaders of Middle-earth can decide what to do about destroying the Ring, though they all agree that it must be done, and it must be done by taking it to the heart of the Dark Lord's realm of Mordor. Faced with this task, everyone falls silent. Then Frodo stands up, filled with dread, and says, "I will take the Ring … though I do not know the way."

- Unlike Bilbo, Frodo is not on his own and he's not in the dark, but he shows a similar kind of understated courage. What Frodo must overcome is his own fear, and he gets no help in doing so. And that continues to be his style. He plugs through the Dead Marshes, around the Black Gate, past Shelob the spider, and into Mordor itself.

- In addition to his own fear, Frodo must also overcome temptation. He is offered repeated opportunities to avoid his duty—to hand over the Ring or use it himself. He and Sam are also tempted, in the Land of Shadow, to do the expedient thing and kill Gollum.

- They have every excuse for doing so, because Gollum would not hesitate to kill them if he could get back the Ring. But another lesson learned in Tolkien's time was that just because the other side does something, it doesn't mean you should do it, too.

- Frodo and Sam feel pity for Gollum, and they spare him, as Bilbo did in *The Hobbit*. The hobbits are big enough—spiritually, not physically—not to take advantage.

- Ironically, pity for Gollum is vital because Frodo fails at the last temptation and chooses not to destroy the Ring. It is Gollum, in the end, who destroys it.

- It's striking that after achieving his quest, which makes him, in a way, the major hero of *The Lord of the Rings*, Frodo increasingly fades out. He plays very little part in the liberation of the Shire. Back home, his deeds aren't recognized. He never really recovers from the physical and mental wounds he has suffered. And Sam is pained to discover how little respect he gets.
  - Frodo receives the kind of treatment that our own veterans have often received: not much in the way of thanks, honor, or rehabilitation.

  - That's part of the modern heroic style, as well. Heroism is lonely while you're doing it and unrecognized once it's over. But that just makes it more heroic because there's nothing to keep you at your duty except your own sense of duty.

- Tolkien created characters who expressed the feelings and experiences of the men and women of the last century's citizen armies. They were not professionals and not necessarily volunteers, yet they were often called on to perform tasks that the warrior elites of the past would have regarded as impossibly brave.

Essential Reading

Tolkien, *The Hobbit*.

———, *The Lord of the Rings*.

Suggested Reading

Colebatch, *Return of the Heroes*.

Garth, *Tolkien and the Great War*.

Haber, ed., *Meditations on Middle-earth*.

Shippey, *Tolkien*.

Questions to Consider

1. What do you think makes a hero or heroine? What qualities do you most admire?

2. This lecture argues that ideas of heroism changed in Tolkien's lifetime (1892–1973). Have they changed in yours?

Frodo Baggins—A Reluctant Hero
Lecture 1—Transcript

What makes some fictional characters unforgettable? Not just successful, but super-successful, lastingly successful. Why do some characters in some stories grab our attention and then hold our attention, not just for a few days or months, but for decades, even generations?

In this course we're going to try to figure that out. We'll look at some of literature's most compelling heroes and legends, characters as diverse as Beowulf and Elizabeth Bennet, and we'll try to understand just what it is about them that captures our imagination. Why did the adventures of Odysseus enthrall the ancient Greeks, and why have they continued to captivate all kinds of readers right up to the present day? Or think about Sherlock Holmes. What made him a veritable celebrity in Victorian England? And why does he continue to be a bankable hero in 21st-century Hollywood? These are just a few of the topics we'll be tackling together.

But where to begin? Well, I suppose we could go back to the classic myths of Greece and Rome, and we will be spending some time with those stories. But I thought we'd start with a less likely work of fiction, indeed, with the biggest and most unlikely literary success of my lifetime, which by now is quite a long one. I'm referring to JRR Tolkien's *Lord of the Rings*.

Now, the central protagonist of this work, Frodo Baggins, is probably not the first character who pops into your head when you think of the word "heroic." And that's precisely the reason he's such a great character to start with. By exploring what makes Frodo an appealing hero for millions of Tolkien fans worldwide, we can gain fresh, even unexpected insights into that important question I asked a few moments ago. What makes some fictional characters, some heroes and heroines, unforgettable? Let's see what Frodo Baggins has to teach us.

The Lord of the Rings is a long book, originally printed as three separate volumes, a thousand pages and more than half a million words. And if you asked a hundred people what was its pivotal moment, you'd probably get a hundred different answers. But for me, the moment is this one. It comes near the end of the second volume. Frodo and his companion Sam have gone off on their own, away from all their friends and supporters, to try to carry out their mission, which is to get to the very heart of Mordor, the land of the Dark Lord, and there throw the Ring of Power into the fires of the Cracks of Doom. This is the only way to destroy it, and so break Sauron's power for ever.

They've made their way over the mountains and through the Dead Marshes. They've been joined by Gollum, the only creature who may be able to guide them into Mordor, though they know he's very untrustworthy. They've been captured and released again, and they've seen terrifying signs of the power of the Dark Lord and his servants, the Ringwraiths. They know they're facing thousands of goblins and trolls and the Dark Lord himself, and there's another threat they don't know about, caused by the treachery of Gollum. That's Shelob, the giant spider, who guards the secret entrance. Even if they get past her into Mordor and then through all the Dark Lord's inner defenses and manage to destroy the Ring, they don't even have the beginnings of a plan about how to get back; it's a suicide mission.

They pause to rest where there's a bit of cover between two tall rocks, though the place they're resting is a barren waste, where even the air and water smell bad. And then, Frodo and Sam start to talk, not noticing that Gollum has slipped away; they're talking about legends, old tales, and adventures. "Why," says Sam to Frodo, "we're in one now. The star glass the elf-queen Galadriel gave you, that has some of the light in it from the Silmaril, the long-lost jewel of ancient times. So we're in a legend too." Sam asks, "Don't the great tales never end?" "Why," he says, "maybe someone will write a book about us one day. And people will say, tell us about Frodo and the Ring. Maybe someone will say to his little boy, 'yes, son, Frodo was the famousest of the hobbits, and that's saying a lot.'"

Of course, it's not saying a lot at all, because in the wider world, hobbits, which is what Sam and Frodo are, just aren't famous. No one's ever taken any notice of them except Gandalf the wizard. But when he hears what Sam is saying, Frodo laughs. And it's a good laugh, not sarcastic, long and clear and from the heart. Frodo just thinks the idea of him being a hero in a book is genuinely funny. Now that laugh, there in the ruined land on the outskirts of Mordor, has a startling effect; it's just so out of place. Nothing like it has ever been heard in those parts for thousands of years. To Sam it seems as if even the stones are listening and the barren rocks are leaning over them, as if they can't believe what they've heard. And Frodo laughs again and carries on the joke saying, if he's going to be in a story, then Sam will have to be in it too, and people will ask to hear more about "Samwise the stouthearted," and hear more of the funny way he talks, because it makes them laugh.

In such a place and such a position, that laughter is a kind of exorcism. It dispels the gloom and depression and defeatism, which is one of the chief weapons of the Dark Lord, which makes people give up before they're beaten. And shortly, Sam and Frodo go off to sleep with their minds at rest. It's a very undramatic moment, but then hobbits are undramatic by nature. When the old Ent Treebeard has to make up a line or two to describe the hobbits in the long list he has of the creatures of Middle-earth, he calls them "the laughing-folk, the little people." He's got them exactly right.

This scene, though, does shed light on the question of what makes some characters unforgettable and some stories, like *Lord of the Rings*, super successful. I don't think there will ever be a one-line answer to that, and I'm not going to try to give one now. By the end of this course we will have a much better idea of the many factors that may create a super success. But let's say one thing right away; nothing beats a new idea; nothing has the same charm as the completely unexpected.

Unless it's something completely unexpected which people have been waiting for, waiting for without knowing they were waiting for it, something unexpected which you immediately recognize. That's the ace of trumps. And that is the case with Frodo Baggins and his uncle and predecessor, Bilbo, the hero of Tolkien's much shorter and earlier work, *The Hobbit*.

Let me pick up first on unexpectedness. I don't think anything in the history of world literature has ever been as unexpected as the success of *Lord of the Rings*: hundreds of millions of copies sold in scores of languages; converted into three movies, which themselves set records for sales and viewing figures; regularly top of the list whenever there's a survey of popular favorites; and recognized by fellow authors as having broken the mold of publishing, for Tolkien made heroic fantasy mass market. A typical endorsement came from George Martin, creator of *Game of Thrones*, who said, very generously, of himself and his fellow authors, "We are all still following in Bilbo's footsteps."

And all this came from an Oxford professor who began the whole sequence as tales told to his children. The professional critics just didn't know what to make of him or the work he'd written. Most of the first reviews he got were terrible. It didn't matter. His book became more and more of a cult, the cult spread to the general public, the movies directed by Peter Jackson made the books alive again for a whole new generation, so, unexpected success, even unparalleled success. But what was the secret of it? Many things, I'm sure, but top of the list must be the characters of Bilbo and Frodo, the hobbit heroes of *The Hobbit* and then *The Lord of the Rings*.

But what am I saying? Can hobbits be heroes? We know what heroes are, don't we, at least traditional basic male Mark I heroes? They're big; they're strong; they're fearless. The *Oxford English Dictionary*, which Tolkien worked on, and which he often referred to, says, heroes are "men of superhuman strength, courage, or ability," which hobbits are not. Big and strong? No, hobbits are little, only in exceptional circumstances growing more than four feet tall; nor are they strong and burly, like dwarves. Fearless? Far from it. When Gandalf the wizard tells Bilbo he's going to send him on an adventure, Bilbo says, "I don't want any adventures, thank you," and scuttles back inside his hobbit hole as fast as ever he can, shutting the door firmly behind him. Besides, hobbits are utterly un-warlike. Many years later, at the end of *Lord of the Rings*, when the hobbits have to take back their country, the Shire, from human occupiers and hobbit collaborators, Frodo says, "No hobbit has ever killed another on purpose in the Shire, and it is not to begin now."

As heroes, old style, hobbits seem to have no credentials at all. But they are the heroes just the same. What I'm saying is, they were certainly unexpected heroes, but they were also the kind of hero people had been waiting for without knowing they were waiting for them. Now, why should that be? Here I have to change my tune and talk about something which isn't very laughable at all, and that is Tolkien's own life and, more important, the lives of his contemporaries, the people he wrote for. And though we're no longer his contemporaries, that includes us as well.

Literary talent and literary inspiration are, of course, part of the requirements for lasting success, for unforgettability. But nobody writes in complete isolation. Response to events, response to changing cultural values, that's another requirement as well. And one last generalization here, writers don't just respond to changing cultural values, they also help to change them. As we shall see many times during this course. What I'm talking about this time is war. The major events of Tolkien's life were two world wars. It is hard to convey now the shock effect of World War 1 in particular.

As it happens, I think I am a good person to try to convey that shock effect. It's just chance, but I went to the same high school as Tolkien, King Edward's School, Birmingham. As I'm saying all this, I'm wearing my Old Edwardians tie. I own a copy of the School Service Record 1914–1919, which lists all the alumni who served in World War I. The basic list is 161 pages long, about ten names to the page, and on every page there are names with crosses by them: killed in action. As by chance, it's 11th November today, Armistice day, or Veteran's Day. You'll see I'm wearing a Flanders Poppy in remembrance of the dead. The total number of King Edward's alumni who died in World War I was 254, about three complete graduating classes.

What's even more significant for my purpose today is not the total number, but the way they died. Of Tolkien's three closest friends, one joined the Navy, which was not quite as risky as the Army. The other two became infantry subalterns, like Tolkien. Rob Gilson was shot dead on July 1st 1916, the first day of the Battle of the Somme, leading his platoon into the machine guns. Geoffrey Smith was even unluckier. He was well behind the lines in December 1916 when a German shell landed nearby, and he was nicked by shell splinters. He walked to a dressing station, sent a postcard to his mother saying he'd been slightly wounded but was okay, and died a few days later of gas gangrene—no antibiotics in those days.

Tolkien also fought on the Somme, and survived because he came down with trench fever, a kind of typhus spread by lice, and was sent home to recover. But my point is this: There was no romance or glory about the way Gilson and Smith died. They never saw the men who killed them. It was impersonal. It led to a paradox. On the one hand, and this applied to World War II as well, more and more people were being required to behave heroically, to advance into the machine guns, run convoys through the U-boats, fly bombers into the flak and the fighters. On the other hand, after all those impersonal and mechanical deaths, it was no longer possible to believe in the traditional images of heroism, brave charges, gallant stands. So much so that the dominant mood was expressed, post 1918, in the war memoir by the novelist Robert Graves, which he called *Goodbye to All That*. I met Graves, by the way, as he was an Honorary Fellow of St John's College, Oxford, of which I was also a Fellow. I've talked to both him and Tolkien and another of their contemporaries whom I'll mention later.

But going back to Tolkien and heroism, my point is this. After 1918, traditional heroism seemed to be impossible. The most common reaction was cynicism, as with Graves, goodbye to all that. But not everyone likes being cynical. What people wanted, what they were waiting for, whether they knew it or not, was an image of a new style of heroism, which they could believe in and not feel cynical about. That's what Tolkien provided with the hobbits. And although he also found ways of bringing back very traditional images, like the death in battle of Théoden King, or the lady Éowyn's fight with the foul Dwimmerlaik, the hobbits were totally unexpected.

Now, the new heroic style. The one suddenly relevant to the twentieth century and the twenty-first. How does that work? How is it shown in Frodo, and before him in his uncle Bilbo? I'll take Bilbo first because his trajectory is easiest to describe. In the early stages of Tolkien's novel *The Hobbit*, he is anything but a hero, as compared with the fierce, grim dwarves, creatures from the old heroic world. In fact, Bilbo does the worst thing you can do in the old heroic world, which is lose self control. When Thorin tries to recruit him for their expedition to kill the dragon Smaug and says it's an expedition from which some "may never return," he shrieks and falls down, "shaking like a jelly." Right at the start, on an old heroic scale of 1 to 10, Bilbo is a zero. He does a little better in the expedition's first adventure, an encounter with three man-eating trolls, but not much. Just the same, through the book he rises steadily up the scale, with maybe five main turning points.

In chapter 5, when he's gotten separated from the dwarves as they try to make their escape from the goblins, deep under the mountains, he comes round, on his own, in the dark, in a goblin tunnel. He draws his elvish blade, finds it comforting, and goes on to meet the strange creature Gollum, win a riddle-contest with him, and make his own escape.

He takes another step at the start of chapter 6. He has just made up his mind that it is "his duty," having escaped from the tunnels, to go back into them and look for the dwarves, when he hears them discussing what to do. And one of them says, "if we've got to go back into the tunnels to look for him, let's just ditch him." Here Bilbo, for the first time, is definitely one up on the dwarves when it comes to courage.

More clearly marked is the moment in chapter 8, when Bilbo wakes up to find himself being attacked by a giant spider and manages to kill it, "all alone by himself in the dark." He feels "a different person," enough of an old-style hero by this time to give his sword a name, Sting. But Bilbo's peak of courage, clearly signaled as "the bravest thing he ever did," comes in chapter 12 when he conquers his own fear and goes on down the tunnel to the cave of Smaug the dragon to steal the cup. By this time, on our heroic scale, Bilbo must be up to a seven or even an eight. Nevertheless, he still has one step more to take. This comes when he creeps away from the dwarves and hands over the priceless Arkenstone jewel to Bard and the Elvenking for them to use as a bargaining point against the dwarves. This is courage of a different kind, for it could be seen as dishonorable, even treacherous.

I won't try to say where Bilbo now is on the heroic scale, because I think we're now on a different scale. Bilbo's heroism is different from traditional saga-style heroism in important ways. Note that none of Bilbo's five main turning points, except to some extent the last, is recognized by the outside world. They all take place when he is alone, and most of them, when he is in the dark. His courage is shown in conquering his own fear.

His style is markedly non aggressive, except for spiders. No one can imagine Bilbo ever being called *Víga-Bilbo*, "Killer-Bilbo," like a saga hero. What he shows is what some call "cold courage" or "three-o'clock-in-the-morning courage." As for his decision over the Arkenstone, this is clearly "moral courage," doing what many would call wrong in defiance of general opinion and accepting the risk of blame. Both these styles of courage can be seen as especially relevant to the modern world, and here I have a very serious authority to back me up. I mentioned the King Edward's School service book and Tolkien's close friend Geoffrey Smith. If you look across the page from Smith, Geoffrey, you see the entry for Slim, W. J., much later to be Field Marshal Sir William Slim. Slim is generally accepted as the most professionally competent British general of World War II. One thing Slim said about courage was this. The dominant feeling on a modern battlefield, he told his officers, is loneliness—no drums, no bugles, and especially in jungle warfare, no one looking. It calls for a new style of courage—Bilbo's style, lonely courage, and also moral courage. Tolkien very much valued old-style heroic courage, the sort the dwarves would recognize, but he knew something else was needed now as well. Cultural values had changed, in response to changing circumstances.

What about Frodo, Bilbo's successor, in *The Lord of the Rings*? He too starts off pretty low down the scale. When Gandalf first explains to him about the Ring and the danger which it creates, his response is, "I wish it need not have happened in my time." Now, that's a loaded phrase for people in Tolkien's time. It was bound to remind them of what the British Prime Minister Neville Chamberlain said when he came back from a meeting with Hitler in 1938. He waved the agreement which they had made and said he brought "peace in our time." Of course he hadn't. Ever since then, that phrase, "in our time, in my time," has been automatically associated with appeasement, with shirking your duty.

Gandalf tells Frodo that everybody feels like that, but what we all have to do is decide what to do with the time that is given us. Director Peter Jackson used the phrase very effectively in his first *Lord of the Rings* movie. It's remembering what Gandalf says that gives Frodo the courage to go on. Like Bilbo, Frodo improves slowly. But his first real step up comes at the end of the Council of Elrond. What's happened is that after a very long meeting called by the elf-lord Elrond, none of the leaders of Middle-earth can decide what to do about destroying the Ring, though they all agree that's what has to be done, and it has to be done by taking it to the heart of the Dark Lord's realm of Mordor. Faced with this, everyone, all the leaders and the heroes, all fall silent. Then Frodo stands up, filled with dread, and really only wishing that he could stay safe in Rivendell, and says, "I will take the Ring [...] though I do not know the way."

Unlike Bilbo, Frodo is not on his own, and he's not in the dark; but he shows a similar kind of courage. It's understated. It's not obviously heroic. What Frodo has to overcome is his own fear, and he gets no help in doing so. That continues to be his style. He goes on, not quite on his own, because he has Sam with him, but they plug on through the Dead Marshes, round the Black Gate, on past Shelob the spider, and into Mordor itself. And what Frodo has to overcome is not just his own fear, it's temptation. He's offered repeated opportunities to avoid his duty. To hand over the Ring, or to use it himself.

He and Sam are also tempted in the Land of Shadow to do the expedient thing and kill Gollum. They have every excuse for doing so, because Gollum would not hesitate to kill them if he could get back the Ring. But something we again learned during Tolkien's century was that just because the other side does something, that doesn't mean you should do it too. Frodo and Sam feel pity for Gollum, and they spare him, as Bilbo did in *The Hobbit*. The hobbits are big enough—spiritually not physically—not to take advantage. And ironically, pity for Gollum is vital. Because Frodo fails at the last temptation and chooses not to destroy the Ring. It is Gollum, in the end, who destroys it.

It's striking that after achieving his quest, which makes him, in a way, the major hero of *The Lord of the Rings*, Frodo increasingly fades out. He plays very little part in the liberation of the Shire. Back home his deeds aren't recognized. He never really recovers from the physical and mental wounds he's suffered, and Sam is pained to discover how little respect he gets.

I said, didn't I, that Tolkien was a veteran. Frodo gets the kind of treatment that our own veterans have often received, not much in the way of thanks, honor, rehabilitation. That's part of the modern heroic style as well—lonely while you're doing it, and unrecognized once it's over. But that just makes it more heroic, because there's nothing to keep you at your duty except your own sense of duty. What Tolkien did, putting it very briefly, was create characters who expressed the feelings and the experiences of the men and women of last century's citizen armies, not professionals, not all of them even volunteers, but often called on to do tasks which the warrior-élites of the past would have regarded as impossibly brave. Tolkien's world is in obvious ways early medieval, full of knights and dragons and creatures out of fairy tale. But what I'm saying is that it's very strongly contemporary as well, especially in the picture it gives of the nature of true heroism. And that's been a major reason for his success. People recognized what he was saying, both about the new nature of heroism and about the new nature of evil, though that last bit is another story.

He brought back the heroes in a way we can understand, and that new way is framed for me, as it happens, by three men I've actually met, talked to, shaken hands with. Robert Graves, who said "goodbye to all that." Slim, who told us, "No, things are the same as they always were, only they've gotten harder." And Tolkien, who brought the two together: the heroic style of Thorin, Théoden, and Aragorn, which Graves thought we'd said "goodbye" to, and the heroic style of Frodo and Bilbo, the one Slim would have recognized—lonely, in the dark, understated, and now, as in Tolkien's time, awfully familiar to millions of veterans, and civilians too.

In this course we'll be looking at many different heroes, and heroines, and villains too, and we'll see many different styles. Many different responses as well to changing cultural values. We'll see as well that while authors respond to those changing values, the characters they create also help to shape them, sometimes decisively. The way I'd put it is just to remember what Sam asks, "Don't the great tales never end?" And the answer is, "No. They don't."

Odysseus—The Trickster Hero
Lecture 2

The legendary Greek hero Odysseus is one of the few literary characters who have given a word to the English language—in this case, "odyssey," meaning a long journey, full of exciting adventures. Odysseus himself has also become something of a symbol. For us, he symbolizes the urge to explore, to know, to push beyond the boundaries. In this lecture, we'll focus on what makes Odysseus different from the other Greek heroes who surround him, such men as Achilles, Ajax, and Diomedes. They fit our standard definition of hero: strong and fearless. Odysseus is those things, too, but he's also something else: *polymetis*, "the man of many wiles." Odysseus is a trickster.

Background to *The Odyssey*

- The starting points of European literature are *The Iliad* and *The Odyssey*, two epic poems in ancient Greek, long said to be by the blind poet Homer. Odysseus is a prominent figure in the first and the central figure of the second.

- *The Iliad* tells the story of a pivotal moment in the first known event in European history: the Trojan War. In that war, a Greek alliance besieged and, after 10 years, destroyed the city of Troy through the famous stratagem of the wooden horse, a stratagem that was, of course, devised by Odysseus.

- *The Odyssey* then tells the story of Odysseus's return home after the war to the island of Ithaca, a voyage that took him 10 years. *The Odyssey* starts near the end of that 10-year return trip, for most of which Odysseus has been held captive by the nymph Calypso on her island.

- Odysseus has been absent from Ithaca for 20 years, and the nobles there want him declared dead. They also want his wife, Penelope, to choose one of them as her husband, who will inherit

Odysseus's property. To force her into this decision, a crowd of prospective suitors has moved in, demanding to be feasted every day. The suitors also mean to kill Penelope's son, Telemachus, as a potential avenger.

- Thus, the poem has three strands: (1) At the start, it follows Telemachus's attempts to dodge the suitors and round up support; (2) at the end, it details Odysseus's return and the cunning tactics he uses to eliminate Penelope's suitors; (3) in between, it tells of Odysseus's release by Calypso and his eventual washing up on the shore of Phaeakia.

- At the Phaeakian court, Odysseus is asked to tell his story, which he does. This central core of the poem is the real odyssey. It covers Odysseus's 10 adventures from leaving Troy to reaching Calypso, including his dealings with Circe the witch, his survival after hearing the song of the Sirens, and other famous stories.

Encounter with the Cyclops

- After leaving Troy, Odysseus and his crew are blown off course to the Land of the Lotus-Eaters. There, the inhabitants eat a plant that makes them so happy they never want to leave. Odysseus manages to escape with his addicted crewmen and lands his ships on an island, from which they can see smoke rising from another island nearby. Curious, Odysseus sets off with one ship to explore the other island and look for provisions.

Because his fellow Cyclopes have no social organization, they fail to help Polyphemus after he has been blinded by Odysseus.

- Odysseus finds the land of the Cyclopes. These are giants

who have only one eye, in the middle of their foreheads. They're completely uncivilized, with no social organization. Each lives by himself in a cave, herding flocks of sheep and goats and living off milk and cheese. They don't know how to make bread or wine. They're also man-eaters.

- Odysseus finds the cave of the giant Polyphemus and notes the sheep pens, the pails of milk, and the racks of cheeses. His men want to take the provisions and return to the ship, but Odysseus decides they should wait inside the cave to see the giant. When Polyphemus returns, he seals the cave with an enormous boulder.

- Odysseus appeals to Polyphemus, reminding him that they are guests, and Zeus, father of the gods, is the protector of guests. Polyphemus is unmoved; he seizes two crewmen, dashes their brains out, and eats them raw. He plans to eat the men two at a time, at breakfast and dinner.

- Polyphemus falls asleep as soon as he's eaten, but Odysseus can't kill him because he and his men will still be trapped in the cave. And although Polyphemus will open the cave in the morning, he'll guard the entrance to prevent the men from sneaking out.

- Odysseus considers his resources, notes his enemy's weakness—his one eye—and makes a plan. He and his men fashion a stake from an olive tree Polyphemus has in the cave. Odysseus then offers Polyphemus wine, to which the giant is unaccustomed. Polyphemus asks Odysseus's name and promises him a gift in return for the wine. Odysseus says that his name is Nobody, and Polyphemus says that his return gift will be to eat Nobody last.

- During the night, as Polyphemus lies drunk, the men heat the olive spike in the fire and thrust it into the giant's one eye. He howls for help, and other Cyclopes come from their caves nearby and ask who has attacked him. Polyphemus, of course, shouts out, "Nobody did it," and the other Cyclopes simply return to their caves.

- In the morning, Polyphemus rolls the rock aside to let the sheep out; he sits by the door, running his hands over the sheep to ensure that there is no man with them. But Odysseus has tied the big rams together in threes, using strips of willow from the giant's bed, and slung a man under each one. He goes out last, under the biggest of the rams.

- Having escaped, the Greeks round up as many sheep as they can, load up their galley, and row for saltwater. In spite of the pleas of his crew, Odysseus taunts Polyphemus, telling him who blinded him. The giant, whose father is the sea god Poseidon, prays to his father to put a curse on Odysseus. Although the hero's divine protector, Athene, will not allow Odysseus to be drowned, Poseidon sees to it that it takes 10 years for him to reach home. And in those 10 years, he loses all his companions.

Cultural Values

- As this story shows, Odysseus is certainly tricky and resourceful, but is he a good leader? He's a survivor, but the people who are with him often don't survive for long. This brings us to the issue of differences in cultural values. A hero in one culture may be very different from a hero in another.

- Odysseus's cultural values are those of a Heroic Age, meaning a particular set of social circumstances. These circumstances have arisen only twice in European history: once after the fall of the Roman Empire (400–600 A.D.) and once earlier, at a time that is difficult to pinpoint.
  - Most people think that Homer created his poems about 750 years before the birth of Christ. The Trojan War took place perhaps 300 years before that.

  - Archaeology has revealed that the Greek cities that launched the assault on Troy—Mycenae, Tiryns, and Knossos—supported a complex and incredibly bureaucratic civilization, yet Homer knew nothing about their advances.

- The heroes in Homer's poems don't seem to have heard of writing, and most scholars think that Homer himself couldn't read or write. His poems were composed and passed on for centuries by word of mouth.

- The old city-civilizations that Homer's poems commemorate collapsed—so completely that their treasures weren't found until the 19th century. What happened, and what effect did it have?

- Hesiod, a Greek poet from about the same time as Homer, gives us a clear answer: imperial overreach. He tells of a race of heroes destroyed by "grim war." The great cities of southern Greece wasted their energy trying to capture the lands of central Greece (Thebes) and launching a naval attack on Troy, perhaps hoping to seize control of the grain trade with the Black Sea area. The survivors were sitting ducks for new enemies. Since that time, says Hesiod, man had been living in an age of cruelty, deceit, and anarchy.

- In a Heroic Age—a post-collapse age—a primary cultural value is this: Every man for himself. In such a time, there's not much more social organization than the Cyclopes have. Anyone who strays outside his kin group is likely to be made a slave. Authority has no basis except personal violence, and the only moral restraint is the idea that the gods may punish cruelty to guests and strangers.

- These circumstances may account for some of the complexity of Odysseus's character. He might like to be more civilized, but in a Heroic Age, what makes a hero are a sword, spear, and shield and the ability to use them.

Odysseus's Return
- In the time of Odysseus, the Greeks had invented neither democracy nor aristocracy. The Greek heroes were autocrats; for them, power was personal. But that presents a problem for Odysseus when he returns home. He can't reveal himself to his wife and suitors and attempt to claim his rights. The suitors will merely cut his throat. Odysseus must rely on himself and a few advantages: He's tricky;

he has friends among the slaves; and he possesses the useful quality of self-restraint.

- Odysseus returns to Ithaca disguised as an old beggar. He is kicked by his own goatherds, and the suitors throw things at him, but he keeps up his act. His old housekeeper sees through his disguise, but she keeps quiet about Odysseus's identity. Touchingly, his old dog, Argos, also recognizes his master and wags his tail.

- Still, getting rid of more than 100 suitors will be trickier than escaping from the cave of Polyphemus. Odysseus has Eumaeus the swineherd on his side, Eumaeus's friend the cowherd, and Telemachus—all now in on the plot. The hero develops a four-point plan to trap the suitors in the hall where they feast and trick them into allowing him to shoot his old war bow. Once he has the bow and starts shooting, his supporters will fend off the suitors until he has shot all the arrows. By then, the suitors will be panicked, and Odysseus and the others will finish the job.

- The plan doesn't go exactly as expected, but it works. Odysseus is merciless. When those who have been disloyal to him are dead, he rescues his old father from the hovel where he's been living, rejoins Penelope, and resumes his rule over Ithaca.

Essential Reading

Homer (Fitzgerald, trans.), *The Odyssey.*

Suggested Reading

Bradford, *Ulysses Found.*

Finley, *The World of Odysseus.*

Fox, *Travelling Heroes.*

Graves, *Homer's Daughter.*

Hall, *The Return of Ulysses.*

1. Is being a hero compatible with having survival qualities?

2. Have trickster heroes (such as Brer Rabbit or Old Man Coyote) dwindled nowadays to being figures of fun, or do they still exist as role models?

Odysseus—The Trickster Hero
Lecture 2—Transcript

The figure I'm going to talk about in this lecture is the legendary Greek hero Odysseus. He's one of the very few literary characters who have given a word to the English language, and the word is "odyssey." We use "odyssey" to mean a long journey full of exciting adventures. You might say that the long epic poem about Odysseus, which we call *The Odyssey*, was the first "On the Road" story; only Odysseus wasn't riding a Harley or driving a pick-up truck, he was steering a ship, a twenty-oar Greek galley. Long after that first poem about him, though, Odysseus also became something of a symbol. For us, he symbolizes above all the urge to explore, to know, to push beyond the boundaries.

First, though, I want to focus on what makes him different from the other Greek heroes who surround him, the heroes of the Trojan War, men like Achilles and Ajax and Diomedes. They're all capital-H Heroes. As I said in the last lecture, they're big; they're strong; they're fearless. Odysseus is all those things too. But he's something else as well. He's *polymetis*, "the man of many wiles." He's a trickster.

I'm going to concentrate on two examples of his resourcefulness, out of many. But first I need to just give you some background. The very start of European literature are the two long epic poems in ancient Greek, almost three thousand years old, and long said to be by the blind poet Homer, called *The Iliad* and *The Odyssey*. Odysseus is a prominent figure in the first and the central figure of the second.

The Iliad tells the story of a pivotal moment in the very first known event in European history, which was the Trojan War, fully 3,000 years ago. In that war, a Greek alliance besieged and after ten years destroyed the great city of Troy through the famous stratagem of the Wooden Horse, a stratagem which was, of course, devised by Odysseus. *The Odyssey* then tells the story of Odysseus' attempt to return home after the war to the island of Ithaca. Ithaca is only about 1,000 miles from Troy, but the voyage took Odysseus 10 years. So he was away from home for twenty years—ten years spent besieging Troy, another ten trying to get home again.

The Odyssey follows the rule of ancient epics, which is not to start at the beginning. It starts near the end of that 10-year return trip, for most of which Odysseus has been held captive by the nymph Calypso on her island the Navel of the Sea, which many people think must be Malta, at the center of the Mediterranean.

But meanwhile, back in Ithaca, Odysseus has been absent for twenty years, and the nobles of Ithaca want him declared dead. They also want his wife Penelope to choose one of them as her husband, who will inherit Odysseus' property, and to force her into this, a whole crowd of prospective suitors have moved in, demanding to be feasted every day, and literally eating their way through Odysseus' herds and stores. The suitors also mean to kill her son Telemachus, as a potential avenger.

So the poem has three strands. One, at the start, follows Telemachus' attempts to dodge the suitors and round up support. Another, at the end, details Odysseus' return and the cunning tactics of his wipe out of Penelope's suitors. In between, Odysseus is released by Calypso, and eventually washed up on the shore of Phaeakia, which many people think must have been Corfu. But at the Phaeakian court he is asked to tell his story, which he does. This central core of the poem is the real odyssey. It covers Odysseus' adventures from leaving Troy to reaching Calypso, and there are ten of them.

I should say that, to ancient Greeks, these must have been particularly interesting, because they're set in what was, to them, the Wild West, the western Mediterranean, into which Greek sailors were only just starting to probe. Some people think we can still identify the places Homer heard of, like Malta, like Corfu, but also Sicily, the Straits of Messina, Corsica. Odysseus calls up the ghosts of the dead at a great rock by the "Fire-Flamer" river *Pyriphlegethon*, and it sounds very like the Rock of Huelva, in southern Spain, by the Red River or Rio Tinto.

Odysseus' ten adventures include his dealings with Circe the witch, who turns men into beasts; his calling up the ghosts of the dead to get advice from the dead prophet Tiresias; the way he became the only man to hear the Song of the Sirens and survive; and other famous dangers, like the Land of the Lotus Eaters and sailing between the man-eating monster Scylla and the deadly whirlpool Charybdis.

But to highlight the unusual heroic quality I mentioned earlier—Odysseus' trickiness—the adventure I want to detail is his encounter with the Cyclops. What's happened is that after leaving Troy, Odysseus has been blown way off course to the Land of the Lotus-Eaters. There, the inhabitants eat a plant which makes them so happy they never want to leave, or work, or do anything ever again.

As soon as Odysseus realizes, he ties up his addicted crewmen, he shoves them under the rowing benches, and he sets off once more. They find a beach where they can pull up their ships on an island, close to another island, from which they can see smoke rising. Remember that smoke. And Odysseus, curious as always, sets off with one ship to explore and look for provisions. What he has come to is the land of the Cyclopes. They are enormous giants who only have one eye in the middle of their foreheads. They're completely uncivilized with no social organization. Each lives by himself in his cave, herding flocks of sheep and goats and living off milk and cheese, curds and whey. They don't know how to make bread or wine. They're also man eaters.

Odysseus finds the cave of the giant Polyphemus and notes the sheep pens and the pails of milk and racks of cheese. His men, very sensibly say, "let's take the lambs and kids and cheeses and get out of here, back on good salt water." But Odysseus, typically nosy, decides to stick around inside the cave to see the giant. This is a mistake. Polyphemus comes back, brings his sheep inside to milk them, and immediately seals the cave from inside with an enormous boulder. Two dozen ox teams couldn't move it, says Homer.

Odysseus appeals to Polyphemus, reminding him that they are guests, and Zeus, Father of the gods, is the protector of guests. Polyphemus, who, as I said, is completely uncivilized, says he doesn't give a hang for Zeus, seizes two crewmen, dashes their brains out, and eats them raw. He's going to eat the men two at a time, at breakfast and dinner time.

So, you can see, Odysseus has a tactical problem. He's got his sword, and Polyphemus falls asleep as soon as he's eaten. But if Odysseus stabs him or cuts his throat, how are they going to get out? They won't be able to roll the rock aside. And although Polyphemus will open the cave in the morning, to let his sheep out, he guards the entrance so the men don't sneak out with them. But remember, he's only got one eye. So what Odysseus does is what they tell you to do in officer-training courses. He considers his resources, notes his enemy's weakness, and makes a plan. Remember again, Cyclopes don't know about wine. And wine is one of the things Odysseus has been carrying, part of the rations. It's strong wine too, which the Greeks would drink diluted, 20 parts water to one part wine if you believe Homer.

Polyphemus also, like most giants, carries a club, and he's brought an olive tree back to the cave to make into a club. While he's away with his flocks, Odysseus and his men cut a length from the tree, smooth it, sharpen it with their swords, and then hide the stake. Where to hide it? Under the sheep dung, which covers the floor of the cave. Then, when Polyphemus comes back, and after he's had his usual two-man dinner, Odysseus approaches him and offers him the wine, which Polyphemus glugs down, and which, remember, he is not used to. Even the hopelessly uncivilized know they have to make a return gift, and Polyphemus asks Odysseus' name, and promises him a return gift. Odysseus says his name is "Nobody," and Polyphemus says okay, his return gift will be to eat Nobody last. That's a giant joke.

In the night, as Polyphemus lies drunk, the men go to the fire—Cyclopes have fire; remember the smoke rising? They heat up the 6-foot olive spike till it glows, and then they thrust it in the giant's one eye. He howls for help, and other Cyclopes turn up from their caves nearby and ask him who's attacked him. Polyphemus, of course, shouts out, "Nobody did it." And the other Cyclopes—remember, they're a surly lot, with no social organization—they say, "oh, well then," and go away.

In the morning Polyphemus, who is a good shepherd for all his faults, he rolls the rock aside to let the sheep out, but he sits by the door, running his hands over the sheep to see there's no man with them. But Odysseus has tied the big rams together in threes, using strips of willow from the giant's bed, and slung a man under each one. He goes out last, under the biggest of the rams. Then the Greeks do what they should have done at the start, round up as many sheep as they can, load up their galley, and row for salt water.

But Odysseus, typically, won't leave it at that. He has to taunt Polyphemus and tell him who blinded him. So in spite of the crewmen saying, "don't bait him, skipper, he's throwing rocks and you'll give him the range," he shouts out, "if anyone asks you who took your eye, say it was Odysseus of Ithaca, son of Laertes, sacker of cities." And Polyphemus, whose father is the sea-god Poseidon, prays to his father to put a curse on him. So Odysseus incurs the enmity of Poseidon, and although his divine protector, Athene, will not allow Odysseus to be drowned, Poseidon sees to it that it takes ten years for him to return home, and in those ten years he loses all his companions.

You can see, this is a Jack-the-Giant-Killer story, but it's very well told. Everything has its place: the smoke, the wine, the giant boulder, the one eye, the "Nobody" trick, even the sheep dung. Odysseus is certainly tricky and resourceful. But is he a good leader? He's a survivor, but you notice that people who are with him don't survive for long.

This brings up an issue which is going to concern us many times during this course of lectures, which is, different cultural values. A hero in one culture may be a very different thing from a hero in another. Frodo Baggins wouldn't have lasted long as a crewman for Odysseus, and I very much doubt that Odysseus would have been prepared to go over the top with Tolkien's own Lancashire Fusiliers. Odysseus' cultural values are those of a Heroic Age, that's Heroic Age in capital letters, and I mean, a particular set of social circumstances. These circumstances have only arisen twice in European history.

A Heroic Age comes about after the fall of an empire and a traumatic collapse of civilization. So the second European Heroic Age is the one which came about after the fall of the Roman Empire, say about 400–600 AD, the age of King Arthur and of Beowulf. The first Heroic Age is harder to date. Most people think that Homer created his poems about 750 years before the birth of Christ. The Trojan War took place maybe 300 years before that. The strange thing is that archaeology has revealed to us that the Greek cities which launched the assault on Troy—Mycenae and Tiryns, and even more remarkably Knossos on the island of Crete—supported a complex and incredibly bureaucratic civilization.

We know about the civilization from things like the gold death masks of Mycenae and the frescoes of Knossos, with their images of acrobats leaping over bulls' horns in a way which cattlemen say is flat out impossible. We know about the bureaucracy because these ancient cities left thousands of records on baked clay tablets.

The shock is because Homer knew nothing about all this. The heroes of his poems don't seem even to have heard of writing, and most scholars think that Homer couldn't read or write as well. His poems were composed and passed on for centuries just by word of mouth. As for the old city civilizations the poems commemorate, they had collapsed, so completely that no one even found their treasures, not till the 19th century. You have to ask, what happened, and what effect did it have?

Hesiod, a Greek poet from about the same time as Homer, gives a clear answer to what happened. His answer, in a phrase, is what we would call "imperial overreach." Once upon a time, he says, there was a race of capital-H Heroes. "Grim war destroyed them, some […] at seven-gated Thebes, some […] when they crossed the sea to Troy for the sake of Helen. There death shrouded them."

The great cities of southern Greece, in other words, wasted their energy trying to capture the corn lands of central Greece—that's Thebes—and then, in a great naval attack on Troy, maybe hoping to seize control of the grain trade with the Black Sea area. The survivors were sitting ducks for new enemies, wild men coming down from the north. Ever since then, says Hesiod, we've been living in an iron age of cruelty and deceit and anarchy; he wishes he'd never been born into it.

But going back to Odysseus, the point about the cultural values of a Heroic Age, a post-collapse of civilization age, is that it's every man for himself and devil take the hindmost. In a Heroic Age, there's not much more social organization than the Cyclopes have. Anyone who strays outside his kin group is likely to be made a slave. Raiding for women is normal. The fate of women and children, once their protectors have been killed, is very bad.

Old people too. The fate of Odysseus' father Laertes may seem strange to us. At start and end of *The Odyssey* we're reminded that he's living in poverty, out of town, up in the hills of Ithaca, with one slave woman who acts as his carer. But he was a great hero himself! He sailed with Jason and the Argonauts! He was King of Ithaca! Yes, but he's old, and his son is missing In action, and his grandson is too young.

In a Heroic Age your authority has no basis, except personal violence. There's no police, no law except custom. The only moral restraint is the feeling, which Odysseus appealed to with Polyphemus—that the gods look out for guests and strangers and may punish cruel treatment of them. But of course, you can't count on that.

These circumstances may account for some of the complexity of Odysseus' character. I'd put it like this. He'd quite like to be Mr. Nice Guy, but in a Heroic Age, what can you do? If people were to start thinking you're a wimp, you'd be in a slave pen, quick time. In a Heroic Age, what makes a hero? Sword, spear, and shield, helmet, armor, and ability to use them. Lose those, and you can forget about human rights. Democracy hasn't been invented yet.

Odysseus himself certainly isn't democratic. His big intervention in Homer's other poem, *The Iliad*, is to beat up and silence a low-rank soldier who starts talking about going home. However, to be fair, the Heroic-Age Greeks hadn't gotten very far with inventing aristocracy either. It's true, there seems to be a gulf between the ones who call themselves heroes and the rest. I think "heroes" just means the guys with full armor and battle chariots, the ones who fight in the front rank. But even they know what work is. For example, there's a scene when Odysseus, back in Ithaca and disguised as a beggarman, is being taunted by one of the suitors. How does he respond? He says, I'm a beggarman now, but I was a hero once. We could have a match at scything. I bet I could mow more hay than you. We could have a match at plowing. I bet I could plow a straighter furrow.

Later, British noblemen wouldn't talk like that, still less French seigneurs. These Greek heroes aren't democrats or aristocrats. They're autocrats. Power is personal. This means that Odysseus has a problem once he returns home. What's he going to do to get rid of his wife's suitors, reveal himself and claim his rights? What rights? They'll just cut his throat. Call the Ithacan assembly and demand help? His son tried that, and was told, "You're on your own, son."

No, Odysseus has to rely on himself. He does have several advantages. One is, he's tricky. He's a master of deceit, disguise, and tactics. Another is, the nobles of Ithaca may be scheming to replace him, but he has friends among the lower classes. In fact, the slaves. One of the best passages in the poem comes when Odysseus has returned to Ithaca. He's been ferried over by the Phaeakians, who were impressed by his own account of his "odyssey." Now, heavily disguised as an old beggarman, Odysseus is hiding out in the hills with Eumaeus the swine herd, and the two are just chatting.

Odysseus, sticking to his role as a beggarman, tells a pack of lies about his life story but says that he has seen Odysseus, and he is coming home. Eumaeus says, "Good story, but I wish you hadn't put that bit in about Odysseus, I know you're only doing it to get a good reception." Odysseus says, "if I'm telling a lie," which of course he is, "throw me off a rock." And Eumaeus says, "that would get me a good name, wouldn't it, feeding a guest one day and murdering him the next?"

The swine herd really wins that argument. He's dirt-poor; he can't even spare the beggarman a shirt, because he hasn't got one to spare, but he gives what he can. And he very much resents having to send his prize hogs downtown for those idle suitors to eat.

Odysseus has one other useful quality, rare in a capital-H Hero, and that is self-restraint. Normally, you hit a Hero, he hits you back. But Odysseus can keep up his act. Going down into town to make a reconnaissance, still dressed as a beggarman, one of his own goat herds kicks him. Odysseus takes it. A suitor throws a footstool at him, and Odysseus takes the hit. Another throws a cow hoof at him, and he just dodges. There is a dangerous moment when another beggarman sees Odysseus as a competitor and tries to drive him off his pitch. The suitors think this is funny and call for a match, the prize to be a haggis, a kind of blood pudding. Some of them notice, as Odysseus reluctantly strips off, that this old guy looks like a boxer.

But even then Odysseus shows restraint. He thinks to himself, "shall I kill the other beggar? Better not. I'll just knock him down and collect the haggis." But danger is there all the time. His old housekeeper sees through his disguise and recognizes a scar. She keeps quiet. Touchingly, at least to an Englishman like me, his old dog Argos also recognizes him. Argos is twenty now, he was only a puppy when Odysseus left for Troy, and now he's been thrown out on a dunghill to die. But he knows his master, and he just has the strength to wag his tail. Odysseus, old softy that he is, silently wipes away a tear.

Yes, but what about the tactics? Getting rid of more than a hundred suitors is going to be trickier than escaping from the cave of Polyphemus. Odysseus has Eumaeus the swineherd on his side, and Eumaeus' friend the cowherd, and also his son Telemachus, all of them now in on the plot. But they're still outnumbered about a hundred to four. Odysseus develops a four-point plan. First, there are weapons on the wall of the chamber where the suitors continually feast. Get them out. Take them off to be cleaned.

Second, Odysseus is a famous archer. But he left his own great war bow behind when he sailed for Troy. If he can get that back in his hands, okay, tell Penelope to make this a final test for the suitors. The one who manages to string it and pass a complex shooting test will be her husband. Odysseus is confident that no one will be able to do it, but after a few have failed, he'll go up and have a try himself, the old beggarman, just as a joke.

Third, no one must escape to go for reinforcements or weapons. The cowherd will slip out and quietly bar the outer door and lash the bar down. Finally, once Odysseus has the bow and starts shooting, the suitors will still have swords at their belts, and if they have any sense, they will rush him. Odysseus' supporters will put on full armor, with spears and shields, and keep them off till he has shot all his arrows. By then the suitors will be panicked, and Odysseus and his armored helpers will finish the job.

It doesn't work quite according to plan, but it works. Odysseus is merciless. Surrenders are not accepted, except for the bard and the herald, whose office is protected by Zeus. The maidservants, who lay disloyally with the suitors, are strung up to a ship's hawser and hanged. A famous line in the poem is

"Their feet danced for a little while, but not for long." And then Odysseus can rescue his old father from the hovel where he's been living, almost like the old dog Argos; rejoin his faithful wife Penelope; resume rule over Ithaca. Odysseus can be grim, he can be tender hearted—about his old dog, anyway. He can show restraint in the face of provocation. But above all, he's tricky. He's a survivor.

Later ages, I have to say, were not too happy about this. Stern moralists, like Plato, thought that Homer should be banned altogether. Greek dramatists played up Odysseus' reliance on deceit, and as we shall see in the next lecture, the Roman poet Virgil created a kind of anti-Odysseus in his hero Aeneas. Aeneas moves in the same world as Odysseus, Cyclopes included, but his social values are far different from those of a real Heroic Age. And yet Odysseus, under the Roman form of his name, Ulysses, continued to fascinate. Two thousand years after Homer, the Italian poet Dante encountered Ulysses where you might expect to find him, deep down in Hell, in the circle reserved for false counselors. But not even hellfire can break Ulysses' spirit. Dante has him describe, speaking from the heart of the fire in which he burns eternally, how he set out in old age, on one last voyage, for no reason but to see new things. To boldly go, as they say in *Star Trek*, our modern *Odyssey*, where no one has been before.

Another seven centuries later, and Tennyson rewrote the scene without the condemnation in his poem, "Ulysses." Its concluding words are, "To strive, to seek, to find, and not to yield." And we will come across those lines again even later in this course of lectures, set very much in our own time.

"Don't the great tales never end?" Well, you know the answer to that. But they change; they get adapted, often in ways their first creators could never even have imagined, as we shall see in the next lecture. They still speak to us, and their heroes and heroines come back revived. Almost like Dracula, and we shall hear much more of him as well.

Aeneas—The Straight Arrow

Lecture 3

As we've said, the great tales continue, but they may be continued in a different spirit from their originals. Those who decide to continue the great tales may do so in a way that contradicts or even reverses what has been told before. They may fill a gap in an original tale or add new elements that no one could have predicted. In this lecture, we'll explore Virgil's attempt, in his Latin epic the *Aeneid*, to continue—and compete with—*The Iliad* and *The Odyssey*. Virgil's hero, Aeneas, is a kind of anti-Odysseus, an archetypal straight arrow. We'll also see that Virgil writes into the gap, filling in the story of the fall of Troy.

Pius Aeneas

- Homer left a time gap between *The Iliad* and *The Odyssey*. At the end of *The Iliad*, Hector, the great Trojan hero, is dead, and it's certain that Troy is going to fall. *The Odyssey* starts with Odysseus on his way home, after Troy has fallen. Homer does not deal with the Greeks' invasion of Troy or the final destruction of the city, but that's where Virgil starts.

- Just like Homer, Virgil tells his story in flashback, through Aeneas speaking at the court of Queen Dido. The Greeks, including Odysseus, have exploded out of the wooden horse and poured into Troy. The situation is hopeless. Hector, the dead hero, appears to Aeneas in a dream and tells him it's his duty to Troy to get out.

- Aeneas fights his way through the streets but is unable to rescue King Priam, Queen Hecuba, or Princess Cassandra. He is about to take revenge on Helen—the cause of the war—when his mother, the goddess Venus, appears to him in a vision and tells him to consider his own family.

- Aeneas makes his way through the burning city to the house of his father, Anchises. His father also wants to go back to the fight, but Aeneas's wife, Creusa, begs him to save their son and her. One more vision confirms that Aeneas's son, Iulus, must be saved.

- Aeneas makes his way out of Troy. He carries his father on his back and leads his son by the hand. Anchises carries the household gods, and Creusa follows behind. To the Romans, this order of priorities and Aeneas's behavior represented a model of *pietas*. Indeed, at the start of book I, Virgil calls Aeneas *insignem pietate virum*, "man distinguished for *pietas*."

- *Pietas*, in this context, means "propriety." Aeneas, unlike Odysseus, always does what is socially correct. He demonstrates the social values that Virgil (and his imperial patrons) thought most important: respect for the past, for age, and for ancestry; concern for the future destiny of one's bloodline; respect for the gods; and respect for the institution of marriage.

Aeneas and Dido

- In the confusion of the sack of the city, Aeneas holds on to his father, his son, and the household gods, but Creusa goes missing. Of course, he returns to Troy to look for her, but her ghost appears to say goodbye to him. Creusa's death is convenient given the fact that Aeneas is telling much of his story in flashback at the court of Queen Dido, a Phoenician princess who is in the process of founding Carthage. Dido, a widow, falls in love with Aeneas—so much so as to forget propriety.

- The Trojans and Phoenicians go hunting but are caught in a sudden thunderstorm. Aeneas and Dido take shelter in the same cave, and readers are left to guess what happens next. Later, Virgil puts all the blame on Dido. That day was fatal, he says, the cause of lasting grief. But it's Dido who forgot her good name. Nor did she have the decency to keep the affair a secret. According to Virgil, "she calls it marriage, and with that name veils her sin."

- The local king, who was contemplating an alliance with Dido, hears about the affair, as does Jupiter, the father of the gods. He sends

Aeneas a message, telling him that his job is to build Rome, not Carthage. Aeneas prepares for a silent departure, but Dido realizes his intent. Aeneas tells her that his leaving is the will of the gods: *Italiam non sponte sequor*; "I do not seek Italy of my own free will." Dido then commits suicide, falling on her sword.

Virgil's Hidden Agenda

- The *Aeneid* was written during the years 29 to 19 B.C.E. specifically for the emperor Augustus and as a national epic. Among its goals was the wish to give Rome a noble origin—one that would have all the prestige of Homer but not be Greek.

- We can see that Virgil is competing with Homer. Aeneas's itinerary largely follows Odysseus's, and episodes throughout the *Aeneid* echo those in *The Odyssey*. Virgil is attempting to show that he can do just as well as Homer.

- A large part of the aim of the *Aeneid* is to specifically define Roman virtue, an area where the Romans considered themselves superior to the Greeks. That's where *pietas*—social propriety—comes in. But *pietas* also includes social duty: subordinating private wishes and personal happiness to public service, to the *res publica*, the "common good."

- The Romans would say that they invented republican virtue. And they believed that whatever happened to their society, it would still be rooted in that virtue. The proudest thing anyone, including Saint Paul, could say was this: *civis Romanus sum*; "I am a Roman citizen." Thus, Aeneas, for all his royal birth and divine ancestry, never forgets what he owes to the future of Rome.

The Situation in Rome

- The traditional founding of Rome was attributed to Romulus and Remus in 753 B.C.E. There was a belief that Rome was a kind of outlaw offshoot from the nearby city of Alba Longa, which explains the need for a story of noble origins.

After its legendary founding by Romulus and Remus, Rome gained a reputation among its Mediterranean neighbors of refusing to accept defeat.

- The Romans spent many centuries fighting their neighbors, ultimately becoming the "top barbarians" in Italy. They then ran into conflict with established Mediterranean powers, namely, the Carthaginians and the Greeks.

- By about 100 years before Virgil, the Romans were well on their way to ruling a Mediterranean empire, but it's been suggested that they did so perhaps too easily. In contrast to the Greeks, who had been through the kind of Heroic Age we discussed in the last lecture, the Romans did not know "the reverse side of glory, the bitterness of lost battles, the sting of the master's lash."

- That difference would become even more acute in Virgil's time. Julius Caesar had conquered Gaul. The Roman Civil Wars had been terminated by Augustus's victory over Mark Antony and Cleopatra at the Battle of Actium. The Roman Republic had effectively been abandoned, and the Roman Empire was about to be imposed.

Knowing this history, perhaps we can see some of the anxieties that Virgil was trying to alleviate: remorse for the destruction of Carthage, an inferiority complex toward Greece, and guilt over the Trojan War.

- There was also the issue of republican virtue. Rome had been a republic, run politically by the Senate and the people. Would it lose its republican virtue if it became an empire? Virgil's answer was no. The main republican virtue is subordinating one's private wishes to one's public duty, and that's exactly what Aeneas does.

Manifest Destiny

- There is also a strong sense in the *Aeneid* of what we would call "manifest destiny." This idea is heavily reinforced by Aeneas's descent into the underworld.

- In this sequence, we note again a strong sense of competition with Homer. Odysseus did not descend into the underworld but only called up spirits from there. Aeneas goes all the way. What's more, Aeneas's Golden Bough enables him to exit the underworld—a much more difficult task than entering it.

- As Aeneas walks through the underworld, the road forks. To the left is a kind of hell, where sinners are punished. To the right are the Blissful Groves, the homes of the virtuous. It's a very Roman and republican virtue that lands one in the groves, above all, suffering wounds while fighting for one's country. There, Aeneas meets his father, who gives a long prophecy about the glorious future of Rome.

- Once Aeneas emerges from the underworld, we find much more of the idea of manifest destiny: He fights wars to establish himself in Italy and marry Lavinia, the daughter of the Latin king.

Legacies of the *Aeneid*

- For thousands of years Virgil, along with the Bible, was the foundation of Western education. And one major effect of the

Aeneid was to make European countries feel the need for a similar myth of origins, which several of them tried to bolt on to Virgil's story. The British version of this was the "Brutus books."

- The Virgilian ideology was rivaled in popularity by the Virgilian visions, especially his vision of the underworld, which gave so much to Dante's *Inferno*. The figure Dante chooses as his guide through hell is Virgil, because Virgil was the acknowledged expert on the underworld.

- As mentioned at the beginning of the lecture, some writers may choose to continue a story by adding new elements that no one could have predicted. This is what the author Richard Adams did when he turned the great heroes of Virgil and Homer into rabbits in his novel *Watership Down*.
  - The novel begins with a puny rabbit, called Fiver, having a vision of utter disaster coming to his warren. Because he cannot get the chief of the warren to believe him, he and a few others, led by a rabbit called Hazel, make the decision to flee on their own and set up somewhere else.

  - Two similarities are immediately obvious: The rabbits fleeing the doomed warren are like Aeneas and his companions fleeing Troy, and their setting up a new warren on Watership Down is like Aeneas founding a New Troy, which will become Rome. Getting to the new warren is clearly an odyssey, and it's quite like Homer's.

  - One close similarity to *The Odyssey* is that the warren the refugee rabbits reach is much like the land of Homer's Lotus-Eaters. What the rabbits there know but won't admit is that humans feed them to be snared and eaten later. Their comfort and luxury carry a price: death.

  - Like hobbits, Hazel's group of rabbits provides another model of heroism for us. Rabbits are prey, not predators. They're not good at long marches because they scatter, or dawdle, or freeze. But they're more cooperative than human beings. Their weapons are craft and cunning. They're tricksters, like Odysseus, but they use cunning to achieve the goal of Aeneas: to found a new city. Their victory is to survive and breed.

Essential Reading

Virgil (Fitzgerald, trans.), *The Aeneid.*

Suggested Reading

Griffin, *Virgil.*

Quinn, *Virgil's Aeneid.*

Spargo, *Virgil the Necromancer.*

Questions to Consider

1. E. M. Forster once wrote that if he ever had to choose between betraying his country and betraying his friends, he hoped he would have the courage to betray his country. How do you see the balance between public duty and private emotion?

2. What modern stories can you think of that involve descent into the underworld or into an imagined afterlife?

Aeneas—The Straight Arrow
Lecture 3—Transcript

Just picking up on what I said at the end of the last lecture, first, the great tales continue, but they may be continued in a quite different spirit from their originals. Continuators may decide to continue in a way that contradicts, or even reverses, what has been told before. Second, a very productive way of continuing a great tale is to look at it, to see a gap in it, and then to write into the gap. And third, you just can't tell how inspiration will work. Regardless of changing cultural values, someone may add to a tale an element which no one could have predicted. Least of all the original author, hundreds or thousands of years before.

Now, this lecture is about the Trojan hero Aeneas. He is the hero of Virgil's Latin epic, the *Aeneid*. We know a lot more about Virgil and about the *Aeneid* than we do about Homer and the origins of the *Iliad* and the *Odyssey*. But it's clear that Virgil was trying to continue and to compete with the *Iliad* and *the Odyssey*—both at once, a tall order!

Going back to my point one, about continuing in a different spirit, Aeneas is a kind of anti-Odysseus. Odysseus was a trickster. Aeneas is your archetypal straight arrow, the kind of guy they put on recruiting posters. Going back to my point two, what Virgil was doing was writing into a gap. There's a time gap between the *Iliad* and the *Odyssey*. At the end of *the Iliad*, Hector, the great Trojan hero, is dead, and it's certain that Troy is going to fall. The *Odyssey* starts chronologically—though as I said in the last lecture, that's not the way it's narrated—with Odysseus already on his way home, after Troy has fallen. Homer does not deal with the wooden horse, with the Greeks getting into Troy, with the final destruction of the city.

That's where Virgil starts. Though, just like Homer, he tells the story in flashback. Odysseus tells the tale of his odyssey, in flashback, at the Phaeakian court. And Aeneas tells the story of his escape from Troy, in flashback, at the court of Queen Dido. This tale starts with what you might call an enduring "straight arrow" image. The Greeks, Odysseus among them, have exploded out of the Wooden Horse, opened the gates of Troy, and let in the whole Greek army. The situation is hopeless. Hector, the dead hero, appears to Aeneas in a dream and tells him to get out, it's his duty to Troy to get out.

Aeneas fights his way through the streets but is unable to rescue old King Priam, or old Queen Hecuba, or the Princess Cassandra. He is about to take revenge on Helen, the cause of the war, when his mother appears to him in a vision—his mother is the goddess Venus—and tells him to think of his own family. So, he makes his way through the burning city to the house of his father Anchises. His father also wants to go back to the fight, but Aeneas' wife Creusa begs him to save their son and her. One more vision confirms that Aeneas' son Iulus must be saved. And so, Aeneas makes his way out of Troy. He carries his old father Anchises on his back. He leads his little son Iulus by the hand. His father carries the household gods. His wife Creusa follows behind.

That's the image; the man leaving the burning city with all that's precious to him. But note the order of priorities, one, old father; two, little son; three, household gods; and four, wife. We might think that this is not the natural order. But then, we're not Roman straight arrows. To Romans, Aeneas is behaving as a model of *pietas*. And that's exactly what Virgil emphasizes. He calls his hero *pius Aeneas* 20 times during the *Aeneid*, very different from Odysseus *polymetis*, "man of many tricks." Right at the start of book 1 Virgil calls Aeneas *insignem pietate virum*: *virum* = man; *insignem* = distinguished; *pietate* = for *pietas*. Aeneas is the man distinguished by his *pietas*.

But what did Virgil mean by *pietas*? It's an absolutely vital concept in Roman cultural values. Well, *pietas* gives us our word pity. But Aeneas doesn't show much pity for anyone. In fact, in our terms, he'd be a war criminal. Romans were not big on pity. They crucified people, right? *Pietas* could also mean piety, and that's a bit closer. But one shouldn't think of it as going to church and listening to the preacher. It's a more everyday quality, not specifically religious. I would translate the word as "propriety." Aeneas, very unlike Odysseus, always does what is socially correct. He demonstrates the social values Virgil and his imperial patrons thought most valuable, and these are respect for the past, for age, and ancestry; concern for the future destiny of Aeneas' bloodline, which will eventually found Rome; respect for the gods; and last, respect for the institution of marriage. But that last one, like Aeneas' wife fleeing from Troy, comes a long way last. In the confusion of the sack of the city, Aeneas holds on to father, son, and household gods. But his wife Creusa goes missing.

Of course he goes back into the city to look for her. But her ghost appears; this is the fourth ghost or vision to turn up and tell him what to do, and she says, it's no good. "Banish your tears for me. […] Farewell, and love our child." He tries three times to embrace her, but she disappears. One has to say, this is quite convenient. For Aeneas—remember, I said that, like Odysseus, he tells much of his story in flashback—Aeneas is telling the story of his escape from Troy at the court of Queen Dido. Dido is a Phoenician princess who is founding a new city in North Africa, which will become the city of Carthage. And Dido is a widow. So now she knows this stranger is not only a capital-H Hero and the son of a goddess; he is also a widower.

In brief, Dido falls for Aeneas very heavily, so much so as to forget propriety; the Trojans and the Phoenicians go hunting; there's a sudden thunderstorm; Aeneas and Dido take shelter in the same cave; And Virgil does what Hollywood filmmakers used to do long ago, he averts his eyes and lets you guess what happened next. When Aeneas and Dido are back in the frame, however, what Virgil does is put all the blame on Dido. That day was fatal, he says, the cause of lasting grief. But it's Dido who forgot her good name; nor did she even have the decency to keep things secret, to enjoy a *furtivum amorem*, a furtive or secret love. No, "she calls it marriage, and with that name veils her sin."

In an age of very different cultural values one might well say, hold on here, Aeneas did it too. And Dido may have consorted with Aeneas before marriage, that's putting it politely, but marriage is what she wants. Did Aeneas think, "she's just a one night stand?" Anyway, people start to talk. The local king who was contemplating an alliance with Dido gets to hear about it. More importantly, Jupiter, father of the gods, sends Aeneas a message which says: "what are you doing building Carthage? Your job is building Rome! Set sail now!"

Aeneas then, note this, gives orders to get ready silently for departure, but Dido, of course, realizes. Aeneas answers her reproachful and desperate speech by saying, in effect: "I wasn't trying to sneak off," but it looks as if he was. "I never said anything about marriage. Anyway, it's not my fault. You're founding a city. I'm founding a city. And it's the will of the gods." *Italiam non sponte sequor*; "I do not seek Italy of my own free will."

I may have removed the epic dignity which Virgil tries to give to this incident, but I'm not the only person to feel that Aeneas here behaves badly. There's a long mediaeval poem, *Le Roman d'Eneas*, which retells the story, but to a mediaeval audience, not a Roman one, an audience which has been brought up on chivalry, on courtesy, on the duties knights owe to ladies, Well, to such an audience, Aeneas' behavior was all very bad form indeed. Dido then commits suicide, falling on her sword, just like a Roman would. Aeneas, at sea, sees the flame of her funeral pyre.

Perhaps this is the time to consider Virgil's hidden agenda. Hidden from us, may be, very obvious to the people for whom it was written.

The *Aeneid* was written in the 10 years, 29 to 19 BCE, Before the Christian Era. It was very much a poem written for, and read aloud to, the Emperor Augustus. It was also very deliberately, a national epic. Among its goals are the wish to give Rome a noble origin. One, furthermore, which would have all the prestige of Homer, but not be Greek. And as I said at the start, we can see that Virgil is competing with Homer. Aeneas' itinerary largely follows Odysseus'. He even rescues one of Odysseus' crewmen, whom Odysseus left behind in the land of the Cyclopes; typical irresponsible Greek, Virgil hints, how different from reliable, straight arrow Aeneas.

Episodes like Virgil's funeral games for Anchises follow Homer's funeral games for Patroclus in detail, boxing match, check; running race, check; decided by a slip and a fall, check. Homer's chariot race has become a rowing match, but accusations of cheating, check; last boat straggling in damaged to collect a consolation prize, check. And so on. Virgil is showing he can do just as well as Homer, and at the same time, trying to avoid what we call "cultural cringe."

A large part of the aim, however, is to define specifically Roman virtue, an area where the Romans thought they were much superior to the Greeks, and everybody else as well. That's where *pietas* comes in, social propriety. But *pietas* also includes social duty. Subordinating private wishes and personal happiness to public service, to the *res publica*, the common good, civic responsibility. You notice, even now, we can't talk about such things without using Latin words. The Romans would say, we invented republican virtue, and whatever happens to our society, our society will still be founded on it. The proudest thing anyone will be able to say, St. Paul included, is *civis Romanus sum*, "I am a Roman citizen."

And so Aeneas, for all his royal birth and divine ancestry too is the small-r republican hero. He never forgets what he owes to the future of Rome. However, one final part of Virgil's agenda, and perhaps this one really was relatively hidden, may have been to gloss over feelings of guilt. I'll come back to that, but just let me check you out first on the Roman situation in those years leading up to 20 BCE. Rome had been founded traditionally in 753 BCE by Romulus and Remus. There was a belief that it was a kind of overspill or offshoot from the nearby city of Alba Longa. But it did look rather like a settlement of outlaws, bandits, and riffraff, all of which naturally explains the need for a story about noble origin.

Romans then spent many centuries fighting their neighbors the Latins, the Volscians, the Sabines. Remember the rape of the Sabine women? Bandits have to capture women from somewhere. They fought their way up to being "top barbarians" in Italy, rather like the English did in Britain, and then they ran into conflict with the established Mediterranean powers, namely, the Carthaginians and the Greeks. The wars against Greece were relatively civilized, but gave the Romans their reputation for never being beaten easily. The Greek Pyrrhus won a victory over them, but at such a cost, he declared he couldn't afford another win like that; that's where we get the term "Pyrrhic victory," one which leaves you played out.

The three Carthaginian wars were especially nasty, Rome getting a serious fright from Hannibal, and they ended with Carthage completely destroyed, never to rise again. The very site was sown with salt to make sure nothing would ever grow there. Some said that this genocidal victory, brought about by fear and treachery, had called down on Rome a curse from which she never recovered. But curse or no curse, nasty or civilized, 100 years before

Virgil, Romans had become top dog, well on the way to Mediterranean empire. This may not have been entirely good for them.

The great scholar Gilbert Murray thought that the difference between the Latin epic and the Greek epic was accounted for by the fact that the Greeks had been through the kind of Heroic Age which I discussed in the last lecture. "The Romans," he said, "had an almost steady history of stern discipline, of conquest and well earned success." But by contrast, the Greeks had, as Murray put it, "passed through the very fires of Hell." They knew something Rome did not know: "the reverse side of glory, the bitterness of lost battles, the sting of the master's lash."

That difference, in Virgil's time, was just about to become even more acute. Julius Caesar had conquered Gaul; the Roman Civil Wars had been terminated by Augustus' victory over Mark Antony and Cleopatra at the battle of Actium, just two years before Virgil started *the Aeneid*; The Roman Republic had effectively been abandoned; and the Roman Empire was about to be imposed. Knowing all that, we can perhaps see some of the sore points and the anxieties which Virgil was trying to massage.

Should Rome feel guilt over the destruction of Carthage? Not at all. It was all Dido's fault. By her amorality she had created a lasting enmity. Should Rome feel an inferiority complex towards Greece? Not at all. Our epic is as good as theirs. And as for war guilt, they did to us first! If they hadn't attacked Troy, the Trojans would have stayed at home, and Rome would never have been founded. More seriously, there was the issue of republican virtue. Rome had been a Republic, run politically by the Senate and the people. Rome was very proud of having expelled the Tarquin Kings. Rome's great strength, very different from the Greeks, had always been its dedication to the *res publica*, the public weal, the Commonwealth. We'd say, Rome was distinguished by its social cohesion. Was Rome going to lose its republican virtue now that it was turning into an empire? Not at all, the main republican virtue is subordinating one's private wishes to one's public duty, and that is exactly what Aeneas does.

Finally, there is also a very strong sense in the *Aeneid* of what we would call "manifest destiny." What I'm talking about is heavily reinforced by a third great sequence in the *Aeneid* after the sack of Troy, after the affair of Dido, and this is Aeneas' descent into the underworld, led there by the prophetess known as the Sybil. Once again, there is a strong sense here of competition with Homer. Odysseus did not descend into the underworld; he only called up spirits from the underworld. Aeneas goes all the way.

Odysseus had a magic herb which protected him from the witch Circe, and Aeneas is given a similar magic herb. But his Golden Bough enables him not only to enter the underworld, but, and as Virgil says, this is the harder job, to exit from it again. So, down Aeneas goes with the Sibyl as his guide. He sees Charon, the ferryman who takes souls over the river Styx, only those who have been properly buried, though. The rest, the unburied dead, stretch out their hands in longing for the other shore, but Charon will not take them over. In another reminiscence of Odysseus, Aeneas here meets his helmsman, Palinurus, who fell overboard. The Sibyl promises him a tomb.

They go on past the three-headed dog, who has to be fed a drugged offering to send him to sleep—did J.K. Rowling remember that in the first Harry Potter book? They meet the infant dead, the suicides, those who died for love, Dido among them, but she refuses Aeneas' attempt at apology. Aeneas meets a fellow Trojan who did not escape from the city. And then the road forks. To the left is a kind of Hell where sinners are punished: fratricides, misers, adulterers, traitors. To the right are the Blissful Groves, the homes of the virtuous. But it's a very Roman and republican virtue which gets you there; above all, suffering wounds while fighting for your country. There Aeneas meets his father, who tells him that some spirits will be reincarnated once their sins are erased. And he also gives a long prophecy of the glorious future of Rome, right up to Virgil's own day.

The whole underworld sequence ends with a really egregious bit of patron pleasing, for the last figure Aeneas sees is a youth of great majesty but a sad face; it's Augustus' nephew Marcellus, who, in fact, never achieved anything, but died while the *Aeneid* was being composed. It's said that when this passage was read to the imperial royal family, Marcellus' mother, Augustus' sister, fainted. But Virgil has to work very hard at saying what Marcellus would have achieved, were it not for "the harsh bonds of fate." And once Aeneas emerges from the underworld, we switch much more to the idea of "manifest destiny," as Aeneas fights wars to establish himself in Italy and marry Lavinia, the daughter of the Latin king.

One final difference between Greek and Roman epics, the *Iliad* contains an atrocity, the mutilation by Achilles of the corpse of Hector. But it ends with Achilles handing the corpse back to Hector's old father, as if in apology. But the *Aeneid* ends with what we would call a war crime. Aeneas has overcome his great rival Turnus, who surrenders, and asks, not for mercy exactly, but for respect. But then Aeneas sees that Turnus is wearing a belt taken from the body of his friend Pallas, and cuts him down. And that's the end. Turnus dies, his spirit passes *indignata*, indignant, to the shades of the underworld. I did say the Romans were big on piety. Not on pity.

Well, for thousands of years, Virgil, along with the Bible, was the foundation stone of Western education. Even more so than Homer, because Latin remained the language of the Church, even after the Roman Empire had passed. One major effect of the *Aeneid* was to make European countries feel they really needed a similar myth of origins, which several of them tried to bolt on to Virgil's story. After all, we know there were other Trojans. Perhaps some of them founded countries as well. The British version of this was what was called the Brutus books, which insisted that Britain had been founded by a Trojan called Felix Brutus; that the old name for London was Trinovantium; and that this must mean "New Troy;" and that the British were accordingly the new Romans and eventually the heirs of Empire as well. They weren't the only Europeans to invent similar stories. So, the Virgilian ideology was very powerful for centuries.

However, and this is part of what I mean about the legacy of great tales being quite unpredictable, the Virgilian ideology was rivaled in popularity by the Virgilian visions, especially his vision of the underworld, which gave so much to Dante's *Inferno*, the first part of his famous poem, *La Divina Commedia*. When Dante wrote his poem about descending into Hell, the figure he chose as his guide through Hell was, naturally, not Aeneas, but Virgil, because Virgil was the acknowledged expert on the underworld. Later, Virgil guides Dante through Purgatory as well, but he cannot enter into Paradise because he was a pagan. The Christian Paradise of Dante contrasts with, is even in opposition to, the Blissful Groves of Aeneas, full as they are of politicians and senators and generals. Ideas of virtue change, just like ideas of heroism.

However, I'd like to mention yet one more turn of the wheel of heroic imaginings. So far I've talked about continuation in a different spirit; I've talked about writing into the gap; but I've said nothing about the third qualification with which I began this lecture, the one about not being able to tell how inspiration will work, maybe in ways absolutely unthinkable to the person who originated that inspiration. Could Virgil, or Homer for that matter, ever have imagined someone who imitated their great epics but decided to turn the heroes into rabbits?

Well, that's what author Richard Adams did with his novel *Watership Down*. The novel starts with a little puny rabbit, called Fiver, having a vision of utter disaster coming upon his warren. He cannot get the chief of the warren to believe him, so he and a few others, led by a rabbit called Hazel, make the decision to flee on their own, and set up somewhere else. Two similarities are already obvious. The rabbits fleeing the doomed warren are like Aeneas and his companions fleeing Troy, and their setting up a new warren on Watership Down is like Aeneas founding a New Troy, which will become Rome. As for getting there, well, that is clearly an odyssey, and it's quite like Homer's.

Adams actually mentions the *Odyssey* twice as he tells the story, but one close similarity is the warren the refugee rabbits reach, where all the rabbits are well fed and healthy, but also strange, passive. The rabbits in this warren are like Homer's Lotus Eaters. What they know, but won't admit, is that humans feed them, so they're there to be snared and eaten. Their comfort and luxury carry a price-tag. It's death. Later on Hazel and his rabbits reenact scenes like the Rape of the Sabine Women, and the long struggle with General Woundwort parallels Aeneas' long struggle against the Latins and the Italians in the second half of the *Aeneid*.

What gives *Watership Down* its charm, though, is the addition to the whole brew of rabbit psychology, which I'm sure Virgil and Homer would have regarded as way beneath their dignity. But like hobbits, Hazel's rabbits do provide another model of heroism for us. Rabbits are prey, not predators. They're not good at long marches because they scatter, they dawdle, they freeze. But, they're more cooperative than human beings. Their weapons are craft and cunning; they're tricksters, like Odysseus, but they use cunning to achieve the goal of Aeneas, to found a new city. Their victory is to survive and breed, and their hero is El-ahrairah, the Prince with a Thousand Enemies, who in the end takes Hazel to join his great Owsla, not his bodyguard, so much as his Council, in the sky. Valhalla it isn't, nor the Blissful Groves, nor the Elysian Fields either. I guess many would still prefer it to Odysseus' gloomy and hopeless Heroic Age underworld, or Aeneas' heaven, inhabited only by models of republican or imperial virtue.

So far in this course, then, we've seen a humble hero, Frodo Baggins, with his predecessor Bilbo; a trickster hero, Odysseus; and a straight arrow hero, Aeneas. They all have their good points and their limitations. Aeneas' good points are his reliability, his propriety, his concern for duty, not very popular virtues nowadays, but just as necessary as they always were. Most of us probably think he would be improved by a touch of Frodo Baggins' humility or Odysseus' ability to talk to slaves man to man. But all heroes are affected by their time and place, which makes it all the more remarkable when we see them being adapted.

The next lecture will focus on a heroine and on a change in cultural values which would have shocked both Homer and Virgil, and which even Tolkien found difficult to take.

Guinevere—A Heroine with Many Faces
Lecture 4

I n the 15th century, the Italian poet Matteo Boiardo asked himself why the story of King Arthur and his knights was popular across Europe, whereas the legend of King Charlemagne had never caught on. To Boiardo, the answer was obvious. Arthur and his knights became glorious *per l'arme e per l'amore*, "through arms and through love." What the Arthur story had that the Charlemagne story didn't was a love interest: Guinevere. In this lecture, we'll trace Guinevere's disastrous affair with Lancelot across 10 centuries. In the process, we'll see the effects of what may be the greatest change in cultural values in our history, one that still marks off the Western world from most other cultures on the globe.

The Knight of the Cart

- The definitive early account of Lancelot and Guinevere came in the 12th century from a French poet, Chrétien de Troyes, in a long-verse romance called *Le Chevalier de la Charette*, "*The Knight of the Cart*."

- Guinevere has been carried off by a knight called Meleagant to a strange country. Attempts are made to rescue Guinevere by other knights and, then, by Lancelot. In the pursuit, Lancelot loses his horse but goes on, on foot, in armor. He sees a dwarf driving a cart and asks whether he has seen the queen. The dwarf invites Lancelot into the cart, and he hesitates briefly before climbing in, knowing that for a knight to ride in a cart is utterly disgraceful.

- Lancelot goes through many adventures in his attempted rescue, but he presses on, inspired by love. When he finally reaches the castle where Guinevere is being held prisoner, he fights a duel with Meleagant but almost loses because he cannot take his eyes off the queen.

- Once Lancelot has won the duel, Guinevere refuses to see him! In despair, he tries to hang himself by being dragged from his horse's saddle-bow. In the end, the two manage to get together, and Lancelot asks Guinevere why she wouldn't speak to him after all the efforts he made on her behalf. Her answer is that he hesitated before getting into the dwarf's cart. The disgrace of riding in a cart should count for nothing against his desire to please his lady.

- The story continues with more adventures, but the important point here is that it is set in a world where cultural values have changed significantly with regard to the status of ladies.
  - This change is perhaps explained best by Reepicheep, the mouse in C. S. Lewis's Narnia stories. Reepicheep has been insulted by a boy called Eustace and is about to take the matter further, when it is realized that Eustace's girl companion, Lucy, is cold and wet and must be taken off to be dried.

  - Reepicheep, who is the soul of honor, says, "to the convenience of a lady, even a question of honor must give way." In this, he expresses the central tenet of chivalric love.

  - In an academic work, Lewis himself wrote, "the lover is always abject. Obedience to his lady's lightest wish, however whimsical, and silent acquiescence in her rebukes, however unjust, are the only virtues he dares to claim."

- In Chrétien's story, Lancelot apologizes to Guinevere for his hesitation—behavior that would be viewed as insane by such heroes as Odysseus and Aeneas. The emergence of courtly love in medieval literature marks a significant development in European attitudes toward women that in some ways continues today. The cult of love has marked Western civilization deeply and is still one of its main differences from other cultures.

Guinevere's Attraction
- Guinevere was irresistibly attractive to Lancelot and has remained so to storytellers up to the present day. What's the secret of her attraction?

- One possible answer is that she has always retained an element of the mythic. Her name, Guinevere, seems to be Welsh Gwenhwyfar, which may mean "the white enchantress."

   o The first mention of her is in a saint's life, in which we are told that Guinevere is carried off by a king called Melwas (Meleagant) to the Summer Country.

   o There's a hint here of the myth of Persephone, the fertility goddess who is captured at the end of every summer and taken down into the underworld, from which she must be rescued and released every spring.

- There have been many attempts to explain Guinevere and comment on her, but the canonical version in English is Sir Thomas Malory's *Le Morte Darthur*, written in the late 15th century and one of the first books ever to be printed in English.

   o Malory also tells the tale of the Knight of the Cart, but he tells it with a strong sense of tactics. According to Malory, Lancelot was ambushed by archers, who managed to kill his horse but not him. When the cart comes by, Lancelot asks for a ride, but the carter addresses him rudely, and Lancelot strikes him and kills him.

   o The carter's assistant offers Lancelot a ride, which he accepts. One of Guinevere's maids, looking out the window, sees the cart and thinks it is a tumbril, an execution wagon. Guinevere, however, recognizes Lancelot, and tells the maid off for thinking that the noblest knight in the world might come to a shameful death. The motif of the hesitation has disappeared completely, but somehow, the story can't do without the cart.

   o Nor can it do without the motif of serious tension between the two lovers. Once Lancelot has burst into the castle, Guinevere's abductor, Sir Mellyagaunce, begs for mercy, and she grants it. Lancelot tells her, rather sarcastically, that if he had known she would make a deal with Mellyagaunce so readily, he would not have come to her with such haste. Guinevere replies, also sarcastically, "Why do you say that? Are you sorry for your good deeds?" She's still in control but no longer on a pedestal.

o   For the first time, Malory gives us a recognizable picture of what we would call a relationship. Lancelot and Guinevere often talk to each other with a mix of anger and even scorn, yet they can't leave each other alone. We can see why Guinevere needs to hold on to Lancelot—he's her protector—but what causes Lancelot's infatuation? It seems to be some supernatural or magic power.

Guinevere and Lancelot

- Let's look at a few snapshots from Malory of Guinevere in her "relationship" with Lancelot, beginning with a moment when Lancelot removes himself from court to let the affair cool down.

    o   To disguise himself, Lancelot accepts a token from another lady, the Fair Maid of Astolat, in the form of a red sleeve. It's a good disguise because it's generally known that Lancelot, unlike all the other knights, never ever wears a lady's token.

    o   The court is pleased that Lancelot has met a nice girl, but Guinevere is furious. Lancelot refuses to marry the

Guinevere's association with the white enchantress may explain her seemingly magical power over Lancelot.

Fair Maid or become her paramour, and she commits suicide. Guinevere rebukes Lancelot, saying that he might have saved the maid's life if he had shown her any kindness—although we know that she would have flown into a jealous rage had he done so.

o Arthur defuses the situation by saying that Lancelot must see to the funeral. But once again, we can see that Guinevere is horribly unfair—which doesn't stop the pair from making up.

- In Malory's tale, the Knight of the Cart affair rumbles on until a duel must be fought between Lancelot and Mellyagaunce. Mellyagaunce has rashly accused Guinevere of adultery with one of her bodyguards, which is half-true: She has committed adultery but with Lancelot. Of course, Lancelot must then challenge Mellyagaunce.

  o Almost immediately, Mellyagaunce gives up and asks for mercy, which chivalry obliges Lancelot to grant. But Guinevere wants Mellyagaunce dead—he knows too much—and she signals her wish to Lancelot.

  o Lancelot offers to take off his helmet and half his armor and tie his left hand behind his back if Mellyagaunce will fight to the death. Mellyagaunce accepts the offer and, of course, loses the duel.

- The point here is this: Guinevere is in a horribly vulnerable position. Repeatedly, she finds her life at risk for her adultery, until Lancelot rescues her. But she shows no sign that she recognizes the weakness of her position, and she never says she's grateful to Lancelot. We must admire her courage and confidence and—perhaps this is the secret of our fascination—recognize her very human reactions. Guinevere is a complex character—more like a woman in a modern novel than a medieval romance.

Changing Perceptions of Guinevere

- Guinevere's role as an adulteress left her at the mercy of changing cultural values, especially in the Victorian era. In Lord Tennyson's popular cycle of poems about King Arthur, *Idylls of the King*, Guinevere became the scapegoat for everything that went wrong with the Round Table. Victorians still practiced veneration of the lady, but they didn't tolerate the medieval idea of the mistress.

○ The 11th of Tennyson's 12 poems opens with Guinevere having fled from her husband. When Arthur comes searching for her, she grovels at his feet.

○ In Arthur's long rebuke of Guinevere, he says that he can't possibly excuse her because to do so would be a betrayal of public morality.

○ Tennyson leaves us with an unpleasant picture of Guinevere, reduced to the status of a dreadful warning. She is allowed no repentance and no painful parting from Lancelot.

• In the 20th century, there was a vigorous reaction to this Victorian treatment, the best example of which comes from T. H. White's tetralogy *The Once and Future King*. White writes the scenes of the cart, the duel, and the Fair Maid's suicide in a modern idiom. He also asks whether Lancelot and Guinevere's relationship changed over the many years it lasted.

○ White's Lancelot and Guinevere still bicker, but gently, like an old married couple. The sexual infatuation is gone and has been replaced by tenderness.

○ White also invents a new scene to explain the start of the relationship. As a young man, Lancelot treats Guinevere badly, then realizes that he has hurt her: "She was not a minx, not deceitful, not designing and heartless. She was pretty Jenny, who could think and feel."

• In her long trajectory, Guinevere has gone from being a goddess, to an unreasonable dominatrix, to a proud queen, to a wicked adulteress, and finally to a young girl married off too soon and trying to find her own happiness. Always there is the mix of sexual allure and physical weakness. Always she is under threat, of being abducted, being discarded, or being executed, but she never compromises.

Essential Reading

Chrétien de Troyes (Owen, trans.), *Arthurian Romances*.

Malory (Vinaver, ed.), *Le Morte Darthur*.

Suggested Reading

Cross and Nitze, *Lancelot and Guenevere*.

Field, *The Life and Times of Sir Thomas Malory*.

Walters, ed., *Lancelot and Guinevere: A Casebook*.

Questions to Consider

1. Has feminism killed completely the idea of *la belle dame sans merci*, the fascinating but unreasonable mistress?

2. Can you think of any modern story in which a woman is torn between two men, all three of them honorable and admirable people?

Guinevere—A Heroine with Many Faces
Lecture 4—Transcript

The subject of this lecture is Guinevere, Queen of King Arthur. Why not King Arthur himself? I'll let an Italian poet give the answer to that, not Dante this time, but Matteo Boiardo. In the later 15th century, Boiardo asked himself why the story of King Arthur and his knights was popular all over Europe, whereas the legends of King Charlemagne and his paladins had never caught on. And Boiardo said the answer was obvious. Arthur and his knights became glorious, he wrote, *per l'arme e per l'amore*—through arms and through love. Virgil's Aeneid began with the words *arma virumque cano*—I sing of arms and the man. But Boiardo says that to arma we now have to add amore, or the story won't take off. In other words, what the Arthur story had that the Charlemagne story didn't was a love interest, and that centered on Guinevere and her disastrous affair with Lancelot, the affair which destroyed the Round Table. Today we'll trace that affair across ten centuries. And in the process, we'll see the effects of what may be the greatest change in cultural values in our history. One which still marks off the Western world from most of the other cultures on the globe.

The definitive early account of Lancelot and Guinevere came in the twelfth century from a French poet, Chrétien de Troyes, in a long verse romance called *Le Chevalier de la Charette*—the Knight of the Cart, and the cart is vital. What's happened is that Guinevere has been carried off by a knight called Meleagant to a strange otherworld country. I ought to just pause at this point and say that everyone has always had trouble with Meleagant. Any name which sounds a bit like him, it's him. I won't stop to explain this every time.

Anyway, attempts are made to pursue Meleagant and rescue Guinevere, first by Sir Kay, then by Sir Gawain, and then by an unnamed knight who turns out to be Sir Lancelot. In the pursuit, Lancelot loses his horse but presses on, on foot, in armor. He sees a dwarf driving a cart and asks, "have you seen the Queen?" The dwarf just says, "get in the cart; you'll find out." At this point Chrétien tells us that for a knight to ride in a cart instead of riding a horse, like a proper chevalier or caballero, was seen as utterly disgraceful. In those days, he says, anyone who committed a crime was put in a cart and led through the streets, and after that, he lost all his legal rights and was never welcome again in any court. If you even saw a cart, you were supposed to cross yourself. And so, when Lancelot is invited to get into the cart so he can continue his rescue of Guinevere, and don't forget that a knight on foot, in armor, is not likely to get very far very fast, he hesitates for just two steps. And then he climbs in.

After this he goes through many adventures in his attempted rescue. He is almost speared by a fiery lance, which strikes down at him as he lies in bed. He rescues a damsel from rape. He has to cross a bridge made of a sword to get into the strange land of Gorre, and the sword cuts his hands open. He presses on, inspired by love. When he finds a hair left by Guinevere in a comb she has used, he feasts his eyes on it. When he finally reaches the castle where Guinevere is being held prisoner, he fights a duel with Meleagant, but he almost loses it because he cannot take his eyes off Guinevere, who is watching.

But, then, once he's won the duel, Guinevere refuses to see him! In despair, Lancelot tries to hang himself by being dragged from his horse's saddle bow. The Queen hears he is dead; she faints from grief; Lancelot hears she is dead, and so on. In the end, they manage to get together and have a conversation, and Lancelot finally gets round to asking why she wouldn't speak to him after all the efforts he has made on her behalf. And the answer is, it's because he hesitated to get into the cart. That is not the way a lover is supposed to behave. Disgrace, loss of legal rights, humiliation, all these should count absolutely nothing against the desire to please his lady.

The story goes on with Lancelot coming by night to Guinevere's bedroom, breaking the bars on the window with his hands, which split open because of the cuts he got while crossing the sword bridge. So Lancelot gets blood on Guinevere's sheets, and when this is seen in the morning, Guinevere is accused of sleeping with Sir Kay, who is lying wounded in an antechamber, etcetera. But the important thing we can see from this central part of the story of the Knight of the Cart is that we are in a world where cultural values have changed very much in one particular area, and that area is the status of ladies. The change is put best, I think, by Reepicheep, the talking mouse in C. S. Lewis's Narnia stories. Reepicheep has been insulted by a boy called

Eustace, and is about to take the matter further, when it is realized that Eustace's girl companion, Lucy, is cold and wet, and has to be taken off to be dried. Reepicheep, who is the soul of honor, nevertheless says at this point, "to the convenience of a lady, even a question of honor must give way."

That's right. Reepicheep is expressing the central tenet of chivalric, or courtly, love. Lewis himself wrote in an academic work that the rule of courteous behavior is, and I quote, "The lover is always abject. Obedience to his lady's lightest wish, however whimsical, and silent acquiescence in her rebukes, however unjust, are the only virtues he dares to claim." And so, of course, when in Chrétien's story Lancelot is rebuked by Guinevere for hesitating, he doesn't say, "Think of all the things I did for you." Instead he says, "You are absolutely right, please accept my apology; tell me if you will ever pardon me for my wrongdoing."

Now, to the heroes we have been talking about earlier on in this course, this behavior would seem simply insane. Odysseus makes every effort to get home to his wife Penelope, but I think home is more important than Penelope. The whole second half of the Aeneid is dominated by the conflict over Lavinia. But Aeneas and Turnus are fighting over Lavinia; she's politically valuable. They're not fighting for her. The emergence of courtly love in medieval literature marks a significant development in European attitudes towards women, or at least towards ladies. And the medieval love cult hasn't quite gone way; it remains a staple of pop music, and especially of country and western. The George Jones classic, "He Stopped Lovin' Her Today" has exactly the theme of inextinguishable love, even of a lady who has deserted you, which would be completely comprehensible to the likes of Lancelot. The cult of love has marked Western civilization very deeply and is still one of its main differences from other cultures.

But going back to Guinevere., what is the secret of her attraction? What makes Lancelot put up with her? In terms of the love cult, this is a stupid question. For the true lover, there is no question why! Love is love, and it's not meant to be sensible. That's why in pictures and statues Cupid is regularly given a blindfold, because, you never know where Cupid's arrow will strike, and it may well be in exactly the wrong place.

Just the same, I ask the question again; what is the secret of Guinevere's attraction? And not just to Lancelot, because after all, that's just made up. But she's remained irresistibly attractive ever since to story tellers and to readers as well, right up to now. I cannot think of another heroine who has remained so consistently intriguing. Helen of Troy is just a name, by comparison. One possible answer is that Guinevere has always retained an element of the mythic. Her name, Guinevere, seems to be Welsh Gwenhwyfar, which may mean "the white enchantress." The very first mention of her is in a saint's life, the life of St. Gildas, written by a Welshman called Caradoc. In this we are told that Guinevere is carried off by a king called Melwas to the Summer Country—Melwas is Meleagant, again, though I won't keep saying that. So, Guinevere is the captive Queen of the Summer Country. Now, that could be a real place, the English county of Somerset, and the story does seem to be associated with the Somerset town of Glastonbury. But there's a hint also of the myth of Persephone, the fertility goddess who is captured at the end of every summer and taken down into the underworld, from which she has to be rescued and released every spring.

Chrétien probably wouldn't have known anything about that. But some things seem to be built into a story so deeply that you can never get them out. This story of the rescue of Guinevere, for instance, is retold in the movie First Knight. I thought it was a very bad movie, most of it being an ego trip for Richard Gere, who was playing Lancelot. But just the same, when it came to the scenes where Guinevere was being held prisoner deep underground by someone called Malagant, I thought there was a kind of shudder about it, as if we were still in the presence of a powerful archetype to which we cannot help responding.

There have been many attempts to explain Guinevere and comment on her between Chrétien and the Hollywood movie I just mentioned, but the canonical version in English is Sir Thomas Malory's *Le Morte Darthur*, written in the late 15th century and one of the first books ever to be printed in English; it has never been out of print since. Now I have to say that Malory is quite out of the ordinary run of authors. Unlike most medieval writers, he was not a cleric; he was a knight. And he was also, in his own words, "a knight prisoner." He wrote the book in jail.

What was he in jail for? If one believes the many medieval records of him, he was in jail for pretty well everything. And as for jailbreaks, he made *Cool Hand Luke* look like the amateur he was. But I'll sum up a long story by saying that Malory was obviously a very tough guy. And the best excuse I can make for his many crimes is that all this took place in the middle of a bitterly fought civil war, the War of the Roses, in which Malory changed sides more than once, probably because both sides thought he was really worth having on the team.

Now, Malory tells the tale of the Knight of the Cart as well, but as you could expect from what I've just said, he tells it a different way, with a strong sense of tactics. He says that what happened was that Lancelot was ambushed by archers. They shot his horse, but they couldn't shoot him because he was wearing top-quality, full-plate armor. For the same reason, he couldn't catch the archers. He desperately needs a ride. So when the cart comes by, he asks the carter fairly politely what the carter will take to carry him two miles. But the carter says, "Thou shalt nat go with me!" This was a bad idea. Middle English, like modern French, had two forms for "you," and as in modern French, you use one form—"thou" and "thee"—to intimates or to people of inferior status, and you use the other form—"ye" and "you"—for equals or social superiors. So the carter addressing Lancelot as "thou" is extremely rude.

Lancelot is not one to put up with impoliteness, and he immediately hits the carter, "reremayn," or backhand, with his steel gauntlet, with the result that the carter "felle to the erthe starke dede." The carter's assistant then says, carefully using the "you" form, that he will take Lancelot wherever he wants. Lancelot then rides on in the cart. One of Guinevere's maids, looking out of the window, sees the cart coming and says, "se, madam, where rydys in a charyot a goodly armed knyght, and we suppose he rydyth unto hangynge." She thinks the cart is a tumbril, an execution waggon.

Guinevere looks out, recognizes Lancelot, and tells the maid off for being so foulmouthed as to think that the most noble knight in the world might come to such a shameful death. The motif of the hesitation has disappeared completely, but somehow, the story can't do without the cart. Nor can it do without the motif of serious tension between the two lovers. Once Lancelot has burst into the castle, incidentally, breaking the porter's neck with his trusty gauntlet, for he scorns to draw sword on mere menials, the abductor, Sir Mellyagaunce, very sensibly begs for mercy, and Guinevere grants it.

Lancelot, however, is not at all pleased and says rather sarcastically— Chrétien's hero would never have dared to say anything like this to his lady—"if I had known you would make a deal with him so readily," "I wolde nat a made such haste unto you." Guinevere replies, equally sarcastically, "why do you say that? Are you sorry for your good deeds?" She's still in control, you notice. But she's not on a pedestal any more.

What strikes me about this and about a whole string of similar incidents, is that for the first time Malory is giving us a very recognizable picture of what we would call a "relationship." Lancelot and Guinevere often talk to each other with a mix of simmering anger, and even scorn. Yet they can't leave each other alone. One can see why Guinevere needs to hold on to Lancelot, best knight of the world, her protector when King Arthur refuses to intervene. But what causes Lancelot's infatuation?

Maybe infatuation is a good word. At the center of it is the word "fata," which in French becomes the word "fée," which in English becomes "fairy," and also "fate." It's as if there is some kind of supernatural or magic power which explains the infatuation. And we remember that Guinevere's name may mean "white enchantress." Another way of putting it is that Guinevere is a femme fatale. Like Helen of Troy, who caused the Trojan War; or like Cleopatra, whose affairs with Julius Caesar, Mark Antony, and potentially Augustus Caesar helped bring about the end of the Roman Republic. Guinevere, meanwhile, in most stories, is responsible for the fall of the Round Table. But what gives her her power? What does she have that other women haven't? I'll give a few snapshots from Malory of Guinevere in her "relationship" with Lancelot.

There's a moment when Lancelot goes away from court to let things cool down. In order to disguise himself, he accepts a token from another lady, the Fair Maid of Astolat, in the form of a red sleeve. It's a good disguise, because it is generally known that Lancelot, unlike all the other knights, never, ever wears a lady's token. Well, the whole court is quietly pleased when they find out. They've all been hoping for years that Lancelot would meet a nice girl—repeat, nice; repeat, girl, not a cougar, not a married woman, and especially, please God, not a woman married to the King. But when Guinevere finds out she is furious.

Nevertheless, Lancelot absolutely refuses to marry the Fair Maid or to become her paramour, as she suggests, so she dies of grief. She arranges to have herself drifted down the river to Camelot in a boat with a suicide note in hand. This is then read out aloud to Arthur, to Lancelot, to Guinevere, and everyone else present. And everyone looks at Lancelot. And he says to Arthur, I feel, breathing very hard, "I am ryght hevy of the deth of thys fayre lady. And God knowyth I was never causar of her deth be my wyllynge...I woll nat say nay...but that she was both fayre and good...but she loved me oute of mesure." And Guinevere says, still very formally, "Sir...ye myght have shewed hir some bownté and jantilnes whych myght have preserved hir lyff."

Everybody knows that if Lancelot had shown any lady any kindness or gentleness at all, Guinevere would have flown into the mother of all jealous rages. And so Lancelot has to make rather a long speech defending himself, after which Arthur defuses the situation by saying Lancelot must see to the funeral. In another century, I feel he would have said it was time for us all to have a nice cup of tea. He knows about his wife's affair. He just doesn't want a public scandal. But once again, one can see that Guinevere is being horribly unfair. Which doesn't stop them from making up.

Another snapshot, the Knight of the Cart affair, in Malory, rumbles on until a duel has to be fought between Lancelot and Mellyagaunce. Mellyagaunce has seen the blood in the bed after Lancelot has ripped out Guinevere's window bars and rashly accused her of adultery with a wounded knight, which is half true; it wasn't one of her wounded bodyguards, it was Lancelot. Of course Lancelot then has to challenge him. The duel is naturally a no contest, with the best knight in the world fighting a no hoper, and almost immediately Mellyagaunce gives up and asks for mercy, which of course, chivalry obliges Lancelot to grant. And the whole court is watching.

But Guinevere wants Mellyagaunce dead. His accusation was basically true. He knows too much. Lancelot looks at her to see what she wants, "And anone the queen wagged hir hede upon Sir Launcelot, as ho seyth, 'sle hym'." Kill him! But he can't! It's not knightly! But he's got to, he knows what she wants. Lancelot says he'll take off his helmet and half his armor and tie his left hand behind his back if Mellyagaunce will fight to the death. Mellyagaunce takes the offer, and you can guess what happens next. By medieval standards, legally okay. But I would call that murder. And there are other scenes I could cite. But my point is this. Guinevere is in a horribly vulnerable position. Again and again she finds herself on trial for her life or standing at the stake waiting to be burned alive for adultery until Lancelot rescues her. But she shows no sign that she has recognized the weakness of her position. She doesn't try to conciliate Lancelot. She never says she's grateful.

You have to admire her courage. Wonder at her confidence. And also, and maybe this is the secret, recognize her very human reactions. We've all answered sarcastically when we shouldn't. We can all understand, I think, why Guinevere feels a sudden wave of sympathy for the poor dead Fair Maid of Astolat and scores a cheap hit on her lover. She likes to win arguments and have the last word. She never asks herself, what would be the best plan here. We all know people like that. Passionate, strong willed, often, people say, her own worst enemy. So though she's a puzzle in all kinds of ways, people, especially in our time, basing themselves on Malory, have felt they can work her out. We can understand her feelings, and understand why she can't control them, even if it's not sensible. She's a complex character, like someone in a modern novel, not a medieval romance.

I have to say that her role as adulteress left her very much at the mercy of changing cultural values, especially, of course, in the Victorian era. In Lord Tennyson's extremely popular cycle of poems about King Arthur, Guinevere became the scapegoat for everything that went wrong with the Round Table. Victorians still practiced veneration of the lady, you might say. But there was no toleration at all for the medieval idea—Victorians would say, the French idea—of the mistress, the woman to whom you are not married, but to whom you owe absolute devotion.

So, the eleventh of Tennyson's twelve *Idylls of the King* opens with Guinevere having fled from her husband. And when Arthur comes in search of her, "prone from off her seat she fell, / and grovell'd with her face against the floor," Tennyson never allows her to get up. If you ask me, this is all very ungentlemanly. But perhaps the strangest thing King Arthur says in his long rebuke of Guinevere is that he can't possibly excuse her, because it would be a betrayal of public morality. "I hold that man the worst of public foes / who either for his own or children's sake, / to save his blood from scandal, lets the wife / whom he knows false abide and rule the house."

The worst of public foes? Really? Not a private matter? No, says Arthur, here being an even straighter arrow than Aeneas. She must not be forgiven, because "she, like a new disease, unknown to men, / creeps, no precaution used, among the crowd." Perhaps the idea of the new disease explains Tennyson's obsession. Later on in this course I shall remark on the Victorian fear of syphilis, and that may partly account for the much stricter 19th-century sense of sexual morality. It's still a very unpleasant picture of Guinevere, who has been reduced to the status of dreadful warning. She is allowed no repentance, no painful parting from Lancelot.

I'm happy to say that there's been a vigorous reaction to this in the 20th century, and the best example comes from T. H. White, in his tetralogy *The Once and Future King*, which began as *The Sword in the Stone*. White keeps all the scenes I've mentioned already—the cart, and the duel, and the Fair Maid's suicide—writing them all into a modern idiom. But he also, very cleverly, does what I call "writing into the gap." White asks, did Lancelot and Guinevere's relationship change over the many years it lasted? Yes, it did. Towards the end, his Lancelot and Guinevere are still bickering, but gently, like an old married couple. The sexual infatuation has gone and been replaced by tenderness.

But how did the relationship start? What made them fall in love in the first place? White invents a whole new scene to explain it. Lancelot, a young man, is out hawking, like half the Round Table—White was an accomplished falconer himself. Guinevere, who has been asked by Arthur to be nice to his new recruit, decides to help Lancelot out. But Lancelot is in a bad temper. Things have gone wrong; hawks themselves are angry creatures;

their trainers catch bad temper from them. Guinevere starts to wind up a ball of twine for Lancelot and does it all wrong. He snatches it from her, says "That's no good," and began to unwind it, her hopeful work, with angry fingers. His eyebrows made a horrible scowl. And everything stops. Guinevere, Lancelot, even the hawk. In that moment Lancelot realizes he has hurt someone, and hurt a real person. "She was not a minx, not deceitful, not designing and heartless. She was pretty Jenny, who could think and feel."

I don't know what Chrétien de Troyes would have made of a scene like this, not dignified enough, I dare say, and anyway, that's no way to talk to a lady. But we understand it. In her long trajectory Guinevere has gone from being a goddess and then a totally unreasonable dominatrix,   to being a queen who will not give in to her own vulnerability; a wicked adulteress; and finally, a young girl married off too soon and trying to find her own happiness. Always there is the mix of sexual allure, and physical weakness. Always she is under threat of being abducted, being discarded, being executed. She never compromises.

We're going to look at other examples of strong women in this course and at least one weak one, or maybe unlucky one, depending whose side you take. But Guinevere is the one who has most consistently provoked reinterpretation. It is odd that though everyone knows her name, it's very rare for parents to give it to a girl baby. Not because they think it's unlucky, but because it's too presumptuous. It would be a hard name to live up to.

The Wife of Bath—An Independent Woman
Lecture 5

The Wife of Bath is one of the most interesting characters in *The Canterbury Tales*, and Chaucer may have worked harder on her than on any of his other characters. For most of the characters, we get two perspectives: a description in the General Prologue and the insight we get from his or her tale. But for the Wife of Bath, Chaucer gives us four perspectives. In addition to her description and her tale, we get her tirade about marriage and the tale told by the Shipman, which was clearly originally meant to be told by the Wife. In this lecture, we'll use these sources to fill out a picture of one of literature's most memorable female characters.

The General Prologue

- As most of us know, *The Canterbury Tales* focuses on a group of pilgrims heading from London to Canterbury, with Chaucer himself among them. Each of the pilgrims is individually described in what is called the General Prologue. Then, all the pilgrims agree to tell tales as they ride along.

- In the General Prologue descriptions, Chaucer likes to pretend that he is simply making remarks at random and leaving readers to draw their own conclusions. He pretends to be naïve and gullible, simply repeating what people tell him, sometimes using their own words. In this way, he avoids responsibility for what is often biting satire, especially of the rich and corrupt churchmen on the pilgrimage.

- The description of the Wife of Bath contains about 20 bits of data in 32 lines of poetry. We learn, first of all, that she's a wife, not a maid or a nun, perhaps a widow; she comes from Bath; she's rather deaf; and she is better at making cloth than the big producers in Flanders. Note that cloth making was one of the few trades open to women, and it was lucrative.

- As Chaucer's description continues, we learn that in her parish church, the Wife of Bath was the first woman to go up and make an offering. Indeed, other women didn't presume to go up before her. She wore elaborate Sunday headgear, scarlet hose, and new shoes. Chaucer tells us that she was a "worthy woman" who had had five husbands.
  - What does Chaucer mean by "worthy"? He has a trick of using words in different senses according to the senses in which the characters themselves use them.

  - For instance, Chaucer uses the word "worthy" seven times in his description of the Knight, and each time it clearly means "brave." For some of the other characters, "worthy" means "well-off."

  - For the Wife of Bath, it may mean that her reputation has never been challenged, although she's been married five times and, as Chaucer tells us, has had other unmarried partners in her youth. Drawing our own conclusions, we might say that she's gotten away with having it all.

- We also learn that the Wife has been on many pilgrimages, even traveling as far as Jerusalem. She knows a lot, says Chaucer, about "wandryng by the weye"—perhaps straying off the straight and narrow?

- The Wife has gapped teeth; she rides an ambler; she has an enormous hat and a mantle wrapped around large hips; and she's good company to laugh and chat with. Finally, Chaucer tells us, she knows all about the "olde daunce" of love.

- Obviously, this is a sexually experienced and independent woman, and not all of her experience was gained legitimately. She is also financially independent, and her clothes and demeanor display dominance. Chaucer gives us an unusual medieval portrait—a woman not like Guinevere at all.

The Wife's Personal Prologue

- The autobiography the Wife tells before her tale is truly shocking. She begins by denying authority, a word that, at the time, still had a strong connection with the word "author." The suggestion here is that she denies "book learning," which would have been largely under the control of celibate and often misogynist clerics. She is saying that she doesn't need book learning; she knows things firsthand, and she knows better!

- Of course, the book that was the foundation of all book learning at the time was the Bible, and the Wife even takes issue with it, specifically with John 4 and 1 Corinthians 7. She can't read these chapters, but she's been told what they say by male clerics, and she won't have it.
  - The story of the Samaritan woman in John 4 seems to be saying that a woman cannot have five husbands, as the Wife of Bath did, because only the first is truly her husband. But the Wife has had five husbands, all of them perfectly legal and proper. She demands to know how many husbands a woman is allowed to have. Men may try to "define" a number, but she knows that God told us to wax and multiply.

  - As for Saint Paul, he may have recommended virginity, but, says the Wife, it wasn't a commandment. Maybe a woman must be a virgin to be perfect, but the Wife doesn't mind being imperfect.

- After this aggressive start to her prologue, the Wife next gives us an account of her five husbands.
  - Her first three were all old and rich, and she controlled them completely. She says that she made them pay when they wanted to have sex with her, and she made them have sex with her whenever she felt like it. She seems like a terrible partner, but what makes her sympathetic is that she enjoys herself so much.

  - Her fourth husband was a womanizer, and the Wife seems glad that he's dead. The fifth husband turns out to be a bit of a paradox. He was an Oxford student, that is, a cleric but not yet committed to the priesthood. He was 20 when he married the 40-year-old Wife, and she gave him all her property.

- o Being young and rich, this fifth husband has the upper hand. And though he never became a priest, he's studied for the priesthood and believes in authority. He likes to read to her from a book about wicked wives. In fact, she's deaf because she once tore a page from the book, and he hit her.

- o But the Wife gets control just the same. She pretends to be dead, and when her husband bends over her, she hits him back. In the end, he agrees to give her complete control, and she makes him burn his book. But once she's got control, she says, she turns into the perfect wife. Control—not independence—was what she wanted all along. Her word for this is "sovereignty."

The Wife of Bath's Tale

- The tale Chaucer eventually assigned to the Wife is about sovereignty, and it follows the story of the fifth husband fairly closely.

- In King Arthur's time a knight rapes a maiden. The penalty for this is death, but he is handed over to the queen and the court of ladies to decide his fate. They give him a year to learn what women desire most. If he discovers the correct answer, he'll be allowed to live.

- The knight asks everyone he can find and gets all kinds of answers, until he meets a strange, ugly old woman. She promises to tell him the answer, but in return, he must do what she asks of him.

- The knight returns to the queen and gives the correct answer: that women desire sovereignty. But the old woman asks the court to make the knight keep his promise; she wants him to marry her.

- On their wedding night, the old woman gives the knight a choice: She can be old and ugly and faithful or young and beautiful, but he'll have to take his chances on fidelity. Of course, the knight gives her the sovereignty to make the choice herself, and she becomes both beautiful and faithful.

The Wife's Original Tale

- The tale that Chaucer originally wrote for the Wife of Bath is a fairly widespread story, well told by the Italian writer Boccaccio in the *Decameron*. Boccaccio's version is a very misogynist story, in which a wife is tricked into infidelity with a man she believes is in love with her. She promises to have sex with the man for money, but he secretly borrows the money from her husband and sets her up in such a way that she is forced to return it.

- Obviously, this isn't a good story for the Wife of Bath, so Chaucer changed it. He removed the witness who had originally seen the man give the money to the wife and whose presence forced her to give it to her husband in the end. In the last scene of Chaucer's version, when the lover says that he repaid the money to the wife, she claims that she thought the money was gift and has spent it all. She tells her husband, "Score it upon my taille," meaning, "I'll pay you back in bed."

- The strong point of this story is the answer from the wife, who gets out of a tricky situation, quite unlike the wife in Boccaccio's story. And it uses a basic idea of the Wife of Bath, namely, that sex and money are interconvertible. Money can be turned into sex, which is what the lover does. Sex can be turned into money, which is what the wife does.

- Chaucer has turned a misogynist story about a helpless female into a story about a dominant female who knows how to give a smart answer. Why would he decide to replace this story with the one about what women most desire?

- One answer might be that the tale she ends up telling is the one the Wife herself would like best—not because it's about sovereignty, but because it's about an old woman who becomes young and beautiful again.

- The Wife of Bath has been a great warrior—and winner—in the war of the sexes, but she knows she's getting old. She says of herself: "The flour is goon, ther is na-more to telle. / The bran, as I best can, now moste I sell." By "flour," she means the best part of the wheat. What's left after the flour has been ground out is the bran. Still, something can be done with the bran, and the Wife will use it.

- The Wife of Bath is dominant, independent, aggressive, and irrepressible. She's also a little bit sad and a little bit vulnerable. Chaucer's shift from the "smart answer" tale to the "happy ending" tale brings out in her an element of yearning and makes her a more complex and sympathetic character.

Essential Reading

Chaucer (Allen and Kirkham, eds.), *The Wife of Bath's Prologue and Tale.*

Suggested Reading

Dinshaw, *Chaucer's Sexual Poetics.*

Questions to Consider

1. Do you think Chaucer understood women, or is he just presenting a frightened male view of a strong woman in the Wife of Bath?

2. Is it a good idea to "grow old gracefully" or to carry on cheerfully, like the Wife of Bath?

The Wife of Bath—An Independent Woman
Lecture 5—Transcript

The Wife of Bath is one of the characters in Geoffrey Chaucer's *Canterbury Tales*, some would say the most interesting character. Maybe Chaucer would have said so too, because there is evidence to show that he worked harder on her than on any of his other characters. He kept changing his mind about her, he kept adding bits on.

The basic plan of the *Canterbury Tales* is that there is a group of pilgrims heading from London to Canterbury, and Chaucer himself is one of them. The pilgrims each get an individual description, as they appear to Chaucer, in what is called the General Prologue to the *Canterbury Tales*. Then all the pilgrims agree to tell tales as they ride along, and though Chaucer never finished the project, most of them get to tell a tale.

Chaucer's new idea is that each tale in some way or other fits its teller. The Knight tells a chivalrous tale; the Franklin, who is just on the edge of being upper class, tells a tale about what it means to be a gentleman; the Friar and the Summoner, who are professional enemies, tell tales against each other; and so on. The tales match up with the descriptions in the General Prologue to illuminate character.

For most pilgrims, then, we have two perspectives; there's the General Prologue description, and then the tale they tell. But with the Wife of Bath we have 4 perspectives. As usual, there's her description in the General Prologue. As usual also, there's the tale she tells. But before she tells the tale, she launches into a long tirade about the "wo that is in mariage," and this turns into a kind of sexual autobiography—our third perspective. Not something you find very often in the middle ages, especially not from a woman.

And then, our fourth perspective, we have one of Chaucer's changes of mind. He clearly meant the Wife of Bath to tell another tale, which is very suitable to her and matches what is said in her autobiography. Then he must have thought to himself, "I've got a better idea!" And he switched this first tale to another character, the Shipman.

But he forgot to make all the necessary changes, so the Shipman's Tale still seems to be told by a woman. The Wife of Bath is the only woman on the pilgrimage apart from the nuns and their Prioress, who definitely would not tell the story, which is now the Shipman's Tale. So we can look at the Shipman's Tale as well as the Wife of Bath's Tale and wonder why Chaucer decided that what is now the Wife of Bath's tale was an even better idea for her than the one which has become the Shipman's Tale. We have four sources, then, for the Wife of Bath's character. Today, we'll use those sources to fill out a composite picture of one of literature's most memorable female characters.

Now, usually, I start these lectures by fixing on the scene which defines a character, like Odysseus tricking Polyphemus or Guinevere despising Lancelot for hesitating to get into the cart. But this time I'm going to do things Chaucer's way. In the General Prologue descriptions, he likes to pretend he is just making remarks at random and leaving you to draw your own conclusions. He pretends to be naïve, wide eyed, gullible, just repeating what people tell him, sometimes using their own words. That way, he's not responsible for what is often biting satire, especially of the rich and corrupt churchmen on the pilgrimage. The Wife of Bath was not a churchman, but frankly, she was a pretty hot potato in the 14th century as well.

So, I'll just tell you, to start with, what Chaucer says about her, the way he says it, and then I'll draw my own conclusions. So, the description of the Wife of Bath in the General Prologue: This contains about twenty separate bits of data in 32 lines of poetry, and here are the first four lines, this time, translated.

> 'There was a good wife from nearby Bath, / but she was rather deaf, which was a shame. / She was so good at cloth making / That she was better than the Flemings from Ypres or from Ghent.'

Well, that tells us four things. She's a wife, not a maid, not a nun, maybe a widow, but anyway, she has some status; she comes from Bath. This may have meant something to Chaucer, but it no longer means anything to us. We also learn, and this appears to be completely disconnected from everything else, that she's rather deaf.

The fourth thing we learn is quite important: she was so good at making cloth that she was better than the big producers in Flanders. This is important, because cloth making was one of the few trades a woman could do and was also a big money earner. Chaucer knew all about this. In his day job, he was Controller of Customs for wool, which was England's major export, and his wife was Flemish by birth. So we're getting a line on the Wife of Bath's status.

Chaucer's description continues, and we get even more data. In her parish church, the Wife of Bath was the first woman to go up and make an offering. Indeed, if any woman presumed to go up before her, then she was "out of alle charitee." In other words, she wouldn't give anything. Her Sunday headgear was so elaborate, it must have weighed 10 pounds. She wore scarlet hose and new shoes. "Boold was hir face, and fair, and reed of hewe." We're getting a picture, as well as a line, but then it starts to get more problematic. Chaucer says, "She was a worthy womman all hir lyve; / Housbondes at chirche dore she hadde fyve." And then Chaucer, pretending to be embarrassed, adds, "not counting other company in youth. But we don't need to speak of that right now."

The question here is, what does Chaucer mean by "worthy." He has a trick of using words in different senses according to the senses which the characters themselves put on them. So, for instance, Chaucer uses the word "worthy" seven times in his description of the Knight. Each time it clearly just means brave. To the Knight, "worth" comes from bravery and nothing else. For some of the other characters, "worthy" means well off. What does it mean for the Wife of Bath? Possibly it means that her reputation has never been challenged, although she's been married five times, and she has had other unmarried partners in youth. You might say, she's got away with it. She's had it all. But that's me saying that, not Chaucer. As I said, he leaves you to draw your own conclusions.

Going on, the wife has been on many pilgrimages, as far as Jerusalem. She knows a lot, says Chaucer, about "wandryng by the weye." What's that supposed to mean? Straying off the straight and narrow? She also has gapped teeth; she rides an ambler, which is a horse trained to amble, a more comfortable gait than trotting; she has an enormous hat; a mantle wrapped round large hips; and she wears sharp spurs; she's very good company to laugh and chat with; and, final remark from Chaucer, she knows all about "the olde daunce" of love.

Well, all these scattered observations add up pretty well. This is an experienced woman, a sexually experienced one; not all of the experience was legitimate; she had other partners in youth; she knows a lot about wandering by the way; so she's sexually independent.

And she's financially independent as well. But we don't know which came first. Did her wealth come from her husbands, or from her trade of cloth making? Whichever, she is a very dominant person. Her clothes display dominance; the enormous hat, the scarlet hose, the Sunday headgear, which she wears for show. We know she demands priority even in church.

And she wears sharp spurs. Maybe they're not just for the horse! Right at the start we were told she's a bit deaf. Does that mean anything? It does, but we don't yet know what. It's a very unusual medieval portrait, not like Guinevere at all. Are we supposed to admire her or be shocked?

Let's turn from the General Prologue to the second source of information we can use to create our portrait of the Wife of Bath. The start of her autobiography, her personal prologue, before she tells her tale, is seriously shocking. This is how it starts. "Experience, though noon auctoritee / Were in this world, were right y-nough to me / To speke of wo that is in mariage." Now, "experience," then, meant pretty much what it does now, but "authority" had a rather different sense. Back then, it still had a strong connection with the word "author," someone who writes things down, and so, what has been written down.

Remember, medieval England was still a wholly Catholic country, dominated by a church staffed by male priests—male celibate priests. And though there were literate laymen, like Chaucer himself, book learning, that is to say, "authority," was still very largely under the control of celibate and often misogynist clerics.

The Wife of Bath starts off by denying their authority. What she is saying is, I don't need book learning. I know things first-hand. And I know better! Now, what's the book, which is the foundation at this time of all book learning? It's the Bible. And the next thing the Wife of Bath does in her prologue is to take issue with the Bible, specifically with the Gospel of John, chapter 4, and then St. Paul's First Epistle to the Corinthians, chapter 7. Of course she hasn't read them. She can't read. But she's been told what they say by male celibate clerics, and she won't have it.

The story of the Samaritan woman, in John chapter 4, seems to be saying that a woman cannot have five husbands, like the Wife of Bath did, because only the first is really her husband. That is to say, a woman should only marry once. But the wife has had five husbands, all of them at church door, all perfectly legal and proper. So, she demands, how many husbands are you allowed to have? She contemptuously parodies the academic language of her time. I've never heard tell, she says, a "definition" for this number. Men may define as much as they like, she says, but what I know is that God told us to wax and multiply. Now there's a text I understand!

Jesus didn't say anything, she insists, about bigamy. Or, being sarcastic again, "octogamy." Anyway, she goes on, look at Solomon, or Abraham. I wish I'd had as many partners as they had. And as for St. Paul, in Corinthians, he may have recommended virginity. But, says the Wife of Bath, it wasn't a commandment. Maybe you have to be a virgin to be perfect. That's all right, she says, I don't mind being imperfect.

After this very aggressive start to her prologue, the Wife of Bath next gives us an account of her five husbands. I'm only going to give you the gist of what she says, but this is very briefly it. Her first three husbands, she says, were all the same, old and rich. And she controlled them completely; they were all under her thumb. She says that she made them pay when they wanted to have sex with her, and she made them have sex with her whenever she felt like it. But, she knew how to string them along. If she went out by herself, she told her husbands that she was spying on them to see if they had girlfriends. And this, it's a favourite phrase of hers, "tickled their hearts," because they thought she was jealous. Maybe the old guys were flattered that she thought they were still capable of having girlfriends. And she knew how to calm them down as well, and assure them of her doubtful fidelity.

Well, all this sounds like the partner from hell. But what makes her sympathetic still is that she enjoys herself so much. Using her own words again, "When I remember me about my youth, and all my jollity, / It tickles me about my heart-root. / Up to this day it does my heart good / That I have had my world as in my time." The word for her is "merry." And don't forget, her aggressive behaviour to men, and husbands, and celibate clerics, it's all a backlash. It's hard to blame her for resisting professional and social misogyny.

Now, she says, I'll tell you about my fourth husband. Well, cutting it short, he was a womanizer. I fried him in his own grease. He's dead and buried. And I didn't spend much on the funeral! Now, for the fifth husband, and he turns out to be a bit of a paradox; the Wife says he was an Oxford student. This means that he's a cleric, but he's not yet committed to the priesthood. At the funeral, she says, "he followed the bier of my fourth husband, and when I saw his legs as he walked in the procession, well—I gave him my heart. He was 20 and I was 40 and we were married within the month—and I gave him all my property."

But this led to another contest for dominance, because he now has the whip hand, being young and rich. And though he never became a priest, which would have barred him from marriage, he has studied for the priesthood, he believes in authority. He likes to read to her from a book, which is all about wicked wives. And now we find out why the Wife of Bath is deaf. It's a battle scar from the war between the sexes. Because she loses her temper when he's reading this darn book, this authority, and she tears a page out of it. At which he hits her, and presumably he bursts her eardrum, for which there was no medieval cure.

But she gets control just the same. She pretends to be dead, and when he bends over her, she hits him back. And in the end, he agrees to give her complete control of everything. She even makes him burn his book, and so much for authority. But once she has control, she says, she turns into the perfect wife. Control was what she wanted all along, not independence, Control. Her word for this is "sovereignty."

Now the tale Chaucer eventually assigned to her is about just that, so you can see why he picked it. It follows this fifth-husband scenario fairly closely. It goes like this, again, very briefly. In King Arthur's time, a knight rapes a maiden. The penalty for this is death, but he is handed over to the queen and the court of ladies to decide his fate. They say, you've got a year. Tell us what women most desire. Get it right, "and keep thy nekke-boon from yron." Get it wrong… So the knight asks everyone and gets all kinds of answers, until he meets a strange, ugly, old woman. She says, I know the answer, and I'll tell you, satisfaction guaranteed. But if the queen lets you off, you have to do what I ask.

He goes back to the queen, she asks, what's the answer and he says, "Wommen desyren to have sovereyntee / As wel over hir housbond as hir love, / And for to been in maistrie him above." The queen and the ladies agree; that's correct, so he keeps his head. But then the old woman says, make him keep his promise. I'm old and poor and ugly, but he has to marry me.

The knight tries to get out of it, but it's no good. On their wedding night she says to him, choose. I can be old, and ugly, and faithful; or young and beautiful, and you have to take your chance. Which do you want? And the right answer, of course, is, you choose, dear. I give you sovereignty, and mastery. And she says, that's the right answer, so I'll be both, young and beautiful, and faithful too. The perfect wife, just like the Wife of Bath was with her own fifth husband.

This is all very neat. The description in the General Prologue feeds into the personal autobiography of her own prologue, and the tale she tells dramatizes the story of her own life in fairytale terms, very neat indeed. But as I said at the start, Chaucer had a very neat story drafted for the Wife of Bath before he decided on this one. So what is it in the "what women most desire" story that made him prefer that one? The answer to that, I think, plays back to the wife's autobiography in a way that makes her a more sympathetic, and a more vulnerable, and a more courageous character. I'll come back to that.

I'll tell you briefly, again, about the story Chaucer first constructed and then rejected for the Wife of Bath. It's a fairly widespread story, very well told by the Italian writer Boccaccio, author of the famous collection the *Decameron*, which Chaucer almost certainly read. In Boccaccio's story, not Chaucer's story, this is what happens. A soldier falls in love with the beautiful wife of a merchant friend of his, and makes a pass at her. She says, okay, but it will cost you 200 gold florins. The soldier is disgusted at this and decides to teach her a lesson. So he secretly borrows 200 gold florins from her husband—that is, his friend the merchant. This money he then hands over to the wife, and this is an important bit, in the presence of a third party. And he says, as he hands the money over, "that's what I owe your husband."

The wife thinks he's just saying that because there's someone else there, and the money is really hers. She then goes through with her side of the bargain, we are told, many times. But when the husband comes back from his journey, the soldier calls on him, with the wife there, and the witness there as well, and says to the merchant, "I brought the 200 florins back and gave it to your wife. So my debt is cancelled. Okay?" The wife can't deny it, because there was a witness to the handover, and he's there looking at her, so she just has to say, "I got the money. Sorry, I forgot to tell you."

Now this as told by Boccaccio is a very misogynist story. The big scene is the one where the woman faces three pairs of masculine eyes—husband, lover, and witness—and realises all at once she's been had; she's got nothing for it; and her lover set her up for it all along. So he despises her, and there's nothing she can do about it.

Well, this was never any good as a story for the Wife of Bath! So Chaucer changed it. What he did was, take out the witness. In his last scene there's only the three of them there—husband, wife, and lover. So when the lover says to the husband, "I gave your loan back to your wife," she could logically say, "No, he never gave me any money at all." It would be his word against hers. But what Chaucer has the unfaithful wife say to her husband is, "Oh, that money. I didn't know he was paying back the loan to you. I thought that was a present for me. And I spent it all on clothes."

But then she tells her husband, and in Middle English she's making a pun, never mind, "I am your wyf. Score it upon my taille." Now, "tail" in Middle English means butt, or rear end, as it still does in vulgar modern English. But in Middle English it also meant "tally." So she saying, put it on my bill. I'll pay you back in bed. And the husband just has to go along with that.

Now, this would have made a pretty good tale for the Wife of Bath. The strong point is the back answer from the wife, who gets out of a tricky situation, quite unlike the wife in Boccaccio's story. And it uses the basic idea of the Wife of Bath, namely that sex and money are inter convertible. Money can be turned into sex, which is what the lover does. Sex can be turned into money, which is what the wife does. Chaucer has turned a misogynist story about a helpless female into a story about a dominant female who knows how to give a smart answer.

Okay, so why did Chaucer decide to drop this rather neat story for the "what women most desire" story? Because, we might think, the "what women most desire" story is the story the wife herself would like best, not because it's about sovereignty, but because it's about an old woman who becomes young and beautiful again. The Wife of Bath knows she is getting old. She's been a warrior in the great sex war. She's got the scars to prove it. She's always been a winner so far, but now. Well, she says, age has robbed me of "my beautee and my pith. / Lat go, farewel, the devel go therwith. / The flour is goon, ther is na-more to telle. / The bran, as I best can, now moste I sell. / But yet to be right mery wol I fonde."

"Flour" is another pun. You might think it means "flower," as in "rosebud," or as in "the flower of my youth." But the Wife of Bath means "flour," as in 'the best part of the wheat. What's left after the flour has been ground out is the bran. Still, you can do something with the bran, and she will. The Wife of Bath is dominant, independent, aggressive. She's also irrepressible, a little bit sad, a little bit vulnerable. Chaucer's shift from the "smart answer" tale to the "happy ending" tale brings out in her an element of yearning. It makes a more complex and more sympathetic character. We don't see another female character like her for many years.

The Wife of Bath has been a very popular character in recent times, but she also made a considerable impact on her own time. There's even a kind of sequel to her in a poem by the Scottish poet William Dunbar. It's called, and this title is in Middle Scots, not Middle English, "The Tretis of the Tua Mariit Wemen and the Wedo."

In this, a thoroughly cynical widow gives advice to two thoroughly disenchanted married women. I can only say that this comes over as the porno version of the Wife of Bath, in which the widow ends up with a fantasy of herself surrounded by, well, I don't like to say what she fantasizes herself being surrounded by, but let's tactfully call it willing and ready young men.

The fantasy is prefaced by long complaints from the two married women, which are exercises in exaggeration well beyond anything the Wife of Bath says about any of her husbands. The first one says, and she says it in Middle Scots, which is a very evocative language for insulting people in, but not easy to follow, that her husband is like the Wife of Bath's first three. He's a tired out old wreck, a bag of phlegm, good for nothing but scratching his own scabs and making vulgar noises, and a great deal else we need not go into! As for the second married woman, she says that her husband is like the Wife of Bath's number four. He's an ex-womanizer, who is now not so much worn out as played out. His sexual abilities were used up on other women before he ever got married, and now there's nothing left.

And the widow who gives them advice? Well, her advice is just, get revenge. This may seem to be a poem sympathising with women, but it isn't. It's a poem saying, this is what women are really like, insatiably lecherous, grasping, hard as nails. It's a misogynist poem. By, of course, a supposedly celibate cleric. Dunbar was a very skilful poet, but not Mr. Nice Guy. What his poem comes down to is the Wife of Bath with the fun taken out. Which shows, by contrast, how much the picture of the Wife of Bath relied on fun.

I'm sorry to say that the fun doesn't creep back into the relationship between the sexes for some considerable time. Not, indeed, until women start writing from their side, as we shall see later on in this course.

Cressida—A Love Betrayed
Lecture 6

In the last two lectures, we've met a *femme fatale* in Guinevere and a strong woman in the Wife of Bath. There's a third medieval heroine—or villainess?—who attracted the attention of two of the greatest poets in the English language, Geoffrey Chaucer and William Shakespeare, as well as a third, the late-medieval Scottish poet Robert Henryson. This medieval heroine is Cressida, caught in a love triangle between an honorable and a dishonorable man. In this lecture, we'll look at Shakespeare's play *Troilus and Cressida* as a kind of commentary on the story and character of this woman, but we'll focus more closely on the portraits of her painted by Chaucer and Henryson.

Chaucer's *Troilus and Criseyde*

- Chaucer's *Troilus and Criseyde* is a long poem, written in the 1380s and set during the 10-year siege of Troy by the Greeks. But this is not the Trojan War that Homer would have recognized. The whole setting is medieval, including the conventions of war and love.

- Criseyde is a Trojan, but her father, Calchas, is a traitor, which makes her vulnerable. Calchas is an astrologer, and he's seen in the stars that the Greeks are going to win. Thus, he's fled from Troy

In Chaucer's Trojan War, armored knights fight by arrangement outside the city, as they did in the Hundred Years' War.

and joined the Greeks, leaving Criseyde behind. She is a widow but has powerful friends, including the great Trojan champion Prince Hector, who assures her that she will be protected. But there are Trojans who distrust her, and she won't be safe if the city falls.

- The first time we see Criseyde, she has gone to the temple. She's dressed in black, and although she's sure of herself, she's trying not to be noticed. This kind of ambiguity marks her throughout the poem. She seems and is vulnerable, but there's a sense that she's always in control.

- Of course, as Criseyde stands in the temple, she is noticed by Troilus, a Trojan prince, who gapes at her. She returns his gaze, then drops her eyes demurely. In Shakespeare's version of the story, there's no doubt that she is deliberately playing hard to get. Troilus immediately falls in love with her. His friend Pandarus, who is Criseyde's uncle, volunteers to set Troilus up with his niece.

- The conversation between Pandarus and Criseyde concerning Troilus again shows the ambiguity that haunts this rather skillful young woman. She wants to know what he's talking about but refuses to ask outright. Just after Pandarus has left, Troilus rides by in armor, his helmet battered and his shield full of arrows, blushing at the cheers of the bystanders. Criseyde falls in love.

- As the courtly love affair slowly progresses, tremendous pressure is put on Criseyde. She's lured into a private meeting with Troilus by threats of legal action being taken against her. She's lured again to Pandarus's house, where the weather forces her to stay the night. Her room has a secret door, and the affair is consummated. Criseyde looks like a victim, but we have to wonder. Does she really believe her uncle when he says that Troilus is out of town?

Reading Criseyde

- At this point, our sympathies might be with Criseyde, but then, the situation changes. The Trojans have a bad day in the war and lose many noble prisoners. Calchas, the traitor, persuades the Greeks to offer to swap one of them for his daughter. The Trojan mob immediately demands that she be used as an exchange and sent out of Troy.

- Troilus is in despair and ready to commit suicide. He suggests that they run away together, but Criseyde won't have it. Troilus, she argues, will be disgraced forever if he runs away. She assures Troilus that he can trust her, and Chaucer tells us, "That al this thyng was seyd of good entente"—she really meant it.

- Readers have a moment of doubt in Criseyde in a scene in which Troilus prepares to commit suicide; Criseyde has fainted, and he thinks she must be dead. When she comes around and he stops, Criseyde says that if he had killed himself, she would have done the same with his sword. But is that true? Chaucer has already told us that she is "the fearfullest of creatures." She then immediately changes the subject, telling Troilus they should go straight to bed. Shakespeare has no doubt that she's being deceptive.

- Criseyde leaves Troy, escorted by the Greek Diomedes, to whom she soon begins to turn her affections. This change of heart is made to look especially disgraceful by Shakespeare. He writes a scene in which she arrives in the Greek camp and is kissed by the warriors; she's passed from man to man, flirting coyly but making no objection.

- Criseyde is made to look even worse by the normally nonjudgmental Chaucer. He presents Diomedes as dishonorable, a man who views women as conquests about which he likes to brag, yet Criseyde falls for him. Does she do so out of fear, or is she just a weathervane? Does she not know what love is? Chaucer uses the trick of making excuses for her, which serves to call attention to what she's doing wrong. She then sends a letter to Troilus, who is back in Troy, going mad with worry.

- Criseyde's is the first "Dear John" letter in English, and it's confusing and full of clichés. Having received the letter, Troilus doesn't realize that she's broken off the affair. He finds out only when he sees a brooch he had given to her being worn by Diomedes on the battlefield. This is the only moment when Chaucer expresses criticism of his heroine; he writes, "and that was litel nede," meaning, "There was little need for her to do that."

- From there, the story drifts to an end. Troilus is killed in battle by Achilles. His soul looks down and laughs. Criseyde tells herself that she'll get it right the next time: "to Diomede, anyway, I will be true." Perhaps she means it, but she never seems to mean anything for long.

Robert Henryson's *The Testament of Cresseid*

- At the end of his poem, Chaucer comments that the story is one about pagans who did not know God. Robert Henryson, 100 years later, believed that wasn't a satisfying ending. In response, he wrote *The Testament of Cresseid*. Most people think it is a harsh and cruel poem, a kind of reproof to Chaucer for being too soft on his heroine, but it seems sad, as well.

- In Henryson's poem, Cresseid receives a cruel "Dear Jane" letter from Diomedes. Alone and deserted, she is passed from man to man. At last, she goes home to her father, who welcomes her. But then she makes a complaint against the gods, and the pagan gods call a parliament to punish her. She has a dream in which the god Saturn touches her with his frosty wand, and the touch turns her into a leper.

- One of the poem's dreadful moments is that Cresseid then wakes up from her dream, looks in the mirror, and discovers it wasn't a dream. In medieval circumstances, she has no option but to join the lepers, among whom she makes another long complaint. This is answered only by a female leper, who tells her that she must live the law of the lepers and always wear a clapper to warn others away.

- As Cresseid is sitting among the lepers, who are begging by the wayside, Troilus rides by. He sees the lepers, but the disease has changed Cresseid so much that he does not recognize her. Just the same, she reminds him of Cresseid, and he throws her all the money he's got and rides on. The disease has made Cresseid almost blind, and she asks the other lepers who has just ridden by. They reply that it was the noble and generous Sir Troilus.

- At this, Cresseid makes a final lament, and then we get her testament, her last will. She leaves her body to the worms and toads, as if she's disgusted with it. She leaves her gold to the lepers, to see her buried. She leaves her ruby ring to Troilus so that he will know about her death. She leaves her spirit to Diana, the goddess of virginity, hoping that after death, she can walk with Diana in the waste woods and streams, as if she never wants to see anyone again.
  - The last clause is a kind of non-bequest. She says, "O Diomed, thou hes baith broche and belt / Quhilk Troilus gave me in takning / Of his trew lufe."

  - She dies saying the word "love," which she has betrayed. She dies unable to bequeath something she gave away for nothing. It's a terrible picture of remorse that comes too late.

- The poem ends with a series of nonstatements. Troilus is bitterly upset by the news of Cresseid's death, but all he can manage to say is, "I can no moir; / Scho was untrew, and wo is me thairfoir." On the gravestone is written "Cresseid of Troyis toun ... / Under this stane, lait lipper, lyis deid." And at the very end, Henryson writes, "Sen scho is deid, I speik of hir no moir."

- We could read the poem as a classic male revenge fantasy, but it seems that Henryson was also trying to answer the basic question: What made her do it? Why did she give up Troilus for Diomedes? The answer seems to be signaled by the gods assigned to carry out the sentence and by the nature of the punishment.
  - In the Middle Ages, leprosy was often thought of as a sexually transmitted disease, while in Henryson's time, the late 15th and early 16th centuries, syphilis had also started to become common. The symptoms of syphilis could look rather like those of leprosy, as could the results of age.

  - One of the two gods assigned to carry out the sentence on Cresseid is Cynthia, who is also the moon. The moon, the only heavenly body medievals knew that waxes and wanes, is a symbol of change.

- ○ The other god who passes sentence is Saturn. But Saturn in Greek is Kronos, and though this is actually a mistake, Kronos was taken to be the same as Chronos, which means "time." Thus, Cresseid is punished by change and time.

- Cresseid's mistake is summed up in the accusation she makes against the gods. She says, "You gave me once a divine guarantee / That I should be the flower of love in Troy." But there is no such divine guarantee for anyone. At bottom, Cresseid was led astray by feelings of entitlement. She seems to have thought that she would meet more men like Troilus and, perhaps, do better. She found out too late that was not the case.

Essential Reading

Chaucer (Barney, ed.), *Troilus and Criseyde*.

Henryson (Fox, ed.), *Poems*.

Suggested Reading

Gordon, *The Double Sorrow of Troilus*.

Lewis, "What Chaucer Really Did to *Il Filostrato*."

MacQueen, *Robert Henryson*.

Questions to Consider

1. In addition to Madame Bovary and Anna Karenina, can you think of any other cases, in literature or in real life, of a woman choosing a bad man when she already has a good one?

2. Do you believe in "the wages of sin" or "bad karma"?

Cressida—A Love Betrayed
Lecture 6—Transcript

In the last two lectures we've met a femme fatale in Guinevere, we've met a strong woman in the Wife of Bath. There's a third medieval heroine—or is she a villainess?—who attracted the attention of two of the greatest poets in the English language, Geoffrey Chaucer and William Shakespeare. And in between, one who on his day could rise above them both, the late medieval Scottish poet Robert Henryson.

Perhaps contrary to expectation, I am not going to give Shakespeare top billing. I'm going to treat his play, *Troilus and Cressida*, as a kind of commentary on the story and on the character and work it in to what I have to say about Chaucer and Henryson. Cressida, or Cresseid, or Criseyde, is something of an archetypal figure. She's the woman in a love triangle, like Guinevere. But Guinevere was torn between two honorable men. Criseyde is caught between a true lover and, well, I have to say, a creep. And she chooses the creep, just like Flaubert's Emma Bovary and Tolstoy's Anna Karenina.

It's a recurrent situation, and quite common in real life. There are some things which are far more common in fiction than in fact. People call these "quicksand motifs." You find far more quicksands in fiction than you are ever likely to meet in reality. But conversely, there are some things which are much more common in real life than in fiction. One of them, for instance, is the "Dear John" letter, or the "Dear Jane" letter. People in reality write and receive these all the time, but they are not so common in fiction, though there is a famously cynical one in *Madame Bovary*. Criseyde, anyway, writes one in Chaucer's poem *Troilus and Criseyde*, as far as I know, the first one ever recorded in English. I'll talk about it later, but one of the strange things is, that although it is so early, it contains most of the clichés with which too many of us are familiar.

In the Guinevere lecture, I commented on the way that cultural values changed in the Middle Ages as regards courtesy, chivalry, attitude to ladies. In *Troilus and Criseyde*, Chaucer himself goes out of his way to remind his readers that, "in sundry londes, sundry been usages." In different times and places we find different ways of expressing love. Well, actually, not so very different. As I read Chaucer, I can't help thinking every now and then, this is like a modern pop song, or even a country and western number. It's as if Troilus, the true lover, who's been dumped, could come out with a bit of the Beatles song, "Yesterday," or even, "You picked a fine time to leave me, Lucille."

So, in Chaucer's poem we have a familiar situation—female central character, masculine complaint, male self pity. But Criseyde is also a *My Fair Lady* figure, the heroine her creator—Chaucer anyway—falls in love with. Chaucer wasn't exactly her creator. Like Malory with Guinevere, he had a book in front of him. An Italian one, once again, by Giovanni Boccaccio, called *Il Filostrato*—the man prostrated by love. Chaucer, though, again like Malory, thought he understood the story better and decided to tell it his way.

The result is a long poem in Middle English called *Troilus and Criseyde*, written in the 1380s. It's set in the Trojan War, like Homer. Troilus is a Trojan prince during the 10-year long siege of Troy by the Greeks. But it's not the kind of war Homer would have recognized, no chariots, no infantry in bronze. The knights ride out to battle in plate armor, as in the Hundred Years War in which Chaucer served, and fight by arrangement outside the city. "The long day, with spears sharp and ground / With arrows, darts, and swords, and maces fell / They fight and bring down horse and man to ground / And with their axes out the brains they spill." The whole setting is medieval, including the conventions of war and of love.

Criseyde, however, has a problem which Guinevere did not. She's vulnerable. She's a Trojan. But her Trojan father, Calchas, is a traitor. He's an astrologer, and he's seen in the stars that the Greeks are going to win. So he's fled from Troy and joined the Greeks, leaving Criseyde behind. She's a widow and a lady, and she has powerful friends, including the great Trojan champion Prince Hector, who assures her she will be protected. But there are Trojans who distrust her. And if the city falls, well, ladies in a city given over to sack are never safe, remember Aeneas's wife Creusa.

The first time we see Criseyde, then, she's gone to the temple. Like going to church, but Chaucer knew those people were pagans. She's wearing black, as a widow, and she stands "behind other folk […] near the door," trying not to draw attention. Just the same, Chaucer tells us that her looking and her manner are "ful assured." So, she's very sure of herself, but she's trying not to be noticed. This kind of ambiguity marks her all the way through. She seems, and is, very vulnerable. But there's a sense that she's always in control. She really knows what she's doing. She's certainly much sharper than her lover Troilus, maybe too sharp for her own good.

Of course, as she stands in the temple she is noticed, by Troilus, who gapes at her so obviously that she notices. And she responds coolly but provocatively. Chaucer says she looks rather "deignous," which means disdainful, "for she let her look fall / A little aside in such a manner / Askance," as if to say. "What! May I not stand here?" It's the dropping-your-eyes-trick. You see someone looking at you; you hold his eye for a moment; then you drop yours demurely. Then you count three and you look up again. It's devastating if done properly.

But in the case of Criseyde, you wonder. Is she really frightened, or is she playing hard to get? Shakespeare, at least, was in no doubt. He wrote in a scene in which Cressida soliloquizes, saying that although she already has her eye on Troilus, she knows not to make herself cheap. "Men prize the thing ungain'd more than it is." So for Shakespeare, she's definitely and deliberately playing hard to get from the start.

But back to Chaucer, Troilus, on beholding Cressida, falls in love in the proper medieval way, which is, at first sight. And the effect is that of a thunderbolt, or if you like, a dart from Cupid's bow. Love has pretty much the effect on him of fever, or maybe anorexia, or possibly clinical depression. His state is actually recognized by his friend Pandarus, who is Criseyde's uncle. Pandarus likes to get mixed up in love affairs, in a voyeuristic sort of way, and he says, he will set Troilus up with his niece.

But the first conversation between Pandarus and Criseyde shows again the kind of ambiguity that haunts this rather skillful young woman. It goes like this. I'll try to do the two speakers in slightly different voices.

Pandarus says: "I've got a secret. I could tell you something that would really cheer you up."

Criseyde: "The Greeks! Are they giving up the siege?"

Pandarus: "Oh no, much better than that! You'd really like to know!"

But Criseyde doesn't take the bait. She doesn't ask him what the secret is, obviously, because she knows he wants her to ask him. Pandarus goes on to give Troilus a very heavy plug, but then, since she doesn't pick up on it, he says he's leaving.

Criseyde: "What, so soon? Sit down. We need to talk."

Pandarus: "No, you need to dance. Do stop wearing widow's black. I really want to give you some good advice."

Note, she does the eye trick again by looking down and not responding. But as Pandarus continues to beat about the bush, in the end she says, "Come off, and tell me what it is!"

Pandarus: "Troilus is dying for love of you. Now, can't you—do something to make him feel better?"

Criseyde: "You're supposed to protect me! Not set me up!"

Pandarus: "Oh well, if you don't trust me, I'll go, and I'm not coming back!"

Criseyde: "Well, tell me more. How do you know?"

Perhaps you can see my point. It looks as if Pandarus is running this conversation against Criseyde's will. But is he? She wants to know what he's talking about but is not going to ask. But if he tries to leave, she catches hold of his coat. And then, just after Pandarus has left, Troilus rides by, in armor, on a wounded horse, with his helmet battered and his shield full of arrows, blushing at the cheers of the bystanders. And Criseyde says to herself, "who gave me drink?" She means, have I just been fed a love potion?

This does not speed matters up very much, for a courtly love affair requires prolonged agonizing, just like modern Hollywood rom-coms. But during this period, what we're made aware of is the pressure being put on Criseyde. First, she's lured into a private meeting with Troilus by threats of legal action being taken against her. She needs support. She's persuaded to visit Troilus's brother Deiphebus. Troilus just happens to be there, and they're left together while Deiphebus and Helen are out in the garden discussing something. And just to remind us that Troy is a dangerous place, they're discussing a death sentence.

Then she's lured again, to Pandarus's house, and Pandarus has checked that it is certain to rain hard so she can't go home. He has a room for her, and another one for her maids, and of course he's her uncle, so she's quite safe. But her room has a secret door. It's then that the affair reaches consummation, with the very active assistance of Pandarus, whose voyeurism here becomes obvious. So, Criseyde looks like a victim, pressured, betrayed, seduced. But you have to wonder, she asks whether Troilus really is out of town. But does she really believe the answer? She knows her uncle is trying to set her up.

Well, so far, for all the ambiguities, one's sympathies might well be with Criseyde. Alone, vulnerable, pressurized, let down by her protector. But now it changes. The Trojans have a bad day in the war and lose many noble prisoners. Calchas, the traitor, persuades the Greeks to offer to swap one of them for his daughter. The Trojan mob immediately demands that she be used as an exchange and sent out of Troy. Troilus is in despair and ready to commit suicide. Then he suggests, let's run away together. But Criseyde won't have it. She says, "No, I'll go." Troilus, she argues, will be disgraced forever if he runs away. "What will people say? Anyway, you can trust me! No, I can see you don't trust me! Can I trust you?" Chaucer adds, "And treweliche […] al this thyng was seyd of good entente." She really meant it. Hmmm.

One very doubtful moment is when Troilus gets set to commit suicide, because Criseyde has fainted, and he thinks in his over-dramatic way that she must be dead. When she comes round and he stops, Criseyde says, if you had killed yourself, believe me, "with this same sword, myself I would have slain." Would she really? Chaucer has already told us that she is "the fearfullest' of creatures." And Criseyde immediately changes the subject, saying, "[w]hoo, for we han ryght ynough of this. / And lat us rise, and streght to bedde go." Well, that's one sure way of distracting attention.

Once again, Shakespeare is in no doubt about this. He writes in a scene where Troilus is trying to explain why he's anxious, and he gets a severe brush off from Cressida and another one, earlier, where she makes a very powerful statement of her fidelity, which is undercut by the way she says to Troilus, if I play you false, in times to come let people say, "as false [...] as fox to lamb, as wolf to heifer calf, / Yes, let them say, to stick the heart of falsehood, / 'As false as Cressid'." Which, of course, they will.

Anyway, she leaves Troy. Her Greek escort is Diomedes. Pretty soon, she has taken up with Diomedes. And this change of heart is made to look especially disgraceful by Shakespeare. He writes in another scene in which she arrives in the Greek camp, having just said goodbye to Troilus, and is kissed by the Greek general, Agamemnon. Our general has kissed her, says Ulysses, on the make as usual, so she should be kissed "in general." We'll all kiss her. So she's passed round, flirting coyly, but making no objection. After she's gone, Ulysses says, in effect, "you can see that one's a party girl." "There's language in her eye. [...] Her wanton spirits look out / At every joint and motive of her body."

In a later scene Ulysses stands by sympathetically as Troilus overhears Cressida playing the same tricks on Diomedes that she used on him. Shakespeare presents her as shallow, a practiced flirt, hopping from one alpha male to the next, as opportunity serves. But she's made to look, if anything, worse, by the normally non-judgemental Chaucer. What Chaucer does is present Diomedes as a grade-A creep of a familiar modern type. There are two signs of this. When he first turns up to act as Criseyde's escort, he says to himself, "well I might as well make a pass at her. At worst it will pass the time." A familiar notion. "Always try your luck, there's nothing to lose." But he also says to himself, anyone who gets her, "He myghte seyn he were a conquerour." Criseyde would be a grade-A conquest. Furthermore, Chaucer notes, "som men seyn he was of tonge large." In other words, not only does Diomedes see women just as conquests, if he succeeds, he likes to tell everyone all about it. Another familiar notion.

And the creep is the guy she goes for! Out of fear? Or is she just a weathervane? Does she not know what love is? Chaucer uses the trick of trying hard to make excuses for her, all of which call attention to what she's doing wrong. The culmination of this is the letter which she sends to Troilus, who is meanwhile back in Troy, going mad with worry. As I said earlier, it's the first "Dear John" letter in English. Now, "Dear John" letters and "Dear Jane" letters are difficult things to write. They are, of course, letters sent— nowadays it's probably text messaging on a smart phone—to break off a relationship. Very often they are sent to someone who is far away, and I think the phrase "Dear John letter" became common during wartime, when women sent them to their lovers abroad on military service. But if you write one, you know you're doing something cruel and possibly something cowardly, because you don't want to say it face to face. So the writer is a prey to conflicting emotions—guilt, embarrassment, a wish to make excuses—very likely what the psychologists call projection—accusing the other party of doing what you're doing yourself.

Well, Criseyde's letter has it all. It's confused—Chaucer is very good at pretending to write badly—and it's full of clichés. She says, cutting out the rhetoric and the repetitions, "I'm really upset! I got your letter. I can't come to see you, but I can't tell you why. I know you're just thinking of yourself! Please don't be angry! People are talking about us. (Again), don't be angry. I know you've just been fooling me. I'm sorry this is so short." And of course, the classic line, "I hope we can still be friends."

Having received this letter, Troilus, not surprisingly, still docs not know what is going on or that he has, in fact, been dumped. He only finds out when he sees, on the battlefield, a brooch he gave to Criseyde, which is being worn by Diomedes. That's the only moment when Chaucer expresses criticism of his heroine. He says, "and that was litel nede." And then the story just drifts to an end. Troilus is killed in battle by Achilles. His soul looks down and laughs at it all. And Criseyde tells herself, as people do, I'll get it right next time, "to Diomede, anyway, I will be true." Perhaps she means it. The trouble is, she never means anything for long.

Chaucer leaves it at that, commenting only that the whole thing is a story about pagans, who did not know God. But is that a satisfying ending? A hundred years later Robert Henryson thought not and wrote his poem *The Testament of Cresseid*. Note the word Testament. The poem builds up to her death, and her will. Most people think it is a harsh and cruel poem, a kind of reproof to Chaucer for being too soft on his heroine. We are fairly sure that Henryson was a Scottish schoolmaster.

Now, my first dialect was Scottish, because at the age of seven I was sent to a boarding school in central Scotland while my parents remained in India. And I always tell people that mine was not a sissy boarding school like Harry Potter's Hogwarts, where the kids go home for holidays and are disciplined by losing house points. We stayed at school 365 days a year; we saw our parents only every three years, and the thought of being disciplined by losing house points would just have been laughed at. So, no one needs to tell me about the harshness of Scottish schoolmasters.

But I think people have got Henryson wrong. His poem is harsh, but it's sad as well. The story is very simple, though it's told in between long passages of rhetorical description. It goes like this (and I will revert to my native Scottish when I quote from it). Henryson has a habit, note, of shortening the names of characters. So, here goes. "Quhen Diomed had all his appetyte / And mair, fulfillit of this fair ladie," he sent to her "ane lybell of repudie / And hir excludit fra his companie." In other words he sent her a "Dear Jane" letter, but it was a cruel one. A letter of repudiation, which said he did not want to see her again.

Cresseid, alone and deserted, is then passed from man to man. At last she goes home to her father, who welcomes her, as fathers often don't in these circumstances. All okay, it seems. But then she makes a complaint against the gods, and the pagan gods call a parliament to punish her. She has a dream in which the god Saturn touches her with his frosty wand, and the touch turns her into a leper. One of the poem's dreadful moments is that Cresseid then wakes up from her dream, looks in the mirror, and discovers it wasn't a dream. Henryson comments with his usual understatement, "Gif scho in hert was wa aneuch," God knows.

In medieval circumstances she has no option but to join the lepers, among whom she makes another long complaint. This is answered only by a leper lady, who says, "Sen thy weiping dowbillis bot thy wo, / I counsell the mak vertew of ane neid, / To leir to clap thy clapper to and fro / And live efter the law of lipper leid." She means, the law of the leper people, who must always clap a clapper to warn people to keep off.

So Cresseid is sitting among the lepers, who are begging by the wayside, and Troilus rides by. He's just had a good day against the Greeks. He sees the lepers, with Cresseid among them. But the disease has changed her so much that he does not recognize her. Just the same, she reminds him of Cresseid: "For knichtlie pietie and memoriall / Of fair Cresseid, ane gyrdill can he tak, / Ane purs of gold, and mony gay jowall, / And in the skirt of Cressid doun can swak ..." He throws her all he's got, and rides on.

The disease has made Cresseid almost blind, so after he's gone, she asks the other lepers, who was that? And the lepers say, that was Sir Troilus, noble and generous. At this, she makes a final lament, and then we have her Testament, her last will. It has five clauses. She leaves her body to the worms and toads, as if she's disgusted with it. She leaves her gold to the lepers to see her buried. She leaves her ruby ring to Troilus so he will know about her death. She leaves her spirit—sadly and ironically—to Diana, as the goddess of virginity, hoping that after death she will be able to walk with Diana in the waste woods and streams, as if she never wants to see anyone anymore.

The last clause is a kind of non bequest. She says, "O Diomed, thou hes baith broche and belt / Quhilk Troilus gave me in takning / Of his trew lufe," and with that word she swelt, she died. She dies saying the word "love," which she has betrayed. She dies unable to bequeath something which she gave away for nothing. It's a terrible picture of remorse which comes too late.

The poem ends with a series of non statements. Troilus is bitterly upset by the news of Criseyde's death, but all he can manage to say is, "I can no moir. / Scho was untrew, and wo is me thairfoir." On the gravestone is written, "Cresseid of Troyis toun / Under this stane, lait lipper, lyis deid." And at the very end all that Henryson can manage to say is, "Sen scho is deid, I speik of hir no moir."

Well, that's Scotland for you. Understatement there is an art form. When Henryson says that Diomed had "all his appetite / And more, fulfilled," "and more" means "much too much." When he says, "if she in heart had woe enough," "woe enough" also means "much too much." Human grief and divine cruelty, run through the poem. Now you could say, this is a classic male revenge fantasy. The prom queen who sent you the "Dear John" letter, years later as you're driving by in your BMW, you see her looking shabby and standing at a bus stop. It's like that, only raised to a much higher power.

One thing which scholars have noted is that in the Middle Ages leprosy was often thought of as a sexually transmitted disease, while in Henryson's time, the late 15th and early 16th century, syphilis had also started to become common. And the symptoms of syphilis could look rather like those of leprosy. But you could say, they also look rather like the results of age.

Who are the two gods assigned to carry out sentence on Cresseid? One is Cynthia, who is also the moon. The moon, the only heavenly body medievals knew which waxes and wanes, is a symbol of change. The other god who passes sentence is Saturn. But Saturn in Greek is Kronos, and though this is actually a mistake, Kronos was taken to be the same as Chronos, which means time. So Cresseid is punished by change and time. Isn't Henryson here suggesting that women who trade on their beauty will find it runs out?

Cresseid's mistake is summed up in the accusation she makes against the gods. She says, "you gave me once a divine guarantee / That I should be the flower of love in Troy." But there is no such divine guarantee for anyone. I conclude, that at bottom, Cresseid was led astray by feelings of entitlement. As if she'd said to herself, "I can get away with this. I can do better. I'll meet guys like Troilus on a regular basis." She found out too late, as many people do, women and men, that's not the case.

So what Henryson says is certainly harsh but not necessarily stupid. It may be that tragedies like hers, like "Dear John" and "Dear Jane" letters, are something all too common, if not in the highly exaggerated form that Henryson gives it, in real life male-female relationships. Different customs in different times and places, says Chaucer. But some things remain terribly familiar.

Beowulf—A Hero with Hidden Depths
Lecture 7

*B*eowulf is not an easy poem to understand, and Beowulf himself is not an easy character to read. On the surface, he's an even more classic case of the "basic male hero" than any of the ones we've seen so far. He's big and strong and seems fearless; his response to danger and difficulty is, invariably, action. But in this lecture, we'll look for other aspects of Beowulf's personality. In his heroic façade, is he, perhaps, overcompensating for early neglect? Are there hints of vulnerability beneath the surface? And what moral can we draw from the poem? Does Beowulf provide us an example of wisdom gained through age?

Beowulf as Hero
- On the surface, Beowulf seems like a classic example of the "basic male hero"—big, strong, and fearless. We find a good example of his courage about a third of the way through the poem.

- Beowulf has wrestled and defeated the man-eating giant Grendel in the hall of King Hrothgar. In fact, Beowulf has torn off Grendel's arm, and it's been nailed up as a trophy. After 12 years of terror from Grendel, this is cause for great celebration, and King Hrothgar organizes a feast.

- But in the night, after the feast, Grendel's mother sneaks into the hall. She takes the arm and one of the Danish warriors, Aeschere, and flees back to her home beneath a lake.

- When the king informs Beowulf of this renewed attack, his response gives us the heroic attitude in a nutshell: Heroes fight for glory; death is a certainty, so heroes don't worry about it; and revenge is an obligation.

- Beowulf then tells Hrothgar that they should follow the track wherever it leads. When they reach the monster's lake, the hero puts on his armor, borrows a famous sword from a bystander, and asks Hrothgar to see that his armor is sent home and that the borrowed sword is replaced if he doesn't return. With that, he dives into the lake and eventually finds himself in a strange submarine hall.

- He sees Grendel's mother and strikes out at her with his borrowed sword, but it bounces off. He throws it down and immediately grapples with her, but she is too strong even for Beowulf. She draws her sax (a short sword) and tries to stab him; Beowulf is saved by his armor.

- Beowulf struggles back to his feet, takes up a giant's sword that is leaning against the wall, and cuts off the hag's head. The poem tells us: "It broke the bone-rings; it sheared through the flesh. She fell to the ground. The sword was bloody. The man rejoiced."

Beowulf's Deeper Personality
- Although Beowulf is self-confident, he seems to lack a defined sense of self. He regularly defines himself by reference to someone else, apparently his king or lord, whose name is Hygelac. We could take Beowulf's repeated mentions of Hygelac as a sign of his loyal nature, but it also seems like a kind of emotional dependency.

- At one point in the story, Beowulf has a verbal clash with Unferth, one of the Danes at Hrothgar's court. Unferth asks Beowulf rudely if he once had a swimming contest with a man called Breca. They risked their lives, Unferth says, for *dolgilpe*, "a foolish boast," and Beowulf lost the contest.
  ○ Beowulf replies, strongly and confidently, that he didn't lose, and in fact, he killed the sea-beasts that attacked him. In his reply, though, we can hear notes of self-criticism. Twice he says that he and Breca were both just boys, and he does not entirely reject the accusation of *dolgilpe*.

  ○ Later in the poem, we are told that Beowulf did not have a good reputation in his youth; the nobles of his tribe considered him lazy.

- Is Beowulf the hero overcompensating for early neglect? Are there hints of vulnerability beneath his intimidating façade?

Background to *Beowulf*

- Although *Beowulf* is in Old English (Anglo-Saxon), the poet never mentions England and seems to know nothing about it. He does, however, know about Scandinavia. Half the poem is set among the Danes, and the other half among Beowulf's own people, the Geats, who must be the inhabitants of what are now the Swedish provinces of East and West Götaland.

- The poet has detailed information about four Scandinavian royal houses: the kings of the Danes, Geats, Swedes, and another people called the Bards. All these remained well known to later Scandinavian tradition, except for the kings of the Geats, who vanished without trace.

- We might think that the Geats were fictional, except for the fact that halfway through the poem—after Hygelac has been mentioned at least 10 times—the poet lets slip that Hygelac is the son of Beowulf's maternal grandfather, the king of the Geats. This makes him Beowulf's mother's brother, a relation of special importance to the Germanic tribes. This relationship explains Beowulf's emotional dependence on Hygelac.

- Although Hygelac was completely forgotten in his homeland, he's not fictional and was remembered in England. It's likely that the poet did not bother to explain who he was because he assumed that everyone already knew.
  - Hygelac (called Chochilaicus by a Latin chronicler) was the leader of a disastrous piratical raid on what is now the Netherlands sometime around the year 525. He and most of his men were killed.

  - As a young hero, Beowulf does not know that this event will occur, but the original audience of the poem did. To those who first listened to the poem, Beowulf's emotional dependence on his uncle made him vulnerable.

- This point is underscored when Beowulf, after killing Grendel and his mother, offers to bring thousands of soldiers to the aid of King Hrothgar if trouble arises. He says he knows that Hygelac will back him up. Hrothgar compliments Beowulf on his wisdom and says, "if by any chance Hygelac should die, and you survive, the Geats will have no one better than you to select as king—if, that is, you should want the job." Hrothgar sees Beowulf's future accurately, down to Beowulf refusing the kingship in favor of Hygelac's young son.

- Hrothgar sees the shadow hanging over Beowulf, but he doesn't see the shadow hanging over himself. Once again, the poet does no more than hint at this, probably because the situation was as familiar to Anglo-Saxons as the story of King Arthur is to us.
  o It looks as if the kingdom of the Danes is destined to tear itself apart through civil war, just as the Geats will destroy themselves with rash aggression.

  o The fact is that everyone in the poem is vulnerable—Beowulf, Hygelac, and Hrothgar—but they don't know it. One person who does know it is the Danish queen, Wealhtheow. As the poem makes clear, in Heroic Ages, it's women who pay the highest price for defeat.

Beowulf and the Dragon
- As a young hero, Beowulf assumed he was invulnerable, even against monsters. In the last third of the poem, he squares off against another monster, the dragon. By this time, he is old, and almost everyone in his family is dead. He has become king of the Geats, as Hrothgar predicted, by default. He has defeated the Swedes, but he has neither wife nor child.

- In retaliation for a robbery from its lair, a dragon burns down Beowulf's hall. When he receives the news, we get one fleeting

As a young hero, Beowulf was confident in his strength, but as he ages, he must steel himself for battle.

glimpse of his inner life. The poet says, "The wise man thought that he must have bitterly offended God the Ruler, the eternal Lord. His breast boiled inside with dark thoughts, as was not his custom." Beowulf orders an iron shield and sets off to certain death—for both him and the dragon.

- How is this older Beowulf different from the young hero he used to be? Before the fight, he sits down outside the dragon's lair. His mind, we are told, is gloomy. He knows fate is near. In repeated speeches, he thinks over his own long life, full of disasters, but he still takes savage satisfaction in his actions. At last, he pushes himself up with his shield—a stiff-jointed old man?—and orders his men to stay back.

- Just as Bilbo and Frodo showed us that you don't have to be big and strong to be a hero, so Beowulf shows us that you don't have to be young and strong either. Heroes can also be old and tired.

What counts is not *mægen*, "youthful strength," but *mod*, "spirit unaffected by time."

- Beowulf's heart is strong, but he's not what he once was. The dragon fire is almost too much for him; his iron shield gives less protection than he hoped; and his sword fails him. The dragon bites him in the throat with its poisoned teeth.

- Beowulf is saved by a young relative, Wiglaf, who distracts the dragon while Beowulf draws his sax and stabs the worm in its belly. The dragon is dead, but Beowulf's wound starts to swell. He then makes three death speeches, mixing grief and triumph.

- Scholars have long argued about whether the poet, probably an 8th-century Christian, believed that the pagan Beowulf's soul might be saved. The poet seems to have admired Beowulf, but he knew that salvation was in the hands of God.

Assessing *Beowulf*

- Some people would like to think that *Beowulf* reinforces the idea that those who live by the sword shall die by the sword. But for a hero in a Heroic Age, that's the point; there's no alternative.

- Others have argued that the poem's message is that a good young hero does not make a good old king. Beowulf's decision to fight the dragon by himself is certainly disastrous for his people. His death creates a power vacuum. When the messenger announces Beowulf's death, he predicts that the Geats will be conquered, and the poet says, "He was not far wrong."

- We might also feel that Beowulf the man shows us how we gain wisdom—insight into the true nature of life and death.
  - The hero begins with an emotional dependency that makes him vulnerable and a confidence that is ill-founded.

  - He learns better, but in a way, he doesn't change. He becomes even more self-reliant, although he also knows the limits of his self-reliance. His wisdom isn't perfect, but it may be as good as we can get.

Essential Reading

Anonymous (Ringler, trans.), *Beowulf*.

Suggested Reading

Fulk, ed., *Interpretations of Beowulf*.

Irving, *A Reading of Beowulf*.

Niles, ed., *Beowulf and Lejre*.

Shippey, *Beowulf*.

Tolkien, J.R.R. (Tolkien, C., ed.), *The Monsters and the Critics*.

Questions to Consider

1. Heroes must be brave, but at what point does recklessness become irresponsible?

2. What kind of leaders do you most admire, and what are the most essential leadership qualities?

Beowulf—A Hero with Hidden Depths
Lecture 7—Transcript

Woody Allen famously said, "Don't take any course where they make you read *Beowulf*." He was nearly right. What he should have said was, "Don't take a course where they make you read *Beowulf* if it's taught by someone who's never read *Beowulf*." And I'm afraid many such courses are taught by people who haven't read the poem; and even more by people who've read it but have not been able to understand it. It's not an easy poem to understand, and Beowulf himself is not an easy character to read.

On the surface, though, he's an even more classic case of the Basic Male Hero than any of the ones we've seen so far; is he big, is he strong, is he fearless? He's certainly big. When Beowulf first shows up on the shores of Denmark, come because he's heard of the monster Grendel who is terrorizing the hall of the Danish king, the Danish coast guard looks at Beowulf and his companions and says, "I've never seen a bigger man on earth than that one among you. He is no hall lounger fitted out with weapons—unless his looks belie him."

So, Beowulf is certainly big. He's also certainly strong. Beowulf is directed by the coastguard to the hall of the Danish king, where he meets the door guard. The door guard goes in and announces his arrival, and the King of the Danes, whose name is Hrothgar, responds immediately, saying "I've heard of him. Our seafarers who visited his country said that he has the handgrip of 30 thanes." Something which turns out to be true. Beowulf prefers to fight hand to hand and notoriously does not have much luck with weapons. Later on the poet will excuse this by saying his hand was too strong, and swords broke when he used them. In fact, I may as well say right now that Beowulf, with the strength of a bear, seems to have crept into this epic from a fairy tale in which he was a were bear, or maybe a bear's son. His name could mean "the wolf of the bees," and as we know from *Winnie the Pooh*, the enemy of the bees is the bear, because he comes to steal their honey. Being only semi human, at least in origin, would explain quite a lot about Beowulf.

So, big, check; strong, check. Is he fearless? Well, it's hard to say. In this culture—did I mention that *Beowulf* is an English poem? In this culture people do not show their feelings. Beowulf might be afraid, but if he was, you can be sure he wouldn't show it. His response to danger and difficulty is in fact invariably action. There's a good example about a third of the way through the poem. Beowulf has waited for the man-eating giant Grendel in the hall of King Hrothgar, has wrestled him and defeated him. In fact, has torn his arm off, and it's now been nailed up as a trophy. After twelve years of terror from Grendel, this is a cause for great satisfaction, and King Hrothgar organizes a feast and a party.

What he doesn't know, though, is that Grendel has a mother. And in the night, after the feast and the party, when everyone is sleeping it off in the hall, she comes back. She comes for two things. One is revenge. And the other, naturally enough, is she wants her son's arm back. She takes the arm and flees back to her home deep beneath a lake, but she also seizes one of the Danish warriors, whose name turns out to be Aeschere, and carries him off as well.

Beowulf does not know anything about this renewed attack, because as an honored guest, he has been found another place to sleep, not in the hall with all the others. In the morning, accordingly, he arrives to greet King Hrothgar and, one might think rather tactlessly, asks if he had a pleasant night. The King responds, and you can hardly blame him, "Don't talk to me about pleasant! Sorrow has been renewed for the Danish people. Aeschere is dead. He was my adviser and my confidant, he stood at my side when we defended our heads in battle. Everything a nobleman should be, Aeschere was." And now he's dead.

Hrothgar goes on to say that the monster has fled to a terrible place. Windy slopes where a stream pours down under the earth, where the very air seems to weep, where the trees hang over the water, and where even more ominously people have seen not just air and water mixed, but also fire in the flood. You don't know the place, he says to Beowulf. Seek it if you dare.

Beowulf's response is, as always, very brisk. "Do not sorrow, wise man," he says. "It is better for everyone to avenge his friend than to mourn too much. Each one of us has to endure an end to his life in this world. Let him who can gain glory before death. That is best for a man once he is dead."

That, you might say, is the old heroic attitude in a nutshell. What heroes fight for is glory. Death is a certainty, so don't worry about it. And revenge is an obligation. He says to Hrothgar, let's go and follow the track. he promises to follow the track wherever it leads—wood, mountain, fiery lake, whatever. He ends up with the words, "Have patience this day in all your woes, as I expect of you."

This is not an entirely tactful speech either. But it has an immediate and electrifying effect. The poem says, and I will give the actual words, *Ahleop ða se gomela*, the old man *ahleop*, he leapt up. And off they go through the frightening landscape Hrothgar had already described. When they get to the monster's lake, though, there's a further shock. The first thing they see on the shore is Aeschere's head; nor is the lake uninhabited. They can see strange creatures of some kind swimming in it. Beowulf promptly harpoons one of them, and his men drag it out with barbed spears. Everybody looks at it. In this culture, they don't say anything. They just look at it.

Beowulf's response, again, is to put his armor on; borrow a famous sword from a bystander with whom he had a violent verbal clash two days before; and then ask Hrothgar, if he doesn't come back, to see that his belongings are sent home and that the borrowed sword is replaced. "I will gain glory," he says, "or death will take me."

Having said which, he doesn't wait for an answer. He just dives in. The strange creatures harass him, but he fights his way through them, and finds himself in a strange submarine hall. It has air in it, because he sees a fire burning. He also sees Grendel's mother, the mighty lake woman, the horror from the deep. He strikes out with his borrowed sword, but it bounces off. He throws it down and immediately grapples with her, but she is too strong even for him, and she throws him down. Nor does she only fight barehanded like her son. She draws her sax—the short sword from which the Saxons take their name, the people of the sax—and stabs at him with it. He is saved only by his armor. He would have died far underground, says the poet, if it had not been for God.

Beowulf struggles back onto his feet; sees a giant's sword leaning against the wall, a sword so big no ordinary man can wield it; but he gets his hands on it; and cuts the hag's head off. "It broke the bone rings," says the poem, quite a good phrase for vertebrae; "it sheared through the flesh. She fell to the ground. The sword was bloody. The man rejoiced." All this is very powerfully described, but it does seem to be a description of a very simple and straightforward capital-H Hero—big, strong, undaunted, sure. But is there any sign of anything else in Beowulf's personality?

One give away is that although Beowulf is very self confident, he does seem to lack a defined sense of self. He regularly defines himself by reference to someone else, whom he mentions frequently, apparently his king or his lord, whose name is Hygelac. When Beowulf arrives on the Danish coast and the coastguard asks him who he is, he says, "we are the hearth companions of Hygelac." He does not mention his own name until later on. When he is allowed in to speak to King Hrothgar, he says, "I am Hygelac's kinsman." He goes on to say that he would like permission to stay in the hall and fight Grendel, and since he has heard that Grendel fights without weapons, he will do the same, "so that Hygelac will be glad at heart with me." If he does not survive, he asks Hrothgar to send his armor and his weapons back to Hygelac. Beowulf mentions Hygelac repeatedly, and though we could take this just as a sign of his loyal nature, it does look very like a kind of emotional dependency. And this turns out to be an important fact.

Earlier I mentioned a verbal clash between Beowulf and one of the Danes. The character's name is Unferth, and he seems to have an official position at Hrothgar's court. In any case, Unferth challenges Beowulf early in the poem. He asks Beowulf rudely if he is the Beowulf who once had a swimming contest with a man called Breca. They risked their lives, he says, for *dolgilpe*, for a foolish boast. And anyway, Beowulf lost the contest. Beowulf replies strongly and confidently, as we would expect. He didn't lose; he won. And he killed the sea-beasts who attacked him. In his reply, though, you can hear notes of self-criticism. Beowulf says twice, we were both just boys then. He does not entirely reject the accusation of *dolgilpe*, foolish boasting.

We are told later on in the poem that in fact Beowulf did not have a good reputation in his youth, but that the nobles of his tribe considered him to be, the poet's word is "slack," lazy, as is often the case with bear's sons in fairy tale. Anyway, back then it seems he was, the poet says again, "a prince of no great promise." Is Beowulf overcompensating for early neglect? Are there hints of vulnerability beneath the intimidating surface? I think there are.

To explain this, I have to give some background. We know even less about the origins of this poem than we do about Homer. We don't know who wrote it, or when, or where. One very strange thing about it is, although it's all in Old English, or Anglo-Saxon, the poet never mentions England and seems to know nothing about it. What he does know about is Scandinavia. Half of the poem is set among the Danes and the other half among Beowulf's own people, the Geats, who must be the inhabitants of what are now the Swedish provinces of East and West Götaland, centered on the city we call Gothenburg.

The poet also has detailed information about four Scandinavian royal houses, the kings of the Danes, Geats, Swedes, and another people called the Bards. All of these remain well known to later Scandinavian tradition, except for Beowulf's own relatives, the kings of the Geats. They vanished almost without trace. We would be entitled to say they were all pure fiction, except for another odd fact, which takes me back to Beowulf's emotional dependency on Hygelac. It's only half way through the poem, after Hygelac has been mentioned at least ten times, that the poet lets slip who he is. He is the son of Beowulf's own maternal grandfather, the king of the Geats, which makes him Beowulf's mother's brother, a relation of special importance to the Germanic tribes. So that explains the emotional dependence.

But there's another thing we know about Hygelac. Although he was completely forgotten in his homeland, he's not fictional at all. He was remembered in England. I am sure the poet did not bother to explain who he was, because he assumed everyone knew that already. What made Hygelac famous was his death. He sails into real history in the pages of a Latin chronicler who recounts a big piratical raid on what is now the Netherlands somewhere round the year 525—almost 300 years before the Vikings. That date puts the events of the poem right in the middle of the 200-year-long Heroic Age which followed the collapse of the Roman Empire, beginning about the year 400. This particular raid from the north was led by a man called Chochilaicus, which is not a bad try in the Latin alphabet for Hygelac, and it was a disaster. Hygelac was killed, as were most of his men.

As a young hero, Beowulf does not know this is going to happen. But the original audience of the poem did. So to those who first listened to the poem, Beowulf's emotional dependence on his uncle made him vulnerable. The point is rubbed in when Beowulf, after killing Grendel and his mother, goes to King Hrothgar and says, "If you have any trouble, I can bring thousands of warriors to your help. I know Hygelac will back me up." Hrothgar, the wise old king, compliments Beowulf on his wisdom, and goes on, "If by any chance Hygelac should die and you survive, the Geats will have no one better than you to select as king, if, that is, you should want the job." Hrothgar sees Beowulf's future absolutely accurately, down to Beowulf refusing the kingship in favor of Hygelac's young son.

Hrothgar sees the shadow hanging over Beowulf. What he doesn't see is the shadow hanging over himself. Once again, the poet does no more than hint at this, I think because the whole situation was as familiar to Anglo-Saxons as the story of King Arthur is to us. But it looks as if the kingdom of the Danes is booked to tear itself apart by civil war, just as the Geats will destroy themselves by rash aggression. The fact is that everyone in the poem is vulnerable—Beowulf, Hygelac, and Hrothgar too. They just don't know it. One person who does know it is the Danish queen, Wealhtheow. As the poem makes very clear, in Heroic Ages, it's women who pay the highest price for defeat.

As a young hero, Beowulf assumed he was invulnerable, even against monsters, confident in his strength. But in the last third of the poem he squares off against another monster, the dragon. By this time he is old, and pretty well everyone in his family is dead. He has become king of the Geats, as Hrothgar predicted, by default. He has, however, done the main duty of a king of the Geats, which is defeat the Swedes, and everything is okay, except he has neither wife nor child.

Then some fool goes and robs a dragon's lair, just like Bilbo Baggins, though without provocation. and the dragon burns down Beowulf's own hall. When he gets the news, we have one fleeting glimpse of an inner life. The poet says, "The wise man thought that he must have bitterly offended God the Ruler, the eternal Lord. His breast boiled inside with dark thoughts, as was not his custom." That's right, depression and self analysis are not Beowulf's custom. His custom is to act, and that is what he does. Fire-breathing dragon? Wooden shields obviously no good. "The protector of warriors ordered a shield to be made, all of iron." And Beowulf sets off, to certain death, for him and the dragon both.

How is Beowulf, in old age, different from the young hero he used to be? The main thing is, he now has to psych himself up. He takes 11 men, plus the one who stole the cup and provoked the dragon in the first place and heads for the dragon's lair. But when they get there, he sits down, and like dark thoughts, that hasn't been his custom. But Beowulf's mind, we are told, is gloomy. He knows fate is near. In repeated speeches he thinks over his own long life, full of disasters.

Some of these have already been detailed by the poet—the death of Hygelac, killed by the Franks; Beowulf, famous swimmer that he is, got away from what may have been a naval defeat; Hygelac's widow offered him the throne, but he turned it down in favor of his cousin Heardred, but Heardred took sides in a Swedish civil war and picked the losers. The Swedes killed him too, though Beowulf avenged him. Beowulf remembers it all, but in remembering all these deaths, he nevertheless takes savage satisfaction in his own part.

> "I paid back the gifts they gave me," he says, "and the land I was granted. Hygelac never needed to look for a foreign champion. I always went before him, alone in the front. And so I always will, as long as this sword holds out. As I always have, ever since I killed Dayraven, champion of the Franks, the standard bearer. He took no booty home; he fell on the field. Nor did the edge kill him, but my war grip broke his bone house, crushed the pulses of his heart."

In fact Beowulf bear hugged him. "Broke his bone house" is a good way of saying "shattered his rib cage."

But now, says Beowulf, still psyching himself up, "the edge of the sword will fight for the treasure [...] I endured many battles in youth. Still I will, old guardian of the people, do a famous deed." He orders his men to stay back. And then he gets up. You will remember how Hrothgar *ahleop*, "leapt up," when Beowulf's speech electrified him. That doesn't happen this time. Beowulf *aras bi ronde*, "got up by his shield." Pushing himself up on his shield rim, maybe, like the stiff-jointed old man he is.

We have to ask ourselves what the poet meant by this picture of an old hero, approaching battle in a spirit very different from his youthful carelessness. Not that Beowulf takes anything back, you notice. He challenges the dragon just as he pursued Grendel's mother, and he is still in search of glory, still set on revenge. If Beowulf had been around in Middle-earth to deal with Smaug, Gandalf wouldn't have needed Bilbo.

But I'd suggest that just as Bilbo and Frodo, showed us that you don't have to be big and strong to be a hero, you can be one even if you are little and weak, so Beowulf shows us that you don't have to be young and strong. Heroes can be old and tired as well. What counts is not *mægen*, "youthful strength," but *mod*, "spirit unaffected by time." Of course, being an old hero gets harder. Nowhere in this course, I think, will we come across a more moving picture of weakened but still undaunted old age.

So, Beowulf's heart is strong, as is his battle cry of challenge, but he's not what he was. The dragon fire is almost too much for him; his iron shield gives less protection than he hoped; and his sword Nailing fails again, broken on the dragon's head. The dragon bites him in the throat with its poisoned teeth. Beowulf is saved by his young relative Wiglaf, who ignores the order to stay back and advances through the dragon reek, to distract the dragon while Beowulf draws his sax and stabs the worm in the belly, cutting it in two. That's the end of the dragon, but the bite wound starts to swell. Wiglaf undoes his lord's helmet, and he splashes him with water, but it's no good.

Beowulf then makes three death speeches, which mix grief and triumph. We should remember that the poet was a Christian, writing no earlier than the eighth century, but he must have known that back in the sixth century all his heroes, Beowulf included, must have been pagans. How do pagans die? Can they make a good death?

Beowulf's first death speech has six sentences, and the first four all begin with 'I.' "I'd like to give my armor to a son, if I had one." That's sad. "I guarded this people for fifty years, so no one dared attack them." That's good. "I kept what was mine; I never practiced treachery; I swore no false oaths." That's good too. "When I die the Lord of men will not be able to accuse me of murdering my kin." That's good too, though a Christian shouldn't say, well, God can't blame me for anything. The last two sentences are addressed to Wiglaf, and they start with "you." "Go and fetch out the dragon's hoard. Hurry, so I can die easier, seeing what I've won for my people." Not perhaps a Christian sentiment either, but not a bad one.

In the second death speech, Beowulf thanks God for the treasure. He tells Wiglaf to make him a barrow on Whale-Ness, so that seafarers can call it Beowulf's Barrow—pagan concern for a memorial, though of course Christians can feel the same urge too. But Beowulf's last four-line speech to Wiglaf is just flat, not boastful, not hopeful, just the way things are. "You are the last of our family, the Waegmundings. Fate has swept all my kinsmen to their destiny, warriors in their pride. I must follow them."

It's hard to read the emotions here. I don't think I'm even going to try. Scholars have argued for a long time about whether the poet thought his pagan hero Beowulf's soul might be saved. I think the poet deliberately refused to comment. He knew that was up to God. He admired Beowulf; he thought he was a good man. But without grace, is that enough? Not our call.

What kind of moral are we to draw from the poem, and what assessment should we make of it here? Many would like to think that the poem is telling us, those who live by the sword shall die by the sword. I can't help thinking that if you said that to a hero in a Heroic Age, he'd reply, "Well, yes. But what's your point? Is there an alternative?" To quote the god Odin's advice, "The coward thinks he will live forever, if he stays out of fights. But age gives no man mercy, though spears may spare him." In other words, you're going to die anyway, so as Beowulf said to Hrothgar, gain glory before your death. That's what's best. There's a kind of logic in that, but it's not our cultural values.

Many have gone on more acutely to argue that the poem is telling us a good young hero does not make a good old king. Beowulf's decision to fight the dragon, not leave it alone, and to fight it by himself, not send in a squad, is certainly disastrous for his people. His death creates a power vacuum. When his death is announced, the messenger says, now we have no great protector, and we've made enemies of the Franks and of the Swedes. Our warriors will be food for ravens; our women will be made slaves.

That's what happens to the losers in a Heroic Age. The poet says, seemingly from personal knowledge, "he was not far wrong." That's why the descendants of the Geats are now living in what's called Sweden. My own feeling is that Beowulf the hero, not Beowulf the poem, shows us how you gain wisdom, insight into the true nature of life, and death. The hero begins with an emotional dependency which makes him vulnerable, and a confidence which is ill founded. He learns better, but in a way he doesn't change. He becomes even more self-reliant, but he also knows the limits of that self-reliance. His wisdom isn't perfect, but it may be as good as we can get.

I think I'd give the last word to Wealhtheow, the Danish queen. She is one of several women in the poem booked for an ill fate, and she can see it coming. She begs Beowulf to help her sons, hold their joy. But you can't hold joy. It slips away. Here in the hall, she says, "every noble is true to the other, mild of mood, loyal to their lord. The thanes are united, the people all ready, the warriors drinking do as I ask." She's quite wrong. Soon the Danes in the hall will all kill each other. That's what happens in a Heroic Age. Still, says the poet, musingly, "They were good people. Even heroes can only do their best. As Tolkien so rightly said, "until the dragon comes.""

Thor—A Very Human God
Lecture 8

One reason for including Thor, the Norse god of thunder, in our course is that he has been reinvented as a superhero in modern times. Another reason for including him is that the Norse gods were unusually heroic. In fact, we could say that the whole Norse religion existed to express a consciously heroic ethos. The Norse gods know they can die—and that they will die at Ragnarök—but they fight on nevertheless. That's what makes them heroic. Still another reason for examining Thor is that, in addition to being big and strong like some of our other basic male heroes, he is also funny.

A Tale of Thor from Snorri
- Most of what we know about Old Norse mythology comes from two connected sources.
  - In the 1230s, an Icelandic politician called Snorri wrote a handbook for aspiring poets that we call the *Prose Edda*. Snorri worked into his handbook about 20 stories concerning gods and legendary heroes, about half of which center on or mention Thor.

  - The second important source for Norse mythology is the so-called *Poetic Edda*—a collection of older poems that Snorri clearly knew. The poems in the *Poetic Edda* add several Thor stories to those in the *Prose Edda*.

- In the first tale Snorri tells about Thor, the god sets out on a journey with his fellow god Loki. The two are traveling in Thor's chariot, which is pulled by two goats, and they stop for the night at a peasant's house.
  - Thor slaughters his goats, skins them, puts them in a pot, and invites the peasant family to share the meal. He then tells them to put all the bones in the goatskins. But Thjalfi, the son in the family, splits one of the bones with his knife to get the marrow.

- In the morning, Thor blesses the goatskins and the bones with his hammer, and the goats come back to life. But one of the goats is lame because Thjalfi had split its bone.

- When Thor realizes what happened, he is furious. The peasants are terrified and beg for mercy, and when he sees how frightened they are, Thor calms down and takes Thjalfi as a bond servant by way of compensation.

- Note that in this story, Thor is quite friendly, but he is also short-tempered. Still, he can control himself, and he accepts human companions.

- The group carries on with the journey until nightfall. They find shelter in an oddly shaped empty building, but during the night, there's an earthquake. When dawn comes, the companions go outside and see a giant lying in the forest; the earthquake was the noise of the giant snoring.

- Thor puts on the magic belt that multiplies his strength and gets ready to strike the giant with his hammer, but at that moment, the giant wakes and stands up. Thor hesitates to use the hammer and instead asks the giant's name. The giant replies that his name is Skrymir.

- The members of the group have breakfast together, and Skrymir suggests that they put all their food in one bag, which he will carry. They travel on until nightfall again, and when they stop, Skrymir goes to sleep and tells the others to get on with their supper. But Thor can't get the bag of provisions open; the knots won't come undone.

- Thor becomes angry, and strikes the sleeping Skrymir with his hammer. The giant wakes up and thinks that a leaf must've fallen on his head. Twice more in the night, Thor strikes Skrymir with his hammer, but Skrymir believes he's been hit with an acorn or, perhaps, bird droppings.

- In the morning, Skrymir advises the group that their destination, the castle of Utgard-Loki, is peopled with even larger giants than he. Skrymir tells his companions that they shouldn't act big, or the giants of Utgard-Loki will be angry. He then leaves the group.

- Thor, Loki, and Thjalfi travel on to an enormous castle. They wriggle in through the bars of the gate and find themselves in the giants' hall. The head giant, Utgard-Loki, tells them that no visitors are allowed in the castle unless they can demonstrate a skill.

- Loki volunteers to have an eating contest with one of the giants, Logi, but Logi wins. Thjalfi offers to run a race but loses to a runner called Hugi. Thor tries to drain a drinking horn, to lift a giant cat, and to wrestle with Utgard-Loki's nurse, Elli, but fails at all three.

- In the morning, Thor prepares to go, and Utgard-Loki accompanies him outside the castle. Thor admits that they have not done well, but then Utgard-Loki reveals that the contests were fixed.
  - *Logi* is the word for "fire," and fire eats faster than any person can.

  - *Hugi* is the word for "thought," and no one can outrun thought.

  - The drinking horn was connected to the sea, and Thor's attempt to drain it caused the tides.

  - The cat was the world-girdling sea serpent Iörmungandr.

  - The name of the nurse, Elli, means "age," and age has indeed put down many people who seem as strong as Thor.

- The tone of this story is a kind of friendly disrespect. Most of the time, the joke is on Thor, and he becomes increasingly frustrated.
  - In the end, Thor is a god who thinks with his hammer and can be fooled, but as Utgard-Loki admits, he's still immensely powerful.

- To humans, Thor is good-natured, and most of all, he's on our side against the monsters who continually threaten the human world.

A Modern Tale of Thor

- Two American fantasy writers, Lyon Sprague de Camp and Fletcher Pratt, recast this story in a modern idiom. Interestingly, the tone of the 20th-century story seems almost identical to that of the tale told in the 13th century.

- De Camp and Pratt followed the main outline of Snorri's story, but they introduced a modern American character, Harold Shea. He has figured out how to travel between dimensions and finds himself in the world of the *Eddas*, where—until he learns the laws of magic— he is out of his depth.

- De Camp and Pratt posed and answered some obvious questions about the story: What was the whole expedition for, and given Thor's temper, why doesn't he use his hammer? Their answers drew on another Thor story, one from the *Poetic Edda* called *Thrymskvitha*.
  - This story starts with Thor waking up and finding his hammer gone. In the traditional poem, Loki finds out that a giant called Thrym has stolen it. He'll give it back, but only in exchange for Freyja, the goddess of love. When Freyja objects, Heimdall proposes that they disguise Thor as Freyja.

  - Thor assumes the disguise and travels to the land of the giants, but he's not very good at staying in character as a blushing bride. Ultimately, the marriage ceremony starts, and the stolen hammer is brought out to bless the marriage. But of course, as soon as Thor gets his hands on his hammer, he kills the giant who stole it.

  - Borrowing from this story, de Camp and Pratt answered two of the earlier questions: Thor doesn't use the hammer on Utgard-Loki because the giants have stolen it, and the purpose of the expedition is to get it back. The American, Harold Shea, saves the day because he can see through Utgard-Loki's illusions and recognize the hammer.

Thor and the Giant Hrungnir

- In another story given to us by Snorri, the giant Hrungnir gets drunk in Asgard and behaves rudely, but because he is under safe conduct, he and Thor agree to fight a duel outside. Each of them will have a second.

- The giants make an enormous clay giant called Mokkurkalfi to be Hrungnir's second, but they give him only the heart of a mare. Mokkurkalfi wets himself when he sees Thor and is finished off by Thor's assistant, the human Thjalfi.

- Hrungnir, however, has a stone heart, a stone head, and a stone shield, and his weapon is a whetstone. When Thjalfi cunningly tells him that Thor will attack from underground, Hrungnir stands on his shield. Thor and Hrungnir then throw the hammer and whetstone at each other simultaneously, and Hrungnir's skull is shattered. But a piece of the whetstone is embedded in Thor's skull, and he can never get it out.

- A German poet long ago suggested that all this was an allegory. Killing the stone giant meant, in rocky Scandinavia, creating cultivable soil. The clay giant was the unworkable heavy clay that defeated farmers. Thjalfi stands for the ordinary peasant, who knows that Thor will help him because Thor is the friend of humanity and, especially, of the working man.

Thor the Superhero

- In 1962, Stan Lee and Jack Kirby latched on to Thor as a new idea for a superhero. His alter ego in Lee and Kirby's work is Don Blake, an American doctor with a lame leg. Blake, vacationing in Norway, sees aliens land. He hides in a cave, where he finds a stick; when he picks it up, it turns into the hammer Mjollnir, and he turns into Thor. NATO fails to drive the aliens off, but Thor succeeds.

- In what ways is the modern Thor different from the ancient one? We've already seen that 20th-century writers have not really found a problem with changed cultural values. Still, the comic-book Thor is much more showily violent than his original, and the two sides— the gods and giants—seem much more polarized.

- More important, the tricky combination of friendly disrespect in stories about Thor has nearly vanished. Comic-book Thor is much more like the basic male hero, perhaps because comic books are written for a teenage or sub-teen market.

- At the same time, the comic-book Thor must conform to modern ideas of propriety. For example, he must earn his place, not just inherit it. He is exiled to earth by this father, Odin, and can get his hammer back only if he is found worthy. Thor has to prove his worth by being responsible, a virtue of which there is no sign in the ancient stories. What this means is that Thor is no longer funny. He's a superhero, but he's one who shares the social anxieties of middle America.

- Still, the myth has proved curiously adaptable. Thor crops up repeatedly, even in adult science fiction, and always positively. His image as the friend of humanity remains potent and is set against his uncertain and unreliable relatives, such as Odin in Neil Gaiman's *American Gods*. Although Thor has come a long way from the Old Norse *Eddas*, one thing has remained constant: his heroic defense of the vulnerable.

Essential Reading

Anonymous (Auden and Taylor, trans., *Norse Poems*), *The Poetic Edda*.

Snorri Sturluson (Faulkes, trans.), *The Prose Edda*.

Suggested Reading

Arnold, *Thor*.

Davidson, *Gods and Myths of Northern Europe*.

O'Donoghue, *From Asgard to Valhalla*.

Questions to Consider

1. Would you say that fantasies (such as the superhero fantasies) are myths for our time, or are they just not serious enough?

2. People still have different ideas about what's funny. Do you think that humor is among the cultural values that have changed?

Thor—A Very Human God
Lecture 8—Transcript

Already in this course we've had a number of variations on the Basic Male Hero. We had Odysseus; he's big, he's strong, he's fearless, but he's also cunning and resourceful. We had Aeneas; he's big, he's strong, he's fearless, and he's also socially responsible. We had Beowulf; he's big, he's strong; he's not quite fearless, but he grows to be a sadder and wiser person. And in today's lecture we have Thor, Mighty Thor, as he is often now known. He's definitely big and strong, like Beowulf, not quite fearless. But at least in his far-off origins, he's also funny.

This is unexpected, for several reasons. We've had a heroine who has a touch of the mythical about her in Guinevere, but Thor has more than a touch; he's a god. He's a member of the old Norse pantheon, along with his father Odin, his brothers Heimdall and Baldur, and a number of others, including Loki, whose parentage is in doubt. Not only is he a god, it's very obvious what kind of a god he is; he is the God of Thunder. Thor in Old Norse just means Thunder, and everyone can see that the hammer Miollnir, which Thor throws and which always comes back to him, represents the lightning bolt. If he's a god, should we count him as a hero, which is what this course is about? Well, one reason for doing so is that in the last century, and continuing into this one, Thor was reinvented as a superhero. It's interesting to see how the $20^{th}/21^{st}$ century figure stacks up against his original from the Dark Ages.

The other reason for having him here is that the Norse gods were unusually heroic. In fact, you could say that the whole Norse religion was there to express a consciously heroic ethos. We know about this now because we know about Asgard, the home of the gods; the Bifröst bridge, which leads to the home of the gods; we know about the gods and the giants and the monsters, which the gods continually combat—the wolf Fenrir, the world encircling sea serpent Iörmungandr. Most of all, we know about Ragnarök, when gods and men will march out to fight the giants and the monsters and both sides will destroy each other. Not all Odin's hosts of warriors gathered after death into Valhalla, the halls of the slain, can bring victory.

So, Norse gods are mortal. They can die, like Baldur the beautiful, and when they die, they go down to hell, like Baldur, and not even Odin can get them out. And the Norse gods know they can die and that at Ragnarök they will die, but they fight on nevertheless. That's what makes them heroic.

What I just said explains why we're counting Thor as a hero. But it doesn't explain what I said about him being funny. I'll start on that now. Most of what we know about old Norse mythology comes from two connected sources which were lost for centuries. In the 1230s an Icelandic politician called Snorri son of Sturla wrote a handbook for aspiring poets, which we call the *Prose Edda*. You couldn't be an Icelandic poet without a good grasp of mythic references. So, Snorri worked into his handbook about twenty stories concerning gods and legendary heroes. About half of these center on Thor, or at least, mention him. Our second important source for Norse mythology is the so-called *Poetic Edda,* a collection of older traditional poems which Snorri clearly knew. The poems in the *Poetic Edda* add several Thor stories to Snorri's.

Here's the first tale Snorri told about Thor. See if his behavior matches what you'd expect of a mighty god of thunder. It seems that long ago Thor set out on a journey with his fellow god Loki. They were travelling in Thor's chariot, which is pulled by two goats; one of Thor's names is Öku-Thor, which means Thor the Driver. They stopped for the night at a peasant's house. Thor slaughtered his goats, skinned them, put them in the pot, and invited the peasant, his wife, and their two children to share the meal. But, he said, here are the goat skins. Put all the bones on the skins, which they did. But Thjalfi, the peasant's son, split a hambone with his knife, to get the marrow.

In the morning when Thor got up, he blessed the goat skins and the bones with his hammer, and the goats came back to life. But when the goats got up, one of them was lame in the hind leg, because Thjalfi had split the bone. When Thor realized this, he was furious. His eyebrows sank down over his eyes, and he clenched his hand on his hammer so hard that his knuckles whitened. The peasant family were all terrified and begged for mercy, and when he saw how frightened they were, Thor calmed down and took Thjalfi as a bond servant by way of compensation. There are several things to note about the story so far. Thor is really quite friendly, ready to share his meal with human beings. He is also short tempered, but he can control himself, and he accepts human companions.

Anyway, they carry on with their journey, until nightfall. They find shelter in a big empty building, which has a wide entrance, with a kind of side chamber about halfway inside it. During the night, there's some kind of earthquake, and Thor gets his hammer and stands in the entrance to defend them. But when dawn comes, they go out and see someone lying in the forest, and Snorri remarks "he was no midget." In fact, he is a giant, and the earthquake was the noise of him snoring. Thor puts on the magic belt, which multiplies his strength, and gets ready to strike the giant with his hammer, but at that moment the giant wakes and stands up. And Thor was, for once, we won't say afraid, but he hesitates to use the hammer, and instead asks the giant's name. The giant says, it's Skrymir, and he also says he doesn't need to ask Thor's name. But he goes on, "What are you doing with my glove?" The building, with the strange side entrance, was Skrymir's glove, and the side chamber must have been the thumb.

They have breakfast together, and Skrymir suggests they pool their food and put it all in one bag, which he will carry. They all go on together until nightfall again, and when they stop, Skrymir goes to sleep and tells the others to get on with their supper. But Thor can't get the bag of provisions open. The knots just won't come undone. He gets angry at this, goes over to where Skrymir is sleeping, and strikes at his head with his hammer. Skrymir wakes up and says he thinks a leaf must've fallen on his head. So they all go to sleep with no supper, and once again Skrymir snores heavily. Thor gets angry again, strikes again at Skrymir with his hammer, and feels it sink deep into his head. But Skrymir wakes up and says, "Did an acorn fall on me, or something?'

Thor is now seriously angry, and when he sure Skrymir is fast asleep he goes over again and hits him as hard as ever he can with his hammer, which sinks in up to the handle. Skrymir wakes up and says, "I'm sure I felt something, bird droppings, maybe?" "Well," says Skrymir, "I've got some advice for you. You're going on to the castle of Utgard-Loki, and I've heard you say that I'm not small. But in Utgard-Loki's castle you'll meet some people who are really big, so don't you act big. Those guys won't put up with cheek from shrimps like you. Maybe you should turn back. If you go on, that's the way over there, but I leave you now." And off he goes.

Thor and Loki and Thjalfi go on together and find themselves in front of an enormous castle. They can only get in by wriggling through the bars of the gate, but then they find themselves in the giants' hall. The head giant, Utgard-Loki, looks at them and says, "Huh, little guys. No one is allowed to come here unless they're good at something. What can you show us?" Loki steps forward and says, "I'm prepared to have an eating contest. Let's see if anyone can eat quicker than me." "All right," says Utgard-Loki, and he calls up a giant called Logi and puts a trough of meat in front of both of them, one at each end. They start eating, and they meet in the middle. But while Loki has eaten the meat and the bones, Logi has eaten the meat and the bones and the trough as well, so he is the winner.

Next contest, Thjalfi offers to run a race with anyone, and Utgard-Loki brings out a runner called Hugi. They race three times, but Thjalfi is outdistanced every time by bigger and bigger margins. Time for Thor to take a test. He says he'll compete with anyone at drinking. "All right," says Utgard-Loki. "Here's a horn. See if you can drain it in one." Thor tries, but after one drink the level has hardly gone down. After two, well, you could at least carry the horn without it spilling. But even after three drinks the horn is still not empty. "Not very good," says Utgard-Loki, "what do you want to try next? I've an idea. See if you can lift my cat off the floor."

Well, it's a big cat, but when Thor tries to lift it up it just arches its back, and all he can do in the end is get one paw off the ground. By this time Thor is losing his temper again, and he says, "How about a fight?" "Well, all right," says Utgard-Loki. "You can wrestle my old nurse Elli. She's put down many men who look as strong as Thor is." The wrestle goes on for a long time, but in the end, Thor falls to one knee, and Utgard-Loki says, "That will do."

In the morning, Thor gets ready to go, and Utgard-Loki accompanies him outside the castle. Thor admits that they have not done well. "Better than you think," says Utgard-Loki. "If I had known you were as strong as you are, I would never have let you inside my hall. But now we're outside I'll tell you the truth. I was Skrymir. I fastened the provision bag with magic wire. When you struck at me three times in the night, I put a mountain in the way by magic, and you can see the craters in the mountain where your hammer struck."

As for the contests, well, and this is me speaking now, not Utgard-Loki, anyone who spoke Old Norse would have realized the contests were fixed. Logi is the word for fire, and fire eats faster than any person can. Hugi is the word for thought, and no one can out run thought. The horn was connected to the sea, and Thor's attempt to drain the horn is what has caused the tides. The cat wasn't a cat; it was the world-girdling sea serpent Iörmungandr. But as for the old nurse, her name Elli means age. And age has indeed put many people down who look as strong as Thor.

Well, we can see this is a funny story. The tone of it is a kind of friendly disrespect. Most of the time, the joke is on Thor, and the joke is that Thor gets more and more frustrated. He slugs the giant Skrymir harder and harder, and all that happens is that Skrymir says, "Bird-droppings, maybe?" It's ignominious that they can only get into the giants' castle by wriggling through the bars like small children. And what kind of god is it who can't even lift a pussy-cat off the floor?

The joke is especially funny because Thor opts for such macho tests. "I can drink anyone under the table!" No, he hardly makes an impression on the giants' horn. "I can out-wrestle anybody in this bar!" Except the old lady. It's a joke, really, on the basic male hero. And that's exactly what Thor is; he's not even tricky like Odysseus, and although he wrestles Old Age, we don't see him grown old, like Beowulf.

Just the same, it's a friendly joke. Sure, he's a guy, or a god, who thinks with his hammer, and he can be fooled, or taken aback. But as Utgard-Loki admits, he's still immensely powerful. He's quite good natured, at least to us humans. And most of all, he's on our side against the monsters who continually threaten the human world, Middle-earth. Besides, Thor is a god who reacts like a person. His rage when he finds that his magic goat has had its hambone split, it's just like someone nowadays who finds his new Lexus has been scratched in the carpark.

One result is that the story could easily be recast into a modern idiom, as it was by two American fantasy writers called Lyon Sprague de Camp and his partner Fletcher Pratt. Their retelling of it became the first part of a sequence eventually published as *The Incomplete Enchanter*. I mention it here because so often in this course I talk about the way stories and heroes, are changed by changing cultural values. But the tone of the 20th century de Camp and Pratt story seems to me almost identical to that of the 13th century story told by Snorri. De Camp and Pratt followed the main outline of Snorri's story, but they introduced a modern American character into the story, called Harold Shea. He has figured out, so to speak, how to travel between dimensions and finds himself in the world of the Eddas, where, until he figures out the laws of magic in this world and starts to apply them, he is quite out of his depth.

De Camp and Pratt posed and answered some obvious questions about the whole story, like, what was the whole expedition for? And given Thor's temper, why doesn't he use his hammer in Utgard-Loki's castle? Their answers were beautifully clear, and they drew on another Thor story, this time from the *Poetic Edda*, not from Snorri's *Prose Edda*. There's a poem called *Thrymskvitha*, which starts off with Thor waking up and finding his hammer is gone. I'll give you a couple of lines in the original language, just to show you that Old Norse is not so very different from modern English:

Vreiðr vas þá Ving-Þórr / es vaknaði / ok sins hamars / of saknaði.

Wroth was then Wing-Thor / as he wakened / and his hammer / he found missing.

In the traditional poem, Loki finds out that a giant called Thrym has stolen the hammer. He'll give it back, but only in exchange for Freya, the goddess of love. The gods are okay about this, but Freya definitely is not. Heimdall says, "I have an idea, let's disguise Thor as Freya." But Thor immediately looks worried. "If I let myself be dressed as a bride," he says, "the gods will call me …' Well, I don't like to say what Thor thinks the gods will call him, but there are many rude modern expressions which would cover it. Once again, no translation problem; it's just that the gods' cultural values are not politically correct at all. Loki tells Thor to shut up and do what he has to.

Off they go, then, to the land of the giants in the goat chariot, but it turns out that Thor is not very good at staying in character as a blushing bride. When they have the pre-marriage feast, Thor eats a whole ox, eight salmon, and he drinks three barrels of mead. The giant says, "I've never seen a bride eat like that." Loki says quickly that Freya has been so anxious to get to Giantland that she hasn't eaten for eight days. The giant then tries to look under the bride's veil and leaps back, because he can see fiery eyes beneath it. Loki says quickly that Freya has been so anxious to get to Giantland that she hasn't slept for eight nights. In the end the marriage ceremony starts, and the stolen hammer is brought out in order to bless the marriage. But of course, as soon as Thor gets his hands on his hammer, that's the end of the giant thief.

Borrowing some of this story, de Camp and Pratt decided to answer the two questions I just put by saying that Thor doesn't use the hammer on Utgard-Loki, because the giants have stolen it! And the purpose of the expedition is obviously to get it back. They can't find it because Utgard-Loki is a shape shifter. And that's where the American, Harold Shea, saves the day and redeems himself. He can see through the illusions, recognize the hammer, and point it out. In a way, though this is a coincidence, Harold Shea is like Bilbo in Tolkien's story. He starts off completely out of his depth in the heroic world in which he finds himself. But he gains status, and in the end, control, by using his modern rational intelligence to work out the laws of magic and become an enchanter. Though, as the title says, only an incomplete one.

Well, so much for Thor being funny. One final joke at the expense of the Basic Male Hero pattern, there's one thing Thor is really frightened of, which is being laughed at. The bristling beard, the fiery eyes, the whitened knuckles, they all give a picture of an angry man who doesn't know quite what to do. He's a god, right, but he's a very human god. And unlike some of the other gods—Loki, Odin—he's on our side.

Snorri tells several other Thor stories. There's Thor goes fishing, he hooks the giant sea-serpent Iörmungandr and pulls so hard on the line his feet go through the bottom of the boat. There's how Thor got his hammer Mjollnir, it was made by dwarves to settle a bet with Loki, but Loki cheated. He changed himself into a fly and so pestered the dwarf blowing the bellows that he stopped blowing to swipe at him, and that's why Mjollnir is short in the handle, and so on.

But I'll pick out just one more Dark Age story, to illustrate Thor being on our side. It's about the giant called Hrungnir. Hrungnir gets drunk in Asgard and behaves rudely, but since he is under safe conduct, he and Thor agree to fight a duel outside, each combatant to have a second. The giants decide to make an enormous clay giant called Mokkurkalfi to be Hrungnir's second, but they give him only the heart of a mare. This is a bad idea. Mokkurkalfi just wets himself when he sees Thor, and is finished off by Thor's assistant, the human Thjalfi.

Hrungnir, however, has a stone heart, a stone head, a stone shield, and his weapon is a whetstone. Thjalfi cunningly tells him that Thor is going to attack from underground, so Hrungnir stands on his shield. Thor and Hrungnir then throw the hammer and a whetstone at each other simultaneously, and Hrungnir's skull is shattered. But a piece of the whetstone is embedded in Thor's skull, and he can never get it out. That's why you must never throw a whetstone, because when you do, the fragment in Thor's skull moves.

Does this mean anything? Remember the names Logi and Hugi and Elli. A German poet long ago suggested that all this was an allegory. Killing the stone giant meant, in rocky Scandinavia, creating cultivable soil. The clay giant was the unworkable heavy clay which defeated farmers. Thjalfi stands for the ordinary peasant, who knows Thor is there to help him, because Thor is the friend of humanity, and especially of the working man.

The witch who tries to get the whetstone out of Thor's skull is called Groa, which means to grow, or as the German poet put it, "growth and greening and the harvest to come." And she has a husband Aurvandil. Thor was carrying him home in a basket across a frozen river, but his toe stuck out and got frostbite. Thor broke it off and threw it into the sky to become a star. An allegory, said the German poet, of the seed sown too soon and nipped by frost. Over-poetic? But it makes a fair point. Thor, in his careless kind of way, is the friendly god. Little Norse boys were often called after him, as they still are—Thorstein, Thorgeir, Thormod, etc.

The recovery of the old Norse mythology is a long story, and attitudes to Thor are a big part of it. All these stories became very familiar during the 19th and 20th centuries, so the material was there for people like de Camp and Pratt. It was also there for Stan Lee and Jack Kirby, the Lennon and McCartney of comic books.

Thor, in comic books, and now in Marvel movies, is almost impossible to summarize, but very briefly, in 1962 Lee and Kirby latched on to him as their new idea for a superhero. Now, what does a 20th-century superhero need? He needs an alter ego. Superman was also Clark Kent, and in the first Lee and Kirby story, Thor was also Don Blake, an American doctor with a lame leg. Blake, vacationing in Norway, sees aliens land. He hides in a cave. There he finds a stick, and when he picks it up, it turns into the hammer Miöllnir, and he turns into Thor. NATO fails to drive the aliens off, but Thor succeeds.

Yes, but apart from an alter ego what else does a superhero need? He needs a love interest, and this is the nurse Jane Foster. Yes, but it's known that back in Asgard Thor is already married to Sif, a problem here for family values.

Fortunately, by the late 20th century, the whole complex was very open to take over from science fiction. Bifröst, the magic bridge to Asgard? Must be a wormhole. The belt of strength, which Thor puts on so as to wield Miöllnir? It's a bionic exoskeleton.

Well, I won't try to paraphrase 600-plus comic book plots, which were quite clearly made up as the scriptwriters went along, so they are full of inconsistencies. But a question which remains is, in what ways is the new superhero Thor different from the ancient one? I've already said that there's no real problem with changed cultural values; some 20th century writers have found Thor easy to deal with.

Just the same, the comic book Thor is much more showily violent than his original. The two sides, gods and giants, are also much more polarized. It's quite clear in the old Norse stories that gods and giants are often on close terms and frequently interbreed. More important, maybe, the tricky combination of friendly disrespect has pretty much vanished. Comic book

Thor is much more like the Basic Male Hero, maybe because comics are written for a teenage or sub-teen market.

At the same time, the comic book Thor has to conform to modern ideas of propriety. One of these is that he has to earn his place, not just inherit it. So when his father Odin exiles him to Earth, he'll only get his hammer back "if he be found worthy." Thor has to prove his worth by being responsible, a virtue of which there is no sign in the ancient stories. What this means is that Thor isn't funny any more. He's a superhero, but you might say, one who shares the social anxieties of middle America. So, comic book Thor has father/son issues with Odin. He has sibling issues, with Loki. He reflects the image both of the troubled male wage earner and the unsocialized suburban teenage geek, probably a large part of the comic books' intended audience.

Yet the myth has proved curiously adaptable. Thor crops up again and again even in adult science fiction, always positively. His image as the friend of humanity remains potent, and is set against his uncertain and unreliable relatives, like Odin in Neil Gaiman's fantasy *American Gods*. You might say, Thor has been thoroughly naturalized by now as an American citizen, his story still undergoing continuous movie development.

Yet, although Thor has come a long way from the Old Norse Eddas, one thing has remained constant; this is his heroic defense of the vulnerable, in other words, humanity. Thor is the god who is on our side. And he's on our side because at bottom he's just like us—means well, often frustrated, needs help, and gives it.

Robin Hood—The Outlaw Hero
Lecture 9

No one knows the origins of the hero we'll discuss in this lecture, Robin Hood. By the time stories about Robin Hood started to appear, he was already an established figure. Paradoxically, this may be one reason he has remained popular with writers: There are so many gaps in his story that it's easy to write into them. Another reason people continued to add stories about Robin Hood is that from the start, he looked like a bundle of contradictions. As we'll see, these were apparent contradictions only, but they still provoked writers to provide explanations.

The Original Robin Story?

- Many of the questions surrounding the character of Robin Hood appear in a scene from a poem called *A Gest of Robyn Hode*, probably written around 1425 and the nearest thing we have to the original Robin story.

- Near the end of the poem, the king visits his private deer park and finds it completely depopulated by Robin Hood and his Merry Men. The king is not pleased and decides to look for Robin himself. He disguises himself as an abbot and rides into the greenwood with five of his knights, disguised as monks.

- Of course, Robin and the Merry Men hold up the king's party. But Robin's approach is to invite the king and his men to dinner, then tell them that they have to pay for it. With all his victims, those who reply honestly to Robin that they can't pay for dinner are allowed to keep what money they have. Those who lie about their money lose all of it. The disguised king tells Robin that he has only £40, and when it turns out he's telling the truth, Robin splits the £40 with him.

- To round off the entertainment, Robin proposes a shooting match. Anyone who misses his target will lose his arrow and get a clout on the head from Robin. When Robin misses, he gives his guest the opportunity to hit him. The "abbot" rolls up his sleeve and—because he's a warrior-king, probably Edward III—deals Robin a good blow.

- At that moment, Robin recognizes the king. He kneels down and asks for mercy. The king pardons all the men on condition that they enter his service, which of course, they are glad to do. And off they ride together to Nottingham.

- On the way, they play a game called pluck-buffet that involves taking alternate shots at a target. The one who misses or shoots widest gets another clout on the head.
  - o We can see the appeal of this detail. Robin is keen on male bonding in a typically rough and violent way, but both he and the king are sportsmen and play fair.

  - o Robin is also loyal in a disloyal kind of way. He shoots all the king's deer, and he kills his officers, but he insists that he loves the king.

Robin as a Yeoman

- The *Gest* mentions repeatedly that Robin is a yeoman, an abbreviated form of "young man." The term probably derived from the name a local lord or leader might call his squad of enforcers. Yeomen gained status by doing a good job for the boss and earning land as payment.

- What did yeomen look like in the 1370s, when we first hear about Robin Hood? As it happens, we have a good description of one, written by Geoffrey Chaucer in the General Prologue to *The Canterbury Tales*. The Yeoman there is a forester; he wears green and carries a bow. Robin Hood himself has always been defined by his characteristic weapon, the English longbow.
  - o For several generations, the specialized class of English longbowmen ruled the battlefields of England, Scotland, France, Spain, and even further afield.

We often hear that knights were the medieval equivalent of tanks, but the English longbow was the antitank gun.

- o This meant that the rural yeomen of medieval England became increasingly confident and even aspirational in the 14th and 15th centuries. And Robin Hood was their hero. He expresses all their prejudices, which appear to us as a bundle of contradictions.

Contradictions in Robin Hood

- In the *Gest*, Robin Hood won't have his dinner until he's robbed someone to pay for it. Here, he is imitating an aristocratic custom. King Arthur also would have dinner served to his guests but would not sit down to eat his own dinner until he'd seen a marvel of some kind. What the poem is telling us is that yeomen are just as good as their social superiors, especially at having good manners.

- We're also told that Robin always hears three masses before dinner, the third of them in honor of Our Lady. Robin is devoted to Our Lady and never robs any company that includes a woman. In fact,

Robin tells Little John that he can rob only churchmen and the Sheriff of Nottingham. Just as Robin loves the king but hates his officials, he's a devout Christian but can't stand the officials of the established church.

- As the story continues in the *Gest*, the Merry Men go off to rob someone on the highway. The next traveler to go by is a knight but a sorry-looking one. Little John courteously kneels down and invites him to dinner, after which Robin tells the knight he must pay. The knight, Sir Richard at Lee, says that he has only 10 shillings, and when Little John checks, this turns out to be true.

  o The knight tells Robin that his son has killed someone, and he has pledged his lands to St. Mary's Abbey in York, a rich Benedictine monastery, to pay for lawyers and compensation. He's due to pay the money back, but he will have to ask for an extension, which he knows he won't get.

  o Robin offers to lend the knight the money if he has a guarantor. The knight replies that God is his guarantor, but Robin rejects that response. When Sir Richard then says that "Our Lady" will be the guarantor, Robin accepts and immediately lends him £400.

  o Sir Richard goes to St. Mary's and is treated rudely by the abbot, who takes delight in the prospect of repossessing Sir Richard's lands. The abbot has a justice sitting by him, just to show that the law is on his side. In the end, Sir Richard brings out the money lent him by Robin Hood. The abbot is chagrined, and his annoyance worsens when the justice refuses to hand back the legal fee that the abbot has paid him.

  o We can see that Robin is devoted to justice in the elementary sense of playing fair, but he also has no faith in the corrupt legal system. His complaint about lawyers and justices is the same as it was about senior churchmen. Robin is a devout Christian, but they aren't; they're just in it for the money. As for the officials who enforce the law, their bribe-taking and harshness to the poor were notorious.

○ Robin is protesting against corruption in the Church, the law, and the administration. But he has a strong belief in true religion, true justice, and true authority. Thus, it's not Robin who is contradictory but his hypocritical enemies.

- A year later, Sir Richard is on his way to repay Robin when he is held up by having to protect a yeoman. Robin is rather surprised that Our Lady, Sir Richard's guarantor, seems to have let him down. He sends Little John off again to see what's on the road.
  ○ Little John finds a monk and brings him to have dinner with Robin. Of course, the monk lies about how much money he has and forfeits it—£800, double the money Sir Richard owes. Robin says that he knew Our Lady wouldn't let him down.

  ○ But then Sir Richard turns up. Robin accepts his excuse that he has been protecting a yeoman and refuses to take the money back, saying he's already gotten it from Our Lady. In fact, he even splits the takings from the monk with Sir Richard.

  ○ Robin certainly isn't behaving like a proper social bandit here. Instead of robbing the rich to feed the poor, he robs the rich to help the gentry. But Robin is a conservative bandit—and quite recognizable in modern America. He is loyal and patriotic but has no time for the government or Washington. The underlying appeal to justice and protest against corruption in Robin Hood's actions have remained vital even after the circumstances of the medieval yeomanry ceased to be relevant.

Robin Hood's Fortunes

- Eventually, the longbow was replaced by firearms, and the yeomanry of England failed to continue their upward trajectory. This didn't put an end to Robin Hood, but after the 15th century, he began to seem lower class. In 1598, a playwright called Anthony

Munday, perhaps trying to push him upmarket again, added the notion that Robin Hood was really the outlawed Earl of Huntington.

- In his novel *Ivanhoe*, Walter Scott offered a solution to the continuing puzzle of Robin's ambivalent relationship with royalty.
  - If Robin was hostile to the king's officers but loyal to the king, then there must be two kings: the real king, for some reason absent or in exile, and the king acting in his place, the regent. The obvious place in English history when this was true was when King Richard Lionheart was away on the Crusades and his brother King John was acting as regent.

  - Scholars have often noted how many mistakes Scott made, but it hasn't made any difference. The very openness of the Robin Hood story has been a standing provocation for many writers to try to fill in the blanks.

- Given that Robin Hood emerged from a particular class in a particular place at a particular time, how has he managed to retain his appeal centuries later?
  - Robin represents a strong desire for justice, which is only made stronger by distrust of the law, a feeling that has not gone away.

  - In addition, Robin is strongly associated with merriment, laughter, and jokes, even if the jokes are often violent. Life in the greenwood, for the Merry Men, is carefree.

  - Robin and his men live in an agricultural society, but they never do any agricultural work; instead, they are hunter-gatherers. To people who have to work every day, that form of existence looks fairly attractive.

  - In modern times, Robin has also been made to look good as a democratic hero, almost an honorary American.

- Modern depictions of Robin Hood still show the radical uncertainty of plot that we've seen, but the essentials don't change: the bow, the forest, the sense of justice, and the idea of freedom from control and from care.

Essential Reading

Anonymous (Knight and Ohlgren, eds.), *A Gest of Robyn Hode*.

Suggested Reading

Dobson and Taylor, eds., *Rymes of Robyn Hood*.

Holt, *Robin Hood*.

Keen, *The Outlaws of Medieval England*.

Questions to Consider

1. What modern cases can you think of where outlaws are presented sympathetically (Jesse James, Ned Kelly, Butch Cassidy and the Sundance Kid)? What makes them sympathetic?

2. Has anything replaced "the greenwood" as the ideal hideout or getaway location?

Robin Hood—The Outlaw Hero

Lecture 9—Transcript

This lecture is an anomaly within this course. All the other lectures are either based on a single work of art, like Beowulf, or else on a collection of stories about a single figure, like Sherlock Holmes or James Bond. This is not the case with the hero I'm going to discuss today—Robin Hood. We don't know where he came from. People have tried to identify him as a real-life person, but without success. By the time stories about Robin Hood start to appear, he's already an established figure.

Paradoxically, this may be one reason why he stayed popular with writers, and from the 20th century on, with scriptwriters for films and TV. There were so many gaps in the story, that it was easy to write into the gaps, as Virgil did with Homer. And another reason why people kept adding on stories about Robin Hood was that from the start he looked like a bundle of contradictions. I'm going to say that they were only apparent contradictions which can readily be explained, even in very modern terms. But still, on the surface, the contradictions were there, they needed explaining, and writers were provoked into doing so.

Let's try this. What do we know about Robin Hood? He's an outlaw. He lives in the greenwood. He lives off the King's deer. He has a band of Merry Men, like Little John. Most important, he robs the rich to feed the poor. And his deadly enemy is the Sheriff of Nottingham. Okay, let's consider what we don't know. His deadly enemy is the Sheriff of Nottingham, but do we know the Sheriff's name? Some say it's Guy of Gisborne. But maybe that's a different person.

Anyway, why is Robin an outlaw? Was he made an outlaw because he poaches the King's deer, or does he poach the King's deer because he's an outlaw? Is there any chance of a pardon for him? And, given that he's a highway robber, why was he so popular? Is there any way of making all this look realistic?

Many of these issues appear in a scene from what is the nearest thing we have to the original Robin story. It's a poem called *A Gest of Robyn Hode*.

It's quite a long poem, nearly 2,000 lines, but it looks as if it's really several short poems stuck together. We think it was probably written about 1425, a generation after the death of Chaucer. I'm not going to get into dates, but I'll just say that the first definite mention of Robin Hood is about 50 years earlier than that. There's a long poem from Chaucer's time called *Piers Plowman*. In it, there is a character who represents the deadly sin of sloth.

Sloth is a parish priest who can't be bothered to learn his psalter and can't read his mass book, but, he says, "I know rhymes of Robin Hood and Randolph Earl of Chester." We don't know what Sloth meant by these rhymes, but it does show that by the 1370s there were already popular poems about Robin Hood in circulation.

Going back to the *Gest of Robyn Hode*. Near the end of the poem the King hears about Robin and comes North from London to see what he can do about it. He visits his private deer park and finds it completely depopulated. To quote the poem, "There our kynge was wont to se / Herdes many one, / He coud unneth fynde one dere / That bare any good horne." The king is not pleased about this, and he decides to look for Robin himself. He knows Robin holds up everyone who goes into the greenwood and has a particular dislike of men of the church. So he disguises himself as an abbot, with five of his knights disguised as monks, and they ride into the greenwood looking like a soft target.

Sure enough, Robin and the Merry Men hold them up. However, Robin has his own way of working. He doesn't say "your money or your life," like highwaymen did in later days. What he does is say, "come and have dinner." After dinner, of course, he says "Now you have to pay for it." And Robin's rule is that if you say honestly, "I have no money, or I only have a few shillings," and this turns out to be true, then you don't have to pay. If on the other hand you say, "I have no money" and Little John then discovers riches in your saddlebags, then Robin takes the lot for lying.

The disguised King, however, says "I have £40, and it's all I have left, because I've been with the King in Nottingham and have spent most of my money there on entertainment." Robin then, very fairly, splits the £40 with him. Half goes to the Merry Men, and half he gives back. To round off the greenwood entertainment, Robin says "let's have a shooting match." The rules of the match are, if you miss your target, you lose your arrow, and you get a clout on the head from Robin.

So the match goes on, and several of the Merry Men collect a clout on the head from Robin, including Little John, and then Robin, for once, misses the target himself. The Merry Men say, "Fair is fair, Robin," and Robin says, "well, our guest can hit me." So the King, still disguised as an abbot, rolls up his sleeve, and because he's a proper warrior-king—probably Edward III—he hits Robin a good one. Robin is very impressed and says, "you have a good arm for an abbot." But at that moment he takes a good look at the supposed abbot, and so does his aristocratic friend Sir Richard, who happens to be there, and they recognize the King. They don't shoot him, like they would the Sheriff. They kneel down at once, and Robin asks for mercy. The King pardons them all on condition that they enter his service, which of course, they are glad to do. And off they ride together, to Nottingham.

On the way, so the poem says, they play a game called pluck-buffet. The rules of this seem to be that as you ride along, you take alternate shots at a target, and the one who misses, or shoots widest, gets another clout on the head. This is a game with rules which could easily be adapted to golf , but somehow I don't think it's going to catch on. The King loses all the time, of course, and Robin pays him out, but because he's a proper English king, and therefore a good sport, he takes it well, remarking only, "I could shoot all year and not get one up on you."

I hardly need to say that all this is very, very unlikely. But you can see the appeal of it. Robin is an honest robber. He is also keen on male bonding in a typically rough and violent way. But he plays fair. He's a sportsman. And so is the King. So they understand each other. Robin is also very loyal, in a disloyal kind of way. He shoots all the King's deer, and he kills his officers— earlier on in the poem he killed the Sheriff of Nottingham. But he insists that he loves the King. This is just one of his apparent contradictions, and I'll mention a couple of others later. Now, can we explain any of this? Is it the product of particularly medieval circumstances? Has it got any resonance in modern times? Well, I've asked three questions, and the answers are, yes, yes, yes. We can explain it. There is something particularly late medieval about it. But the whole complex of contradictions has lasted very well into modern times, even into modern America.

I have up to this point deliberately concealed two important facts about the medieval Robin. One of those is his social status. This is stated repeatedly in the *Gest*, almost obsessively. Robin is a yeoman. The next question is, what's a yeoman? And there are two meanings which have survived in England right up to the present day. One is, he's a bodyguard. The Queen's formal bodyguards are called the Yeomen of the Guard. The other meaning survives as a collective noun given to military regiments. My own county, Dorset, still has the vestige of a regiment called the Dorset Yeomanry. Many counties have these, and they continued to serve right up to and through World War II, where they often did surprisingly well, some said because their troopers were mostly poachers. So that sounds like Robin Hood already. Poachers who can be recruited as bodyguards.

How did these meanings come about? Historians argue about this, but I think it's quite easy. Yeoman is just an abbreviated form of "young man." And it's followed the same sort of development as the word "knight." The word "knight" comes from the Old English word *cniht*, which just meant "boy," exactly as "yeoman" comes from "young man."

What's happened is pretty obvious. In a society without an effective police force, a local godfather, whether he's a good one or a bad one, has to have a squad of enforcers. And he is very likely to call these, "my boys." A thousand years ago he called them my *cnihtas*; six hundred years ago he called them "my young men." So how does this rather simple meaning develop to mean a "person of high social rank," like "knight," or "'man of good standing," which is what one of my dictionaries offers for "yeoman"? Again, I think it's quite obvious. If you're an enforcer for a local godfather, and you do a good job for him, the payoff is that he gives you a farm or a landholding of some kind. All this meant that first knights, and then yeomen, worked their way up the social ladder.

Now we come to the other thing I've been concealing. What did yeomen look like in the 1370s when we first hear about Robin Hood? As it happens, we have a very good description of one, written at about this time, by Geoffrey

Chaucer. Just as he described the Wife of Bath in the General Prologue to his *Canterbury Tales,* he also described the yeoman who accompanies the knight and the squire on the pilgrimage. And Chaucer describes him very well. He wears green; he's a forester; he carries a horn, just as Robin does. Chaucer adds, "His arwes drouped noght with fetheres lowe / And in his hand he bar a mighty bowe."

Robin Hood has always, like some characters we shall meet later, been pretty much defined by his characteristic weapon, the English longbow. And this deserves respectful attention. We know from archaeological finds that medieval bows had a draw weight which might be double that of a modern competition bow, and since you had to pull the string all the way back to the ear, the arrows were 3-feet long, the Gest says, three feet nine. It's a very lethal weapon. I have seen demonstrations of them, and even in modern hands they will punch through anything but the most top-quality steel breastplate, like maybe Sir Lancelot's

But they weren't in modern hands. Archer skeletons have also been found, and these men were deformed. The only way you could learn to shoot bows like that was start in childhood and practice all the time. So medieval archers had forearms like Popeye the Sailor Man, and they had twisted spines, because they'd spent all their lives heaving back and twisting. The result of all this was that for several generations the specialized class of English longbowmen ruled the battlefields of England, Scotland, France, Spain, and even further afield. You often hear that knights were the medieval equivalent of tanks. But the English longbow was the anti-tank gun.

All this meant that the rural yeomen of Medieval England became, in the 14th and 15th centuries, increasingly confident and even aspirational, and Robin Hood was their hero. He expresses all their prejudices, which appear to us as a bundle of contradictions. To explain them I need to go back to the start of the *Gest of Robyn Hode.* This begins, of course, with Robin Hood in the greenwood. But he hasn't had his dinner. He won't have his dinner until he's robbed someone to pay for it. Robin is here imitating an aristocratic custom. King Arthur also would have dinner served to his guests but would not sit down to eat his own dinner until he'd seen a marvel of some kind. What the poem keeps saying is, yeomen are just as good as their social superiors, especially at having good manners.

We're told Robin has another custom, which is that he always hears three masses before dinner, the third of them in honor of Our Lady. Robin is devoted to Our Lady and never robs any company which has a woman in it. In fact, Robin is so picky about who he robs, that you wonder how he makes a living. His instructions to Little John are, he's not to rob any ploughmen or peasants. He's also not to rob any knight or squire "That wol be a gode felawe." So don't rob the lower classes; don't rob the upper classes. Who's left? Robin says, "These bishoppes and these archebishoppes / Ye shall them bete and bynde, / The hye sherif of Notyingham, / Hym holde ye in your minde."

Just as Robin loves the King but hates his officials, so he's a devout Christian, who can't stand the senior officials of the established church. That's two contradictions, with a third to come. Little John and the others accordingly go off to rob somebody on the highway, which we know incidentally, from references in the poem, to be the modern A1 road just south of the village of Wentbridge in Barnsdale in Yorkshire. The poem even mentions the local place name where they keep watch, nowadays Sayle's Plantation, from which you have a good view of the bridge and the road.

The next traveller to go by is a knight, but a sorry-looking one. Just the same, Little John courteously kneels down and says, "My master Robin Hood is waiting dinner for you." Off they go; they have a very good dinner, venison being a main part of it, and then Robin does his usual trick and says, "You're a knight, you must pay for it; it wouldn't be proper for a yeoman to pay for a knight." The knight, Sir Richard at Lee, says he only has 10 shillings, and when Little John checks, this turns out to be true.

Robin asks, "You're a knight, how come you're so poor?" The knight says his son killed somebody, and all his money has gone on paying lawyers and compensation. He could only raise the money by pledging his lands to St. Mary's Abbey in York, a very rich Benedictine monastery. He's due to pay the money back; he hasn't got it; and he's going to have to ask for an extension, which he knows he won't get. Robin says, "I can lend you the money, but have you a guarantor?" "Only God," says Sir Richard. Robin says, rather rudely, that's no good. "Fynde me a better borowe"—That's word for guarantor—"Or money getest thou none." "There's only Our Lady," says Sir Richard. And Robin, who is devoted to Our Lady, says, "She'll do," and immediately lends him £400.

The poem then follows Sir Richard, who goes to St. Mary's. He is treated very rudely by the Abbot, who makes him kneel in front of him and takes delight in the prospect of repossessing Sir Richard's lands. He has a justice sitting by him, just to show that the law is on his side. In the end, Sir Richard, of course, brings out the money, to the chagrin of the Abbot, which gets worse when the justice refuses to hand back the legal fee that the Abbot has paid him. And here is our third contradiction, which explains all the others. We can see that Robin is devoted to justice in the elementary sense of playing fair. Tell him the truth, and he won't take your money. But he has no faith in the medieval English legal system at all, Because it's corrupt. Professional lawyers, professional justices like the abbot's crony, these people have no interest in real justice at all.

It's the same complaint about senior churchmen. Robin is a devout Christian, but they aren't. They're just in it for the money, and many English monasteries, like St, Mary's, were amazingly rich. As for the King's officials, who enforced the law, their bribe-taking and harshness to the poor was notorious. Robin is protesting against corruption in the church, the law, the administration. But he has a strong belief in true religion, true justice, true authority. That's what powers his protests. So it's not Robin who's contradicted. His enemies are. They're all hypocrites.

Well, let's go back to the story of the *Gest*, to see how it all turns out. A year later, Sir Richard, who has been able to raise the money, now he's back in possession of his lands, he's on his way to repay Robin when he is held up by having to protect a yeoman, who has won a wrestling contest and is being hassled by the home crowd. Robin is rather surprised that Our Lady, Sir Richard's guarantor, seems to have let him down, so he sends Little John off again to see what's on the road.

What they see is a monk, with a big bodyguard and seven pack horses. The bodyguard all run away when ambushed, and the monk is taken off to have dinner with Robin. Of course he tells lies about how much money he has, and he forfeits his money—£800—double the money Sir Richard owes. "Look at that," says Robin, "I knew Our Lady wouldn't let me down." But then Sir Richard turns up, makes his excuse, which Robin accepts as soon as he hears Sir Richard has been protecting a yeoman, and Robin refuses to take the money back, saying he's already got it from Our Lady. In fact, he even splits the takings from the monk with Sir Richard.

Well, this is all very unlikely again, and it's proved rather disquieting to modern academics, especially Marxist ones. The trouble is, you see, that Robin isn't behaving like a proper social bandit. He doesn't exactly rob the rich to feed the poor; he robs the rich to help the gentry. Robin is a very conservative bandit.

It may look unlikely, but this behavior pattern is also easily recognizable, even in modern America. If Robin was a modern American, he would fly Old Glory from a flagpole; he'd be a member of the NRA; he would very much dislike members of the liberal elite—college professors, lawyers, and the IRS. He'd go to church on Sunday, though of course in America there is no established church, and donations are voluntary. He'd probably vote for the Tea Party. And do I need to say, he'd be a deer hunter. Very loyal, very patriotic, no time for the government, or for Washington. Some folks may think these are contradictions, but we know that they aren't. The underlying appeal to justice and protest against corruption has remained vital, even after the particular circumstances of the medieval yeomanry ceased to be relevant.

Those particular circumstances, in fact, did not last very long. The longbow was replaced by firearms, not because early guns were significantly superior, but because it took such a long time to train archers. The yeomanry of England, unlike their predecessors, the knights, failed to continue their upward trajectory and lost the aggressive confidence which they had had for a while. This did not put an end to Robin Hood, but after the 15th century, he began to go down market. There were many ballads in which he fought some kind of contest with another member of the working class—a potter, a tanner, a peddler etc.—and he invariably fought a draw or lost. In the 17th century he started using the low-class weapon, the quarterstaff.

Maid Marian had been added to his list of associates in the 16th century, drawn in from her role in May Day celebrations. The idea that Robin Hood's name was really Robert Loxley comes from the same period, and in 1598, a playwright called Anthony Munday, perhaps trying to push him upmarket again, added the notion that he was really the outlawed Earl of Huntington. Friar Tuck got into the mix as well.

What continued to puzzle people, however, was Robin's ambivalent relationship with royalty, at once disobedient and deferential. One solution was offered by Walter Scott in his novel Ivanhoe, of 1819, and it has become virtually mandatory ever since. If Robin was hostile to the King's officers, but loyal to the King, then the solution was to say that there must be two kings—the real King, for some reason absent or in exile, and the King acting in his place, the Regent. The obvious place in English history when this was true was when King Richard Lionheart was away on the Crusades, during which period his brother bad King John was acting as Regent. So Robin was being loyal by resisting the bad King and could hope for reward when the good King came back.

Scott added a nationalistic element to the mix by presenting Robin as a kind of guerrilla leader, acting for the Saxons against their French or Norman oppressors. This is why, on film, the Sheriff of Nottingham's men have usually been distinguished by their kite-shaped shields and Norman-style helmets.

Scholars often point out how anachronistic all this is and how many mistakes Scott made, but it hasn't made any difference. As I said at the start of this lecture, the very openness of the Robin Hood story and all the blank spaces in it have been a standing provocation to many writers to try to fill some of them in. We finally have to ask why, if Robin Hood emerged, as he so clearly did, from a particular class in a particular place at a particular time, he's managed to retain his appeal centuries later.

I guess you could say several things. Robin represents a strong desire for justice, which is only made stronger by distrust of the law, a feeling that has not gone away. In addition, something strongly associated with him is merriment, good humor, laughter, and jokes, even if the jokes are usually pretty violent. Life in the greenwood, for the Merry Men, is carefree. Robin and his men live in an agricultural society, but they never do any agricultural work. They are hunter-gatherers, with the emphasis on hunter. To people who have to work all day and every day, that form of existence can look pretty attractive.

In modern times, Robin has also been made to look good as a democratic hero, almost an honorary American, though modern movies like to have their cake and eat it. In the 1991 movie with Kevin Costner in the lead, Robin is an aristocrat; his name is really Robert of Loxley; and his home is Loxley Castle; but he returns from a crusade to find his father dead and his lands stolen. So he's driven into the greenwood, where he takes up with Little John and the others, meanwhile trying to rescue Maid Mariam, who is minor royalty, from the attentions of the Sheriff of Nottingham. But though Robin is an aristocrat, he's very democratic at heart. "Don't call me sire," he says to one of the Merry Men. He takes over the leadership of the outlaw bands just the same, and at the end King Richard comes back to give away the bride, his cousin Marian, and make sure everything ends happily.

Robin Hood movies, of which there have been many ever since 1908, are in some ways very repetitive—quarterstaff duels, jumping off walls into hay wagons, that sort of thing. But they still show the radical uncertainty about plot which I remarked on before. Will Scarlet may be on Robin's side or he may be Robin's traitor half brother. It may be Marian who needs rescuing, it may be Robin, it may be someone else. Every scriptwriter has tried to think of different clever tricks for Robin to play. But the essentials don't change— the bow, the forest, the sense of justice, the idea of freedom from control and from care. In the case of this particular hero, hold on to the scenario, and the rest is optional.

Don Quixote—The First of the Wannabes

Lecture 10

O f all the heroes presented in this course, Don Quixote is one of the most visually recognizable: an old, thin man on a bony horse with a lance in his hand, wearing antique armor and a helmet made out of a brass shaving basin. Like Odysseus, he has given a word to the English language: quixotic, meaning extravagantly romantic, idealistic to the point of absurdity. *El Ingenioso Hidalgo Don Quijote de la Mancha* by Miguel Cervantes may be one of the most influential works in the history of literature, but it's also one of the least read. In this lecture, we'll try to get the flavor of this novel and explore the surprising complexity of the title character.

Becoming a Knight-Errant

- Don Quixote is known, of course, for tilting at windmills. This phrase has become popular, especially in politics, and is used to refer to an attack on a target that exists only in the attacker's mind. Don Quixote tilts at windmills because his mind has been completely warped by reading books. More than that, he's become a wannabe.

- For Don Quixote, becoming a wannabe is disastrous because his literary role models are singularly bad. He has overdosed on a diet of romances, and under their influence, he decides to become a knight-errant.

- To fulfill this role, the hero first changes his name. He then cleans up some old armor and fashions a helmet. He renames his old horse Rocinante, adds "de la Mancha" to Don Quixote, and then realizes that he needs a lady love.
    - He remembers seeing a peasant girl that he once liked, whose name was Aldonza Lorenzo, and he renames her, too: Dulcinea, because that sounds properly romantic.

- He imagines himself defeating a giant and sending him to Dulcinea to fall on his knees before her and admit that he has been vanquished by Don Quixote de la Mancha.

- After these preliminary preparations, one further ceremony needs to be arranged: Don Quixote must be made a knight. He finds himself at an inn, where the only customers are a couple of women of easy virtue. Together with the innkeeper, they play along with Quixote's fantasy, and ultimately he is knighted.

- His first efforts do not go well, but undeterred, the Don goes home and recruits Sancho Panza to act as his squire. The arrival on the scene of Sancho is the magic ingredient that makes the story take off.

- Even this early in the book, we can see the pattern that emerges. The Don continually thinks in terms of vigils, challenges, fair ladies, giants, and enchantments. But he keeps running into issues over money and donkeys and ladies of dubious virtue. The fantasy world and the real world keep clashing.

Reality versus Delusion

- This clash becomes evident in the scene involving the windmills. As the Don and Sancho are riding along, they see 30 or 40 windmills standing on the plain, and the Don tells Sancho that he will fight these "giants."
  - Sancho tries to point out that the giants are actually windmills, but the Don doesn't listen. He charges the windmills and drives his lance into one of the sails, but the wind turns it so violently that it breaks the lance and drags the horse and rider over with it.

  - Sancho rushes to help the Don, and says, "Didn't I tell you they were only windmills?" The Don gives the all-purpose answer that maintains his delusion: "An enchanter must have changed the giants into windmills to deprive me of the glory of my victory." No matter what, he rewrites events into the language of his own fantasies.

- This basic joke is played out repeatedly. The Don comes upon a chain gang being led off to the royal galleys. As a knight-errant, he feels obliged to free prisoners, which he does, helped by the galley slaves, who turn on their soldier escort. Another time, he attempts to fight lions that are being transported to the royal zoo, but the leader of the pride doesn't even emerge from its cage. We can see from these incidents that the Don is insane, but he is genuinely brave and, in a way, goodhearted.

- This basic joke of delusion confronted by reality by itself doesn't tell us much. But note that, insane though the Don may be, people go along with him. He meets others who are fans of romance and share his madness to a lesser degree. There are also some who go along with his illusions in the hope of curing him, cheering him up, or playing tricks on him.

- From the Don's point of view, all this playacting around him makes the distinction between the fantasy world and the real world look rather uncertain. Furthermore, we are all wannabes at one time or another. If Don Quixote was living in the 21st century, he might indulge in virtual-reality role-playing games, and no one would notice his delusions.

Contrasting Characters

- In addition to writing a narrative centered on a wannabe, Cervantes was also responsible for another innovation in the history of literature: creating a contrasting pair of characters. In this case, we have the Don, exaggeratedly romantic, high-flown, and ineffectual, and Sancho Panza, exaggeratedly down-to-earth, vulgar, and worldly wise.

- Such contrasts have been used repeatedly, with many variations. There's the Cisco Kid and Pancho, the Lone Ranger and Tonto, Frodo Baggins and Sam Gamgee, and Mr. Pickwick and Sam Weller. P. G. Wodehouse put a twist on the idea by creating Bertie Wooster, the aristocratic idiot, and his valet Jeeves, who can solve all problems.

Just as all of us have a bit of Don Quixote—the urge to be a hero or heroine in our own imaginary worlds—so all of us have a bit of Sancho—the part that reminds us that the fantasy is not real.

- The pairing of contrasting characters is an immensely useful narrative device and, arguably, psychologically penetrating. Some have said that Don Quixote represents the ego in each of us, while Sancho represents the id. George Orwell skipped the Freudian language and put it like this: "If you look into your own mind, which are you, Don Quixote or Sancho Panza? Almost certainly you are both."

- Further, just as the Don and Sancho are mixed in every one of us, so in Cervantes's work, the Don and Sancho rub off on each other. They can speak each other's language, and Sancho's adoption of his master's speech adds another dimension to Don Quixote's character.
  - In one scene, the Don sends Sancho off to greet Dulcinea; Sancho reflects that this won't work, because there is no Dulcinea, but he decides to play along with the Don's mania. He sees three peasant girls approaching on donkeys, and he

tells Don Quixote that it's Dulcinea coming to greet him with two maids.

- o Sancho describes the girls in great detail, but the Don replies that all he sees are three peasant girls on three donkeys. Sancho tells the Don that he's got it wrong and rides forward to greet the girls, addressing them in speech that is very like his master's.

- o Don Quixote is completely dumbstruck because all he can see is a very ordinary peasant girl who speaks in very non-noble language. He begs her to look kindly on him, even though some enchanter has cast a spell on him to disguise her beauty, but she takes no notice.

- o As the girls ride on, Dulcinea is bucked off her donkey. But she jumps up, runs after the donkey, puts both hands on its rump, and vaults onto the packsaddle, sitting astride just like a man. Don Quixote stares after her and says, very sadly, "Sancho, you can see now, can't you, how the enchanters hate me." They've taken away from him his image of beauty.

- This is the complete opposite of the windmill scene, and it shows that the Don is not completely insane. He can see what's in front of him, but does that make him feel better? Perhaps Sancho's attempt to go along with his master's fantasies is psychologically wiser.

- Sancho, like Samwise Gamgee in *The Lord of the Rings*, is *samwis*, which is Old English for "part-wise." The peasant sayings he's fond of ("If you lie when you buy, it's your purse that will sigh") reveal a vein of cunning quite opposite the Don's gallantry.

- And sometimes Sancho's cunning pays off. For example, he is given a town to rule as governor by the duke who is playing along with Don Quixote's fantasy and turns out to be a perfect Solomon when it comes to lawsuits. Eventually, though, he gives up the job of governor because it gives a man no peace.

- At the end of the story, Don Quixote is freed of his delusion; he takes his own name back and pronounces an anathema on all romances of chivalry. Sancho tries to cheer him up by talking to him again in his own chivalric terms, but it doesn't work. The Don makes his will and dies, and then, in an ironic fulfillment of his thirst for glory, all the towns of La Mancha fight for the right to claim that they were the hometown of the famous Don Quixote.

Cervantes's Influence

- Some of Cervantes's later influence is obvious. When English writers first began to write novels, they usually modeled themselves on Cervantes and seem to have been particularly impressed with the idea of the "picaresque," a road novel full of amusing scrapes and misunderstandings.

  o Henry Fielding's famous novel *Tom Jones* imitates *Don Quixote* quite closely, especially in one scene of misunderstandings, jealous husbands, and predatory females.

  o All picaresque heroes also must have a Sancho in attendance: Tom Jones has Partridge, Smollett's Roderick Random has Strap, and much later, Dickens's Mr. Pickwick has Sam Weller.

- We find buried memories of Cervantes in *Tom Sawyer*. When Tom leads his gang in an attack on a Sunday-school picnic, he says that there were diamonds there, and Arabs, and elephants, but Huck says he couldn't see any. "It's all done by enchantment," says Tom, quoting *Don Quixote* as an authority.

- And *Don Quixote* remained a powerful influence on a larger scale than just scenes and sayings. One of the earliest open imitations in English was *The Female Quixote* by Charlotte Lennox. Her heroine, Arabella, has been reading romances, too, but these are female-oriented romances in which the heroine's virtue is perpetually threatened. In Jane Austen's first novel, *Northanger Abbey*, the young heroine's head has been turned by Gothic novels.

- Cervantes gave us the idea of the picaresque and of satirizing the pernicious influence of popular literature. Even more important, he gave us the ideas of the wannabe as a hero and the anti-hero in Sancho. Both these ideas were present at the birth of the novel and have influenced it ever since, never losing their capacity to create both comedy and tragedy.

Essential Reading

Cervantes (Rutherford, trans.), *Don Quixote*.

Suggested Reading

Byron, *Cervantes: A Biography*.

Predmore, *The World of Don Quixote*.

Williamson, *The Half-Way House of Fiction*.

Questions to Consider

1. Do you know any real-life wannabes or people who seem to have damaged their lives by trying to make them fit a pulp-fiction pattern? (See Kurt Vonnegut, *Slaughterhouse Five*.)

2. What would you identify as the best fictional role models in our time?

Don Quixote—The First of the Wannabes
Lecture 10—Transcript

Of all the heroes and legends presented in this course, Don Quixote, along with Robinson Crusoe, who comes next, must be one of the most visually recognizable—an old, thin man, on a bony horse, with a lance in his hand, wearing antique armor and a helmet made out of a brass shaving basin. He also has the distinction, along with Odysseus, of having given a word to the English language—quixotic. Quixotic behavior is extravagantly romantic and chivalrous, idealistic to the point of absurdity.

And if we were taking this course in a Department of English literature, or even world literature, I reckon I could make out a case for the work by Miguel Cervantes, *El Ingenioso Hidalgo Don Quijote de la Mancha*, being one of the most influential in the history of literature. It certainly marks a pivotal moment in the history of literature. Well, all those are big claims, so I'll deflate them a bit by saying it's now one of the least-read works of all those I talk about. Influential, pivotal, recognizable, yes, but not very familiar. It's not an easy work to summarize, but I'll do my best to convey its flavor, and also, the surprising depth and complexity of the title character.

By the way, I've already called him *Don Quijote*, but from now on, I'll use the English pronunciation I grew up with and call him Don Quixote.

The thing everybody knows about Don Quixote is that he tilts at windmills, and that's become a popular phrase, especially in politics. If you say someone is tilting at windmills, you mean they're attacking a target which exists only in their own minds. So why does Don Quixote tilt at windmills? It's because his mind has been completely warped by reading books. More than that, he's turned into what we call a wannabe. Here's another big claim; Don Quixote is the first wannabe in the history of literature. Not, I'm sure, the first wannabe in real life, after all, we're all wannabes, or we have all been wannabes, at some level and at some stage, little kids playing Batman, or my little grandson running round shouting incessantly "Spiderman, Spiderman." They're wannabes. People who turn up at science fiction and fantasy conventions dressed as Darth Vader or Galadriel; they're kind of wannabes. And I bet this has always existed. Little Greek boys running round shouting "I'm Achilles," Little medieval boys who wanted to be Sir Lancelot, or little girls hoping to be Guinevere. Okay, we grow out of it, or maybe we don't, but in any case, it's just fun. Why does it become so disastrous for Don Quixote?

Well, the first reason is that he has to some extent, even to a dangerous extent, lost touch with the real world. And the other reason is that his literary role models are really bad ones. Don Quixote has overdosed on a diet of late romances. We no longer know very much about these; they were the pulp fiction of the time, the degenerate descendants of poems like "Le Chevalier de la Charette," which I talked about in the lecture on Guinevere. They have titles like *The Exploits of Esplandian*, or *Don Cirongilio of Thrace*, or *The Knight of the.*

Under the influence of all these works, of which he has a considerable library, until his friends and well wishers burn it, Don Quixote decides to become a knight errant to travel round righting wrongs. It's a bit like wanting to be Superman and go round fighting crime, which is behavior not completely unknown in the modern world. But, how does one go about becoming a knight errant? Well, the first thing our hero does is change his name. His real name is Alonso Quijano el Bueno, "the Good," but he changes Quijano to Quijote, which is a variant on the word for "thigh-piece," the piece of armor that protects your upper legs.

Then he finds some old armor, which has been lying around for ages, and cleans it up as best he can. He can't find a helmet, only a steel cap. He makes a visor and face guard out of cardboard, and then puts some iron bars on the inside to make the whole thing look like a proper knight's helmet. He also renames his old horse Rocinante, adds de la Mancha to Don Quixote, and then, most important thing, realizes he needs a lady love. He remembers seeing a peasant girl he once liked the look of, whose name was Aldonza Lorenzo, and he renames her too, Dulcinea, because that sounds properly romantic, and because she comes from a place called El Toboso, she becomes Dulcinea del Toboso. The scene he imagines is himself defeating a giant and sending him to Dulcinea to fall on his knees before her and say, "I, my lady, am the giant Caraculiambro, vanquished in single combat by the never sufficiently extolled knight Don Quixote de la Mancha, who has commanded me to present myself before your Highness."

Those are his preliminary preparations, but there's one further ceremony which needs to be arranged. Somebody has to make him a knight. He finds himself at an inn, whose only customers are a couple of ladies of easy virtue, as they used to be called. The Don, however, takes them to be noble maidens, and they kindly play along with him, even feeding him through his home-made visor, because he won't take it off. One girl has to hold it up all the time, while the other puts the food in his mouth.

The next problem arises when the innkeeper asks if he has any money, and Don Quixote replies that he has never read in any history of knight errants that any of them ever carried money. The innkeeper, also, playing along with the delusion, says, it may not have been written, but just the same, knights must have carried something, even if it was only bandages and ointment for their wounds. Or maybe their squires had saddlebags?

Once that's sorted out, they arrange for Don Quixote to keep the vigil, which is customary before being knighted, in the yard of the inn. This causes some trouble, as the muleteers have to cross the yard to feed and water their beasts, which the Don objects to. But in the end, the innkeeper pretends to knight Don Quixote, the obliging ladies gird him with his knightly belt, and put his knightly spurs on for him. So the Don is finally ready to start his career as a knight errant.

His first efforts do not go very well at all, but, undeterred, the Don goes home and recruits Sancho Panza to act as his squire. There's an immediate problem, because Sancho only has a donkey, and the Don has never heard of a squire riding a donkey. But the arrival on the scene of Sancho is the magic ingredient which makes the story take off.

Even this early on, though, you can see the pattern which emerges. The Don continually thinks in terms of vigils, challenges, fair ladies, giants, and enchantments. But what he keeps running into are issues over money, and donkeys, and ladies of dubious virtue. The fantasy world and the real world keep clashing. The clash becomes evident in the first big scene, which is, of course, the scene with the windmills.

As the Don and Sancho are riding along, they see thirty or forty windmills standing on the plain, and the Don says to Sancho, "Look, there are thirty or more giants whom I'm going to fight, because it is a great service to God to wipe such a breed from the face of the earth." "What giants?" asks Sancho. "Those giants over there," says the Don, "the ones with long arms. There are giants with arms six miles long." "They're not giants, they're windmills," says Sancho, "and what you're taking for arms are their sails. That's what makes the millstones go round." "It's obvious you don't know anything about adventures," says the Don scornfully. "They're giants, and if you're frightened, you go and say your prayers." And saying this, he charges the windmills just as the wind blows and the sails start to turn. He drives his lance into one of the sails, but the wind turns it so violently that it breaks the lance and drags the horse and rider over with it, so that the Don crashes to the ground. Sancho rushes to help him and says, "Didn't I tell you they were only windmills?" The Don replies, it's the all-purpose answer which keeps his delusion going, "An enchanter must have changed the giants into windmills to deprive me of the glory of my victory." No matter what, he rewrites events into the language of his own delusion.

Well, as I say, that's the basic joke, and it's played again and again. The Don comes upon a chain gang being led off to the royal galleys. He decides that his profession as a knight errant obliges him to free prisoners, which he does, helped by the galley slaves who turn on their soldier escort. The slaves aren't at all grateful, and one of them, Ginès de Pasamonte, is a notorious bad character who keeps on turning up in the rest of the story, stealing Sancho's donkey and the Don's sword, among other misdeeds.

Another time, the Don is deluded into fighting what he thinks is a giant who has been oppressing the noble Princess Micomicona, but all he does is slash open wineskins, so that the wine runs all over the floor. He thinks it's blood. Again, he comes upon a cart transporting lions, real lions, to the royal zoo. He bullies the carter into opening the cages to let the lions free so that he can fight them. But as it happens, the head of this particular pride is not very interested, and doesn't bother to come out of his cage, which allows Sancho to boast of his master's knightly courage.

So, the Don is insane, but he is genuinely brave. And also, in a way, goodhearted. We might just note that Cervantes himself had actually been a slave for five years in Algeria after being captured by the Moors. So freeing galley slaves might well have seemed to him a particularly good idea, even if they were petty criminals. I'd add that Cervantes had also fought at the great battle of Lepanto, in 1571, against an enormous Turkish fleet, where he was wounded and lost the use of his left hand. He had a very eventful life, just like Sir Thomas Malory, and just like Sir Thomas, it's thought that he at least began writing Don Quixote in jail.

Now, if all we had was this basic joke of delusion confronted by reality, you might say that it doesn't tell us much. But note one thing. Insane, though the Don may be, people go along with him. He meets other people who are fans of romance. The innkeeper who knighted him was one of them. He tells stories taken from romance with great enthusiasm:

> "You ought to read about what Felixmarte of Hyrcania got up to— with just one backstroke he cut five giants clean through the middle as if they were dolls that children make out of bean pods! And another time he charged at a whole army and defeated more than one million six hundred thousand soldiers all in armor, just as if they were flocks of sheep. And then there was Don Cirongilio of Thrace ..."

And so on. If the Don is mad, there are others who share his madness, if to a lesser degree. Also, some people go along with the Don's delusions in the hope of curing him, like Sanson Carrasco, who disguises himself as a fellow knight errant. He means to fight a duel with the Don, win it, and as penance, order the Don to go home and start living normally again. But as it happens, the Don wins the duel.

Another helpful lady called Dorotea decides to disguise herself as the Princess Micomicona, who has come from the ends of the earth to beg the help of the famous knight Don Quixote against the giant Pandafilando. She hopes by this at least to cheer the Don up. Much of the second part of

Cervantes' work is further dominated by an unnamed Duke and Duchess, who take great pains to go along with the Don's delusion, just so they can play tricks on him.

Well, looked at from the Don's point of view, all this play-acting around him makes the distinction between the fantasy world and the real world look rather uncertain. Furthermore, I've already said that we've all been wannabes once upon a time. So, consider the modern phenomenon of virtual reality role-playing games. It's notorious that many people find the lives they live in the virtual world much more vivid, much more rewarding, than the disappointments of everyday life. Nowadays we can act out our fantasies on computers. If Don Quixote was living in the 21st century, perhaps no one would notice his delusions at all. Or they might join in, like the innkeeper and the kind-hearted girls who act out his vigil. "Hey, he has a good idea for a Multi-User Domain there. I'm not going to be a knight, I'm going to be giant Caraculiambro ..."

Cervantes was responsible, however, for a second great innovation in the history of literature. The first one was centering a narrative on a wannabe. The second was to bring in Sancho Panza, and by doing so, to create a pairing of man and master, which is also a contrast of styles, even of ideologies. The one exaggeratedly romantic, high flown, ineffectual, the other, exaggeratedly down to earth, vulgar, worldly wise.

The trick has been played again and again, with many variations. There's the Cisco Kid and Pancho; or the Lone Ranger and Tonto; there's Frodo Baggins and Sam Gamgee; there's Dickens' Mr. Pickwick and Sam Weller; P. G. Wodehouse put a twist on it by creating Bertie Wooster, the aristocratic idiot, and his valet Jeeves, who can solve all problems. But there are many more pairs, even outside comedy. C. S. Forester paired Horatio Hornblower with Lieutenant Bush. Many will remember more recently Patrick O'Brian's creation of Captain Aubrey and Dr. Maturin. And let's not forget Sherlock Holmes and Dr. Watson. It's an immensely useful narrative device.

It's also arguably extremely psychologically penetrating. People have said that Don Quixote represents the ego in each of us. Meanwhile Sancho represents the id in each of us. George Orwell skipped the Freudian language and put it like this:

> "if you look into your own mind, which are you, Don Quixote or Sancho Panza? Almost certainly you are both. There is one part of you that wishes to be a hero or a saint, but another part of you is a little fat man who sees very clearly the advantages of staying alive with a whole skin."

So just as all of us have a bit of Don Quixote, the urge to be a hero or heroine in our own preferred imaginary world, so all of us have a bit of Sancho, the bit that reminds us it's not true, it's not going to work, you'll still have bills to pay in the morning. Of course, important qualification, the proportions are different in every one of us.

But just as the Don and Sancho are mixed in every one of us, so in Cervantes' work, the Don and Sancho rub off on each other. They can talk each other's language. The Don is quite sensible when Sancho puts forward the suggestion that it might be an idea to pay a Squire a fixed wage. He even uses one of Sancho's characteristic peasant sayings against him. "So long as the pigeon loft does not lack food, it will not lack pigeons." But it's Sancho talking like the Don who adds another dimension to Don Quixote's character, not a funny one, this time.

In one scene the Don sends Sancho off to greet Dulcinea. Sancho reflects that this won't work, because there is no Dulcinea, so he decides to play along with the Don's mania. He sees three peasant girls approaching on donkeys, and he tells Don Quixote that it's Dulcinea coming to greet him with two maids. He describes them in great detail:

> "She and her maids are all one blaze of flaming gold, all spindlefuls of pearls, they're all diamonds, all rubies, all brocade more than ten levels deep, with their hair flowing over their shoulders like sunbeams playing with the wind, and what's more each of them is riding her piebald palfrey."

"All I can see, Sancho," says the Don, "is three peasant girls on three donkeys."

Sancho tells him he's got it wrong and rides forward to greet the three girls, falls to his knees and says to the first of them:

"Oh, Queen and Princess and Duchess of beauty, may your highness be pleased to receive into your grace and good will this your hapless knight, overcome by finding himself in your magnificent presence. I am his squire Sancho Panza, and he is the knight Don Quixote de la Mancha, also known as the Knight of the Sad Countenance."

Sancho here is talking like the Don, and doing it very well. Don Quixote, by contrast, is completely dumbstruck, because all he can see is a very ordinary peasant girl who furthermore speaks in very non-noble language, "get out of the damn way and let us through, we're in a hurry." The Don then breaks in and begs her to look kindly on him, even though some enchanter has cast a spell on him to disguise her beauty. But she takes no notice.

As the girls ride on, Dulcinea herself is bucked off her donkey. But she jumps up, runs after the donkey, put both hands on its rump, and vaults onto the packsaddle, sitting astride just like a man, all in a hopelessly unladylike fashion and trailing a strong smell of garlic. Don Quixote stares after her and says, very sadly, "Sancho, you can see now, can't you, how the enchanters hate me." They've taken away from him even his image of beauty.

This is the complete opposite of the windmill scene, and it shows that the Don is not 100% crazy. He can see what's in front of him. But does that make him feel better? Maybe Sancho's attempt to go along with his master's fantasies is psychologically wiser. Sancho, like Samwise Gamgee, is *samwis*, which is Old English for part wise. At least that's politer than Tonto, which just means "stupid."

I've mentioned Sancho's liking for peasant sayings, of which he has many: "If you lie when you buy, it's your purse that will sigh," or "Many think they'll find bacon when there isn't even a hook," or "The hare leaps up where you least expect it to." I can't always understand what they mean, but he has a vein of cunning quite opposite to the Don's gallantry. And sometimes this pays off. For example, Sancho is given a town to rule as governor by the duke who is playing along with Don Quixote's fantasy. Sancho turns out to be a perfect Solomon when it comes to lawsuits. When two men argue over whether 10 gold escudos have been repaid or not, Sancho notices that the debtor hands the creditor his stick to hold before swearing on oath that he has returned the money. Then he takes the stick back. So Sancho has the stick broken open, and the gold escudos are found inside it. He deals with other disputed cases with the same peasant shrewdness. But eventually, he gives up the job of governor as giving a man no peace at all and goes off with characteristic moderation, with just half a loaf and half a cheese.

There are many other incidents in the novel's thousand pages, and one thing which impressed later novelists was the way in which Cervantes grafted stories on to his main narrative. There's one, for instance, centered on two pairs of lovers, which may have been the source for a lost late play by Shakespeare called *Cardenio*. The end of the story though, is that Don Quixote is freed of his delusion, takes his own name back, and pronounces an anathema on all romances of chivalry. Sancho tries to cheer him up by talking to him again in his own chivalric terms, but it doesn't work. The Don makes his will and dies. And then, fulfilling, ironically, his own thirst for glory, all the towns of La Mancha fight for the right to claim that they were the hometown of the famous Don Quixote, just as the Greek cities, long before, all did their best to claim Homer as one of theirs.

Some of Cervantes' influence is very obvious. When English writers first began to write novels, they usually modeled themselves on Cervantes. The thing which seems to have impressed them particularly was the idea of "the picaresque." A *picaro* was a kind of scallywag, and many 18th-century novels are picaresque novels, which is to say, road novels full of amusing scrapes and misunderstandings. Henry Fielding's novel *Joseph Andrews* acknowledges Cervantes as a source, and his more famous novel, *Tom Jones,* imitates Don Quixote quite closely, especially in one famous scene, set in the inn at Upton, of misunderstandings and jealous husbands and predatory females.

All picaresque heroes also had to have a Sancho in attendance; Tom Jones has Partridge, Smollett's Roderick Random has Strap, and much later and much better, Dickens's Mr. Pickwick has Sam Weller. Sam Weller has also given a word to English, which is the "wellerism." A wellerism is a saying which is given unexpected comic meaning by adding a phrase onto it, like, just to give one example from Dickens, "Now we look compact and comfortable as the father said when he cut his little boy's head off, to cure him of squinting." But although Sam Weller and Dickens get the credit for the wellerism, Sancho and Cervantes were there before them. This is just one of Sancho's: "You're a bit late in chirping, as the Galician soldier said to the chicken who hatched from the egg he'd just swallowed."

And there are many other buried memories of Cervantes. In Huckleberry Finn, which we'll be looking at later, Tom Sawyer leads his gang in an attack on a Sunday school picnic. Tom says there were diamonds there, and Arabs, and elephants, but Huck says he couldn't see any. It's all done by enchantment, says Tom, quoting Don Quixote as an authority. Huck thinks it over for a while before deciding, "All that stuff was only just one of Tom Sawyer's lies. I reckoned he believed in the Arabs and the elephants, but as for me, I think different. It had all the marks of a Sunday school." Tom and Huck are the Don and Sancho come back again.

And Don Quixote remained a powerful influence on a larger scale than just scenes and sayings. One of the earliest open imitations in English was *The Female Quixote*, by Charlotte Lennox, who has been described,—not very convincingly—as the first American novelist. Her heroine, Arabella, has been reading romances too, but of a different kind, female-oriented romances in which the heroine's virtue is perpetually threatened. Near the end, she sees some horsemen, immediately decides that they must be intent on ravishing her, and attempts to swim the Thames to escape, just like one of the heroines she has read about. She has to be fished out, revived, and restored to sanity rather earlier than the Don.

The same joke is the basis for Jane Austen's first novel, *Northanger Abbey*. Though there, the literature which has turned the young heroine's head is the Gothic novel, full of ghosts, mysterious documents, skeletons in cupboards etc., none of which, of course, actually turn up in her perfectly normal English surroundings. She, too learns better.

There have been any number of later novels with "Quixote" in the title, like Richard Graves's *The Spiritual Quixote*, G. K. Chesterton's *The Return of Don Quixote*, Graham Greene's *Monsignor Quixote*. But even if the name isn't mentioned, the influence of Cervantes is often lurking. He gave us the idea of the picaresque; he gave us the idea of satirizing the pernicious influence of popular literature. But the two great inventions of Cervantes for which we can all be grateful were, first, the idea of the wannabe as hero, and second, the idea of the Sancho as anti-hero. They were both there at the very birth of the novel; they have influenced it ever since; they've never quite lost their capacity for creating comedy, and, if one remembers the Don saying sadly, "You see how the enchanters hate me," their capacity for human tragedy as well. We start by laughing at the Don; we end by recognizing ourselves in him.

Robinson Crusoe—A Lone Survivor
Lecture 11

In this course so far, we've had heroes called into being by historical trauma, to express changing cultural values, or to deny or make fun of established values. But with Robinson Crusoe, we have a hero called into being by a new geography. Daniel Defoe's *Robinson Crusoe* is the model for the "desert (deserted) island" story, but such stories weren't possible until people discovered habitable islands that had no inhabitants. This was a New World phenomenon, and the New World itself was a study in contrasts for the first European explorers: fear and danger versus luxury and riches. As we'll see in this lecture, such contradictions, along with new ideas and images, dominate the desert island story.

Contrasts in the New World

- Although we're all familiar with deserted island stories, such stories weren't possible until habitable islands were discovered that had no inhabitants. Such discoveries were a post-Columbus phenomenon.

- The New World was a strange place to the first European explorers. On the one hand, it was terrifying; Europeans encountered destructive tropical weather, sharks, and cannibals for the first time in the 1500s. But the New World could also be alluring, providing such products as potatoes, tomatoes, tobacco, maize, pineapples, and sugarcane.

- Such contradictions probably set many people wondering what it would be like to live in the New World, and these thoughts were fed by accounts of exploration, disaster, and triumph across the sea.

- One such account was certainly a source for *Robinson Crusoe*. It was the story of a Scottish sailor named Alexander Selkirk, who was cast away on an island about 800 miles off the coast of Chile. Selkirk did several things that Crusoe was later to do and become famous for, notably, making his own clothes out of goatskin.

- Defoe's description of Crusoe in his goatskin clothes makes him visually recognizable. Defoe also tells us that Crusoe is bearded and hairy; he looks like a prehistoric wild man. But Crusoe is pretty heavily equipped in a style that is definitely not prehistoric. He has a saw and hatchet; he wears a baldric with pouches for his gunpowder and shot; and besides his basket and umbrella, he carries a gun.

- We can note one other contradiction in Defoe's story of Crusoe: When he finds the footprint of Man Friday, he reacts with fear and alarm at the thought of human companionship.

Crusoe's Personality

- There are many things about Crusoe as a person that make people uneasy now and probably always did. For example, James Joyce said that he was the model of the British colonizer, and there are certainly things about him that remind us of the worst aspects of the history of European colonization and dominance.
  - Crusoe gets his start as a merchant in what he calls the "Guinea trade." He scrapes together £40 that he spends on "toys and trifles" to take to Africa, where he trades them for gold dust worth almost £300.

  - Later on, Crusoe is captured by the Moors of North Africa and escapes from them in a boat, along with a Moorish boy he calls Xury. They are picked up by a Portuguese ship on passage to Brazil. The Portuguese captain deals fairly with Crusoe, buying his boat, which gives Crusoe the means to start a plantation in Brazil. However, Crusoe also sells Xury to the captain. Eventually, a deal is struck that Xury will serve the captain for 10 years, after which he will be freed as long as he converts to Christianity.

  - Crusoe is always high-handed when it comes to dealing with any non-Europeans. After he has set up his plantation in Brazil, even though it's going well and making him rich, he still desires to go back to the Guinea trade, by which he means buying slaves in Africa and shipping them to plantations in South America.

- In addition to being a potential slaver, Crusoe also is, perhaps, a potential capitalist. He certainly has strong feelings about money. We see this in the scene in which Crusoe attempts to salvage as much as he can out of the wreck of his ship.
  - Although he is now a castaway and completely dependent on his own efforts, everyone else on the ship has been drowned; thus, Crusoe has unchallenged title to a great deal of valuable property, if only he can salvage it.

  - Crusoe gets back on board the wreck and starts stripping it of everything he can find: bread, rum, tools, guns, gunpowder, and more. Then he finds some money, about £36, and muses that it isn't worth anything to him now, yet he says, "upon second thoughts, I took it away."

- Crusoe also represents a high degree of the Protestant work ethic and what is often felt to go along with it: a kind of hypocrisy or self-righteousness.
  - In Protestant England, many people were encouraged to write diaries of their spiritual progress, and in this "autobiography," Crusoe is doing something very similar. He keeps an account book of his soul, just as he does of his money and possessions. This gives a new and unusually honest insight into his inner life, but he comes over as a strange mixture.

  - Is he hardhearted? He takes home a small goat with the aim of making it a pet but later kills it and eats it. He arms himself heavily and seems quite confident that he can wipe out many cannibals if he can take them by surprise.

  - But Crusoe also has a Christian conscience. Although he describes the Indians regularly as "naked savages," he wonders whether their dreadful customs are their own fault and whether they deserve the death he means to deal out to them. They don't see what they do as a crime. Still, these reflections don't prevent Crusoe from attacking and killing the Indians who have captured Friday and doing the same thing when he and Friday rescue Friday's father.

- Crusoe seems to be able to practice what George Orwell called doublethink, the useful ability to proclaim one principle and believe in it wholeheartedly even when it's contradicted by your actions.

- None of this makes Crusoe a very likeable character, especially in the modern world, and his most obvious blind spot is his treatment of Man Friday. He does, of course, rescue Friday from certain death, and it's only right that Friday should be grateful to him. But Crusoe portrays Friday with a kind of indulgent patronage. As far as Crusoe is concerned, Friday is a child.
  - Crusoe naturally tries to explain Christianity to Friday but runs into trouble when Friday starts asking questions. Crusoe concludes that "nothing but a revelation from heaven" can form correct opinions in the soul.

  - As for what Friday tells him about his own religion, Crusoe's only comment is to say that the Indians also suffer from "priestcraft," which in Protestant England was an obvious slur on Roman Catholics.

Imitations of Crusoe
- Crusoe is self-righteous, patronizing, money-oriented, distinctly ruthless, and for all his spiritual account-keeping, possibly so hypocritical that he doesn't even notice it himself. We must ask, then, how has he come to inspire so many imitations? In German-speaking countries, imitations of Crusoe were so numerous that a special term was developed for them: *Robinsonaden*.

- The most familiar of these imitations is *The Swiss Family Robinson*, which became a children's classic. Jules Verne wrote one called *L'Ecole des Robinsons*, "*The School for Robinsons*." J. M. Barrie,

Robinson's most lovingly described success on the island is his construction of a kind of fort for himself.

the creator of Peter Pan, added an element of class comedy in a play called *The Admirable Crichton*, in which an upper-class family is stranded with their butler, who turns out to be the most practical and useful member of the party.

- What seems to have made Defoe's book a hit in the popular consciousness was Crusoe's ingenuity. At the heart of the story are detailed accounts of his triumph over his environment: how he learns to grow grain and grind it to make bread; how he learns to make butter, cheese, and baskets; and how he builds a fort for himself.

- There's a moment, too, as Crusoe explores the island and sees its abundance when he feels how lucky he is. We might even say that he has the best of both worlds.
  - He has land of his own to do what he wants, with no human competition and no serious animal competition. At the same time, he has considerable accumulated capital—from all the

things he salvaged from his own wrecked ship and more added from a second wreck that comes ashore years later.

○ He also has what we might call the intellectual capital of the civilization he comes from. Crusoe may not know exactly how to do things, but he knows what can be done, and with the aid of labor and patience and experiment, he manages to supply most of his wants.

○ We've likely all been Crusoes, at least in our imaginations. Building a treehouse or a fort as a child is a Crusoe-style activity, and we can imagine ourselves doing similar things as adults, with better equipment and more know-how. It's an immensely satisfying feeling, and we feel Crusoe's own satisfaction as he rises above his difficulties.

• There are no desert islands left on Earth, which is probably why Crusoe stories have been shifted into science fiction.
  ○ One obvious Robinson spinoff is a book called *No Man Friday* by Rex Gordon. It's about someone who finds himself stranded on Mars, with no resources other than what he can salvage from his wrecked rocket.

  ○ James Blish, one of the first *Star Trek* authors, wrote another book along similar lines called *Welcome to Mars*.

• Crusoe expresses the sense of enormous untapped possibilities that came over the Western world as it broke out of its medieval isolation. He has many of the bad qualities that accompanied the surge into the New World, especially his treatment of the native peoples to whom the Westerners felt so superior, but on his own, competing against nature, he is an admirable figure.

Essential Reading

Defoe, *Robinson Crusoe*.

Suggested Reading

Ellis, ed., *Twentieth-Century Interpretations of Robinson Crusoe.*

Seidel, *Robinson Crusoe: Island Myths and the Novel.*

Souhami, *Selkirk's Island.*

Questions to Consider

1. If you were to be stranded on a "desert island," like Robinson's, what half-dozen pieces of equipment (single items, not a whole toolbox, as Robinson had) would you select as top priority?

2. Do you think that modern science-fictional post-apocalypse stories (Cormac McCarthy, *The Road*; John Varley, *Slow Apocalypse*) are really "Robinsonades"?

Robinson Crusoe—A Lone Survivor
Lecture 11—Transcript

In the course so far, we've had heroes called into being by a historical trauma, like Bilbo and Frodo Baggins. We've had heroines created to express changing cultural values, like Guinevere, or to deny established values, like the Wife of Bath, or even to make fun of them, like Don Quixote. But with Robinson Crusoe, we have a hero called into being, not by a change of culture or by some historical event, but by a new geography. Daniel Defoe's novel *Robinson Crusoe*, 1719, is the model for the "desert island story," of which we have so many in English—Robert Louis Stevenson's *Treasure Island*; R. M. Ballantyne's *The Coral Island*; H. G. Wells's *The Island of Dr. Moreau*, William Golding's *Lord of the Flies*.

I've just called them "desert island stories," but obviously they aren't. By "desert" we mean a place that is uninhabitable. It may be a hot, sandy desert like the Sahara, or a cold, arid desert like the Gobi, but deserts are places where people can't live. By contrast, the islands in all the stories I just mentioned are downright lush; they're perfectly, easily habitable. You can live very well on them. So we don't mean desert islands, what we mean is deserted islands. What I'm saying is that you couldn't have a desert island story, as we call them, until you came across that contradiction in real life. Islands where you could live, which didn't already have people living on them.

This is a New World phenomenon. If it did exist in the old world, it existed so far back that we have no record of it. Even by Homer's time, I suspect that every rock in the Mediterranean which had fresh water on it also had people living there. They might be nymphs, like Calypso, or witches, like Circe, or one-eyed, man-eating giants like Polyphemus, but there was someone there. Islands which didn't have anyone on them are a post-Columbus phenomenon. The first location for them was the Caribbean Sea, from 1492 onwards. Eventually, the Pacific Ocean would also provide a place where explorers would find uninhabited atolls. Long before that, though, the Caribbean and the Americas, more generally, opened up a whole new vision to European eyes.

The New World was a very strange place to the first European explorers. On the one hand it was seriously terrifying. In their flimsy ships the Europeans met hurricanes. "Hurricane" is a word first recorded in English in 1555; also "tornadoes," a word first recorded 1556, and "typhoons," first recorded 1588. And it wasn't just weather. The word "shark" is not recorded in English until 1569. Blue sharks, bull sharks, hammerheads, all came as a major and unpleasant surprise to those who ventured into the warmer waters. And then there were the human man eaters, the cannibals.

That was one side of it. The other side was much more alluring. We know about all the crops which were first found in the New World—potatoes, tomatoes, tobacco, maize, all very useful. But there were sexier products than that. One was the pineapple, another word not recorded in English until the 1660s, when it's described as "the most delicious fruit of all America." Pineapples were a serious luxury item right up to the 20th century. In Victorian times, an aspiring family holding a party might even hire a pineapple. You put it in the middle of the table surrounded by all the lesser foods and fruits, but of course, no one was allowed to eat any of it. It was too expensive for that. It had to be returned to the person who rented it to you. It was just for show.

But on the Caribbean islands, they grew wild, and you could eat as many as you liked for nothing! And then there was sugarcane. Europe very rapidly developed a sugar habit, which had to be fed by the slave plantations in the West Indies. Another great delicacy was the turtle, from which you made turtle soup, the absolute pièce de résistance of the London Lord Mayor's banquet.

So, on the one hand, fear and danger, on the other, luxury and riches, it's contradictions of this kind that dominate desert-island stories. And with them go the new ideas and images with which we are all now perfectly familiar— buccaneers, pirates, castaways, all words which didn't exist in the language until the post-Columbus period I'm talking about. What those contradictions did, I suspect, was to set thousands of people, maybe millions, saying to themselves, "Wouldn't it be nice if … ?" And "What would it be like if…?" These thoughts and fantasies were fed by more and more accounts of exploration, disaster, and triumph in the New World across the sea.

One of the most famous of these was certainly a source for Defoe's *Robinson Crusoe*. It was the story of a Scottish sailor called Alexander Selkirk, who was cast away on an island, not in the Caribbean, but round Cape Horn on the other side of South America, the island Juan Fernandez, about 800 miles off the coast of Chile, now called Robinson Crusoe Island. Strictly speaking, Selkirk was not a castaway. He left his ship because he thought it was unseaworthy, and though he changed his mind, the skipper wouldn't let him back aboard. So he wasn't a castaway; he was a maroon—another new word, like Ben Gunn in Stevenson's *Treasure Island*. But Selkirk did several things that Crusoe was later to do and to become famous for, notably making his own clothes out of goatskin. The goatskins are one of the things that made Crusoe famous. Along with Don Quixote, he must be the most visually recognizable of all the heroes and heroines we deal with in this course. Defoe has Crusoe give a description of himself, which has been an inspiration for illustrators ever since.

> "I had a great high shapeless cap, made of a goat's skin, with a flap hanging down behind [...] I had a short jacket of goat's skin, the skirts coming down to about the middle of the thighs, and a pair of open-kneed breeches of the same [...] I had on a broad belt of goat's skin dried which I drew together with two thongs of the same. instead of buckles [...] At my back I carried my basket [...] and over my head a great clumsy goat's skin umbrella, but which after all was the most necessary thing I had about me[.]"

Crusoe is also bearded, and whiskered, and hairy. All round, he looks like something from the prehistoric past, a wild man of the woods, such as you find in medieval pictures. But as with desert islands, that's only half the story. Because actually, Crusoe is pretty heavily equipped in a style which is definitely not prehistoric, or even mediaeval. In his belt he has a little saw and a hatchet, taking the place of a sword and dagger. He wears a baldric as well, with two pouches for his gunpowder and for his shot, and besides his basket and his umbrella, of course he carries a gun. Crusoe is always heavily armed.

And there's another contradiction which one can see from the picture nearly everyone has of Crusoe. What's he doing in his goatskin clothes, with his gun and his umbrella? In the picture which everyone has seen, he's bending over and looking at a footprint in the sand. It's the footprint of Man Friday. Now, when he sees that, Crusoe has been on his island for 20 without hearing a human voice, except for Poll Parrot, who he's trained to talk to him. Is he lonely, is he pleased at the thought of human companionship? No, his reaction is fear and alarm. The island has definitely had human visitors, but the only visitors likely are native cannibals or European pirates. Crusoe is struck with fear and returns to his fortified home to check his weapons and his gunpowder and wonder what more he can do to make himself safe.

At this point I can say that whatever made Crusoe a lasting success and inspiration, it was not his individual character. There are many things about Crusoe as a person which make people uneasy now, and probably always did. James Joyce said that he was the model of the British colonizer. And there are certainly things about him which remind one of the worst aspects of the history of European colonization and dominance.

Crusoe gets his start as a merchant in what he calls "the Guinea trade." What he does is to scrape together some £40, which he spends on "toys and trifles" and takes off to Africa with him. He trades the toys and trifles with the Africans for gold dust, and brings back—Defoe always gives precise details about money—5 lbs. 9 oz. in gold dust, which brings him in almost £300. So Crusoe has made a 700% return on his first voyage, at the expense of the Africans.

Later on he is captured by the Moors of North Africa and escapes from them in a boat, along with a Moorish boy he calls Xury. They are picked up by a Portuguese ship on passage to Brazil, and the Portuguese captain deals very fairly with Crusoe, buying his boat and its contents off him, which gives Crusoe the means to start a plantation in Brazil. However, Crusoe also sells him the boy Xury. He has some compunction about this, and the deal eventually struck is that Xury will serve the Portuguese captain for ten years and after that be freed, as long as he converts to Christianity.

Crusoe tells us that Xury is perfectly happy to be treated like this, but Crusoe is always high-handed when it comes to dealing with any non-Europeans. After he has set up his plantation in Brazil, even though it's going well and making him rich, he still has a hankering to go back to the Guinea trade, by which he means buying slaves in Africa and shipping them over to the plantations in South America. It's while he's on passage to Africa that his ship is caught by a hurricane and wrecked on an island somewhere near the mouth of the Orinoco River, and serve him right, you might well say.

So Crusoe is at least a potential slaver, and he's also, well, what can we say? He's a potential capitalist? He certainly has very strong feelings about money. One scene in the novel which could be seen as funny, though it probably wasn't meant to be, is the one where Crusoe is getting as much as he can out of the wreck of his ship. You might say that this is a capitalist fantasy in itself, because although Crusoe is now a castaway and completely dependent on his own efforts, everyone else who was on the ship has been drowned, so that Crusoe has unchallenged title to a very great deal of valuable property, if only he can salvage it.

Crusoe, then, gets back on board the wreck and very sensibly starts stripping it of everything he can find. The first thing he goes for is bread, and then a shot of rum. Then he makes a raft, fills some chests with provisions, and then finds the carpenter's chest full of tools, which, as he says, is the most valuable thing there. He stocks up with guns, gunpowder, shot, cables and iron, and razors and scissors—all very sensible.

And then he finds money, as usual, described in detail: "about £36 value— some European coin, some Brazil, some pieces of eight, some gold, and some silver." This provides a good opportunity for some familiar moralizing. Crusoe says,: "I smiled to myself at the sight of this money. "Oh drug!" I exclaimed, "What art thou good for? Thou art not worth to me—no, not the taking off the ground; one of those knives is worth all this heap; I have no manner of use for thee—e'en remain where thou art, and go to the bottom as a creature whose life is thing not worth saving." "However," Crusoe goes on, "upon second thoughts I took it away." He never forgets the money and is careful to take it with him when he is finally rescued.

Was Crusoe's change of mind intended as a kind of joke by Defoe? One can't be sure. But once again, many people have thought that Crusoe is not only a kind of archetypal colonizer and a kind of archetypal capitalist, but that he also represents in high degree what people call "the Protestant work ethic" and what is often felt to go along with it, a kind of hypocrisy, a kind of self-righteousness.

We might just note what a tour de force it was for Defoe to write the whole core of his book with no human interactions at all. It becomes a kind of autobiography, and a kind of journal. Now, in Protestant England many people were encouraged to write diaries of their own spiritual progress, of which the most famous is John Bunyan's *Grace Abounding to the Chief of Sinners*, and Crusoe is doing something very like that. You might say, he keeps an account book of his own soul, just as he does of his money and his possessions. This gives a new and unusually honest insight into his inner life, but he comes over as a strange mixture.

Is he hardhearted? He does seem to shoot at anything as a kind of instinctive reaction. One cannot blame him for shooting a goat to feed himself. But then, having shot the goat, he feels sorry for the kid standing by its mother. He takes it home with some aim of making a pet of it. But then he kills and eats it too.

On a more serious level, once he realizes that his island is sometimes visited by cannibals as a place to kill their prisoners and hold their feasts, Crusoe has a bloodthirsty urge. As I mentioned before, he's very heavily armed, and has no qualms about attacking even twenty or thirty of the Indians. He loads up his muskets with a brace of slugs each and four or five pistol bullets, and loads his fowling piece, a kind of shot gun, with "swan shot of the largest size." Then he loads his two pistols with about four bullets each and makes certain he has spare ammunition. With all this, and his sword as well, he seems quite confident about being able to wipe out whole canoe-loads of cannibals, if he can take them by surprise. But Crusoe also has a Christian conscience. Although he describes the Indians regularly as "naked savages," he does wonder whether their dreadful customs are their own fault and deserve the death he means to deal out to them. They don't see what they do as a crime.

And after a long inner debate, Crusoe decides,

"It followed necessarily that I was certainly in the wrong in it; that these people were not murderers, in the sense that I had before condemned them in my thoughts, any more than those Christians were murderers who often […] put whole troops of men to the sword, without giving quarter, although they threw down their arms and surrendered."

Actually, we would think that Christians who did that were war criminals. But in any case, none of these reflections prevent Crusoe from attacking and killing the Indians who've captured Man Friday and doing the same again when he and Man Friday rescue Friday's father. Crusoe seems to be able to practice what George Orwell called doublethink, the very useful ability to proclaim one principle and believe in it wholeheartedly, even when it's contradicted by your own actions.

None of this makes Crusoe a very likeable character, especially in the modern world, and his most obvious blind spot is his treatment of Man Friday. He does, of course, rescue him from certain death, and it's only right that Friday should be grateful to him. But Crusoe portrays Friday with a kind of indulgent patronage. He's the perfect servant.

"Never man had a more faithful, loving, sincere servant than Friday was to me; without passions, sullenness, or design […] His very affections were tied unto me, like those of a child to a father, and I dare say he would have sacrificed his life for the saving of mine upon any occasion whatsoever."

As far as Crusoe is concerned, Friday remains a child. Crusoe naturally tries to explain Christianity to him but runs into trouble when Friday starts asking questions. Crusoe concludes that "nothing but a revelation from heaven" can form correct opinions in the soul. As for what Friday tells him about his own religion, Crusoe's only comment is to say that the Indians also suffer from priestcraft, which in Protestant England was a pretty obvious slur on Roman Catholics.

Crusoe is self-righteous, patronizing, money-oriented, distinctly ruthless, and for all his spiritual account keeping, possibly so hypocritical that he doesn't even notice it himself. One has to ask, how, then, has he come to inspire so many imitations? Well, one clue is that Defoe wrote a sequel, called *The Further Adventures of Robinson Crusoe*. It's a travelogue, in which Robinson goes to the Far East, visits many countries, and has adventures. And Man Friday, as we might have expected, sacrifices his life for his master. But the book was never popular; people have never been interested in those "further adventures."

By contrast, Robinson Crusoe on his island has generated a very large number of imitations, so many, in German-speaking countries especially, that a special term was developed for them. They were called *Robinsonaden*, and they all follow the basic pattern of being stranded on a desert island with limited resources, and turning it into a kind of Utopia.

The most familiar is *Swiss Family Robinson*, which became a children's classic. Jules Verne wrote one which was called *L'Ecole des Robinsons*, "the school for Robinsons."

J. M. Barrie, the creator of Peter Pan, added an element of class comedy in a play which is called *The Admirable Crichton*. In it an upper-class family are stranded with their butler, Crichton, and Crichton turns out to be the most practical and useful member of the party, until they're rescued and the social hierarchy is re-established.

The sequels almost become competitive; everybody tries to do more with less. What all this shows is that what really made Defoe's book a hit in popular consciousness was Robinson's ingenuity. At the heart of the story are all the detailed accounts of how Robinson triumphed over his environment.

He describes the difficulties he has with things which people take for granted. Making bread, first he has no seed, but he finds that some bags of chicken food, which he threw out, contained seeds of barley and rice. He saves the seed, he prepares the ground. He has no plough and no spade, but he makes a spade out of wood. He harrows the ground, like a rake, by dragging a big bough with stubby points over it. He uses one of his swords to reap the grain, and then he has to thresh and grind it.

How to bake it, for he has no oven? He explains how he makes clay pots and fires them, and he makes a replacement oven by piling hot embers round a big flat dish. He makes an enclosure for his goats, and uses them not only for meat, but for milk. He learns how to make butter and cheese to go with his home-made bread.

Robinson has failures, which he describes as well as his successes. He makes a giant canoe by hollowing out a tree trunk with his axe, and then finds it's too big for him to move down to the water. Making planks is immensely difficult for him, because he has to cut each one out by chipping away at solid wood. Still, he does it, so that he can put up shelving. He makes baskets out of woven twigs to hold the grain he eventually gathers. One of his big successes, and this reminds us of the luxuries which people found so surprising on the islands of the New World, is his discovery of grapes, which he can dry in the sun to make raisins, which form a large part of his diet.

Perhaps his most lovingly described success is the way he makes a kind of fort for himself, by driving stakes into the ground and then winding the ship's cable, which he salvaged, round the stakes. He reinforces this with hedging, and in the end, when he becomes more and more afraid of the cannibals who occasionally visit the island, he mounts some of his muskets in loopholes, like cannon.

"It was a great pleasure to me," he says, "to see all my goods in such order, and especially to find my stock of all necessaries so great." Crusoe's motto, you might say, is this: "Every man may be, in time, master of every mechanic art. I had never handled tool in my life, and yet, in time, by labor, application, and contrivance, I found at last that I wanted nothing but I could have made it, especially if I had had tools."

And there's a moment, too, as he explores the island and looks out over it, and sees its abundance of oranges and lemons and limes, when he feels how lucky he is. For he is, in his own words, "King and Lord of all this country indefeasibly, and had a right of possession."

You might even say that he has the best of both worlds. He has land of his own to do what he wants, with no human competition, and no serious animal competition. But at the same time he has very considerable accumulated capital from all the many things which he was lucky enough to salvage from his own wrecked ship, with more added from a second wreck which comes ashore years later. And also from what we might call the intellectual capital of the civilization he comes from. Crusoe may not know exactly how to do things, but he knows what can be done, and with the aid of labor and patience and experiment, he manages to supply most of his wants.

What I feel is that we've all been Crusoes, at least in our imagination. Did you ever build a tree house as a child, or a den? Try to make yourself a bow and arrows? Salvage nails and scraps of metal to help in your constructions? Build yourself a little cart? All these things are Crusoe-style activities, and we can imagine ourselves doing them as adult, with better equipment and more know-how. It's an immensely satisfying feeling, and we feel Crusoe's own satisfaction as he rises above his difficulties.

Alas, there are no desert islands any more on this Earth, which is probably why Crusoe stories, or *Robinsonaden*, have been shifted into science fiction. One very obvious Robinson spin-off is a book by a writer called Rex Gordon, with the title *No Man Friday*. It's about someone who finds himself stranded on Mars, with no resources other than what he can salvage from his wrecked rocket. Though the title isn't quite true, because the spaceman encounters a Martian, actually, a kind of companion animal for the long-extinct Martians, and this helps him to survive.

James Blish, one of the first "Star Trek" authors, wrote another one along very similar lines called *Welcome to Mars*. Obviously survival would be much harder on a frozen world with no oxygen, but Blish, again, uses all his creativity to imagine what human ingenuity could do. One thing everyone seems to have learned from Robinson Crusoe is that the first thing you do in such circumstances is make an inventory of all you possess, down to the last piece of string and paperclip, because everything will come in handy sometime.

Crusoe expresses the sense of enormous untapped possibilities, which came over the Western world as it broke out of its mediaeval isolation. He has, as I've noted, many of the bad qualities which accompanied that surge into the New World, especially his treatment of the native peoples to whom the Westerners felt so superior.

But on his own, competing only against nature, he is an admirable figure. a first and highly concentrated image of the New World pioneer. We're going to see more such images in later lectures, with much more concern than Crusoe could manage for other cultures. In the next lecture, however, we come upon a heroine who takes us firmly back to civilization and to the subject, not of race relations, but of gender relations.

Elizabeth Bennet—A Proper Pride
Lecture 12

Elizabeth Bennet is the heroine of Jane Austen's novel *Pride and Prejudice*. This book was published in 1813, but for more than two centuries, it has been one of the most popular novels written in English. It's had several successful film and TV adaptations, and it's even inspired a kind of remake, under very different social circumstances, in the form of the bestselling novel *Bridget Jones's Diary*. As we'll see in this lecture, there are indeed differences between Jane Austen's social and cultural values and ours; hers are not completely unrecognizable, but they're strange. Perhaps the greatest differences are not found in the realm of love or romance but in class and money.

The Lady/Gentleman Line

- Near the end of *Pride and Prejudice*, Elizabeth, who has poor financial prospects, has received a proposal of marriage from the extremely rich Mr. Darcy. Much to his surprise, she has turned him down. Later on, she realizes that she has been misinformed about him and has misjudged him, and events have started to bring them together again.

  o Mr. Darcy's aunt, Lady Catherine, has heard about this and is extremely displeased because she wants Darcy to marry her own daughter, his cousin Anne, and unite their estates. She calls on Elizabeth to warn her off.

  o Elizabeth refuses to give Lady Catherine a straight answer to the question of whether Mr. Darcy has proposed to her. Lady Catherine declares that Elizabeth and Darcy can never marry because he is engaged to her daughter, although he isn't.

  o Ultimately, Lady Catherine says that Elizabeth is simply not good enough for Mr. Darcy: "If you were sensible of your own good, you would not wish to quit the sphere in which you have been brought up." Elizabeth replies, "In marrying your nephew, I should not consider myself as quitting that sphere. He is a gentleman; I am a gentleman's daughter; so far we are equal."

- An important idea is wrapped up in Elizabeth's statement: There is a dividing line in society. Above it are gentlemen and ladies; below it are just men and women. Everyone above the line is, in theory, equal, and because Elizabeth is above that line, as she says, "so far we are equal." Those last words, however, also imply inequality in other respects, such as money.

- This "lady/gentleman line" was extremely important for 19th- and even 20th-century society in Britain, Europe, and America.
  - These days, "lady" is a polite term for a female person, but in a much more formal sense, "lady" means a certain elevated rank in society; specifically, it applies to the wife of a knight. Elizabeth doesn't use the term in that sense. What she means is that she is above the line; thus, she's eligible to marry a gentleman, however rich he is.

  - One definition of "gentleman" is a member of the officer class, and one privilege of the officer/gentleman class in Austen's time was that gentlemen could fight duels, while military officers could not refuse a duel. Perhaps a simpler definition of "gentleman" is someone who has enough money not to have to work.

  - Working for a living in 19th-century England was liable to disqualify one from being a gentleman. That's another reason that Elizabeth Bennet's world seems strange to us. Today, we assume that everyone has a line of work, but that was not the case in Austen's time.

The Bennets' Finances
- Although the core of Austen's novel is about love and romance, the story is framed and given tension by concerns about money.

- Elizabeth Bennet has poor financial prospects because her parents have five daughters and no sons. Mr. Bennet has an estate worth £2,000 a year, but the estate is entailed. The entail means that the estate must be inherited by a male. Without sons, Mr. Bennet's estate will go to his next male relative when he dies, which is a cousin of his called Mr. Collins. According to Mrs. Bennet, Mr. Collins will put her and her daughters out of their house before Mr. Bennet is cold in his grave.

- Mrs. Bennet has £4,000 capital of her own, and Austen tells us that she can expect a return on that capital of about 5 percent a year, or £200—not much to support six people. Mr. Bennet's £2,000 a year means that his estate—probably farmland that he rents out— is worth about £40,000. Mr. Darcy, meanwhile, who has £10,000 a year, is worth about £200,000. In modern terms, that's the equivalent of about $100 million.

- Another significant difference between Austen's time and our own is that earlier, it was difficult to accumulate capital. Ladies certainly couldn't do it because they weren't allowed to work. And the only professions that gentlemen could enter without losing status were the church, the military, the higher reaches of the law, and "respectable" trade.

- What all this means is that the financial gap between Elizabeth and Mr. Darcy is vast. It was brave of her, then, to turn him down the first time he proposed. She had also turned down a proposal from Mr. Collins, but her friend Charlotte accepts Mr. Collins only three days later, despite the fact that Charlotte knows Collins is stupid and that Charlotte's situation is better than Elizabeth's.

Romantic Core of the Novel
- The romantic core of the novel is the on-again-off-again relationship between Elizabeth and Darcy, which runs in parallel with a similar relationship between Elizabeth's sister Jane and Darcy's friend Mr. Bingley and is confused by the arrival of the adventurer Mr. Wickham.

- At first, Wickham seems to take an interest in Elizabeth, then switches to a lady known to have £10,000, and eventually marries Elizabeth's sister Lydia. We also find out that Wickham had previously tried to elope with Darcy's underage sister Georgiana, which would have been very profitable indeed.

- Meanwhile Elizabeth is not the only lady with her eye on Darcy. There's his cousin Anne and Caroline, the sister of his best friend, Mr. Bingley. Mr. Bingley is attracted to Elizabeth's sister Jane, and Mr. Collins switches deftly from Elizabeth to Charlotte Lucas. The structure of the novel seems rather like an English country dance, with the characters formally pairing off and changing partners, all at arm's length.

- The main theme of the novel, though, is husband-hunting. Its famous first sentence is: "It is a truth universally acknowledged that a single man in possession of good fortune must be in want of a wife." The joke is that this is not universally acknowledged. It's an opinion held strongly by young ladies in need of a rich husband and even more strongly by their anxious mothers.

  © iStockphoto/Thinkstock.

  - Husband-hunting, however, must not be too obvious. Any suggestion of sexual forwardness would ruin a young lady's reputation

  One of the main functions of formal balls in upper-class society was to advance the cause of husband-hunting for young ladies.

  and spoil her chances for good. For example, when Lydia elopes with Wickham and lives with him for two weeks before they are married, even Elizabeth says, "She is lost forever."

- Appearance was certainly important for attracting an eligible man, along with accomplishments, such as playing the piano. But to make a real impact, a young lady needed something more, and that's what Elizabeth has. She chooses the rather dangerous route of speaking her mind and playing hard to get. On more than one occasion, she refuses to dance with Darcy, but he comes to find her honesty bewitching.

- Elizabeth, slightly taken by the new arrival in town, Mr. Wickham, is told by Wickham that Darcy is not to be trusted, and she believes him. She also learns that Darcy has tried to distract Bingley from his interest in her sister Jane. As a result, when Darcy proposes, she turns him down flatly.

- Darcy then writes a long letter justifying his conduct, and Elizabeth realizes that it's correct. She has been deceived, and she was ready to be deceived because of the offense she took against Darcy when she first met him. If he showed pride, she showed prejudice. But it's too late; she seems to have lost her chance.

- Elizabeth and Darcy are drawn together again when Darcy takes charge of finding Lydia and Wickham after their elopement. Darcy bribes Wickham into marrying Lydia and prevents the scandal from getting worse. In the end, Darcy makes a second proposal, which Elizabeth accepts.

- The story in this novel is one of success against the odds. It's also what we might call a Cinderella story in a highly realistic setting. It's given edge and tension by concerns about money, class, and sexual strategies. Finally, it's a story about a kind of female dominance. Elizabeth doesn't flirt and she doesn't make compromises, but she does learn to criticize herself; we might say that she teases her way to success.

Elizabeth Bennet and Bridget Jones

- Interestingly, the plot and some of the characters of Austen's novel were picked up and heavily adapted in Helen Fielding's 1996 and 1999 novels about Bridget Jones.

- The male lead in these stories is actually called Darcy, and he makes a bad first impression, just like Austen's Darcy. There's a Mr. Wickham analog, as well, in the form of the unreliable, womanizing, dangerously attractive Daniel Cleaver.

- Bridget, however, is not at all like Elizabeth Bennet in several important respects. She worries all the time about smoking, about drinking too much, and about putting on weight; she works for a living; and of course, she has had previous sexual partners, including the womanizing Daniel.

- Despite the changed cultural values, is there a lurking similarity? Bridget still has an element of desperation about her, which reminds us of Mrs. Bennet's anxiety transferred to her daughter. It's also true that there is still pressure on a young woman to get married or, at least, to have a stable relationship.

- Another similarity is that Bridget is a modern and independent young woman of the late 20th century, just as Elizabeth was a modern, independent young woman of the early 19th century— or at least as independent as early-19th-century English society would allow.

- Finally, both Bridget and Elizabeth, in different ways, seem to have the odds stacked against them. Bridget has much more money and freedom than Elizabeth, but she still thinks that men have the upper hand in the contest of the sexes. The word we might use for these ladies is "gallant"; each plays the rather poor hand she was dealt as best she can.

Austen, *Pride and Prejudice*.

Honan, *Jane Austen: Her Life.*

Steiner, *Jane Austen's Civilised Women.*

1. Elizabeth Bennet "has it all": wealth, love, integrity, independence. Do you find this realistic?

2. In what ways have cultural values changed in our lifetimes with regard to male/female relationships?

Lecture 12: Elizabeth Bennet—A Proper Pride

Elizabeth Bennet—A Proper Pride
Lecture 12—Transcript

The character I'm going to discuss today is Elizabeth Bennet, the heroine of Jane Austen's novel *Pride and Prejudice*. Let me just note at the start that this is the first time we have a female character described by a female author.

Pride and Prejudice was published in 1813, but for more than two centuries now it has been one of the most popular novels written in English. It's had several successful film and T.V. adaptations, people have written sequels to it, and it's even inspired a kind of remake, under very different social circumstances, in the form of the best-selling novel *Bridget Jones's Diary*.

One of the points I want to stress in this discussion is, indeed, the differences between Jane Austen's social and cultural values and ours. Hers are not completely unrecognizable, but they are strange. I'd say, the biggest differences are not about love and romance, they're about class and money. But class and money affect love and romance. I can illustrate this by looking at a big scene very near the end of the novel. What's happened is that Elizabeth, who has poor financial prospects, has received a proposal of marriage from Mr. Darcy, who is extremely rich, and much to his surprise has turned him down. Later on in the novel, she realizes that she has been misinformed about him and has misjudged him, and events have started to bring them together again.

Mr. Darcy's aunt, Lady Catherine, has heard about this and is extremely displeased, because she wants Darcy to marry her own daughter, his cousin Anne, and so, unite their estates. She accordingly calls on Elizabeth to warn her off. Lady Catherine starts by saying that she has heard that Elizabeth is about to get engaged to her nephew. She says she knows this cannot be true. Elizabeth says, "If you believed it impossible to be true, I wonder you took the trouble of coming so far." What is she here for? Lady Catherine says, "I want you to tell me it's not true." They then spar verbally for a bit, and eventually Lady Catherine says straight out, "Has my nephew made you an offer of marriage?" Which in fact he has. Elizabeth, however, does not answer straight out, but says, "You've already said that was impossible." So, though she doesn't say this, if it's impossible, you don't need to ask.

Lady Catherine realizes that Elizabeth has not said flat out "no," so she continues to try to drag out a more definite answer. She says very firmly that Elizabeth and Darcy can never marry, because "Mr. Darcy is engaged to my daughter." But he isn't. This is only what Lady Catherine intends, and Darcy himself has never agreed to it. Lady Catherine says Elizabeth is simply not good enough for him. She winds up, "If you were sensible of your own good, you would not wish to quit the sphere in which you have been brought up."

Elizabeth now makes her big speech, though it's quite short, and this is what she says. "In marrying your nephew, I should not consider myself as quitting that sphere. He is a gentleman, I am a gentleman's daughter; so far we are equal." There is an important statement wrapped up in this, and it's something like this: There is a dividing line in society. Above it, there are gentlemen and ladies. Below it, there are just men and women. Everyone above the line is, in theory, equal, and since Elizabeth is above the line, as she says, "so far we are equal."

The words, "so far we are equal," imply that she knows that in other respects, like money, they are not equal. But the important thing is whether you are above or below the line. This line, which I shall call the lady / gentleman line, was extremely important for 19th- and even 20th-century society, in Britain, in Europe, even in America. However, it just isn't there any more. This critical division disappeared as a result, I think, of changing economic circumstances.

Okay, what did Elizabeth Bennet mean by the term "gentleman," and what would she mean by calling herself a "lady"? I'm going to take the word "lady" first, because it's a little easier. It's a word which has become very much devalued. Nowadays, "lady" is just the polite term for female person, and is regularly applied to everybody. In a much more formal way, "lady" means a certain rather-elevated rank in society.

One person Elizabeth knows is her neighbor Sir William Lucas, and the "Sir" in front of his name means that he is a knight. If he and his wife were to be introduced at a formal meeting, the right thing to say would be, "May I present Sir William and Lady Lucas?" Darcy's aunt is Lady Catherine in her own right.

Now, if Elizabeth had said "I am a lady," and that is certainly what she means when she says, "I am a gentleman's daughter," she would not mean, "I am a female person," in our modern devalued sense. That would have no force at all. Nor would she mean "I am the wife of a knight," which just isn't true. What she means is, "I'm above the line and so eligible to marry a gentleman. However rich he is."

All right, what's a "gentleman"? You could say he's a member of the officer class. We still often use the words together, as in the film title, *An Officer and a Gentleman*. One privilege of this officer / gentleman class in Jane Austen's time was that, though dueling was illegal in England, gentlemen could get away with it. And military officers could not get out of it. An army officer who refused a challenge would have to resign his commission.

This comes into the plot of Pride and Prejudice, because when Elizabeth's silly sister Lydia elopes with an adventurer called Mr. Wickham, her father Mr. Bennet rushes off after them. Mrs. Bennet becomes very alarmed that they are going to fight a duel, and her husband will be killed, which will be a financial disaster for her and her daughters, as I'll explain in a moment. The point of offering to fight a duel, of course, would be to make Wickham marry Lydia.

But I think there's a simpler test for being a gentleman. A gentleman is someone who has enough money not to have to work. Working for a living in 19th-century England was liable to disqualify you from being a gentleman; that's another reason why Elizabeth Bennet's world seems very strange to us. Today we just assume that everybody has a line of work. In our culture, even really rich people continue to work, not necessarily for a living, but just because that's what they do. But money was different then.

Jane Austen is very clear and open about money, and you could say that while the core of her novel is about love and romance, the whole story is framed and given tension, as it is in the scene between Elizabeth and Lady Catherine, by concerns about money. I said near the start that Elizabeth Bennet has poor financial prospects. This is because her father and mother have had really bad luck. They've had five daughters in a row.

What's the bad luck there? Mr. Bennet has an estate worth £2,000 a year, so he himself is financially more than comfortable, but the estate is entailed. The entail means that the estate must be inherited by a male person. If Mr. Bennet has no sons, and he and his wife are now beyond the age where this can be expected, then when he dies, the estate will go to the next male relative, which in this case is a cousin of his called Mr. Collins. Entails were not uncommon in those days, I suppose because it was a way of ensuring that the estate stayed with the family name. Just the same, Mrs. Bennet and five daughters are on a cliff edge. As Mrs. Bennet says, if her husband dies, Mr. Collins will put them out of their house before he is cold in his grave. And what are they going to live on then?

Jane Austen tells us that as well. Mrs. Bennet has £4,000 capital of her own. We also know how much return she can expect on this. When Lydia Bennet elopes with Wickham, a deal is fixed up by which he will agree to marry her in exchange for having his debts paid, getting a guaranteed £100 a year while Mr. Bennet is alive, and Lydia receiving £1,000 in settlement once he is dead.

Mr. Bennet calculates grimly that there must be a secret element in the deal, because Wickham would not take Lydia for as little as that, now she's, so to speak, damaged goods. £1,000 capital would only bring him in £50 a year, and that's not enough to support a gentleman. So we can take it that return on capital is about five percent, and that's pretty much tops. Mrs. Bennet's £4,000 would bring in £200 a year to support six people.

,Mr. Bennet's 2,000 a year means that his estate, probably farmland, which he rents out, is worth about £40,000. Mr. Darcy, meanwhile, who has £10,000 a year, the first thing we are told about him, is worth about £200,000, or maybe, a quarter of a million. What might that be in modern terms? Anyone will tell you that this is a very hard calculation to make, but my guess is that it's about the equivalent of a hundred million dollars in modern money.

It may have felt like even more than that, because another big difference between Jane Austen's time and our own is that then, it was very difficult to accumulate capital. Ladies certainly couldn't do it, because they weren't allowed to work at all. It was very difficult for gentlemen, because the only professions they could enter without losing status were the church, the army and navy, and the higher reaches of the law. Being "in trade," that is to say a businessman, was only just acceptable, and only if it was a "respectable" trade. Mrs. Bennet's brother is like that, which reminds us that Mrs. Bennet herself, daughter of an attorney, was only just over the vital borderline till she married a rich husband. If he dies, she could sink back below it.

What all this means is that the financial gap between Elizabeth, no prospects at all once her father dies, and Mr. Darcy the multi-millionaire, is extremely great. It was really brave of her, then, to turn him down the first time he proposed. And that wasn't the first proposal she had because she also received one from Mr. Collins, on whom her father's estate is entailed. Mr. Collins is a particularly stupid and boring person, so she has good reason to turn him down, but Jane Austen rubs the point in—that it's a brave thing to do—by having Elizabeth's best friend Charlotte accept Mr. Collins only three days later. Charlotte knows Mr. Collins is stupid and boring, and she is the daughter of Sir William Lucas, so she's not as badly off as Elizabeth, but she accepts Collins just the same. Why? Elizabeth is only 20; Charlotte is 27. For young ladies, marriage is the only possible career, and your chances of marriage start to go down rather early on in life.

I guess I've explained by now just what creates the tension in the scene between Elizabeth and Lady Catherine. It's very satisfying that Elizabeth stands on her rights. It's also very satisfying that she keeps her options open. And it's especially satisfying that no one will ever be able to say she married for money, because she has asserted her independence by refusing Mr. Darcy's first proposal and Mr. Collins's as well.

And now, I'd better turn to the novel's romantic core, which is the long off-on-off-on relationship between Elizabeth and Darcy, which runs in parallel with another on-off-on relationship between Elizabeth's sister Jane and Darcy's friend Mr. Bingley, and which is confused by the arrival of the adventurer Mr. Wickham. This guy, Wickham, first seems to be taking an interest in Elizabeth, then switches to a lady known to have £10,000, and eventually marries Elizabeth's sister Lydia, for the pay off I described. We also find out that Wickham had previously tried to elope with Darcy's under-age sister Georgiana, which would have been very profitable indeed.

Meanwhile, Elizabeth is not the only lady with her eye on Darcy. There's his cousin Anne, though that's her mother's initiative, and there's also Caroline, the sister of his best friend Mr. Bingley. Mr. Bingley is attracted to Elizabeth's sister Jane, and Mr. Collins switches deftly from Elizabeth to Charlotte Lucas. The structure of the novel strikes me as rather like an English country dance, with the characters very formally pairing off and changing partners, all done at arm's length. Its main theme, though, is obviously husband hunting. The novel's famous first sentence is, "It is a truth universally acknowledged that a single man in possession of good fortune must be in want of a wife." The joke is that this is not universally acknowledged. It's an opinion which is held strongly by young ladies in need of a rich husband, and even more strongly by their anxious mothers.

Husband-hunting, however, must not be too obvious. Any suggestion, for instance, of sexual forwardness would ruin a young lady's reputation and spoil her chances for good. When Lydia elopes with Wickham and lives with him for a whole two weeks before they are married, even Elizabeth says, "she is lost forever." Mr. Collins, who is a Church of England vicar, advises her father, "throw off your unworthy child from your affection," and once again he says, "for ever."

So, to attract and hold the attention of an eligible young man, especially a really rich one like Mr. Bingley or Mr. Darcy, what is a young lady to do? Looks are certainly very important. One of the main functions of the formal balls, which everyone in upper-class society attends, is for the young ladies to display themselves under supervision. Accomplishments are important as well. Elizabeth's sister Mary, who we are told is rather plain, has chosen this route—singing, playing the piano, and gaining a reputation for rather sanctimonious learning. Mary's plan does not seem to be working. To make a real impact you need something more than looks and accomplishments, and that is what Elizabeth has.

You could say that she chooses the rather dangerous route of speaking her mind and also playing hard to get. We see this very early in the novel. Mr. Bingley has rented a house close to the Bennets and has organized a ball to mark his arrival. He brings Mr. Darcy with him. The word very rapidly spreads of Darcy's wealth, and everyone admires him very much for a short while, until his behavior makes people conclude that he is insufferably proud.

He certainly is rather aloof. But you might guess, anyone who has £10,000 a year must be used to being chased by ambitious daughters and their anxious mammas, so you could excuse him for trying to keep his distance. However, he gets on the wrong side of Elizabeth because of a remark she overhears. Bingley is trying to persuade him to ask a lady to dance and points Elizabeth out to him. Darcy looks at her and says, without realizing she can hear, "she is tolerable, but not handsome enough to tempt me." No one else has asked her to dance, so why should Darcy?

Elizabeth is sure enough of herself to tell the story to all her friends, because, we're told, "She had a lively, playful disposition, which delighted in anything ridiculous." She gets her own back a little later, at another ball, when Sir William Lucas leads Darcy up to her and tries to actually hand her over to Darcy. She refuses to dance with him. He politely asks of his own accord to be allowed the honor of her hand, but she still turns him down, something he's not used to.

So at least she's got his attention. She fixes it more closely by doing something which is slightly improper for a lady. Her sister Jane has gone to visit Mr. Bingley and his sisters and has caught a cold and had to stay until she's recovered. With 19th-century medicine what it was, you couldn't take a chance with colds and fevers, which might turn into pneumonia. Elizabeth, very worried, decides to go and see her, and since her father's carriage is not available, she walks over. Three miles across the fields, jumping over stiles and springing over puddles. She arrives with wet feet and a muddy petticoat.

Caroline Bingley, anxious to do down a competitor, tells the gentlemen how indecorous she thinks this is. But they don't agree with her. Bingley says that Elizabeth's affection for her sister is very pleasing, and Darcy says her eyes were brightened by the exercise. We might note that one young lady criticizing another to an eligible gentleman is maybe too obvious and likely to be counter effective.

Elizabeth still hasn't forgiven Darcy, however, and she turns him down again when he suggests dancing a reel. She tells him that she knows he only suggested it so that he could despise her taste if she said "yes," and she enjoys frustrating little schemes like that. This is quite close to being cheeky, and, indeed, Caroline Bingley thinks Elizabeth shows "conceit and impertinence." But, Jane Austen tells us, "there was a mixture of sweetness and archness in her manner, which made it difficult for her to affront anybody, and Darcy had never been so bewitched by any woman as he was by her." Everything going swimmingly, in fact, but if it kept on like that, there would be no story.

The next thing that happens is that Elizabeth, slightly taken by the new arrival in town, Mr. Wickham, is told by Wickham that Darcy is not to be trusted and that Darcy has behaved very dishonorably to Wickham himself by depriving him of something which he had been promised in Darcy's father's will. Elizabeth believes this. Worse than that, Mr. Bingley, who appeared to be increasingly attracted to Elizabeth's sister Jane, suddenly returns to London and is not seen again. Elizabeth finds out by accident that Darcy has tried to distract Bingley from Jane as not suitable for him. He has also concealed from Bingley the fact that Jane was for a while in London, which might have restarted the relationship.

The result of all this is that when Darcy does actually make a proposal to Elizabeth in a rather stiff and awkward way, she turns him down very flatly indeed, indicating that she knows about Jane and she knows about his behavior to Wickham as well. That would seem to be that. However, Darcy then writes a long letter justifying his conduct, and Elizabeth realizes that it's correct. She herself has been deceived. She's been ready to be deceived, because of the offense she took against Darcy right at the start. If he showed pride, she showed prejudice. She says to herself, "Until this moment I never knew myself." But it's too late. As we would say, she's blown her chance.

Two things give her a second chance. One is an accidental meeting while Elizabeth is on a trip with her aunt and uncle, which takes them to Darcy's estate, where the housekeeper, showing them around in his absence, speaks very highly of him. The other is Lydia's elopement with Wickham. Mr. Bennet's pursuit of them gets nowhere. But Darcy blames himself for not warning people about Wickham's behavior; he has previously tried to elope with Darcy's own sister, and he takes charge of the matter. He finds the runaway pair, bribes Wickham into marrying her—Mr. Bennet was right in thinking that it must have cost more than he's been told—and prevents the scandal from getting any worse. Which it easily could have done. One of the possibilities which local gossip has entertained is that Lydia could "come upon the town," which is their phrase for being forced into prostitution. The opportunities open for young ladies in this society really were very limited.

So Elizabeth and Darcy start to be drawn together again. Lady Catherine's bullying visit to Elizabeth is another example of counter-effective behavior, and in the end Darcy makes a second proposal, which is naturally accepted. Bingley, meanwhile, gets back together with Jane, Mrs. Bennet's fears are now set at rest, and Mr. Bennet, who has been amusingly sarcastic all the way through the novel, realizes that he should, perhaps, have set a better example—happy ending.

Why has this proved such a long-term charming story and Elizabeth such a charming heroine? It's a story of success against the odds. It's also what you might call a Cinderella story of captivating Prince Charming but removed from a fairytale setting into a highly realistic one. As I've been saying, it's given edge and tension by concerns about money, about class, about sexual strategies. And it's also a story of a kind of female dominance. Elizabeth doesn't flirt, and she doesn't make compromises, but she does learn to criticize herself, and you could also say that she teases her way to success. It's a role model of a kind, a very different one from the Wife of Bath.

Does it make any sense at all in the modern world? The strange thing here is the way that the plot and some of the characters have been picked up, heavily adapted, in Helen Fielding's 1996 and 1999 novels about Bridget Jones, both of them rapidly turned into successful movies. And there's been a third sequel in 2013. The male lead in these stories is actually called Darcy, which is a pretty obvious giveaway. He also makes a bad first impression, just like Jane Austen's Darcy, though it's not from being proud and aloof, it's from being desperately uncool; he's wearing a sweater his mom knitted for him.

There's a Mr. Wickham analog as well in the form of the unreliable, womanizing, dangerously attractive Daniel Cleaver, who several times does more than turn the heroine's head. Bridget, on the other hand, is not at all like Elizabeth Bennet in several important respects. She worries all the time about smoking, about drinking too much, about putting on weight, she works for a living, and of course, she has had previous sex partners, including the womanizing Daniel, all of which is absolutely unthinkable for a Jane Austen heroine.

Is there a lurking similarity which remains despite all these very-much-changed cultural values? Maybe it is that in spite of all the changes, Bridget still has an element of desperation about her, which is like Mrs. Bennet's anxiety transferred to her daughter. You could also say that while money worries have been much eased for Bridget, there is just a lot more money around in the modern world than there was in Jane Austen's. Other worries have gotten worse.

There's still the same old pressure on a young woman to get married, or at least to have a stable relationship. Bachelors, however, have a lot more options than they used to, including being gay, or just dropping out of the marriage stakes altogether. It is no longer a truth universally acknowledged, or even acknowledged at all, that a single man with money must be in want of a wife.

Even Bridget's sexual freedom brings extra risks. For some time it looks as if Bridget could take what we might call, remembering an earlier lecture in this course, the Cressida option and drop the reliable Mark Darcy for the unreliable Daniel Cleaver, a course just as likely to lead to grief as it was with Troilus and Diomedes. Nor was Elizabeth Bennet ever likely to get arrested for drug smuggling and end up in a third-world jail. Helen Fielding nevertheless engineers a happy ending for both her earlier novels, just as Jane Austen did. There are maybe two similarities I could mention to close with.

One is that Bridget is a modern and independent young woman of the late 20th century, just as Elizabeth was a modern independent young woman of the early 19th century, or at least as independent a one as early 19th-century English society would allow. The other is that both of them, in their different ways, seem to have the odds stacked against them. Bridget has much more money and much more freedom than Elizabeth., but she still thinks that the men have the upper hand in the contest of the sexes. The word for both ladies, I think, is "gallant." Each plays the rather poor hand she was dealt as well as ever she can.

Natty Bumppo and Woodrow Call—Frontier Heroes
Lecture 13

So far in this course, we have had Greek and Roman heroes and English and Spanish heroes, but in this lecture, we will turn to American heroes. The first of these shows us that a character can be specifically American, in a way we readily recognize, yet can have roots going back to before Columbus. This is Natty Bumppo, the hero of James Fenimore Cooper's Leatherstocking Tales and the iconic American frontiersman. Along with Natty, we'll also discuss Woodrow Call, Larry McMurtry's hero representing our picture of the Wild West.

An American Robin Hood?

- Nathaniel Bumppo, the hero of James Fenimore Cooper's Leatherstocking Tales, has numerous names, including Natty, Leatherstocking, Hawkeye, Pathfinder, Deerslayer, and *La Longue Carabine* ("The Long Carbine"). Whatever we call him, Natty created a new and powerful image, that of the frontiersman.

- Natty is not big and strong, like the basic male hero we've seen, but lean and sinewy. He is deeply tanned, dresses in buckskin, and has no settled home. He is a creature of the great forests of the eastern United States, from the first stage of Anglo-American settlement—in Cooper's chronology, approximately 1740 to his old age in 1805.

- Although he is typically American, Natty is also similar to Robin Hood; he lives by hunting in the forest. Even more significantly, he is closely identified with his weapon: the American long rifle. Also like Robin Hood, Natty shows his excellence in shooting matches, and like Beowulf's sword or Thor's Hammer, his rifle has a name: Killdeer.

- As far as weaponry goes, Natty is an American Robin Hood, but he's not at all like Robin Hood in other ways. He's not an outlaw or a robber. In *The Pathfinder*, he says that he has had three temptations in his life: to steal a pack of skins he found in the woods, to win a shooting match by deceit, and to take advantage of a band of Iroquois whom he found sleeping. He rejects all the temptations, though in the last case, he shoots the Iroquois after they wake up. Natty has a moral code, but it's one of his own.

Anglo-Americans and Native Americans

- The fact that Natty's code is cross-cultural returns us to the idea that he has roots that go back before Columbus. We learn that he was raised as a Moravian Christian, but he was also brought up by the tribe of Delaware Indians. He is, in a way, intermediate between the Anglo-Americans and the Native Americans, and Cooper uses him to give a markedly sympathetic picture of the latter, though of course, it's one written from the heart of Anglo-American culture.

- A scene from *The Deerslayer* illustrates this point. Natty has reached Lake Glimmerglass in upstate New York. There's a houseboat on the lake, inhabited by a man called Tom Hutter and his two daughters. Natty also has two companions, a white man called Harry March, nicknamed Hurry Harry, and his Mohican friend Chingachgook, also known as *Le Gros Serpent*, "The Great Serpent."

- The Hutters are under threat from a band of Huron Indians, and the whites have behaved badly. Hurry Harry shot a Huron girl for no reason, and he and Tom Hutter, a former pirate, have attempted to raid the Hurons, an attempt that turned out fatal for Hutter. The Deerslayer himself has been captured while trying to rescue Chingachgook's intended bride, the maiden Wah-ta-Wah.

- The Hutter daughters, left alone in the houseboat by the death of their father, are surprised to see the Deerslayer canoe out to them. He has been released to try to make a deal that he knows the daughters cannot accept. He has every reason not to go back because the Hurons plan to torture him to death, but he tells the girls that he must return because he gave his word.

- Here, Natty is honoring his Delaware upbringing. It would be a disgrace, to the Native American mind, to do the sensible thing in this situation, and Natty will not accept disgrace. The point being made by Cooper is that Native Americans—even the Hurons—are more honest and honorable than the whites.

- That's not to say that they are not also more savage. Torture is part of their way of life, as is scalp hunting. In the Leatherstocking Tales, we find a continuing debate about savagery. In numerous scenes, the Deerslayer speaks up for Native American virtues.
  - Cooper expresses himself continually in terms of color and assumes that color equals race and race equals culture. All this is contradictory to modern sensibilities.

  - Still, through the words and actions of his hero, Cooper says that we cannot judge one culture by the rules of another.

  - As a consequence, the Deerslayer believes that what is allowable to his friend Chingachgook, such as taking scalps, is not allowable to himself. Nevertheless, the Deerslayer is well able to see an underlying similarity.

Cultural Conflict

- In the running comparison between the whites and the Native Americans, the latter often come off better. They consider more carefully before they take action, are respectful to their elders, and don't repeat their mistakes. Most of all, unlike the whites, they do not deceive.

- It's true that there are ambiguities of which the Deerslayer is well aware, as we see in *The Last of the Mohicans*. The story here is that Natty is escorting two young women to Fort William Henry when he finds that they are being stalked by a party of Iroquois.
  - In 1757, this fort was surrendered to a mixed force of French and Native Americans on the condition that the British troops and their followers could leave unharmed. But once the troops laid down their arms, the Hurons and others massacred them.

- o This action is very bad faith by European standards. By Native American standards, however, one might say that they kept their word to individuals, but they did not understand the concept of treaties binding on all parties.

- In the Leatherstocking Tales, we get a nuanced picture of cultures and cultural values that are in conflict because they exist at the same time. The Deerslayer and Chingachgook are friends and equals in a way that isn't true of Don Quixote and Sancho, but there's a cultural gap between them.

- We know well that this cultural conflict ended in tragedy: with the dispossession of the Native Americans. Cooper makes this an individual tragedy with the death of Chingachgook's son, Uncas, in a battle against the Iroquois.
  - o Uncas's death foreshadows not only the decline of the Delawares but also the disappearance of whole tribes and languages and the absorption or subordination of others into the modern, dominant culture of North America.

  - o This is not the fault of the Deerslayer, who is caught between the British and the Americans and between the colonists and the natives. He is completely virtuous, but as with the Native Americans, his honesty and integrity don't do him much good.

- Like Chingachgook, the Deerslayer ends childless and is driven steadily out to the edges of his own culture. In the last of the five Leatherstocking novels, *The Prairie*, the Deerslayer dies among the tribe that has adopted him, the Pawnee Indians. As we saw with Beowulf, it's unclear whether or not he dies a Christian death.

The Wild West
- In literary criticism, the word "imaginary" is used as a noun to mean a collective picture of an era derived from books, films, television, and so on. The most powerful imaginary of our time is the Wild West, encompassing gunslingers, wagon trains, rustlers, and, above all, cowboys and Indians. One set of heroes in this

imaginary is Woodrow Call and his sidekick, Gus MacRae, from Larry McMurtry's *Lonesome Dove* series.

- McMurtry seems to have drawn much of his information from a book called *Comanches* by the historian T. R. Fehrenbach. The point this book makes—and McMurtry repeats—is that, entirely contrary to what we've always been told in the Wild West imaginary, the Indians had the cowboys beat.

  o The Comanches, in particular, for decades prevented settlement of large areas of Texas, Oklahoma, and the southern Great Plains. They accomplished this because they were culturally superior, had better horses, were better adapted to the arid prairie, and had a better weapon: the compound bow they used for hunting buffalo.

  o The Deerslayer's long rifle was an excellent weapon for the forests, where there was always cover and where men fought on foot, but on the Great Plains, it was useless. In the time it took an Anglo to reload a long rifle, a Comanche could easily fire off six arrows.

  o Anglo-American expansion halted until the appearance of the other iconic American weapon: the six-gun, a repeating weapon that could be fired accurately at short range from horseback.

- The career of McMurtry's Woodrow Call dramatizes the shift of power that took place with the advent of the six-gun, beginning in 1844. McMurtry tells this story in a series of four novels.

The era of the cowboy became possible only after the advent of the six-gun enabled Anglo-American expansion in the West.

o In *Dead Man's Walk* (chronologically the first in the series), Woodrow and his sidekick, Gus, who are Texas Rangers, fare badly against a Comanche chief and a force of Mexicans.

o In *Comanche Moon*, the Rangers are better mounted, better armed, and more skilled. They manage to defeat a Comanche raid, but much of their manpower is drawn away to the Civil War. Afterwards, the cowboy era sets in, when it became possible to drive large herds of cattle across the Great Plains.

o In *Lonesome Dove*, Woodrow and Gus are independent contractors, whose trail drive parallels the real-life drives of American cattlemen from 1866 onwards. By this time, the dangers on the prairie are white bandits and Indian outcasts rather than organized war parties.

o In the last novel, *Streets of Laredo*, the Comanches are only a memory and so are the Rangers. Woodrow suffers a handicap; he is still furiously independent but without wealth, property, or even respect, except from a few.

• Both of these heroes, Natty and Woodrow, lasted little longer than their enemies, the Hurons and the Comanches. They were brought into being by an entirely new set of circumstances: conflict between agriculturalists with an industrial civilization behind them and Stone Age nomadic hunters, newly empowered by the horses introduced to the continent by the Spanish.

• Theirs was a Heroic Age different from that of Homer or Beowulf but far better recorded—and now immortalized, for good or ill, by our largely inaccurate and self-flattering imaginaries. Both Woodrow and the Deerslayer remain important correctives to both the forest-frontier imaginary and that of the Wild West.

Essential Reading

Note: Essential readings are listed in chronological order of the heroes' lives.

Cooper, *The Deerslayer*.

———, *The Last of the Mohicans*.

———, *The Pathfinder*.

McMurtry, *Dead Man's Walk*.

———, *Comanche Moon*.

———, *Lonesome Dove*.

———, *Streets of Laredo*.

Suggested Reading

Dekker, *James Fenimore Cooper*.

Fehrenbach, *Comanches*.

McMurtry, *In a Narrow Grave*.

Person, ed., *A Historical Guide to James Fenimore Cooper*.

Stegner, *Winning the Wild West*.

Questions to Consider

1. The NRA defends American culture by appealing to the Constitution. Do you think it is the Constitution or the power of the American "imaginaries" that sets limits on gun control?

2. Which "cowboy" hero or heroes do you remember with most affection from childhood and why?

Natty Bumppo and Woodrow Call—Frontier Heroes
Lecture 13—Transcript

So far in this course we have had Greek and Roman heroes and English and Spanish heroes, along with some not easy to classify, like Guinevere or Cressida. But I now want to turn to specifically American heroes, of which there will be several from now on—heroes and heroines too. The first of them that I'm going to select will show that you can be specifically American, in a way we readily recognize, and yet have roots going way back to before Columbus.

In the lecture on Don Quixote I mentioned that Charlotte Lennox had been hailed as the first American novelist, but she wasn't. She just lived in America for a while. The first American novelist to have a European as well as an American reputation was James Fenimore Cooper, born in 1789. His reputation rests largely on a series of five novels with a single hero, often called the Leatherstocking Tales, published between 1823 and 1841.

Their hero has many names. His proper name was Nathaniel Bumppo, B U M P P O, sometimes called Natty. But he's also called "Leatherstocking." One of his Huron enemies gives him the name "Hawkeye." The soldiers and settlers call him "the Pathfinder" or "the Deerslayer," and his French enemies call him, though this is a name he doesn't like, La Longue Carabine, "the long carbine."

Whatever we call him, Natty created a new and powerful image, which deserves to be called an icon—the frontiersman. He's not like the Basic Male Hero, big and strong. Instead, he's lean and sinewy, the first time Cooper described him, he even called him scraggy. But it's better to say that he is tall and rangy, a great walker, tireless, like whipcord. He is deeply tanned, he dresses in buckskin, he has no settled home. He is a creature of the great forests of the eastern United States, from the first stage of Anglo-American settlement, in Cooper's chronology, approximately 1740 to his old age in 1805.

I've said he's typically American, but you could also say that he's very like Robin Hood. He is the Deerslayer. He lives by hunting in the forest.

And even more significantly, like Robin Hood, he is closely identified with, almost defined by, his weapon—the American long rifle. Like the English longbow, this deserves respectful attention.

It's rifled, for accuracy, unlike the smoothbore muskets of contemporary European armies. It's long as well. Natty says it's the same height as he is, six feet. The long barrel gave extra muzzle velocity, which compensated for the relatively low caliber, and this, in turn, allowed the bearer to carry more ammunition on a long trail. The long rifle was the weapon par excellence of the American War of Independence. It created the image of the American rifleman, which still, as we all know, possesses a powerful mystique.

Like Robin Hood, Natty shows his excellence in shooting matches. Indeed I would guess that one of Cooper's intentions was to become the American Sir Walter Scott. In Scott's novel Ivanhoe, there's an archery match, with the bowmen shooting at a wand. Robin's competitor hits the wand, and what can Robin do better than that? Answer, he can split the arrow shot by his competitor.

We get much the same scene in the most famous of the Leatherstocking Tales, *The Last of the Mohicans*. There's a doubt about whether the Deerslayer is who he says he is, and he offers to settle it by showing his skill. The Native Americans hang up a gourd; Natty's competitor shoots at it and gets close to it; and then Natty shoots at it and appears to have missed. Everyone turns on him but he just laughs and says, "Don't look near it, look inside it." Because he's hit it dead center, and the ball from his rifle is inside the gourd. There's a similar scene in the later novel *The Pathfinder*, where we have three competitors shooting. This time, just like Robin, the first one hits the center of the target, the second one plants his ball right over the first one, and then Natty appears to have missed, but only because he shot so straight that his ball has gone through the previous hole without even touching the sides.

Natty never brags about himself, but he does brag about his rifle, which, just like Beowulf's sword, or Thor's hammer, has a name of its own, "Killdeer." This is why he rejects the French name, La Longue Carabine. A carbine is a short-barreled weapon, which used to be issued to cavalry soldiers for ease of management, but Natty thinks nothing of its accuracy or its power. A better name he has, which is what the Iroquois Indians call him, is "Long Rifle."

So, Natty is an American Robin Hood, as far as weaponry goes. But he's not at all like Robin Hood in other ways. He's not an outlaw. He's not a robber. In the novel *The Pathfinder* he says he has had three temptations in his life. The first was to steal a pack of skins, which he found in the woods. The second was to win a shooting match by deceit. And the third was to take advantage of a band of Iroquois whom he found sleeping. He rejects all the temptations, though in the last case what he does is let them wake up, let them keep their arms, and then shoot them fair and square once they are able to defend themselves. You might say that he is like Robin Hood in one other way, which is that he has a moral code, but it's a moral code of his own.

The most distinctive thing about this is that it's a cross-cultural code, and this is what I meat by saying that the Deerslayer has roots which go back before Columbus. We learn that Natty was brought up as a Moravian Christian. But he was also brought up by a tribe of Delaware Indians. He is, in a way, intermediate between the Anglo Americans and the Native Americans, and Cooper uses him to give a markedly sympathetic picture of the latter. Though, of course, it's one written from the heart of Anglo-American culture. There's one scene which illustrates this, which I remember from way back, when I read it as a boy. As for one thing, it taught me a word I didn't know; the word is "furlough." It comes from the novel *The Deerslayer*, subtitled "His First Warpath."

What's happened is that Natty has reached the lake in upstate New York, called Lake Glimmerglass. There's a houseboat on the lake, which is inhabited by a man called Tom Hutter, and his two daughters, Hetty and Judith. Natty also has two companions, a white one called Harry March, nicknamed Hurry Harry, and his Mohican friend Chingachgook, also known as *Le Gros Serpent*, "The Great Serpent."

The Hutters are under threat from a band of Huron Indians. And the whites have behaved badly. Hurry Harry shot a Huron girl for no reason, and he and Tom Hutter, a former pirate, have attempted to raid the Hurons for scalps, which they meant to trade for bounty. This turned out fatal for Tom

Hutter in particular. The Deerslayer himself has been captured while trying to rescue Chingachgook's intended bride, the maiden Wah-ta-Wah. So the Hutter daughters, left alone in their houseboat on the lake by the death of their father, are surprised to see the Deerslayer canoe out to them. Why has he been released? To try to come to a deal, which he knows the daughters cannot accept. But he has been released, "on furlough," which means, he is supposed to go back.

He has every reason not to go back, because the Hurons have a great respect for his abilities, and accordingly, mean not only to torture him to death, but also to see that, "If he is to be tortured, his torment shall be such as no common man can bear." The girls ask him, "So why are you going back?" And he says, as if it's obvious, "Because I gave my word."

I may say that this is a situation famous from antiquity. The classic case is a Roman general called Regulus, who was captured by the Carthaginians and sent back on parole, or on furlough, to persuade the Romans to agree to a peace treaty. But back in Rome he argued firmly for continued war with the Carthaginians and then returned to Carthage, although, the poem says, he knew full well *quae sibi preparabat barbarus tortor*, "what the barbarian torturer had in store for him."

In the case of Natty, though, he does it, not because of some Roman precedent, but because of his Delaware upbringing. It would be a disgrace to the Native American mind to do the sensible thing, and Natty will not accept disgrace. The point being made by Cooper is that Native Americans, even the Hurons, are more honest and more honorable than the whites. This is not to say that they are not also more savage. Torture is a part of their way of life, and so is scalp hunting. The girls in the houseboat have no protector other than the Deerslayer, because their father—this was another scene which I remembered from way back—was scalped alive and left to die, really grisly description of what a scalped head looks like.

So, in the Leatherstocking Tales, there's a continuing debate about savagery. In scene after scene the Deerslayer speaks up for Native American virtues. I have to say that Cooper expresses himself continually in terms of color and assumes that color equals race and race equals culture. All this is very much contradictory to modern sensibilities. Just the same, we should recognize that what Cooper is saying, through the words and actions of his hero the Deerslayer, is that you cannot judge one culture by the rules of another. The Deerslayer himself says that you cannot judge other people's actions unless you understand them.

The effect of this is that the Deerslayer thinks that what is allowable to his friend Chingachgook is not allowable to himself, like taking scalps, or as he puts it, mangling a dead enemy. Nevertheless, the Deerslayer is well able to see an underlying similarity. Why is Chingachgook so determined not only to kill his enemies, but to scalp them? Because the scalps to him are a badge of honor. As the Deerslayer points out to one of his soldier companions, what's the difference between scalps and the colors of a Regiment, which young officers will gladly die to protect and gladly die to seize from their enemies? They're all tokens of honor.

In the running comparison between the whites and the Native Americans, the latter often come off best, as the Deerslayer repeatedly points out. They consider more carefully before they take action. They are respectful to their elders. They don't repeat their mistakes. They have sharper eyes. Where the Scottish soldiers in *The Pathfinder* complain about being fed on salmon and venison and keep wishing they had oats for porridge, a Native American, says the Deerslayer, is always grateful for the food he gets.

Both the Delawares and the Hurons can show tact and consideration. And most of all, we might as well admit, unlike the whites, they do not "speak with forked tongue." Much of this, of course, is telling us that they are much better suited for warfare in the wilderness than the redcoats, or even most of the American colonists serving with the redcoats.

It's true that there are ambiguities of which the Deerslayer is well aware, as in the most famous of these five novels, *The Last of the Mohicans*. The story here is that Natty is escorting two young women to Fort William Henry, when he finds that they are being stalked by a party of Iroquois. Now, the mention of Fort William Henry brings up one of the events most held against Native Americans. That fort was actually surrendered, in 1757, to a mixed force of French and Native Americans from many tribes on the fairly

218

common condition that the British troops and their followers could leave unharmed. But once the troops laid down their arms, the Hurons and others fell upon them in defiance of the treaty and massacred them—very bad faith by European standards. But by Native American standards, one might say, they kept their word to individuals, but they did not understand the concept of treaties binding on all parties.

I've talked quite a lot in this course about the way cultural values change over time and how concepts of the hero change with them. But in Cooper's Leatherstocking Tales we get a nuanced picture of cultures and cultural values in conflict because they exist at the same time. The Deerslayer and Chingachgook are friends and equals in a way that isn't true at all of Don Quixote and Sancho. But there's a cultural gap between them. It's a cultural conflict as well, and we know very well how that conflict ended. In the background of the Leatherstocking Tales is a cultural tragedy—the dispossession of the Native Americans. Cooper dramatizes this by making it an individual tragedy as well.

Why did he choose the title, *The Last of the Mohicans*? Well, after the massacre at Fort William Henry, the two women the Deerslayer was escorting are carried off by the victorious Iroquois, and the Deerslayer naturally tries to rescue them. In the rescue attempt he is joined by his friend Chingachgook and Chingachgook's son Uncas, the son of by Wah-ta-Wah in the earlier novel. The three of them don't stand much chance, but Uncas rallies the remaining Delaware Indians, showing them that he is the last of their old royal line. In the attempted rescue, however, Uncas is killed, and with him dies the last hope of his tribe. His death, then, foreshadows not only the decline of the Delawares, but also the disappearance of whole tribes and languages, the absorption or subordination of others into the modern, dominant culture of North America.

This is not the fault of the Deerslayer, caught, as he is, between the British and the Americans, between the colonists and the natives. He is himself completely virtuous, having honesty, integrity, fidelity, simplicity, modesty, and above all, "a beautiful and unerring sense of justice." But as with the Native Americans, this doesn't do him much good. In novel after novel, he escorts young women through the wilderness, but only in *The Pathfinder* does he think that he might marry one of them. And although in every novel one young woman or another sees all his virtues, even Mabel Dunham, in *The Pathfinder*, eventually chooses another, a younger man, and one with a future in civilization.

Like his friend Chingachgook, the Deerslayer ends childless, And again, like Chingachgook, he is driven steadily out to the edges of his own culture. In the last of the five Leatherstocking novels, *The Prairie*, the Deerslayer is out on the Great Plains and ends dying among the tribe which has adopted him, the Pawnee Indians. Very like the real life Daniel Boone, on whom his story is said to have been based.

Does he die a Christian death? Rather like Beowulf's, his death is ambiguous. The Pawnees have very kindly stuffed his dead dog Hector and put the body at his feet, Not realizing that Hector is dead, the Deerslayer fondles his ear and seems to look forward to being with his dog—where? Will it be in the Christian heaven? Will it be in the Happy Hunting Grounds? We never know. The Deerslayer would probably tell us that it makes no difference. It is the same Great Spirit which he and his Delaware friends respect and pray to. And though he has hardly ever set foot in a church, the Deerslayer reckons that he has always worshipped in the temple of the woods.

James Fenimore Cooper, then, created an icon of the noble frontiersman, not quite the noble savage, but strongly related to him. Though Cooper created an icon, however, there was something he did not create, something we all know all about, something bigger than any individual icon, and that is, the Wild West.

Now, just this once I would like to introduce a term from the modern technical jargon of literary criticism which is actually valuable. It is the word "imaginary," used as a noun, not as an adjective. What I mean by talking about "an imaginary" is a collective picture of an era derived from books, films, TV, anywhere. To give one example, there's a Roman imaginary— gladiators, legionaries, chariot races like in Ben Hur, galley slaves, Elizabeth Taylor being Cleopatra; there's also a medieval imaginary—knights in armor, tournaments, crusaders, Robin Hood, people calling other people "sire," monks and friars and all the rest, all jumbled up together.

But the most powerful imaginary of our time is surely the Wild West imaginary. You know, gunslingers, wagon trains, rustlers, stagecoaches, bounty hunters, and above all, cowboys and Indians. All these have been expressed in innumerable and sometimes interminable TV series: *The Lone Ranger, Gunsmoke, Bonanza, The Cisco Kid.* And then there's all the movies, everything from Bob Hope to John Wayne and Clint Eastwood. And before that, the dime novels. The Wild West imaginary, however, like all the others, jumbles all kinds of things up together with little sense of time or context.

Well, I felt I needed a hero to represent the Wild West imaginary, and one who hopefully would bring back a sense of time and context, someone as carefully set in the 19th century, as the Deerslayer was in the 18th.

The trouble I had was that all the prominent characters in the Wild West imaginary were real people. Billy the Kid, Wyatt Earp, Jesse James, Wild Bill Hickok, and all the rest. Meanwhile, and very surprisingly, in the whole phenomenon there is no single dominant fictional representation. So I just picked the one I thought was best, and that is the "Lonesome Dove" series, written by Larry McMurtry, and turned into a TV serial. Its heroes are Woodrow Call and his sidekick Augustus or Gus MacRae.

One thing I'm pretty sure of is that Larry McMurtry got a lot of his information from a very good book called Comanches by a historian called T. R. Fehrenbach. The point this book makes, and which McMurtry repeats, is that, entirely contrary to what we've always been told in the Wild West imaginary, to start with, the Indians had the cowboys beat. The Comanches, in particular, for decades prevented settlement of large areas of Texas, Oklahoma, the southern Great Plains. They managed to do this because they were culturally superior; they had better horses; they were better adapted to the arid prairie; and they had a better weapon in the short compound bow which they used for hunting buffalo.

The Deerslayer's long rifle was an excellent weapon for the forests, where there was always cover, and where men fought on foot. On the Great Plains it was useless. An Anglo who shot at a Comanche with his long rifle and missed, which he was likely to do against a moving target at 200-yards range, well, in the half minute before he could possibly reload, the Comanche could gallop those 200 yards and shoot six arrows into him, each arrow capable of going right through a buffalo.

Anglo-American expansion, accordingly, halted until the appearance of the other iconic American weapon, not the long rifle, but the six-gun. A repeating weapon, which could be fired accurately at short range from horseback.

Mr. Fehrenbach thinks the vital moment came in June 1844 when a patrol of Texas Rangers, newly armed with Colt revolvers, did not try to take cover when outnumbered by a swarm of Comanches, but charged them on horseback, their leader shouting, "powder burn them." He meant, get up so close you can't miss, and then keep shooting. It was a very destructive tactic, and from that moment, the balance of power on the Great Plains had shifted. What the career of McMurtry's Woodrow Call dramatizes, is that shift of power.

McMurtry tells this story in a series of four novels, collectively known as the *Lonesome Dove* series. The first novel in the series, I mean chronologically first, not in terms of publication order, is Dead Man's Walk, and it includes a scene in which Woodrow and Gus are on their first patrol with the Texas Rangers, along with seven or eight other men. The patrol runs into just one Comanche, the famous chief—and there really was a Comanche chief with this name—Buffalo Hump. Buffalo Hump kills one man without the others even noticing, scalps another without bothering to kill him, wounds Gus with a lance, and leaves the Rangers to make their demoralized way home.

Most of Dead Man's Walk then follows a second Texan expedition aimed at Mexico. This, too, is a total failure, ending with the few survivors forced to draw lots—a white bean out of the bag, you live, pick a black one, you die. Gus and Woodrow are both saved by the luck of the draw. But at this point, the Texans are unable even to survive out on the prairie. Woodrow, though, is a learner. In what is chronologically the second novel, *Comanche Moon*, the Rangers are better mounted, better armed, better skilled. In fact, they are becoming such a threat, that Buffalo Hump organizes a Comanche army to sweep through Texas, even into the capital Austin.

Once again, there really was such a raid in 1840, which got as far as the Gulf coastline, though it was harried mercilessly and ended in failure. McMurtry makes the contest more even. But he also notes that the Comanches received a respite as a result of the Civil War, which drew Texan manpower away to the east. Then, the "cowboy" era really set in, when it became both possible and profitable to drive large herds of cattle across the great plains to the new railheads at Denver or Kansas City, there to be shipped to the meatpacking plants of Chicago.

In *Lonesome Dove*, the third novel chronologically, but the first to be published, Woodrow and Gus are independent contractors, whose trail drive parallels the real-life drives of Charlie Goodnight and Oliver Loving and their successors from 1866 onwards. By this time, the prairie is still full of dangers, but they are white bandits and Indian outcasts, rather than organized war parties. The Rangers are well in control. Pursuing an abducted woman, Gus charges a group of bandits and Kiowa Indians and wipes them out with his pistols as easily as Buffalo Hump dealt with the Rangers a generation before. The main villain by this time is Blue Duck, Buffalo Hump's son by a Mexican mother, who in the end murders his own father, but he's an outlaw, cast out even by the Comanches.

In the last novel, *Streets of Laredo*, the Comanches are only a memory, and so are the Rangers. Woodrow ends up as a cripple, still furiously independent, but without wealth or property or even respect, except from a few. Unlike the Deerslayer, Woodrow is not childless, but he too will die, in effect, intestate, living on charity. Like the Deerslayer, Woodrow has been driven out to the margin of the civilization he defended. At the end, Charlie Goodnight, the real-life character brought into the books, agrees that Woodrow was the greatest Ranger of all. He had his time, says Charlie, and it was a long time too. But the Wild West was in reality a short time, one man's lifetime would cover it, say 1810 to 1880.

Both our two heroes lasted little longer than their enemies, the Hurons and the Comanches. These two American heroes were brought into being by an entirely new set of circumstances, as agriculturalists with an industrial civilization behind them came into conflict with Stone Age nomadic hunters, newly empowered by the horses introduced to the continent by the Spanish.

Theirs was a Heroic Age different from that of Homer or of Beowulf, but far better recorded, and now immortalized, for good or ill, by our largely inaccurate and self-flattering imaginaries.

Fenimore Cooper made out a case for Native American morality, different from ours, but worthy of respect and understanding. Larry McMurtry made out a case for Native American abilities and survival qualities, in some ways and for a time superior to those of their Anglo-American supplanters.

Both Woodrow and the Deerslayer, then, remain an important corrective to both the forest-frontier imaginary and the imaginary of the Wild West.

Uncle Tom—The Hero as Martyr
Lecture 14

In this course, we've seen heroes, such as Robin Hood and Robinson Crusoe, created by particular social and geographical circumstances. But in this lecture, we'll look at a hero created by a particular historical circumstance. He's also a hero who, of all the ones we'll examine, probably had the greatest effect on real political history. Further, this hero is not, like Frodo Baggins, a new type of hero but, in fact, an old type that has become unfashionable. Of course, the hero is Uncle Tom, from Harriet Beecher Stowe's novel *Uncle Tom's Cabin*. The historical circumstance that created Tom was the Compromise of 1850, and his political effect was to contribute to the start of the Civil War.

Uncle Tom as a Christian Martyr

- Uncle Tom, the central figure in Harriet Beecher Stowe's *Uncle Tom's Cabin*, is a different kind of hero, one that has become unfashionable. He corresponds to the medieval hero pattern of the saint: the Christian martyr.

- Hagiography, the writing of saints' lives, was the major form of written narrative for many centuries, but then it fell into disuse. One reason for its disfavor is that its heroes are not active but passive. They show heroism, not through conventional courage, bravery, or gallantry, but through fortitude: the courage of endurance.

- Fortitude has never quite caught on in Western popular culture, despite its great importance for Christianity. When he wrote his Christian epic *Paradise Lost*, John Milton noted that he was swimming against the tide. In telling the story of Adam and Eve, he was rejecting the stories of wars and fabled knights in favor of "patience and heroic martyrdom / Unsung."

A Story of Protest

- The impetus for writing *Uncle Tom's Cabin* is said to have been a vision Stowe had in which she saw Tom's death. But the thunder that preceded this lightning bolt was the Compromise of 1850, legislation that made a significant change to the earlier Fugitive Slave Act.
  - After 1850, northerners were required by law to assist slave catchers, and slave catchers were no longer required to prove the ownership of those they sought.

  - The effect of the legislation was to set up a border zone of anger and indignation, mainly along the Ohio River.

- Uncle Tom is a slave in Kentucky, married to Chloe, with a considerate master, Mr. Shelby. But Shelby gets into debt, and to clear the debt, he plans to sell another slave he owns, Eliza, and her son, Harry. Eliza hears about the plan and runs away. Shelby then decides to sell Tom to a slave trader, and he is taken off in chains. Tom doesn't run away because he knows that if he does, someone else will be sold.

- On the steamboat going down the river, Tom saves a white girl named Evangeline from drowning. He's bought by Eva's grateful father, Augustine St. Clare, and of course, treated well. St. Clare intends to free Tom, but he is killed in a brawl, and Mrs. St. Clare sells all the family's slaves. Tom is bought by Simon Legree, the archetypal slave owner villain. Legree runs a cotton plantation deep in the swamps of the Delta; eventually, he beats Tom to death.

- *Uncle Tom's Cabin* is a novel in protest of the whole institution of slavery. Thus, Stowe takes a broad view, and one way she works is by pairing characters.
  - For example, Tom is a passive hero, but he is paired with an active hero, Eliza's husband, George. Like his wife, George also runs away, and when the slave catchers come after them all, he meets them not with submission but with pistols.

- o   Other contrasting pairs include Mr. and Mrs. Shelby, Senator and Mrs. Bird, and Eva and Topsy.

- These pairings set up a theme of hypocrisy. For example, if the United States is the land of liberty, why do George and Eliza have to flee into Canada, where they are beyond the reach of American law? Stowe points to further hypocrisy in the Senate, in the North, and among slave owners.

- Mixed in with this is the theme of sexual slavery. For instance, one of the northerners who helps Eliza escape remarks, "Handsome 'uns has the greatest cause to run." Another female slave, Cassy, has wound up as a sex slave on Simon Legree's plantation.

- Stowe rarely pulls punches. Later on, some critics, including Henry James, thought that this was inartistic of her, but she didn't care about art; she cared about abolishing slavery. Thus, she punctuates her novel with direct appeals to her audience, often addressing them woman to woman.

Passive versus Active Heroism
- In *Uncle Tom's Cabin*, we are once more in the presence of different cultural values. It's important for us to appreciate the much more powerful force of Christian belief in Stowe's mind and world.

- As we've seen, Tom sacrificed himself for others by not running away when he's sold by Mr. Shelby. He also saves little Evangeline from drowning. Perhaps the only thing we can hold against Tom at the beginning of the novel is that, unlike George, he never rejects the whole institution of slavery.

- Tom's "ministry" starts when he is sold to Simon Legree and marched off to Legree's plantation. Stowe calls the chapter during the march "The Middle Passage," indicating that this is the real start of slavery. The next chapter is called "Dark Places." At the Legree plantation, Tom reaches what other writers call "the heart of darkness."

On his first night on Legree's plantation, Tom begins his "ministry," helping two women who are exhausted from their work in the fields.

- In the 10 chapters that deal with Tom on the plantation, there are a number of recurrent themes, among them, submission versus defiance.
  - We encounter this theme when Legree takes away the clothes and belongings that Tom has acquired during his life with St. Clare.

  - Legree takes away Tom's hymn book, but he does not succeed in taking away Tom's Bible. Legree tells Tom, "I'm your church now!" Tom does not reply, but something within him refuses. The defiance is present, but so far, it's silent.

- Another theme in the novel is temptation, primarily, temptation to give into despair. In addition to the outer struggle of resisting Legree's tyranny, Tom also has an inner struggle: resisting the feeling that God has deserted the slaves. A further and particular temptation for Tom is that Legree bought him because he wants Tom for an overseer, and the quality he desires in overseers is hardness.

- The first test for Tom comes over Lucy, who has been bought to be a sexual partner for one of Legree's slave overseers. She is too old to work in the fields. Tom, against orders, fills her cotton basket from his so that she will not be short on weight at the end of the day. Still, Legree insists that she is short and tells Tom to flog her.

- Tom refuses, and now his defiance becomes overt. Legree demands, "An't yer mine, now, body and soul?" and Tom replies, "My soul an't yours, Mas'r … It's been bought and paid for, by One that is able to keep it." Tom gets his first flogging in Lucy's place.

- Legree's displaced concubine, Cassy, comes to Tom's assistance, bringing him water. But despite her good intentions, she again tempts Tom to despair. She tells him, "There isn't any God, I believe," and Tom almost agrees with her.

- Cassy, though, reads the Bible to him, and Tom remembers what he has been told of the Passion of Christ and the lives of saints and martyrs. They, too, were killed gruesomely. Thus, he concludes, "Sufferin' an't no reason to make us think the Lord's turned agin us."

- Tom defies Legree again, once more refusing to burn his Bible and become an overseer, and at this point, one might expect that his defiance would lead to death and the climax. But Tom sees a vision of Christ in which the crown of thorns turns into rays of glory; after that, he seems to be untouchable by cruelty, his will "entirely merged in the divine."

- Tom has one temptation left to resist. Cassy, herself driven to desperation, wants him to kill Legree with an axe while he's drunk. But Tom refuses, reminding her that we must love our enemies and that victory lies in love and prayer.

- Cassy and another slave, Emmeline, make their escape. Legree suspects that Tom knows what has happened to the runaways and tries to make him talk. But Tom refuses and tells Legree to repent; this time, Tom is beaten to the point of death. And yet, in an *imitatio Christi*, an "imitation of Christ," Tom forgives Legree and the two slave overseers who have flogged him.

A Truthful Ending

- After the beating, George Shelby, the young son of Tom's first owner, turns up too late to save Tom but in time to watch him die. Among Tom's last words are: "Who shall separate us from the love of Christ?" and "What a thing it is to be a Christian!"

- We can see why some have felt this to be an unsatisfactory ending. George Shelby knocks Legree down and takes Tom's body away for burial. Cassy and Emmeline escape, and Cassy is reunited with her long-lost daughter. But Legree is never officially punished, although we're told that he dies raving and desperate. And there is no happy ending for the other slaves on the plantation.

- Nevertheless, we might say that that is exactly Stowe's point. In 1852, slavery had not been abolished, and many slaves were in the hands of people like Legree. Stowe's book was written to shame the collective conscience of America into action against an atrocity that was still continuing. A happy ending would have been a lie and a betrayal.

- Many people also find Tom's obsequiousness to Legree—even at the end—difficult to take. Certainly, that has been the response of many African American writers, including J. C. Furnas and Robert Alexander, who wrote challenges to, or refutations of, *Uncle Tom's Cabin*.

- It's true that Stowe stereotyped, sentimentalized, and offered a role model that later offended African American pride. It's also true, however, that what she did worked. She wasn't trying to provide a role model for African Americans; she was trying to make white

Americans feel ashamed of themselves, and sometimes shame is more powerful than fear.

- Through Uncle Tom, Stowe struck a blow against slavery heavier than John Brown's and a blow for the power and influence of women. Perhaps the short answer to her critics is to ask: Do you want glory and approval, or do you want to achieve your goal? Stowe's goal was achieved in 1865 with the final abolition of slavery in America.

Essential Reading

Stowe, *Uncle Tom's Cabin.*

Suggested Reading

Frederickson, *The Black Image in the White Mind.*

Gossett, *Uncle Tom's Cabin and American Culture.*

Questions to Consider

1. Has Christianity remained as powerful a force in the struggle for civil rights in your time as it was in Harriet Beecher Stowe's? If not, why not?

2. Who are now the most influential role models, in fiction, for African Americans?

Uncle Tom—The Hero as Martyr
Lecture 14—Transcript

In this course so far, we've come across cases of heroes created by particular social circumstances, like Robin Hood. We've also seen one case of a hero created by new geographical circumstances, which is Robinson Crusoe on his "desert island." But today, I'm going to talk about a hero created by a particular historical circumstance, a hero also, who of all the ones we look at, probably had the biggest effect on real political history. And one other anomaly, today's hero is not a new type of hero, like Frodo Baggins, in fact, he's a very old type of hero. But it's a type which has become unfashionable, and he's the only one of that type that we're going to encounter in this course.

I won't be mysterious any more. The hero is Uncle Tom, from Harriet Beecher Stowe's novel *Uncle Tom's Cabin*, published in 1852. The historical circumstance that created Tom was the Compromise of 1850, which among other things, altered the provisions of the Fugitive Slave Act of 1793. And the political effect that *Uncle Tom's Cabin* created was the Civil War of 1861 to 1865. Well, was it? The story often told is that when Abraham Lincoln met Harriet Beecher Stowe in 1862, he said to her, "So you are the little lady who started this great war." There's no definite evidence that this was ever said, though Lincoln did meet Stowe in 1862. The story only surfaced some years later and may have been made up by Mrs. Stowe's relatives.

And of course she didn't create the Civil War, not all by herself. No doubt there were many factors which contributed to the outbreak of the war. Still, I have no doubt that *Uncle Tom's Cabin* was an important factor. Historians nowadays like to think that wars are fought for rational and economic reasons, as is no doubt partly true. But we should remember that wars are predominantly fought by young men, and young men respond better to emotional reasons. They are also much more likely to support a war if it has the support of their wives, and especially their mothers. Harriet Beecher Stowe very much pitched her novel at a female audience, and there's no doubt at all that the female audience in America responded powerfully to it. And not just American mothers, Stowe also influenced British mothers. And this was probably a factor which ensured that Britain did not come to the assistance of the Confederate States. Though that is where Britain's economic interest lay, through the cotton industry. Sometimes emotion trumps economics.

The last thing I need to clear up is the type of hero. Briefly, Tom corresponds to the old mediaeval hero pattern of the saint, the Christian martyr. Hagiography, the writing of saints' lives, was the major form of written narrative for many centuries. It fell into disuse. Why? Well, all the heroes discussed in this course so far have been active ones. They do things to other people, or at the least they aspire to do so, like Don Quixote. This applies even to Elizabeth Bennet. Her big scene is the one in which she defies Lady de Bourgh, in her own interests.

But there can also be passive heroes. Note that the word "passive," like "passion," comes from the Latin word *patior*, "I suffer." The passive hero— or the passive heroine—shows heroism by suffering, by enduring, and by doing so voluntarily. You might say that they show, not courage, not bravery, certainly not gallantry, but something else—related but different. I would use the word "fortitude." Fortitude is cold courage, the courage of endurance raised to a higher power. It's never quite caught on in Western popular culture, despite its great importance for Christianity.

When he wrote his great Christian epic, *Paradise Lost*, John Milton noted that he was swimming against the tide. In telling the story of Adam and Eve, he was rejecting the story of "Wars, hitherto the only argument / Heroic deemed, chief mastery to dissect / With long and tedious havoc fabled knights / In battles feigned; the better fortitude / Of patience and heroic martyrdom / Unsung." Elsewhere he insisted that his subject was "Not less but more heroic than the wrath / Of stern Achilles on his foe pursued / Thrice fugitive about Troy wall." The Christian story, then, says Milton, is more heroic than the Trojan War or the tales of King Arthur and the Round Table, but it's about fortitude, patience, martyrdom.

Well, Milton knew he was swimming against the tide, and so was Harriet Beecher Stowe. As you can see from the way that the phrase "uncle Tom" has been devalued. Calling someone "an uncle Tom" is nowadays strongly disapproving. I looked for definitions of the term on the internet and found lots of them, some too rude for me to quote here. Among them were, "a black man who will do anything to stay in good standing with 'the white man' including betray his own people;" or, "a black person who is regarded as being humiliatingly subservient or deferential to white people;" or, "a race traitor."

These all say pretty much the same thing. Most of the places I looked at, however, also pointed out that this usage in contemporary language is unfair to the original Uncle Tom. Stowe's novel was the first American novel to sell more than a million copies, and its popularity led after the Civil War to what were called "Tom shows," "blackface minstrelsy," and all sorts of humiliatingly stereotypical Tom-descendants. But that is not the fault of the original "uncle Tom."

Going back to our novel, the flashpoint, the lightning bolt which actually started Mrs. Stowe writing, is said to have been a vision which she saw, naturally enough from what I've said about Tom's martyr status, a vision of the death of Tom, the climax and almost the final scene of the novel. But the thunder that preceded it, the gathering storm, if you like, was the 1850 Compromise. This legislation, fought out in Congress between the representatives of the Southern slave states and the Northern free states, did several things. It accepted California into the union as a free state. It provided for New Mexico and Utah to make their own decisions about slavery. But for Mrs. Stowe and many others, the really infuriating part was the change which the Compromise made to the almost 60-year-old Fugitive Slave Act.

Up to 1850, if a slave owner wanted to repossess a slave who had run away to the northern states, he had to prove ownership, and people in the northern states were free to assist runaways if they so chose. After 1850, northerners were required by law to assist slave catchers and could be punished if they did not do so. Furthermore, a slave catcher did not have to prove ownership of a particular person, but only to assert it to a federal commission.

One obvious result was that even free men and women could be claimed as slaves. It didn't help that the federal commissioners were paid ten dollars for agreeing that someone was a slave, but only five dollars for stating that they weren't. Retrospectively, it does seem like a case of poorly drafted legislation. What it did was set up a border zone of anger and indignation mainly along the Ohio River, which will come into my later lecture on Huckleberry Finn. So, the 1850 Compromise set Mrs. Stowe thinking, and the vision she had of its ending was what shaped her novel.

I can tell you the broad outline of Tom's story quite easily. He's a slave in Kentucky, married to Chloe, with a considerate master, Mr. Shelby. But Shelby gets into debt. To clear the debt, he decides to sell another slave he owns, Eliza, and her son Harry. Eliza gets to hear about the plan, and she runs off, in a famous scene, crossing the Ohio ahead of the slave takers, on the ice, which has already started to break. She gets away, but the debt still has to be cleared, and so Shelby sells Tom to a slave trader. Tom is taken off in chains. We might ask, why does he not run off, as Eliza did? And the answer is, and this is his first self-sacrificing decision, because he knows that if he runs off, someone else will be sold. "I s'ppose I can b'ar it as well as any on 'em," he says.

On the steamboat going down the river, and down the river is an ominous phrase for Tom, as also for Huck Finn's friend Jim, Tom saves a little white girl called Evangeline from drowning. He's bought by Eva's grateful father, Augustine St. Clare, and of course, treated very well. St. Clare means to free him. But he gets killed in a brawl, and Mrs. St Clare—lazy, selfish, the worst type of slave owner—sells the whole establishment.

Actually, it turns out she wasn't the worst type of slave owner, after all. That distinction belongs to the man who buys Tom, a character who became the archetypal slave owner villain, Simon Legree. He runs a cotton plantation deep in the swamps of the Delta, and there he works his slaves to death. Or beats them to death, which is what he eventually does with Tom.

That's the outline of the plot, but I've left a whole lot out. This is a protest novel, and what Harriet Beecher Stowe was protesting about was not just the 1850 Compromise, it was the whole institution of slavery. So she takes a very broad view, and one way she works is by pairing characters off.

So, Tom is a passive hero, as I've said, for good reason. But there is an active hero too, and of course, an active heroine. Eliza flees in order to keep her child, for we might note, that if a mother and child were sold, there was no guarantee that they would not be sold separately. George, her husband, flees as well. The slave takers come after them all, but George meets them not with submission but with his pistols. So George and Tom are a contrasted pair. Then there are Mr. and Mrs. Shelby, Senator and Mrs. Bird, and one of the strange pairings, the little white girl Eva and the little black girl Topsy, who became a byword for not knowing where she came from, and saying "I s'pect I grow'd."

What these pairings do is set up a theme of hypocrisy. There's hypocrisy in the United States. If it's the land of liberty, as it so often says, why do George and Eliza have to flee, not only over the Ohio, but into Canada, where they are beyond the reach of American law? There's also hypocrisy in the Senate. In chapter 9, Senator Bird is explaining to his wife that compromises have to be made, that it wouldn't be "Christian and kind" to deprive slave owners of their property, and so on. When Eliza and Harry turn up freezing and exhausted at their backdoor, Mrs. Bird immediately determines to help them, and never mind the law her husband has passed. The Senator, in a shamefaced sort of way, goes along with her. There's hypocrisy in the North too. If a slave owner dies in debt to a Northern bank, what will the bankers in New York do? They'll sell off his slaves to pay their debt. There's hypocrisy even among the slave owners—all of them, except Simon Legree—comfort themselves by saying that whatever they do, there are people who do worse. Simon Legree, we might note, is a New Englander.

Mixed in with this, and remember, this is a novel being pitched to women, white women, in the North, is the theme of sexual slavery. One of the northerners who helps Eliza escape remarks "handsome 'uns has the greatest cause to run." We also meet the female slave Cassy, who, like many women in slavery, has lost all her children. Things can get worse even for her. She has wound up as a sex slave on Simon Legree's plantation, but when Simon buys Tom, he also buys a 15-year-old girl who is going to take Cassy's place. Cassy stops being a house slave and is sent out to pick cotton. We should note that this sexual slavery has been going on for a long time. Eliza's husband George can pass for white, as can Eliza and her son Harry. Insisting on the total separation of the races is just one more form of endemic hypocrisy.

I'd add that Stowe rarely pulls her punches. People like Henry James might have thought later on that this was terribly inartistic of her, but she didn't care about art, she cared about abolishing slavery. So she punctuates her novel with direct appeals to her audience, very often addressing them woman to woman. When Mrs. Bird opens up a drawer to take out clothes to give to Eliza's little son Harry, they are the clothes which belonged to her own little son, dead in infancy. Stowe wrote, "And oh! Mother that reads this, has there never been in your house a drawer, or a closet, the opening of which has been to you like the opening again of a little grave? Ah! Happy mother that you are, if it has not been so." Stowe had, in fact, lost her own little son just three years before, to cholera. She consistently asks, "How would you feel if they took your child away? And never think that slaves don't feel for their children just as much as you do."

But let's get back to Tom's own story and the whole issue of passive versus active heroism, the issue which has given the phrase "uncle Tom" its present negative meaning. I'll just say to begin with that I think we are once more in the presence of changed cultural values. Our values have changed. We need to appreciate the much more powerful force of Christian belief in Harriet Beecher Stowe's mind and world.

I've already said that at the start Tom sacrificed himself for others by going into slavery; that's good. He also saves little Evangeline from drowning; that's good too. So far, I think the only thing one can hold against Tom is that unlike George Harris, with whom he's contrasted, he never rejects the whole institution of slavery. He never says, as George does, "I'm a better man than he is."

Tom's ministry, however, and I think ministry is the right term for it, only starts when he is sold to Simon Legree and marched off to his plantation. Stowe calls the chapter during which they march to the plantation "The Middle Passage," indicating that this is the real start of slavery. And the next chapter is called "Dark Places." At the Legree plantation Tom reaches what other writers call "the heart of darkness."

In the ten chapters which deal with Tom on the plantation, there are a number of recurrent themes. One is submission versus defiance. It begins right at the start. Legree takes away the clothes and the belongings which Tom has acquired during his life with St. Clare, and also takes away his hymn book. But he does not succeed in taking away Tom's Bible. Legree tells Tom, "I'm your church now!" And Tom does not reply, but something within him says. "No!" So the defiance is there, but so far it's silent.

Another theme is temptation, and the main temptation is despair. On his first night on the plantation Tom begins his mission of charity by helping two worn-out female field hands. He grinds their corn for them and lights a fire so they can bake what I guess are griddle cakes. He also reads the Bible to them. One of them has never even heard of the Bible, and when Tom reads the verse "Come unto me, all ye that labor and are heavy laden, and I will give you rest," she asks, "Who said that?" Tom says, "the Lord," and she says, "I jest wish I know'd whar to find him […] I know de Lord an't here."

So Tom has not only an outer struggle in resisting Legree's tyranny, he has an inner struggle not to give in to the feeling all around him that God has deserted them. On this first night Tom is buoyed up by a vision of Evangeline, dead of TB, and Stowe says, "Who's to say that the dead are not allowed to visit us, as ministering angels?"

A further and particular temptation for Tom is that Legree bought him because he was well aware that he is a valuable man, "expert and efficient […] Prompt and faithful. Quiet and peaceable." Legree indeed says, "I paid a little high for him, tendin' him for a driver and a managing chap." But what Legree wants in an overseer is above all, hardness.

The first test for Tom comes over Lucy. Continuing the theme of sexual slavery, she is a woman, a married woman, with children, and a Methodist, who has been bought to be a sexual partner for one of Legree's two slave overseers. She is old and tired and cannot do the work in the fields. Tom, against orders, fills her cotton basket from his so that she will not be short on weight at the end of the day. Legree, however, lyingly insists that she is, and tells Tom to flog her as a test. Tom refuses, and now his defiance becomes overt. Legree demands, "An't yer mine, now, body and soul?" and Tom replies, "My soul an't yours, Mas'r […] It's been bought and paid for, by One that is able to keep it [.]" And so Tom gets his first flogging in Lucy's place, scene which Stowe omits.

The character who then comes to his assistance, bringing water, is Cassy, Legree's displaced concubine. But despite her good intentions she again tempts Tom to despair. She tells him, "There isn't any God, I believe," and Tom for a moment almost agrees with her, saying, "Lord Jesus! Have you quite forgot us poor critturs?" Tom is afraid that if he gives in to Legree's offers, he could grow up to be like Sambo, one of the two slave overseers who whip and beat the others. Cassy, though, reads the Bible to him. She was once well educated, and Tom remembers what he has been told, not only of the Passion of Christ, but also of the lives of saints and martyrs. They too, he remembers, were killed gruesomely, stoned like St. Stephen, or sawn in two like St. Simon. So, he concludes, "Sufferin' an't no reason to make us think the Lord's turned agin us."

Tom defies Legree again, once more refusing to burn his Bible and become an overseer, and at this point one might expect that his defiance would lead to death and the climax. In fact, this time it's Tom who sees a vision, a vision of Christ in which the Crown of Thorns turns into rays of glory, and after that, he seems to be untouchable by cruelty, his will "entirely merged in the divine." Tom lives on the plantation, continuing to do works of charity, giving up his blanket to a woman struck by fever, filling the baskets of others, reading the Bible, and preaching to the others in what little time they have. The other slaves begin to call him, not "Uncle Tom" but "Father Tom."

Tom has one temptation left to resist. Cassy, herself driven to desperation, wants him to kill Legree with an axe, while he's drunk. But Tom refuses, reminding her that we must love our enemies and that the victory lies in love and prayer. Cassy, however, has a plan of escape for herself and her replacement Emmeline, and she puts it into practice. Running away into the swamp is never successful, but she has persuaded Legree that a garret in which he beat a slave to death is haunted. She and Emmeline pretend to run off into the swamp but circle back to hide in the garret. After the hunt has died down, knowing that she can easily pass for white, she intends to head for the river and the steamboat and buy a passage out for both of them with money which she stole from Legree.

Legree suspects that Tom knows what has happened to the runaways and tries to make him talk. Tom refuses, tells Legree to repent, and this time, once again, Stowe omits the vital scene, is beaten to the very point of death. And yet, in what one has to call an *imitatio Christi*—an imitation of Christ—Tom forgives Legree and the two slave overseers who have flogged him. These two, Sambo and Quimbo, are much affected and weep with him. Sambo says, rather like the Roman soldier in the gospels, "Do tell us, who is Jesus, anyhow? Jesus, that's been a standin' by you so […]! Who is he?" George Shelby, the young son of Tom's first owner, turns up just too late to save Tom but in time to watch him die. Among Tom's last words are, "Who shall separate us from the love of Christ?" and, "What a thing it is to be a Christian!"

One can see why some have felt this to be an unsatisfactory ending. George Shelby knocks Legree down and takes Tom's body away for burial. Cassy and Emmeline escape, and Cassy is reunited with her long-lost daughter, who turns out to be Eliza from the start of the novel. But Legree is never officially punished, although we're told that he dies raving and desperate. Most of us would think that he deserves more than that. And there is no happy ending for the other slaves on the plantation, though two of them beg George Shelby to buy them and take them away.

Nevertheless, we might well say that that is exactly Harriet Beecher Stowe's point. In 1852 slavery had not been abolished; slaves were still on the plantations, and many of them were in the hands of people like Legree. Her book was written to shame the collective conscience of America into action against an atrocity which was still continuing. So a happy ending would have been, frankly, a lie and a betrayal. The thing which people find hard to take, I think—remembering some of the "uncle Tom" definitions which I gave earlier—is that Tom still seems to be something like obsequious even to Legree. He says, "If taking every drop of blood in this poor old body would save your precious soul, I'd give 'em freely," and many would think that's going too far.

Certainly that has been the response of many African-American writers, who have written challenges to or refutations of *Uncle Tom's Cabin*. Richard Wright wrote a collection of short stories called *Uncle Tom's Children* in 1938, which he later regretted, feeling he had fallen into the trap of sentimentalizing situations, of which Stowe has often also been accused. Eleven years later, James Baldwin dismissed Stowe's book as "Everybody's Protest Novel." J. C. Furnas called his 1956 analysis of myths about African Americans *Goodbye to Uncle Tom*. And in 1992 Robert Alexander's play, *I Ain't Yo' Uncle* actually put Stowe on trial for creating or perpetuating a stereotype of African Americans.

Most of the charges are basically true. Stowe did stereotype; she did sentimentalize; she offered a role model which later offended African American pride. On the other hand, what she did worked. She wasn't trying to provide a role model for African Americans; she was trying to make white Americans feel ashamed of themselves, and as a wise man of my acquaintance once told me, sometimes shame is more powerful than fear.

Certainly she and her cast of characters, especially Uncle Tom, Eliza and Cassy, had a major impact on literature. Few later novels about race relations in the USA are not in some sense continuing *Uncle Tom's Cabin*, or replying to it.

More important, it worked politically. Without the groundswell of popular opinion in Britain, which Stowe increased by her own tour of Britain, might the British government have decided to support the Confederacy, as many urged? Without her hundreds of thousands of readers in America, might Abraham Lincoln have been obliged to take a weaker line on abolition?

Through Uncle Tom, Harrier Beecher Stowe struck a blow against slavery heavier than John Brown's, and a blow also for the power and influence of women. Perhaps the short answer to her critics is to ask, do you want glory, approval, all those good things?

Or do you want to achieve your goal? Stowe achieved her goal, with the final abolition of slavery in America through the 13th Amendment in 1865: thirteen years and many deaths after she wrote her book. And she achieved it through her creation of Uncle Tom.

Huckleberry Finn—Free Spirit of America
Lecture 15

A s the list of heroes we're exploring gets longer, we should expect to start seeing features of earlier heroes in some later ones, and that's certainly the case with Huckleberry Finn. Like Odysseus, Huck goes on an odyssey, and he's a trickster, staging his own murder to escape his drunken father. Further, much of Huck's odyssey has a sense of Robinson Crusoe about it; his very name suggests that he is a hunter-gatherer. There is also a connection to *Don Quixote*, when Tom organizes the raid on a Sunday school picnic. Above all, though, Huck is emblematic of a free spirit, someone who is comfortable in his own skin.

A Free Spirit

- The one word we most often associate with Huck is "free," and what makes Huck a free spirit most of all is that he's always himself. As we say nowadays—and this is not true of Tom Sawyer—he's comfortable in his own skin. One reason for this may be that from the start, a main element in Huck's character is his freedom from social responsibilities.

Huck's odyssey is much more peaceful than that of Odysseus; as Huck says, "You feel mighty free and easy and comfortable on a raft."

- Although Huck is free of illusions and he frees himself from both his drunken father and the conventions of St. Petersburg, his freedom takes a serious turn.
  - Being a free spirit sounds good, but the price of cutting yourself loose from organized society and drifting along on a raft is that you have to make your own decisions.

- Huck must look inside himself to do that. Seeing clearly about both himself and others—and doing it on his own—is what makes Huck a hero.

Huck's Odysseys

- After the events of *Tom Sawyer*, which made both boys rich, Huck has been adopted by the Widow Douglas, but he misses his freedom. His money attracts his drunken father, who carries him off. Huck decides to run away, stages his own murder to avoid pursuit, escapes, and meets up with Jim.

- Jim, an African American slave, is also on the run but much more seriously. He is the property of the Widow Douglas's sister, Miss Watson, and he's heard that she means to sell him down the river. There, he will become a plantation slave instead of a household slave and will lose all hope of freeing his wife and children. He plans to escape down the Mississippi to Cairo, where he can cross into Ohio and become a free man.

- The most important part of Huck's journey is his deepening relationship with Jim. This inner odyssey progresses in tandem with the outer odyssey of the raft, but it's a much more problematic one.

- Huck begins his inner odyssey with his society's casual assumption of racial superiority. The first time we encounter Jim is when Huck and Tom play a trick on him that is designed to make Jim look stupid. Such tricks are repeated several times, but later, the outcome starts to shift.

- At one point in the story, Huck leaves the raft in a canoe to try to find a place the two can tie up on the riverbank. But Huck gets lost in the fog, and the current carries both the canoe and the raft along swiftly. It's a long while before Huck gets back to the raft again, and when he does, Jim has gone to sleep. When Jim wakes up, Huck pretends that the two were never separated.
  - Huck is so convincing that Jim believes he must have had a dream, which he tries to interpret. The fog, the current,

everything in the experience must stand for something else, and the final return to the clear river stands for Jim getting through to the free states.

○ Huck lets Jim go on, but then he points to the leaves and branches that have landed on the raft while it was crashing along in the current and asks what they stand for. Of course, the leaves and branches prove that all the events in the fog actually happened.

○ Jim looks at the debris and, with great dignity, says that when he thought Huck was lost, his heart was almost broken with grief. He then goes on: "En all you wuz thinkin' 'bout wuz how you could make a fool uv ole Jim wid a lie. Dat truck dah is *trash*; en trash is what people is dat puts dirt on de head er dey fren's en makes 'em ashamed."

○ Here, Jim, the black slave, assumes complete moral superiority over the white boy, and Huck recognizes it. It takes several minutes before he can work himself up to humble himself to a black man, but as Huck says, "I done it, and I warn't ever sorry for it afterwards, neither."

• Huck has always been easy in his own skin, but now he has to put himself in someone else's skin. And it's a skin of a different color, which he's always been told creates an impassable barrier. That's a significant stage in a child's emotional development and a significant stage in the emotional development of America. Huck is starting to become an emblem, not just of the free spirit of childhood but also of the free spirit of America.

Huck's Inner Struggles
• Huck's continuing struggles with his conscience are the focus of several scenes that have been hailed as the great masterstroke of the American novel, a kind of demonstration of what it means to be American.

- The first such scene comes just after the scene with the trash. Jim, by now confident that Huck is on his side, tells Huck that once he is a free man, he plans to save up money to buy his wife, and they will then work to buy back their two children. If their master won't sell them, they'll find an abolitionist to go and steal the children.

  - Huck, who has been brought up in a slave society, finds this plan alarming. Jim is prepared to steal his children, who are the property of another man. Huck decides to paddle ashore and give Jim up.

  - But as he sets off, a couple of white men come along with guns, looking for runaway slaves. Huck dissuades them from searching the raft by implying that his father is aboard and sick with smallpox.

- In the fog, Jim and Huck missed the confluence with the Ohio and drifted into Arkansas, a slave state. Jim is caught, and Huck feels bad about helping a slave run away. He's been told all his life that those who behave in this way will go to hell.

  - Huck decides to write a letter to Miss Watson, telling her where Jim is so that she can repossess him. But then he starts thinking about his experiences with Jim on the river and how grateful Jim was after Huck saved him with the smallpox story. After a long hesitation, Huck says to himself, "All right, then, I'll go to hell" and tears up the letter.

  - Here, Huck is rising above the constraints of his culture. Of course, he did that in one way earlier on, when he apologized to Jim for making a fool of him. But this goes a step further. The earlier apology was a private matter, but in tearing up the letter, Huck is defying what he's always been taught is public morality.

  - Huck takes the action that he's been taught is wrong because he knows in his heart that it's right. This rejection of authority—the idea of the superiority of the individual conscience—is very American. Our own hearts are a better guide than anything we've read or been told.

- Huck tells lies, sometimes for good reason and sometimes not. And he'll go along with other people's deceits, as he does with Tom Sawyer. But at the same time, he sees through others, he sees through himself, and he sees through official morality. Huck is what we might call a soothsayer: He sees the truth and reports it.

Freedom from Illusion
- We see the other side of Huck's freedom from illusion in several scenes of "life on the Mississippi." As he and Jim drift into the southern states, Huck starts to encounter different communities that are bound by their own rules—rules that prevent them from being free.

- The most dramatic example here is the feud between two aristocratic families, the Grangerfords and the Shepherdsons. When one of the Grangerford daughters runs off with a young Shepherdson, the feud is reignited. It ends, as far as Huck is concerned, when his friend Buck Grangerford is shot dead. Huck lays out the body and weeps for his friend.
  - o No one remembers any more what the feud is about. Buck didn't even dislike the Shepherdsons. When Huck says that he thinks one of them is a coward, Buck corrects him sharply: "There ain't a coward amongst them Shepherdsons—not a one."

  - o They're not cowards or fools. But in a way, they're slaves to their own inherited and unexamined beliefs. And unlike Huck and Jim, they can't free themselves.

- We could make a similar point about an attempted lynching Huck observes. The would-be lynchers are faced down by a lone man, another Southern gentleman. Why? Because in a way, they're playacting—acting out what they think is their role. They can't stand up to a lone man, who—right or wrong—isn't playacting.

- Indeed, playacting becomes the dominant image of the later parts of the novel, especially when Jim and Huck meet the duke and dauphin and when Tom concocts the intricate plan to rescue Jim.

- Tom's fantasies prevent a simpler plan from working. Worse than that, after Tom's plan has failed and Jim is once again chained up, Tom confesses that no one has a right to chain Jim up at all. As Tom knew all along, Jim is no longer a slave. He was freed by Miss Watson in her will.

- Unlike Huck, Tom has never had to overcome his own conscience about stealing someone else's property. Further, he seems never to have had a twinge of conscience about using Jim and Huck as extras in his own incompetently produced drama.

- Everyone around Huck is, in a way, self-imprisoned—by their own romantic illusions, like Tom, or by their unexamined and inherited beliefs, like the slave owners and isolated communities along the Mississippi.
  - Huck is different from all of them. He's naïve and inexperienced and easily tricked by showmanship, but he sees into the heart of things.

  - If he knows something is wrong, he doesn't do it. He doesn't condemn people but mostly feels sorry for them because they—the Grangerfords, the duke and dauphin, the Widow Douglas and Miss Watson—can't free themselves.

Essential Reading

Twain, *The Adventures of Tom Sawyer*.

———, *The Adventures of Huckleberry Finn*.

Suggested Reading

Chadwick-Joshua, *The Jim Dilemma*.

Inge, ed., *Huck Finn among the Critics*.

1. Can you think of any examples from your own experience of people who have decided to rebel against the rules under which they were brought up because they decided the rules were morally wrong?

2. How much space is there for real-life Huckleberry Finns in modern societies? Is he now an impossible role model for childhood?

Huckleberry Finn—Free Spirit of America
Lecture 15—Transcript

As the list of heroes and legends we've looked at gets longer, I guess we should expect to start seeing features of earlier heroes in the new ones too; that's the case with Huckleberry Finn. In some ways, he's like Odysseus. The main story about Huck—that's the one in his own novel, *The Adventures of Huckleberry Finn*, which was published in 1884—his main story is a kind of odyssey. It's a much more gentle odyssey than the original one. Huck doesn't have to row or make sail or navigate. On his raft he just floats down the Mississippi River from St. Petersburg, which is Mark Twain's fictional representation of his own hometown of Hannibal, Missouri, and on to somewhere below Cairo, where the Ohio River joins the mainstream.

He does have adventures, like Odysseus. But the story is set in the American Midwest in the time of Twain's own youth, the 1840s, and I guess, that was about as peaceful a place and time as you could find in world history. No great wars to spill the blood of America's young men, though that would change in 1861. Not far to the west it was changing already, as American settlers encountered the Native Americans of the Great Plains.

Still, again, unlike Odysseus, Huck has no problems with one-eyed giant cannibals, or witches who can turn men into beasts, nor does he need to go down into the underworld. Huck's odyssey feels like fun. As Huck says, "You feel mighty free and easy and comfortable on a raft."

Even so, it is an odyssey, a journey that tests Huck's ingenuity and opens his eyes to a wider, and sometimes not very pleasant world. Much of Huck's odyssey also has a strong feeling about it of Robinson Crusoe. In fact, Huck's own name suggests that. Huck is a hunter-gatherer, or maybe we should say, a fisher-gatherer. And the thing about gathering huckleberries is it's not like work. You can do it for free, and "free" is the word I associate above all with Huck. He's an emblem of the free spirit, which he shows in more than one way.

Before I say more about that, I just need to make one more connection with Odysseus. Huck is a trickster. He starts off by staging his own murder so he can get away from his drunken father without being pursued. He tells long stories about himself at least four more times in the course of the novel, just like Odysseus. Sometimes for good reason but sometimes, it seems, just for sport.

So, there's a bit of Odysseus in Huck Finn and there's a bit of Robinson Crusoe. There's also a connection to Don Quixote. As you may recall from my lecture on Cervantes' wannabe hero, there's a famous scene in Twain's earlier book, Tom Sawyer, in which Tom organizes a raid on a Sunday school picnic. Tom tells his gang that a caravan of Spanish merchants and rich Arabs is going to come by St. Petersburg, with elephants and camels and mules loaded down with jewels, and he and Huck and the rest of the gang will ambush them.

Well, as Huck says, "There warn't no Spaniards and A-rabs and there warn't no camels nor no elephants [...] I didn't see no di'monds, and I told Tom Sawyer so." But Tom tells Huck that if he wasn't so ignorant and had read a book called Don Quixote, he'd know that it was all done by enchantment. Huck tries to believe Tom's fables about enchantments and even goes to the length of finding an old lamp and an old ring and rubbing them to see if a genie will appear, "But it warn't no use, none of the genies come. So then I judged that all that stuff was only just one of Tom Sawyer's lies."

You might note that Tom Sawyer hasn't really got the point of Don Quixote, which is that the Don is deluded. Huck goes along with him just for fun, and because he respects Tom's very widespread reading, but he sees clear. He's not weighed down, as Tom is, by the need to be something more interesting and more dramatic than he really is. What makes him a free spirit, most of all, is that he's always just himself. As we say nowadays, and this is not true of Tom Sawyer, he's easy in his own skin.

One reason for this may well be that from the start, a main part of Huck's character is his freedom from social responsibilities. The other boys in St. Petersburg envy him. He's a kind of unofficial role model. He's a juvenile pariah, son of the town drunk. He sleeps on doorsteps when it's fine and in old barrels when the weather is bad. He doesn't have to go to school; he doesn't have to keep his clothes clean; he can smoke a pipe if he wants to, all things which the other boys admire.

The other boys, though, are really integrated into their society. Tom is a naughty boy, but he's the kind of naughty boy who is secretly approved of. Boys will be boys, as people say. Huck, by contrast, is pretty detached from society. He doesn't come into his own until he's run away, and that's in his own book, Huckleberry Finn, not Tom Sawyer. In this book, Huckleberry Finn, though Huck continues to be free of illusions, and he also sets himself free from his drunken father and from the stifling conventions of respectable St. Petersburg, Huck's freedom takes a more serious turn. Being a free spirit sounds good, and it is good. But the price of cutting yourself loose from organized society and drifting along on a raft, "mighty free and easy and comfortable," as Huck says, the price of all that is you have to make your own decisions, and you don't have anyone to do it for you. Huck has to look inside himself to do that. Doing that, seeing clear, not only about other people but about himself, and doing it all on his own—that's what makes Huck a hero.

In Huckleberry Finn, Huck's main companion is not Tom, but Jim, the runaway slave. After the events of Tom Sawyer, which made both the boys rich, Huck has been adopted by the Widow Douglas, but he doesn't like it. He doesn't like clean clothes; he doesn't like church; he can't see why you have to say grace before meals; he wants his freedom back. We can all relate to that. But his money also means that he gets repossessed by his drunken father, who carries him off. Huck decides to run away, stages his own murder to avoid pursuit, escapes, and meets up with Jim.

Jim, an African American slave, is also on the run, but much more seriously. He is the property of the Widow Douglas' sister, Miss Watson, and he's heard, just like Harriet Beecher Stowe's Eliza, that she means to sell him down the river to New Orleans. There, he will become a plantation slave instead of a household slave and lose all hope of freeing his wife and children. He means to escape down the Mississippi to Cairo and then go up the Ohio River, deep into free-state territory, where he will be safe from slave catchers.

The most important part of Huck's journey is his deepening relationship with Jim, white boy, black man. This inner odyssey progresses in tandem with the outer odyssey of the raft, but it's a much more problematic one. We should note that the white-black relationship remained a sensitive subject even in the 1880s, when the book was published, though it was an even more sensitive one in the 1840s, the period in which the book is set.

Huck starts off on what I've just called his inner odyssey with his society's casual assumption of racial superiority. The first time we encounter Jim is when Huck and Tom play a trick on him. They steal some candles, very honestly leave five cents to pay for them, but at the same time, they take Jim's hat off his head while he's asleep and hang it on a tree branch. When Jim wakes up, he decides he was bewitched. Witches rode him all over the state and then put him back where he was before and hung his hat on a branch to show they'd done it. Every time Jim tells the tale, it gets more exaggerated. He keeps the five-cent piece round his neck on a string and says it was a charm the devil gave him with his own hands. Jim becomes extremely famous in the slave community from being the expert on witches.

Well, what this story says is that Jim is stupid—superstitious, easy to fool. This kind of joke is repeated several times. There's one scene when they're taking a break from their raft journey when Huck and Jim get to talking about the famous decision of Solomon. You recall, Solomon finds out who the real mother of a child is by offering to cut the child in two and give half each to the two women who claim him. We all understand the point of this; the real mother is the one who says, "Don't do it." But Jim takes it an entirely different way. He thinks it's because a man with a million wives, like Solomon, well—I'm not going to try to imitate Jim's dialect more than superficially—well, says Jim, "A chile er two, mo' er less, warn't no consekens to Sollermun, dad fetch him!" Huck can't talk him out of this opinion. Joke at the expense of Jim, again, but then the balance starts to shift.

It starts off, once again, with a trick. Jim and Huck are floating down the river on their raft, and when the current gets high, Huck goes off in their canoe to try to find a place where they can tie up, but he gets lost in the fog. The current is racing them along; there are snags everywhere that could rip the bottom out of the canoe; the raft is colliding with the banks and breaking off branches and foliage. Both Huck and Jim keep shouting in the hope the other will hear, but no luck. It's a long while before Huck gets back to the raft again, and when he gets there, Jim has once again gone to sleep. Huck gets back on board, and when Jim wakes up, Huck pretends he's been there all along. Lost in the fog? Never happened. Both of them whooping and trying to make contact with each other again? Never happened. Huck is so convincing that Jim believes that everything that happened in the night must've been a dream, and being superstitious, he settles down to interpret the dream. Everything, snags and whoops and fog, has to stand for something else, and the final return to the clear river, that stands for Jim winning through to the free states.

Huck lets him go through all this, but then he points to all the leaves and branches and brushwood, which has landed on the raft while it was crashing along in the strong current, and says, what's all that stand for? Of course, the leaves and stuff prove that it was no dream, that all the events in the fog did really happen. They don't need interpreting. Jim looks at it all, and says, with great dignity, what do the leaves and branches stand for? He'll tell Huck what they stand for. When he thought Huck was lost, his heart was almost broken with grief, and when Huck came back, he was so glad he could have cried.

Jim goes on, "En all you wuz thinkin' 'bout wuz how you could make a fool uv ole Jim wid a lie. Dat truck dah is trash; en trash is what people is dat puts dirt on de head er dey fren's en makes 'em ashamed." Here Jim, the black slave, assumes complete moral superiority over the white boy, and Huck recognizes it. It takes fifteen minutes before he can work himself up to humble himself to a black man, but as Huck says, "I done it, and I warn't ever sorry for it afterwards, neither."

Huck's always been easy in his own skin, but now he has to put himself in someone else's skin. And it's a skin of a different color, which he's always been told creates an impassable barrier. That's a big stage in a child's emotional development and a big stage in the emotional development of America. Huck is starting to become an emblem, not just of the free spirit of childhood, which he's been all along, but also of the free spirit of America.

Huck's continuing struggles with his conscience are accordingly the focus for several scenes afterwards, which have often been hailed as the great masterstroke of the American novel, a kind of demonstration of what it means to be American.

The first one comes just after the scene with the trash. Jim, by now confident that Huck is on his side, tells Huck that once he is in a free state and a free man, he's going to save up his money to buy his wife back from St. Petersburg, and then they will both work to buy back their two children. And if their master won't sell them—remember, this is all happening in the 1840s, even before the time of Uncle Tom—they'll get an abolitionist to go and steal the children. Huck, who has been brought up in a slave society, as Missouri then was, finds this terribly alarming. Jim is prepared to steal his children, who are the property of another man, a man, who as Huck says, never did Huck any harm. You may recall Senator Bird in Uncle Tom's Cabin saying, freeing slaves, someone else's property, would be neither "Christian nor kind."

So Huck decides to paddle ashore and give Jim up, and the decision makes him immensely relieved. He feels that at last he's doing the right thing. But as he sets off, a couple of white men come along with guns, looking for runaway slaves, and they ask Huck who else is on his raft. Huck says, one man. Is he white? They ask. Huck says yes. They say they'll come and look for themselves. Huck begs them to come, and makes out that he really needs help, because his father is … and then he won't say quite what's the matter with his father. The hunters assume he's trying to cover up the fact that his father has smallpox. So they leave, and Huck, using his wits like Odysseus, has saved Jim and gone against all his upbringing.

Things don't stop there, because the fact is that, in the fog, they missed the confluence with the Ohio and have drifted further south down into the slave states into Arkansas. Down there Jim is caught by someone who turns out to be, and this is a really outrageous coincidence, a relative of Tom Sawyer's. But Huck doesn't know that, and he still feels very bad about helping a slave to run away. He's been told all his life that those who behave like that will go to everlasting fire.

So he decides to write a letter to Jim's owner and tell her where he is, so she can repossess him. But then he gets to thinking about how they floated down the river together and how grateful Jim was the time before when Huck saved him with a story about smallpox. And he decides it's no good; he's just going to have to accept that he's a wicked person. After a long hesitation he says to himself, "All right then, I'll go to hell," and he tears the letter up.

Why is this a critical scene? Well, what Huck is doing here is rising above the constraints of his society, his culture. Of course, he did that in one way earlier on, when he apologized to Jim for making a fool of him. But this goes a stage further. That earlier apology was a private matter, one to one. In tearing up his letter Huck is defying what he's always been taught is public morality, what a Roman would certainly call his civic duty to the republic.

If Aeneas was *pius* Aeneas, the man distinguished for his social propriety, you have to say Huck is *impius* Huck. The boy who denies social propriety. He does what he's been taught is wrong, because he knows in his heart it's right. Well, that's very American—the rejection of authority, the superiority of the individual conscience, a kind of heroic simplicity. Your own heart is a better guide than anything you can read or anything you've ever been told. I don't forget that while the story is set in the 1840s, it was published and read in the 1880s, after the Civil War was over and after a great change in cultural values had been enforced on the battlefield. However, Huck's clear sightedness and independence of opinion have been there all along.

So, right at the start, the Widow Douglas is doing her best to cure what she sees as Huck's bad habits, and one of them is smoking. Huck always has a corn cob pipe. But the widow says it's a mean practice, and it's not clean, and he mustn't do it any more. But Huck notes, the Widow Douglas takes snuff, which is just another form of nicotine addiction. Of course, that's all right, he comments, "because she done it herself."

So, Huck tells lies himself, sometimes for good reason, sometimes not. And he'll go along with other people's deceits, as he does with Tom Sawyer, and later on with the tricksters, who call themselves the duke and the dauphin, just for fun. But just the same, he sees through people, like the Widow Douglas. He sees through himself, as when he humbles himself to Jim. He sees through official morality, as when he tells lies to save Jim and then tears up the letter to his owner. What I'm going to say may sound odd; he's a habitual and enthusiastic liar. But he's what we used to call a soothsayer. He sees the truth and reports it. He doesn't always act on it, but he will if he has to.

We see the other side of Huck's freedom from illusion in several scenes of what we might call—it's the title of one of Twain's other books—*Life on the Mississippi*. As they drift on down into the southern states, Huck starts to encounter different communities, and the thing about them is, they live by their own rules. They're bound by their own rules. Their own rules prevent them from being free.

The most dramatic case comes when the raft is run over by a steamboat. Huck is thrown into the water, and when he comes ashore is sheltered by a family called the Grangerfords. Huck becomes fast friends with one of the Grangerford boys, named Buck. The Grangerfords aren't like anyone he's met before. They have a much more aristocratic ethos, with highly ceremonious behavior, and the head of the family is a colonel. But the main thing about them is that they are engaged in a bitter feud with another local aristocratic extended family, the Shepherdsons, with both sides continually ambushing and shooting each other.

Then, just like Romeo and Juliet, one of the Grangerford daughters decides to run off with a young Shepherdson, and this reignites the feud. It ends, as far as Huck is concerned, with Buck being shot dead. Huck lays out his body and covers his face, and weeps for his friend. No one remembers any more what the feud is about. Buck doesn't even dislike the Shepherdsons. When Huck says he thinks one of them was a coward for shooting an unarmed fourteen-year-old, Buck corrects him sharply, "There ain't a coward amongst them Shepherdsons—not a one."

They're not cowards, and they're not fools. But in a way, they're slaves to their own inherited and unexamined beliefs. And unlike Huck, unlike Jim as well, they can't free themselves. One could make the same sort of point about an attempted lynching Huck observes. The would-be lynchers are faced down by a lone man, another Southern gentleman. Why? Because in a way, they're play acting, acting out what they think is their own role. They can't stand up to a lone man, who, right or wrong, isn't play-acting.

Indeed, play acting becomes the dominant image of the later parts of the novel. Jim and Huck are taken over by a couple of tricksters, who claim to be aristocrats themselves; one says he is a rightful duke, the other, not wanting to be outdone, claims to be the rightful heir to the French throne, so that he calls himself the dauphin. Huck goes along with them, as he usually does, and creates a kind of sympathy for the rogues. After all, most of the people they cheat are cheats themselves. But when they try to swindle completely innocent people, Huck intervenes to save the victims. On the other hand, when he later sees the duke and the dauphin tarred and feathered and ridden out of town on a rail, he feels sorry for them as well. "Human beings can be awful cruel to one another," he remarks.

The last of the play-actors is, once again, Tom Sawyer. Huck, who by coincidence finds himself becoming the guest of Tom's Aunt Sally, actually has to pretend to be Tom. Then Tom turns up and keeps the ploy going by pretending to be his own brother Sid. Meanwhile, Jim has been caught and is locked up again, waiting to be returned to his owner Miss Watson. Huck is determined to rescue him, and Tom is very ready to help him. Unfortunately, Tom's romantic fantasies take over, and he insists on doing the rescue in the most complicated way possible. He's read about the *Man in the Iron Mask*, and the *Count of Monte Cristo*, and he's convinced a proper, elegant rescue should involve tunnels, and rope ladders, and messages in blood, and chains sawn through. It must require immense effort, and if possible, take years. He wants the whole thing to be like *The Shawshank Redemption*.

But the real joke, if it is a joke, is that the whole procedure is completely unnecessary. In the first place, all the boys really have to do is take the key to the lock from Uncle Silas's britches, get Jim's chain loose, and take to the river. Only Tom's fantasies prevent this plan from working. Worse than that, after their plan has failed, and Jim is once again chained up in a shed on bread and water, Tom confesses that they have no right to chain him up at all. Because, as he knew all along, Jim is not a slave any more. After he ran away Ms. Watson, his owner, got to feeling bad about it, and before she died, she put it in her will that Jim was to be freed. So, as Huck observes, Tom had gone to all that trouble to set a freed slave free. So, unlike Huck, Tom has never had to overcome his own conscience about stealing someone else's property. And, very much unlike Huck, he seems never to have had a twinge of conscience about using Jim and Huck as extras in his own incompetently produced drama.

Everyone around Huck is, in a way, self-imprisoned: by their own romantic illusions, like Tom; only slightly more self aware that Don Quixote; by their unexamined and inherited beliefs, like the slave owners and the isolated communities along the Mississippi. Huck is different from them all. He's naive and inexperienced. He's easily tricked by showmanship, as when he goes to the circus and thinks the tricks they put on are fresh and new and have never been done before. But he does see into the heart of things. If he knows something is wrong, he doesn't do it. He backs his own judgment against what people tell him, even if everybody tells him. He doesn't condemn people, mostly he's sorry for them. Because they, like the Grangerfords, like the duke and the dauphin, like the Widow Douglas and Miss Watson, they can't free themselves.

He speaks for a new attitude, an American attitude to authority and old tradition, a child's attitude to the phony and the pretentious. He may tell lies, but he sees the truth. He's the little boy who says the emperor has no clothes. And most of all, he has his own voice—casual, ungrammatical, understated, kind hearted. All these things are what make him the emblem of a new free spirit.

Sherlock Holmes—The First Great Detective
Lecture 16

In the later 1800s, two events occurred that had a significant impact on popular culture. The first of these was the arrival of public education and the creation of a new reading public. In turn, this public created a new set of heroes: the characters of Rider Haggard, Mark Twain, H. G. Wells, Jules Verne, Robert Louis Stevenson, and Bram Stoker. Collectively, these writers are sometimes referred to as the New Romancers. Also in the 1880s, characters began to escape from their creators and belong to their fans. That is certainly the case with the hero in this lecture: Sherlock Holmes.

A New Romance Hero

- By the 1880s, English-speaking countries had reached a high degree of literacy. Most of the authors who created heroes for these new readers can be seen in *The League of Extraordinary Gentlemen*, a movie based on Alan Moore's comic book series. These authors, called the New Romancers, included Rider Haggard, Mark Twain, H. G. Wells, and others.

- One prominent New Romance hero who is missing from the League of Extraordinary Gentlemen is Sherlock Holmes, the creation of Arthur Conan Doyle. He first appeared in the 1886 novel *A Study in Scarlet* and then figured in three more novels and 56 short stories.

- There's almost no need to describe Sherlock because he's become common property to a greater extent than any of our heroes so far. There have been movies, TV series, many sequels, and uncountable imitations related to Sherlock. Many of Sherlock's phrases have passed into common use.

- Sherlock introduced the idea of the private detective, or as he calls it, the consulting detective. He gave us the idea of the clue, the vital fact that explains a mystery. We could even say that he initiated the idea of forensic detection. The center of his novelty and his appeal, however, is the idea that there is always more information in things and people than (almost) anyone realizes.

- The signature moment for Sherlock's methods comes early in *A Study in Scarlet*, when Sherlock deduces that a man outside the window is a retired sergeant of Marines. In *The Sign of Four*, Watson asks Sherlock to tell him about the late owner of Watson's watch. Sherlock correctly guesses that it belonged to Watson's elder brother, who must have been a man of untidy habits, lived mostly in poverty, and died of drink. In a later story, Sherlock tells us that the basis of his method is observation, deduction, and information.

Outguessing Sherlock
- The real thrill of the stories has been the staple of the detective story ever since: trying to outguess Sherlock, almost always unsuccessfully. He always sees something we don't, and what we don't see is often pointed up by the regular police inspectors who compete with Sherlock, don't see it either, and always go for the simple explanation, which is wrong.

- For example, in "The Adventure of the Engineer's Thumb," an engineer describes how he was driven off to an unknown destination, where he lost his thumb. He says he was picked up from the railway station in a carriage, and Holmes asks whether the horse was tired or fresh. There seems to be no point to this question, but the fact that the horse looked fresh when it arrived at the station means that the secret destination cannot really have been 12 miles away. The engineer being taken there must have been driven in a circle.

- In *The Valley of Fear*, a man is found with his head all but blown off in a house that is surrounded by a moat and must be entered by a drawbridge. We might focus on all kinds of questions here, but Sherlock hones in on the fact that the dead man had only one dumbbell. He deduces that the missing dumbbell must have been used as a weight to sink something in the moat.

- For Sherlock, one fact is enough to destroy a hypothesis. In this respect, he is the first of the scientific detectives. In the "Adventure of the Bruce-Partington Plans," a man found dead on a railway track has no ticket in his pocket, although it's impossible to board the train without a ticket. Sherlock deduces that the man was placed on the roof of the train from an overhanging window and rolled off when the train went round a bend.

- In *A Study in Scarlet*, Watson writes that the mist in his mind was slowly clearing away and he began to have "a dim, vague perception of the truth." Sherlock tells him that the mist is the result of his failure to grasp the importance of the single real clue at the start of the inquiry. However, at the end, even most readers can't identify this single clue.

The Metropolis and Gothic Horror

- One of the reasons the world had to wait until the 1880s for a Sherlock-style character is that a private detective needs a metropolis. As Sherlock says several times, in Victorian London, 4 million souls were packed into a few square miles, with every opportunity for strange crimes and strange motivations.

In the ever-present fog of Sherlock Holmes's London, everything becomes mysterious.

- This metropolis is also part of a much wider world, the presence of which is felt surprisingly often in the London of Sherlock Holmes. In "The Adventure of the Five Orange Pips," the Ku Klux Klan pursues an informer. *A Study in Scarlet* brings in the Mormons of Utah. The first half of *The Valley of Fear* is set in Surrey, but the explanation of the man with his face destroyed takes us back to clashes between labor unions and the Pinkertons in West Virginia.

- Along with new settings and circumstances, we also find in the Sherlock stories a large dose of Gothic horror.
  o The best example of this is found in *The Hound of the Baskervilles*, which features an ancient legend, a giant hound, Stone Age huts on Dartmoor, an escaped criminal, and the bog called Grimpen Mire.

  o Sherlock himself is the acme of rationalism. He believes that everything has a natural cause, if only we can discover it. But he operates in a world that appears to others to be inscrutable, even supernatural. His job is often to dissolve the sense of Gothic horror, but the reader gets to shudder at the horrific settings before they're swept aside.

The Character of Sherlock

- Perhaps the main reason for Conan Doyle's extraordinary success is the character of Sherlock Holmes himself: impressive, original, and just barely likeable. Sherlock is a cocaine user and a heavy smoker, and he has a very un-rounded personality.

- Watson notes that although Sherlock knows almost everything about anything to do with his profession, he is both ignorant of, and incurious about, everything else. He knows nothing about literature or philosophy and very little about politics. He's an expert boxer, swordsman, and pistol shot but prone to fits of lethargy. He has no interest in the opposite sex, with the exception of Irene Adler, whom he regards respectfully as a worthy opponent.

- The Holmes/Watson combination is another example of a successful character pairing, similar to the pairing of Don Quixote and Sancho Panza. But Sherlock's relationship with Watson is rather odd. Holmes has a peculiar and callous way of interacting with his associate.
  o For example, Watson writes long reports of the goings-on at Baskerville Hall, but it turns out that they were largely useless. Holmes was hiding out on the moor all the time and hardly needed Watson to tell him what was going on.

- Even more culpably, Holmes allows Watson to think that he is dead at the hands of Professor Moriarty, only to shock him into fainting by turning up disguised as an old bookseller in "The Adventure of the Empty House."

- Narrow-minded, self-centered, an addictive personality—why has Holmes been such a success? Perhaps because he gives his readers a new sense of human potential. We could all be Sherlocks if we could learn to use our eyes and our brains better.

Later Detectives

- Sherlock established the template for the fictional detective. Miss Marple, Hercule Poirot, Nero Wolfe, and many others have followed in his footsteps. The image of the detective has, of course, been much affected by changes in culture and in crime.
  - The detective, whose activities are basically intellectual, mutated into the private eye, with a strong added streak of violence.

  - Opposed to the private eye story was the police procedural, in which results are achieved not by brilliant strokes of genius but by the dogged gathering of information.

  - We see a further stage in such novels and movies as *LA Confidential* or *Pulp Fiction*, when the cops and the robbers are difficult to tell apart, the criminals may be psychopaths, and the plots are so tangled that we feel even Sherlock would not be able to figure them out. Modern society does not have the underlying conviction of rational behavior, even among criminals, that Victorian society had.

- Nevertheless, the basic formula is still powerful. Doyle stories have been converted into many films and TV series, and they have found many authors to continue them. In addition, we should note the phenomenon of Sherlockians, those who treat Sherlock as a real person.

- This phenomenon started as early as 1912, when a scholar named Ronald Knox published "Studies in the Literature of Sherlock Holmes." The pompous title was itself a joke, but it's been followed up by many more such studies.

  - Today, there are many Sherlock Holmes societies, and the Internet is alive with websites where fans discuss problematic issues.

- Doyle actually provoked the continuation phenomenon by having Watson mention cases that he hadn't written up, such as "the affair of the giant rat of Sumatra," for which we are told, "The world is not yet ready."

- Sherlock has also been especially influential in science fiction and fantasy. For example, in the Lord Darcy stories, written by Randall Garrett, Lord Darcy is a Sherlock figure in a parallel universe.

- George MacDonald Fraser's *Flashman and the Tiger* is an affectionate parody of Doyle, in which a Sherlock character makes a mistaken deduction. Perhaps the truth in this story is that in the modern era, we have less confidence that everything can be solved by careful observation and intellectual deduction. Nevertheless, like all the great heroes and legends, Sherlock is capable of mutating into ever-more-successful forms.

Essential Reading

Doyle (Symons, ed.), *The Complete Adventures of Sherlock Holmes*.

Suggested Reading

Baring-Gould, *Sherlock Holmes of Baker Street*.

Klinger, ed., *The New Annotated Sherlock Holmes*.

1. Most of us come into contact with serious crime thousands of times in fiction but rarely or never in reality. Why do you think crime fiction has become such an important part of popular culture?

2. Changes in cultural values have often been mentioned in this course, but they seem to have made no impact on the popularity of Sherlock, clearly Victorian though he is. Why do you think that is?

Sherlock Holmes—The First Great Detective
Lecture 16—Transcript

In the later 1800s, two things happened which had a giant impact on popular culture, an irreversible impact, because the results are still with us. The first was the arrival of public education for everyone. In Britain this was brought about by the Elementary Education Act of 1870. In the USA, the history of public education is much more complicated, but the results were the same. By about the 1880s, the English-speaking countries had reached something like 100 percent literacy. This created a new reading public. And the new reading public created a new set of heroes.

This new reading public and the new heroes it created weren't popular with everybody. In fact, ever since, we've had a split between the English professors promoting highbrow literature, and the new reading public, the latter often written off—by the English professors—as vulgar, lowbrow, semi literate.

Now, there's no doubt about who won the argument, considered democratically. *The Strand Magazine*, for instance, was founded in 1891 and was aimed firmly at the new reading public. It regularly sold half a million copies a month. By contrast, the magazines of highbrow literature, like T. S. Eliot's *Criterion*, rarely reached four figures. Just the same, when I did my undergraduate degree at Cambridge University, we studied "the great tradition" of the English novel—George Eliot, Henry James, E. M. Forster, Virginia Woolf, and so on. We were told that Dickens was just an entertainer. And there was a whole body of famous writers who were never allowed on the syllabus at all.

These are the authors who have provided the famous heroes of our popular culture. You can see most of them in *The League of Extraordinary Gentlemen*, the movie based on Alan Moore's comic book series; there's Rider Haggard's Alan Quatermain, Mark Twain's Tom Sawyer, and contributions from H. G. Wells, Jules Verne, Robert Louis Stevenson, and Bram Stoker, all writers active in the 1880s and 1890s.

Collectively, these writers are sometimes referred to as "the New Romancers." You might say they were a backlash. The literary movement of modernism had created disenchantment. Its world was duller, more introspective, hostile to any form of fantasy. The New Romancers brought enchantment back, and they had good reason to, with an adventurous world opening up everywhere from the Wild West, to Transylvania, and Treasure Island, unexplored Africa and South America; not to mention, outer space, for another part of what the New Romancers did was open up a chink for the growth of science fiction and outright fantasy, which have been so prominent in our time. But till very recently, you would, for instance, never catch a professor of English literature saying a good word for someone like Tolkien. But then, like me, Tolkien was a professor of English language, not literature.

The other thing that happened in the 1880s was that the characters started to escape from their creators and belong to the fans. There's one prominent New Romance hero missing from the *League of Extraordinary Gentlemen*, and I'm told that that's because the creators of the League feared he would unbalance it and completely take it over. His name is Sherlock Holmes. He is the creation of Arthur Conan Doyle. He first appeared in the 1886 novel *A Study in Scarlet* and then figured in three more novels and 56 short stories, these latter collected into five volumes, dated 1892 to 1927. Most of the stories were published originally in *The Strand Magazine*, which I've already mentioned.

I almost don't need to describe Sherlock. He's become common property to a greater extent than any of our heroes so far, even more than hobbits. There have been movies, TV series, many sequels, and uncountable imitations. Well over a hundred authors have written and published Sherlock stories since he came out of copyright. I'll say more about the imitators at the end, but just note how many of Sherlock's phrases have passed into common use. There's "elementary, my dear Watson." This may, in fact, be a slight misquote, but that's what happens when characters become part of popular oral culture; there's, "It is a capital mistake to theorize before one has data;" there's, "When you have eliminated all which is impossible, then whatever remains, however improbable, must be the truth."

But beyond giving us these famous phrases, Sherlock did a lot of things. He introduced the idea of the private detective, or as he calls it, the consulting detective. He gives us the idea of the clue, the vital fact which explains a mystery. You could say that he started off the idea of forensic detection; he always carries his measuring tape and his magnifying glass. Pretty simple, compared with the apparatus which modern detectives routinely deploy, but it's the start of the idea.

I think the center of his novelty and his appeal, however, was the idea that there is always more information in things, and in people, than almost anyone realizes. The signature moment for Sherlock's methods comes early in *A Study in Scarlet*, when he and Watson have just met. Watson looks out of the window and says, "I wonder what that fellow is looking for?" Sherlock replies, "You mean the retired sergeant of Marines." Watson is unimpressed, because he thinks it's just a guess. But then the man comes in; says he's a hotel commissionaire; and Watson asks him what he was before that. He says, "A sergeant, sir, Royal Marine Light Infantry, sir."

How did Sherlock know? Well, he has a pretty big clue to start with, because the man had a blue anchor tattooed on the back of his hand, so he had something to do with the sea. However, he had side whiskers, whereas Royal Navy ratings had to sport a beard and moustache, or else no facial hair at all. He had an air of command as well and looked steady, respectable, middle-aged, all of which added up to being a sergeant of Marines.

That's pretty routine, by Sherlock standards. He does better in *The Sign of Four*, when Watson asks him what he can tell about the late owner of Watson's watch. Sherlock looks at it and says it belonged to your elder brother, which is a fair guess from the initials H. W. on the back and the age of the watch. But Sherlock goes on to say that Watson's elder brother must have been a man of untidy habits, who had good prospects, but threw away his chances, lived mostly in poverty, with short intervals of prosperity, and died in the end of drink.

Watson is offended and thinks that Sherlock must have been making personal enquiries about him. But Sherlock, as always, explains. He wasn't guessing. It's an expensive watch, but dented, which argues that it had a careless owner.

It also has pawnbroker ticket numbers scratched on the inside of the case several times, so the watch must've been pawned repeatedly, which accounts for the periods of poverty. But it was redeemed each time, so there must have been occasional bursts of prosperity. Finally, there are scratch marks all round the keyhole by which the watch was wound up. They indicate an unsteady hand, very likely the effects of drink.

Then there's the scene in "The Adventure of the Greek Interpreter," where Sherlock and his brother Mycroft are looking out of the window and trying to cap each other's deductions from another ex-soldier they see on the street. Sherlock says, an old soldier; Mycroft says, recently discharged; Sherlock says, served in India; Mycroft says, and an NCO; Royal Artillery, says Sherlock; and a widower, says Mycroft; but with a child, says Sherlock; but Mycroft corrects him and says, no, children, so winning the contest. The tricky bit in this, it seems to me, was deducing that he was Royal Artillery. His forehead is tanned more on one side and the other, which means he wasn't wearing a regular infantry helmet. He doesn't walk like a cavalryman, and he's too heavy to be a sapper, so he must've been in the artillery.

But the contest between the two brothers also points to Sherlock's particular abilities. He says that the basis of his methods is observation; deduction; information. Dr. Watson, as Sherlock tells him, sees but neither observes nor deduces. Mycroft does both, but he is physically lazy, which means that he does not gather information. Sherlock does, notably, by employing the Baker Street Irregulars, a gang of street children who see everything and report to him when required.

The real thrill of the stories, it seems to me, has been the staple of the detective story ever since. Which is, trying to outguess Sherlock, almost always unsuccessfully. He always sees something we don't, and what we don't see is often pointed up by the regular police inspectors, who compete with Sherlock, who don't see either, and always go for the simple explanation, which is wrong.

There are dozens of such scenes, so I give only a selection. In "The Adventure of the Engineer's Thumb" the engineer is describing how he was driven off to an unknown destination, where he lost his thumb. He says he was picked up from the railway station in a carriage, and Holmes asks, "One horse? What was the color? Tired or fresh?" There seems to be no point in these questions. What does it matter what the horse looked like? But, the fact that it looked fresh when it arrived at the station means that the secret destination cannot really have been twelve miles away. The engineer being taken there must have been driven in a circle.

In *The Valley of Fear*, a man is found with his head all but blown off by a sawn-off shotgun, in a house which has a moat round it and which has to be entered by a drawbridge. There are all kinds of questions one might think vital at this point, but what Sherlock picks on is the fact that the dead man had only one dumbbell. But dumbbells come in pairs. What does that matter? It means that the missing dumbbell must have been used for something, and what it was used for was to act as a weight, to sink something which must still be in the moat.

One fact, for Sherlock, is enough to destroy a hypothesis. In this respect he is the first of the scientific detectives. So, in the very late "Adventure of the Bruce-Partington Plans," there is the fact that the man found dead on the track in one of London's underground trains has no ticket in his pocket. Though it was considered impossible to board such a train without a ticket. What does that matter? Maybe he dropped it. But Sherlock deduces that he cannot have boarded the train. He was placed on the roof from an overhanging window and rolled off when the train went round a bend.

Back at the start of Sherlock's career, in *A Study in Scarlet*, once again, Watson writes that the mist in his mind was slowly clearing away, and he began to have "a dim, vague perception of the truth," which is what most of us readers get to. Sherlock tells him, it's because at the start of the inquiry, he failed to grasp the importance of the single real clue. It's typical that even though I've read the story, I don't actually know, even at the end, which one was the single real clue. Was it the wedding ring? Was it the tracks made by the cab? It certainly wasn't the word *Rache*, revenge, written in blood on the wall. Even I could see that that didn't help much.

Well, the observation and deduction formula, the scattering of real clues and false clues, have been part of detective fiction ever since. But there are other causes for the outstanding success of Sherlock Holmes and reasons also why such a character could not have existed before. One of the reasons why we had to wait until the 1880s for a Sherlock-style character is that a private detective really needs a metropolis. As Sherlock says several times, in Victorian London you had four million souls packed into a few square miles, with every opportunity for strange crimes and strange motivations.

The atmosphere of the Sherlock Holmes stories is also a large part of their appeal—the ever-present London fog, in which everything becomes mysterious; the gas lamps which give partial light; the horse-drawn cabs in the street, which help the criminals to escape and the detectives to follow—and the national rail service, so much better than anything we have in Britain now!

This metropolis is also very much part of a much wider world. It's surprising how often that wider world makes its presence felt in the London of Sherlock Holmes. In "The Adventure of the Five Orange Pips" we have the Ku Klux Klan pursuing an informer. *A Study in Scarlet* brings in the Mormons of Utah. The first half of *The Valley of Fear* is set in Surrey, but the explanation of the man with his face destroyed takes us back to clashes between labor unions and the Pinkertons in, I would guess, West Virginia. ["The Adventures of Black Peter"] has us involved with whalers in the Arctic, *The Sign of Four* brings in a pygmy from the Andaman Islands in the Indian Ocean, with his deadly poison darts and blowpipe. European royalty is responsible for "A Scandal in Bohemia," and in the background of ["The Adventure of the Bruce-Partington Plans"] lie submarine warfare and the threat of the great conflict which would become World War I.

Along with the new settings and the new circumstances, however, there is a large dose of good, old Gothic horror. "The Adventure of the Speckled Band" is a locked-room mystery with an isolated house, strange low whistles, and a young woman gasping out as her last words, "the speckled band!" It turns out that she's been bitten by a trained Indian swamp adder which comes down a dummy bell-rope. Strange faces are seen at windows in "The Adventure of the Yellow Face" and "The Adventure of the Blanched Soldier."

The best example of Gothicism, however, is *The Hound of the Baskervilles*, which has not only an ancient legend, a giant hound, Stone Age huts on Dartmoor, and an escaped criminal who looks very much like a caveman himself, but also Grimpen Mire, one of the best of those sucking bogs and quicksands, which we find so often in fantasy fiction.

Sherlock himself is the acme of rationalism. He thinks everything has a natural cause, if only we can discover it. But he operates within a world which appears to others to be inscrutable, even supernatural. His job is often to dissolve that sense of Gothic horror, but the reader gets to shudder at the horrific settings before they're swept aside. London atmosphere, wide world outside, Gothic settings and scenarios, still, the main reason for Conan Doyle's extraordinary success is the character of Sherlock Holmes himself—impressive, original, on the edge of not being likeable.

I'm even inclined to call him a sociopath. At the start of *The Sign of Four*, he is notoriously shooting up with a seven-and-a-half-percent solution of cocaine. In the late Victorian period this did not have the aura of criminality which it does now, but even so, it causes Dr. Watson some anxiety. Sherlock is also a heavy smoker, and he's a very un-rounded personality. Dr. Watson notes that while Sherlock knows almost everything about anything to do with his profession, he is not only ignorant of, but also incurious about, everything else. He doesn't know whether the Earth goes round the sun or the sun round the Earth and sees no point in knowing.

He knows nothing about literature or philosophy, very little about politics, and in botany, he knows a great deal about poisons, but nothing of practical gardening. He's an expert boxer and swordsman, and pistol shot as well, but prone to fits of lethargy. He has no interest in the opposite sex, with the exception of Irene Adler, whom he regards respectfully as a worthy opponent.

His relationship with Watson is rather odd as well; though it's worth noting that the Holmes-Watson combination is yet another example of successful pairings, started off as we've already seen by Don Quixote and Sancho Panza. But Holmes has a peculiar and rather callous way of interacting with his associate. Several times Watson takes offense, as well he might, at the way Sherlock uses him. Watson writes long reports of the goings on at Baskerville Hall, but it turns out that they were largely useless. Holmes was hiding out on the moor all the time and hardly needed Watson to tell him what was going on.

Even more culpably, Holmes allows Watson to think that he is dead at the hands of Professor Moriarty, only to return and shock him into fainting by turning up disguised as an old bookseller, in "The Adventure of the Empty House." The explanation given is that Holmes knows he is being stalked by Moriarty's accomplice, Colonel Moran, known as Tiger Moran from his fame as a big-game hunter. Sherlock needs to set a trap in Baker Street, while he and Watson wait in the house opposite, from which Moran will take his shot. And it's true that this reversal was forced on Doyle by his fans. When he wrote about Holmes's death, he was actually trying to kill him off so he wouldn't have to write any more stories. So you might say that it wasn't just Watson who was kept in the dark. Just the same, the trick of appearing in disguise and suddenly throwing it off with no warning seems at best, heartless. Sherlock just likes to show his skill. He has little idea, or concern, about the effect this will have on others.

Narrow minded, self-centered, an addictive personality, why has he been such a success? I think it's because he gives all his readers a new sense of human potential. We could all be Sherlocks if we could learn to use our eyes better, and our brains. We never do it, if we got to the answer before Sherlock did, it would spoil the story. But, we enjoy testing our ingenuity against Sherlock's, and against Conan Doyle's. In that respect, Sherlock established the template for the fictional detective. Miss Marple, Hercule Poirot, Nero Wolfe, and a whole string of others have followed in his footsteps.

The image has, of course been much affected by changes in culture and in crime. The detective, whose activities are basically intellectual, mutated into the "private eye," who had a strong streak of violence added. Opposed to the private-eye story was the "police procedural," in which results are achieved not by brilliant strokes of genius, but by dogged gathering of information.

There's a further stage in novels and movies like *LA Confidential* or *Pulp Fiction*, when the cops and the robbers are hard to tell apart, the criminals may be psychopaths, and the plots are so tangled that you feel even Sherlock would not be able to figure them out. Modern society, you might deduce, does not have the underlying conviction of rational behavior, even among criminals, which Victorian society had.

Nevertheless, the basic formula is still powerful. Doyle stories have been converted into many films and TV series, but they have also found many continuators, and these are not people writing for a franchise. They are just people who want to write about Sherlock Holmes. Along with that, and remembering what I said earlier about characters getting away from their creator, there's the whole phenomenon of Sherlockians, who treat Sherlock as a real person. Of course, it's a joke, but a joke played out with intense seriousness.

This started as early as 1912, when a scholar called Ronald Knox published "Studies in the Literature of Sherlock Holmes." The pompous title was itself a joke, but it's been followed up by many more such studies, including *Dr. Watson: Prolegomena to the Study of a Biographical Problem* in 1931, and *Sherlock Holmes, Fact or Fiction?* in 1932. Writers and scientists and even politicians joined in. Franklin Delano Roosevelt argued that Holmes must really have been an American. There are many Sherlock Holmes societies, and the internet is alive with websites in which fans discuss problematic issues, like the wound which Dr. Watson received in Afghanistan. Was it in the leg, or in the shoulder? Could it have been both? Or could Doyle just have made a mistake? No, that's the one answer which Sherlockians will not accept.

Doyle actually provoked the continuation phenomenon, because Watson is in the habit of mentioning cases which he hasn't actually written up, like "The Affair of the Giant Rat of Sumatra," for which we are told, "the world is not yet ready." So it's no wonder that many people have decided to "write into the gaps," which Watson disclosed for them.

Curiously, Sherlock has been especially influential on science fiction and fantasy. One of my own favorite series is the Lord Darcy stories, written by Randall Garrett, in which Lord Darcy is a Sherlock figure in a parallel universe in which magic works. Naturally, his cases often require a knowledge of magic for their solution, and his Dr. Watson figure is Master Sean, an Irish sorcerer who complements Darcy's knowledge and abilities much more than Dr. Watson ever did for Sherlock.

I'll close, though, with an affectionate parody of Doyle, once again, written by someone who is clearly a fan. It's George MacDonald Fraser, author of the popular Flashman series, whose central character is the coward and bully Flashman first seen in Thomas Hughes' 1850s classic, *Tom Brown's Schooldays*.

In Fraser's collection, *Flashman and the Tiger*, the Tiger is Tiger Moran. And Fraser has inserted Flashman into Doyle's "Adventure of the Empty House." That's the one where Sherlock and Watson have set a trap for Moran after Sherlock has come back from the dead. According to Fraser, there was someone else stalking Tiger Moran. It was Flashman, for reasons of his own. It turned out he didn't have to shoot Moran, because Sherlock caught him first. But as Holmes and Watson come out of the empty house, Flashman has to disguise himself so that he's not exposed.

He's already shabbily dressed; he tips the contents of his hip flask over himself; and lies in the doorway pretending to be a drunk. Will they please just pass him by? No, he reports. Two men bend over him, a tall, thin man— Sherlock Holmes, and a big chap with a bulldog moustache, who must be Watson.

Sherlock then does his trick of deducing things from what he observes. The drunk must be a German he says, who studied at a second-rate German university. This is a deduction from the fact that Flashman has a dueling scar suffered in an earlier adventure, which we know was placed slightly off center, not because it was done at a second-rate university, but because Flashman, as always, dodged and twisted. The drunk must be working as a ship's steward, Sherlock continues, he's recently been in America, he's heading for Hamburg, he's descended to at least the fringes of crime, and is now mis-spending his shore leave.

All this is deduced from the fact that Flashman is wearing a pea jacket, like a sailor, but has particularly good boots on and well-trimmed nails, hair, and moustache. all of which suggests that he has some contact with first-class passengers. He also has a silver hip flask, which Sherlock assumes he must have stolen. The Hamburg destination comes from Sherlock's encyclopedic knowledge of steamer movements. And the idea that he has recently been in America comes from Sherlock's conclusion that the old drunk smells of bourbon whiskey, a taste, he declares, rarely found outside the USA.

Flashman is particularly offended by this latter deduction, as he lies there pretending to be unconscious, because he knows quite well that what was in his hip flask was best brandy; bourbon whisky, thinks Flashman indignantly, "as if I'd pollute my liver with that rotgut." The other half of the joke is that Dr. Watson almost recognized Flashman right at the start, and he keeps saying doubtfully, "well I'm sure you're right, but he does look very like old General What's-his name." What would a general be doing sleeping in an alleyway? asks Sherlock scornfully. Well, Sherlock, there's things even you don't know.

It's a very affectionate parody, and I suppose the moral is, as we often say in the computer era, "garbage in, garbage out." Sherlock went wrong as soon as he mistook brandy for bourbon, and after that, all his deductions went astray. Maybe the truth is that in this modern era of computers we have even less confidence that everything can be solved by careful observation and intellectual deduction. A tape and a magnifying glass just won't hack it any more. Nevertheless, like all the great heroes and legends, Sherlock is capable of mutating into ever more successful forms.

Dracula—The Allure of the Monster
Lecture 17

The origins of Dracula can be traced back to perhaps the most successful literary vacation in world history, which took place in Switzerland in the summer of 1816. At a villa there were assembled Percy Shelley, Mary Wollstonecraft Godwin, Lord Byron, John William Polidori (Byron's physician), and others. When the vacationers grew bored, they decided that they would all write horror stories. Mary started on what would become *Frankenstein; or, The Modern Prometheus*. Byron started a vampire story but abandoned it. Polidori later published a story called "The Vampyre," which was thought to be by Byron and achieved something of a vogue. Other vampire stories followed, priming the reading public for Bram Stoker's 1897 novel *Dracula*.

Structure and Opening of *Dracula*

- *Dracula* is a structurally complex work, almost an epistolary novel. In addition to Dracula and his brides, there are seven main characters: Jonathan Harker, an estate agent; Jonathan's fiancée, Wilhelmina, known as Mina; Mina's friend Lucy Westenra; and three men who want to marry Lucy: Arthur Holmwood, the one she accepts; Jack Seward, a doctor who runs a lunatic asylum; and a Texan called Quincey P. Morris. The final character is a Dutchman and an expert on strange diseases, Professor van Helsing.

- The story of *Dracula* is told through letters between Lucy and Mina, Mina's private journal, Dr. Seward's diary, excerpts from newspaper reports, additional letters, and the journal of Jonathan Harker. Jonathan's journal, the first 60 or 70 pages of the novel, established the ground rules for all future vampire fiction.

- In the journal, we read that Jonathan sets off in a coach, but all the other passengers are terrified at his mention of Count Dracula's castle. The landlady at the inn presses a crucifix on Jonathan before the journey.

- o The count meets Jonathan at a prearranged rendezvous point, and the two drive off; howling wolves escort the carriage until the count commands them to go away.

- o The count's hands are as cold as ice. He has a cruel mouth and sharp teeth. His nails are long and cut to a point. He has hair on the palms of his hands. Jonathan notices that his reflection doesn't show up in a mirror.

- o When Jonathan cuts himself shaving, the blood seems to infuriate the count.

© iStockphoto/Thinkstock.

The first section of Dracula sets up the "rules" for vampires: the cold hands and sharp teeth, lack of reflection in mirrors, and fear of crucifixes.

- o When the two of them sit up talking, the count leaves as soon as he hears a cock crow at dawn. And he is repelled by the crucifix that the landlady at the inn had given to Jonathan.

- o In a scene that became a movie classic, Jonathan sees the count emerging from a window and crawling down the castle wall over a precipice, "*face down*, with his cloak spreading out around him like great wings."

- o Soon, Jonathan realizes that the castle is a prison, and he is a prisoner. But the count is a gentleman, even a gracious host, and it's difficult for Jonathan to turn him down. The count also speaks with great pride of his ancestors.

- Also present in the castle are the brides of Dracula. Jonathan first sees them when he wakes in the night and notes that they are "ladies by their dress and manner." But they don't behave in a ladylike way, and Jonathan does not respond to them as a gentleman should.

- o Although he is engaged to Mina, Jonathan confesses to his journal a "wicked, burning desire that they would kiss me with those red lips." And the three ladies are dead set on doing just that.

- o Jonathan is saved by Dracula, who chases the three women off, saying, "This man belongs to me." Nevertheless, Jonathan has nearly been seduced.

- Later on, in despair at his growing understanding that he has been made a prisoner and reserved for some unpleasant fate, he finds the count in his coffin, looking young, fresh, and gorged with blood. Jonathan tries to kill him with a shovel but fails and escapes over the castle wall.

Hidden Fears

- Obviously, vampire stories are about sex and repression, and they trade on our hidden fears. It's important to note that a vampire can cross one's threshold only if invited in. We might say that's true psychologically, as well as physically. There must be something that welcomes the vampire in.

- What are the hidden fears that vampire stories address? A common one for men is that women are more interested in the "bad boy"— the serial seducer—than the nice guy.
  - o Count Dracula is the bad boy to a higher power. He conquers both Lucy and Mina and boasts about it to the other men: "Your girls that you all love are mine already."

  - o The girls seem innocent in their encounters with Dracula, but we don't know what was in their hearts.

- How does the count gain power over these young ladies? There's more than a suggestion that he creates in them a sexual awakening that their husbands and fiancés cannot match. Stoker repeatedly uses the key word "voluptuous," which derives from Latin *voluptas* and means "sexual pleasure." Note also that the physical descriptions associated with the word "voluptuous" are decidedly not the Victorian female ideal.

○ The brides of Dracula are voluptuous, as we might expect, but they aren't the only ones. After Lucy has encountered the count, her fiancé, Arthur, comes into her room, and she speaks to him "in a soft, voluptuous voice."

○ Later on, when we see Lucy, now dead, possessed, and risen from her grave, we're told that her purity has changed to "voluptuous wantonness." As she lies in her coffin, the men see her "blood-stained, voluptuous mouth" and think that it looks like "a devilish mockery of Lucy's sweet purity."

- Another fear that has a role in the novel is the Victorian fear of syphilis, a disease that has a long incubation period, is asymptomatic for a long time, and was incurable and, eventually, fatal. Like syphilis, the curse of the vampire is passed on; the victim becomes a vampire. Fortunately, if the vampire is killed, then the infected "undead" can be cured. They can die, like the brides and Dracula himself, or they can live naturally, like the children whom Lucy has been preying on since she contracted the vampire infection.

- Both *Dracula* and *Frankenstein* have some basis in the scientific beliefs of their time. In the 19th century, some thought it possible that life could be restored to the dead by "galvanism." That's part of the scenario in *Frankenstein*, and in *Dracula*, van Helsing has ideas about it, too. But in *Dracula*, the question is whether life could be restored or prolonged by blood.

○ People were already experimenting with blood transfusion. Only four years after the appearance of *Dracula*, Karl Landsteiner discovered the existence of the different types of blood, knowledge of which is necessary for safe transfusion.

○ In *Dracula*, Lucy receives several transfusions from her lovers to make up for the blood she has lost to the count. This must have been known to be dangerous in 1897, and when van Helsing is doing it, he mentions that there is no need to "defibrinate" (filter) Arthur's blood for Lucy because the young man's blood is "pure."

- o Van Helsing may mean that Arthur is morally pure rather than physically pure. But just as physical infection doesn't necessarily imply moral infection, so moral purity—which we're prepared to accept that Arthur has—cannot guarantee physical purity and, thus, a safe transfusion.

- o Consider how someone catches syphilis. If one partner in a marriage catches the disease, it means that someone must have engaged in premarital or extramarital sex. Thus, the physical and the moral are strongly connected, and van Helsing's remark is not as naïve as it seems.

Modern Vampires
- With *Dracula*, it's obvious that we have another case of changed cultural values, perhaps created by changed technology. With antibiotics and reliable contraception, the modern world is not as frightened about sexual dangers as the Victorian world was. At the same time, the feminine ideal has also changed, and female voluptuousness is not an automatic sign of evil. Why, then, has the vampire become even more a staple of popular fiction?

- Stoker left several openings for development in his story and in the character of Dracula, and as we've seen, later writers often write into a gap left by a favorite predecessor.
  - o Mina sets up one such development. Near the end of the novel, when Jonathan is cursing Dracula to eternal damnation, Mina points out that Dracula, too, is a victim who needs to be saved. The point is dramatized when the men fight their way through to Dracula's coffin and kill him. Dr. Seward writes in his diary that at the last moment, Dracula's face wore "a look of peace."

- This establishes the idea of the "good vampire," one struggling against his or her nature. This idea has been developed in many contemporary vampire books and movies, such as Terry Pratchett's comic Discworld novels and Stephenie Meyer's Twilight series.

- Another gap that cried out for development is the idea of the *longaevus*, the near-immortal. Stoker's Dracula is immensely proud of his ancestry, but we never know how old he is. Is it possible that when he boasts about his ancestry, he's really boasting about himself?

  - Once people started researching the origins of the vampire belief, the idea emerged that perhaps Dracula had been a historical figure; the 15th-century ruler Vlad the Impaler is often suggested. Dracula, after all, is a nickname. It derives from Latin (as repronounced in Romanian) *draco ille*, "the dragon."

  - If Dracula is a *longaevus*, how many more are there? Interest then started to focus on Professor van Helsing. Stoker brings him in as an expert on infectious diseases, but he seems to know much that is not merely medical. Perhaps he is a *longaevus*, too.

- Finally, later authors have addressed the hidden fears of society, so crucial to the success of Stoker's *Dracula*. We may no longer be terrified of female sexuality, but we have become much readier to believe in secret organizations dedicated to our downfall, such as those in Ian Fleming's James Bond books. Perhaps there are also secret orders dedicated to the fight against the undead; that's the premise of Stephen Sommers's 2004 movie *Van Helsing*.

- Stoker could never have imagined how some of the gaps he left would be developed. But that's what happens when fictional characters become part of the ever-growing global imaginary of Extraordinary Gentlemen—legendary heroes and heroines.

Essential Reading

Stoker (Hindle, ed.), *Dracula*.

Shelley (Hindle, ed.), *Frankenstein; or, The Modern Prometheus*.

Suggested Reading

Clements, *The Vampire Defanged*.

Klinger, ed., *The New Annotated Dracula*.

Questions to Consider

1. What is your own favorite take on the vampire legend, and why does it appeal to you?

2. What kind of fears or other responses are created in a specifically female audience by the vampire legend?

Dracula—The Allure of the Monster

Lecture 17—Transcript

In our last lecture, I introduced you to a group of writers sometimes dubbed the "New Romancers." The character I'm going to talk about today is another creation of the New Romancers. Like Sherlock, he too was not incorporated in the League of Extraordinary Gentlemen. He's definitely extraordinary; he's a gentleman too, but you still wouldn't want him on your side, even if he was available, which fortunately, he isn't. The creators of the League of Extraordinary Gentlemen, nevertheless, gave more than a nod in his direction, for the lady of the League is Mina Harker, who is our character's victim, partner, in a sense, his creation. I'm talking about Count Dracula.

Now, in these lectures I don't usually take too much trouble over sources, but in this case, I think the origins of *Dracula* are worth a look. They go back quite directly to what must be the most successful literary vacation in world history; it took place in Switzerland in the summer of 1816. There, at the Villa Diodati, were assembled, 1) the poet Percy Shelley; 2) his partner, Mary Wollstonecraft Godwin, whom he would soon marry; 3) Mary's stepsister, Jane Clairmont; 4) Jane's lover, the poet and European literary celebrity Lord Byron; and 5) Lord Byron's personal physician John William Polidori, whose nephew and niece, by the way, were the poet Christina Rossetti and the painter Dante Gabriel Rossetti.

Anyway, it was a dull, wet summer, and the party at the Villa got bored. They decided they'd all write horror stories. Mary started on what would become Frankenstein, or the Modern Prometheus, published under her married name of Mary Shelley in 1818. Byron started a vampire story, but abandoned it. Polidori picked the idea up and published a short story called "The Vampyre" in 1819. It really isn't very good. In my opinion, if Polidori had sent it in to the editors of Weird Tales a hundred years later, the editors would have rejected it without hesitation; it's one of those stories which end up with a perfectly obvious conclusion, reinforced by capital letters and an exclamation point to add the excitement which the story had failed to generate: "Aubrey's sister had glutted the thirst of a VAMPYRE!"

Nevertheless, for a while it was thought to be by Byron, the European celebrity and bad boy, so it achieved something of a vogue. Well, there were then further vampire stories in the 19th century, like James Rymer's *Varney the Vampire* and Sheridan Le Fanu's *Carmilla*, so the reading public was pretty well primed for vampires. But the real originator of the vampire craze, which is still with us, was Bram Stoker's 1897 novel *Dracula*.

You see what I mean about the most successful literary vacation. I'm told that, to date, there have been 115 Frankenstein movies, but Dracula beats even that with 161. Where would the horror film industry be without the products of that wet summer? And the number of literary and multimedia adaptations, sequels, versions is past counting—all the way from *Buffy the Vampire Slayer* to Edward Cullen in Stephenie Meyers's *Twilight* series, with a whole host of werewolf and zombie fictions round the margins.

Now, *Dracula* as written by Stoker, is a very complex work structurally; it's kind of an epistolary novel, not told by one narrator, but presented from many different viewpoints. There are seven main characters besides Dracula and his brides. There's Jonathan Harker, sent out to Transylvania to complete a property purchase by Count Dracula himself; there's Jonathan's fiancée Wilhelmina, known as Mina; there's Mina's friend, Lucy Westenra—that makes three; then there are the three men who want to marry Lucy—Arthur Holmwood, the one she accepts; Jack Seward, a doctor who runs a lunatic asylum; and a Texan called Quincey P. Morris. These three men all know and like each other, but when they find themselves out of their depth, they call in the seventh important character, an expert on strange diseases, a Dutchman, Professor Van Helsing, at the suggestion of Dr. Seward, who was once a pupil of his. The story is accordingly told by letters from Lucy to Mina and vice versa, Mina's private journal, Dr. Seward's diary, excerpts from newspaper reports, and other letters backwards and forwards.

The most influential section of the whole novel, though, must be the first 60 or 70 pages, the journal of Jonathan Harker. We might note that it's always a good idea in writing a story to start with the best stuff you have. This section really establishes the ground rules for all future vampire fiction. So, let's quickly review both the events and the general mood of Harker's journal. He sets off in a coach, but all the other passengers are terrified as soon as he mentions Count Dracula's castle. The landlady at the inn before he sets off presses a crucifix on him. The driver speeds up and up as it gets dark and tries to get to the place of rendezvous before the Count does. But it's no good. The Count was expecting this and is there already in his own carriage. Next, Dracula sets off with Jonathan in the dark and into a wilderness, which is full of wolves, which escort the carriage, howling. But they fall silent and disappear as soon as the Count commands them.

The Count himself has a hand as cold as ice. He has a cruel mouth and sharp teeth. His nails are long and cut to a point. He has hair on the palm of his hands. Once they get inside the castle, Jonathan notices there is no mirror in the hall. He has a shaving glass with him, but when he uses it, he notices that the Count behind him does not show up in it. When Jonathan cuts himself shaving, the blood seems to infuriate the count. When the two of them sit up talking, the Count leaves immediately he hears a rooster crow at dawn. And he is repelled by the crucifix the landlady at the inn gave his guest. And in a scene which became a movie classic, Jonathan sees the Count emerging from a window and crawling down the castle wall over a precipice, "face down, with his cloak spreading out around him like great wings." Well, anyone nowadays would know what all this means, and pretty soon Jonathan himself realizes that the castle is a prison, and he is a prisoner.

But there's another side to this. The Count is a gentleman, even a gracious host. It's hard for Jonathan to turn him down, and there's an odd kind of etiquette. On his arrival the Count says very carefully, "Welcome to my house! Enter freely and of your own will!" It's only once Jonathan has stepped over the threshold that he's greeted warmly. The Count also speaks with great pride of his ancestors as defenders of Europe and Christianity against the Turk; it's all very impressive.

But there are other creators of, what shall I call it, moral ambiguity? I mean, the Brides of Dracula. Jonathan has fallen asleep. He wakes up in the moonlight and he sees "three young women, ladies by their dress and manner." You remember what I said before, talking about Elizabeth Bennet, about the vital line that separates ladies and gentlemen from everybody else. Ladies they are, then, two brunettes and one blonde, but they don't behave in a ladylike way, and Jonathan does not respond to them as he should if they were ladies. Although he is engaged to Mina, and he remembers perfectly well that he is, he confesses to his journal a "wicked, burning desire that they would kiss me with those red lips." The three ladies are dead set on doing just that, if only to start with. They argue about who goes first, but they're all intent on kissing him, which he notes "in an agony of delightful anticipation." I feel sure that somewhere someone has made a pornographic film version of this scene, and if Stoker weren't writing a Victorian novel, no doubt even he would have had to go further here.

Jonathan is saved by Dracula, who chases the three women off, saying: "This man belongs to me," at least for now. Nevertheless, Jonathan has been very nearly seduced. Later on, in despair at his growing understanding that he has been made a prisoner and reserved for some unpleasant fate, he finds the Count in his coffin box, looking young, fresh, gorged with blood, and he tries to kill him with a shovel. He fails, however, and escapes over the castle wall. But we have to infer this, because the novel at this point switches suddenly to Mina and Lucy, back in England, writing each other rather flirty letters about men.

I'm sure we all get the idea by now. Vampire stories are really about sex, and about repression. And what they trade on are our hidden fears. Note that there is an important rule, which has been hinted at already – the vampire can only cross the threshold if invited in. We might say that that's true psychologically as well as physically. There has to be something there that welcomes the Count in, or in Jonathan's case, something that welcomed his brides in. We might say that this is very like the Ring in Tolkien's story. The One Ring corrupts anyone who uses it, and no one is immune to it. But it works by focusing on and corrupting some desire which is in the secret heart of the person who uses it; it may be an urge to do good, as is the case with Gandalf or Galadriel, or it may be the urge to protect Gondor, as is the case with Boromir, but there's always something there for the Ring to work on.

Tolkien's Ring, however, is about power. Vampires, as I just said, are about sex and hidden fears. What are these hidden fears? Well, there's a common masculine belief that what women really want, in their secret hearts, is not Mr. Right, Mr. Nice Guy, but Mr. Bad Boy—the unreliable male, the serial seducer, the bedpost notcher. I'm not saying this is true. The belief may well tell us more about masculine insecurity than female behavior. But we've seen it already in this course. There's Criseyde, who throws over Troilus, who really loves her, for Diomedes, who is very clearly a bedpost notcher and will abandon her as soon as he's got what he wanted; and serve her right, said Robert Henryson chauvinistically, no doubt, prompted by his own fears.

There are, of course, no bedpost notchers in Jane Austen. But remember that Elizabeth Bennet, good and sensible though she is, shows signs of being won over by Mr. Wickham. She's very ready to believe him when he tells her bad stories about Mr. Darcy. And Wickham, though he does not succeed in seducing Elizabeth, does seduce and elope with her sister Lydia, whom we might see, if we were feeling Freudian, as a kind of Elizabeth proxy. And in Helen Fielding's makeover of Pride and Prejudice, Bridget Jones' Diary, Bridget Jones does, in fact, sleep with the Bad Boy, Daniel Cleaver, and even shows signs of going back to him after she's hooked up with Mr. Darcy.

Well, putting it briefly, Count Dracula is the Bad Boy to a higher power. He conquers Lucy. He conquers Mina. He boasts about it to the other men, "Your girls that you all love are mine already." Of course, it's not the girls' fault, and they feel really bad about it in the morning. Mina cries out, "Unclean, unclean! I must touch him or kiss him no more." She admits, "Strangely enough, I did not want to hinder him. I suppose it is a part of the horrible curse that such is, when his touch is on his victim." Not my fault, in other words. When Van Helsing puts a consecrated wafer on Mina's forehead to protect her, it burns and scars her, and she cries out again, "Unclean! Unclean! Even the Almighty shuns my polluted flesh! I must bear this mark of shame upon my forehead until the Judgment Day."

As I keep saying, we're told this is not their fault. But who knows what was in their hearts? I might say that I am not the only one to have this kind of suspicion. In one of the many movies made about Dracula, in this case, *Dracula 2001*, there's a scene in which the Count walks into a Virgin record shop; note the name of it. He's dressed normally and has nothing visibly extraordinary about him, but as soon as he walks in, all the young women in the shop turn and look at him. He's a Bad Boy. He has something the rest of us don't.

Let's probe a little deeper into this male fear of the seductive Bad Boy. How does the Count gain power over these young ladies? Well, there's more than a suggestion that he creates in them a sexual awakening, which their loving husbands and fiancés cannot match. There's a keyword here, and it's "voluptuous." Stoker uses this word again and again. Note that it derives from Latin *voluptas*, which means, pleasure, sexual pleasure. Note also that the physical descriptions associated with the word are very much not the Victorian female ideal. Ladies are supposed to be sweet, pale, fragile, and above all pure, not curvy, red lipped and full blooded.

The brides of Dracula are voluptuous, as we might have expected, but they aren't the only ones. After Lucy has encountered the Count, her fiancé Arthur comes into her room and she says to him, "in a soft, voluptuous voice, such as I had never heard from her lips: 'Arthur! Oh, my love, I am so glad you have come! Kiss me!'" But when he stoops to do so, Van Helsing seizes him and pulls him back. Later on, when we see Lucy, now dead, possessed, and risen from her grave, we're told that her purity has changed to "voluptuous wantonness." And as she lies in her coffin, the men see her pointed teeth, her "blood-stained, voluptuous mouth," and think that it looks like "a devilish mockery of Lucy's sweet purity." As I said before, and I say it again, we're told that this is not Lucy's fault. But are we absolutely sure about that? Remember what I said about there having to be something inside which calls to the Count.

In another movie, the excellent 1992 one directed by Francis Ford Coppola, and titled, quite truthfully, *Bram Stoker's Dracula*, the director played Lucy up a bit. She has, after all, got three suitors, and even Stoker has her say, or rather write, in a letter to Mina, "Why can't they let a girl marry three men, or as many as want her, and save all this trouble?" We know she's only joking. But the movie makes her out to be, not unreasonably, what we might call a party girl in the making. She even employs some very heavy double entendres when she's talking to Quincey, who is sporting his big bowie knife. "Isn't it big? Can I feel it?" Yes, I know, this is modern vulgarity, but it's not completely unprovoked or without a source in Stoker's text. So, masculine fear one, fear of the Bad Boy; masculine fear two, he's got something I haven't; masculine fear three, and that something, it spreads.

Maybe you remember the lines from Tennyson, which I quoted when I was talking about Guinevere:

> "I hold that man the worst of public foes / who either for his own or children's sake, / to save his blood from scandal, lets the wife / whom he knows false, abide and rule the house./ She, like a new disease, unknown to men, / creeps, no precaution used, among the crowd."

Save his blood, okay? No precaution used, okay? What is Tennyson talking about? It sounds like the Victorian fear, not of AIDS, but of syphilis. Like AIDS, incurable; eventually fatal; long incubation time; asymptomatic for a long time, so anyone might have it, and you wouldn't know. Creeps among the crowd, okay? This is surely part of the vampire fear. The curse is passed on. The victim becomes a vampire. The infectee becomes an infector. That's kind of what Van Helsing says to Mina, speaking his rather imperfect English, "He have infected you… He infect you in such wise that even if you do no more [he] shall make you like to him."

The good thing is that if the vampire is killed, then the infected undead can be cured. They can die, like the brides, like Dracula himself. Or they can live naturally, like the children whom Lucy has been preying on since she contracted the vampire infection. The cure is possible, as was not the case in Victorian times for syphilis. The sign of the cure, for Mina, is when the scar on her forehead made by the holy wafer vanishes, once Dracula has been beheaded and staked and so released from his own torment.

I have to say that along with the suggestions of syphilis, there go fears or beliefs about blood. Both Dracula and Frankenstein have a kind of basis in the scientific beliefs of their time. In the 19th century, they did not know a lot of what we do now, but they were starting to have ideas about it. So, was it possible that life could be restored to the dead by what they called "galvanism"? That's part of the scenario with Frankenstein, and in Dracula Van Helsing has ideas about it too. He tells his pupil, Dr., Seward, that there are people doing things today with electricity which would have been considered "unholy" by the men who first discovered the phenomenon.

And he was perfectly correct. As Stoker was writing Dracula, Marconi was making wireless transmission possible. I don't know if anyone thought it was unholy, but certainly Kipling, another of the New Romancers, thought it was really creepy. Inaudible voices coming out of the ether? In his 1903 story "Wireless," a young man dying of TB seems to be picking up the thoughts and words of the poet John Keats, who had died of TB eighty-odd years before. Unless he's the sender and Keats was the receiver. Either way, though Keats himself had declared that science was disenchanting the universe, Kipling, and Stoker too, and Mary Shelley before them, were showing that science was putting enchantment back, opening up possibilities the 18th century Age of Reason had discarded, like vampires, and ghosts, and new ideas of life in death.

As for Dracula, the question there is not what could be done with electricity, but whether life could be restored or prolonged by blood. People were already experimenting with blood transfusion. Only four years after the appearance of Dracula, Karl Landsteiner discovered the existence of the different types of blood, knowledge of which is necessary for safe transfusion. In Dracula, though, Lucy receives several transfusions from her lovers to make up for the blood she has lost to the Count. This must have been known to be dangerous in 1897, and when Van Helsing is doing it he says, talking about her fiancé Arthur, "He is so young and strong and of blood so pure that we need not defibrinate it." "Defibrinate"? People had already come to the conclusion that blood transfusions were safer if it was filtered to remove protein fiber. However, when Van Helsing says that Arthur's blood is "pure," we aren't quite sure what he means. He seems to mean physically pure, but that doesn't make much sense. Perhaps he means morally pure.

We might react by saying that just as physical infection doesn't necessarily imply moral infection, so moral purity, which we're prepared to accept that Arthur has, cannot guarantee physical purity, and so a safe transfusion. But then, we should ask ourselves, how did you catch syphilis? By sex. And even if you were having sex entirely legally and morally with your husband or wife and you caught syphilis from him or her... Well, think about it. If your partner had syphilis, then he, or she, or someone in the chain of transmission, must have engaged in some form of pre-marital or extra-marital sex. So the physical and the moral are strongly connected after all, and Van Helsing's remark is not as naïve as it seems.

Well, when it comes to Dracula, it's obvious that we have another case of changed cultural values, perhaps created by changed technology. With antibiotics and reliable contraception, the modern world is just not as frightened about sexual dangers as the Victorian world. Although, back in 1992, when Coppola made his movie, the AIDS epidemic did seem to bring back the same sort of fear as syphilis. More certainly, the feminine ideal has changed markedly from the sweet, pure, fragile female in need of constant protection of Victorian novels. And female voluptuousness is not an automatic sign of evil, striking terror into the masculine heart.

So, we have to ask, how come the vampire has remained, no, has become even more of a staple of popular fiction? I'd suggest that Bram Stoker left several openings for development in his story and in the character of Dracula, and as I've said before during this course, one thing later writers love to do is "write into a gap" left by a favorite predecessor. Mina sets up one development. Near the end, when Jonathan is cursing Dracula to eternal damnation, Mina, who, after all, is on the edge of becoming a vampire herself, points out that Dracula too is a victim who needs to be saved. The point is dramatized when the men fight their way through to Dracula's coffin. Simultaneously, Quincey plunges his bowie knife into Dracula's heart, while Jonathan beheads him with his Gurkha *kukri*. Dr. Seward writes in his diary that he will forever be glad that at that last moment Dracula's face wears "a look of peace," a complete change from his usual glaring ferocity.

So, all vampires can and should be saved; it's not their fault. What this sets up is the idea of the Good Vampire, the vampire struggling against his or her own nature. And this idea has been developed in many contemporary vampire books and movies. For example, in Terry Pratchett's comic Discworld novels, many vampires have become Black Ribboners, like Blue Ribbon teetotallers in the early 20th century. Black Ribboners take the pledge to abstain from blood entirely, female ones swearing, "Lips that touch ichor [not liquor, ichor] shall never touch mine." But much more seriously and romantically, we have Angel in the <u>Buffy</u> TV series. And Edward Cullen from the *Twilight* novels. Such characters retain the allure of the traditional male vampire, but without the fatality, you might say they are Bad Boys trying very hard to be good for the sake of love, a strong combination.

Another gap which cried out for development is the idea of the *longaevus*, the near immortal. Stoker's Dracula is immensely proud of his ancestry, which he takes back to Attila the Hun. But we never know how old he is. Is it possible that when he boasts about his ancestry, he's really boasting about himself? Once people started researching the origins of the vampire belief, which of course, were there in folktales long before Dr. Polidori, the idea grew up that perhaps Dracula had been a historical figure: Vlad the Impaler, a historical figure of the 15th century, often comes into the frame. Dracula, after all, is not a name, but a nickname. It derives from Latin, as repronounced in Rumanian, *draco ille*, which means "the dragon." And if Dracula is a *longaevus*, how many more are there? Interest then started to focus on Professor Van Helsing. Stoker brings him in as an expert on infectious diseases, but he seems to know an awful lot which is not merely medical. Maybe he is a *longaevus* too.

And then there are the hidden fears of society, so crucial to the success of Stoker's Dracula. We may not be terrified of female sexuality any more, but we have become much readier to believe in secret organizations dedicated to our downfall—to take a couple of examples from Ian Fleming's James Bond books, the Russians SMERSH or the criminal organization SPECTRE. Who protects us from these? Perhaps there are secret orders dedicated to the fight against the undead. That's the premise of Stephen Sommers' 2004 movie, *Van Helsing*, which incidentally, borrowed at least one scene from the Bond movies, the one in which the secret agent, whether Bond or Van Helsing, is equipped with an arsenal of new gadgets by the order's armorer.

Stoker, then, left gaps, and hints. He could never have imagined how some of them would be developed. But that's what happens once fictional characters become part of the ever-growing global "imaginary" of Extraordinary Gentlemen, legendary heroes and heroines. "Don't the great tales never end?" asked Sam Gamgee, and the answer is no. But they do mutate, and as with Bond and Dracula, even cross breed.

Mowgli—The Wolf Child
Lecture 18

Rudyard Kipling's Mowgli, the jungle boy, started off as a legend. Like some of our earlier characters, he also has a hint of myth in his background. Yet this character has also, perhaps more than any other, had an institutional impact on the world, starting 100 years ago and continuing up to the present day. The legendary element of Mowgli is that he is a feral child, a child raised by animals. The mythical element is Mowgli's association with Faunus, the Latin woodland deity. As we'll see, his institutional impact can be found in the Boy Scout movement, which echoes Kipling's message to young people to practice self-reliance and cooperation.

"In the Rukh"

- Rudyard Kipling wrote nine stories about Mowgli, the first of which, "In the Rukh" ("In the Forest"), appeared in 1893. Kipling followed that story up with *The Jungle Book* in 1894 and *The Second Jungle Book* in 1895. In terms of the chronology of Mowgli's life, "In the Rukh" is last.

- This story focuses first on a young Englishman called Gisborne, who works for the British Indian government's Department of Woods and Forests. He lives on his own, deep in the jungle of central India, in the Seeonee Hills. There, he supervises new plantations, irrigation, fire control, and sustainable felling. Another of Gisborne's tasks is dealing with man-eaters.

- The story starts with a report of a forest guard killed by a tiger. Suddenly, out of the jungle comes a man, naked except for a loincloth and a wreath of white flowers. He knows this particular tiger and guides Gisborne to a place where he can get a clear shot at it.

- Who is this strange man who knows everything in the jungle? Gisborne's boss, Muller, has the answer. Muller is old and wise, and when he sees the jungle man, he asks to see his elbows, knees, and ankles. He finds the scars he knew would be there. This is Mowgli. The ankle scars are bites from his wolf cub brothers, and the others are from running on his knees and elbows when he was young.

- According to Muller, Mowgli is an anachronism; he comes from a time before the Iron Age, even the Stone Age. Mowgli is Faunus himself, the Latin woodland deity. Muller admits that only Mowgli, not even Muller himself, will ever know the true inwardness of the forest.

- Yet for all of Mowgli's feral nature, "In the Rukh" describes how he finds a human mate and goes into service as a forest guard with the government. He's accepted into society, if only on its outermost edge.

"Mowgli's Brothers"

- It's never absolutely clear where Mowgli comes from. In "Mowgli's Brothers," we learn that somehow, as a toddler, he escapes from the tiger Shere Khan, who has, perhaps, frightened off his parents. He toddles into a wolf lair inhabited by Father and Mother Wolf and their four newborn cubs.

- Mother Wolf is annoyed when Shere Khan comes after the boy and demands his prey. She faces off the tiger and says that from now on, Mowgli is a wolf.

- Mowgli must be accepted by the Seeonee Pack, and he needs two nonrelated sponsors to save him from Shere Khan. Mowgli's two sponsors are Baloo, the bear, who is the wolves' schoolmaster, and Bagheera, the black panther, who has no right to be there but offers to pay a ransom: a fat bull, newly killed, not half a mile away.
  - Bagheera has a fellow feeling for Mowgli because he is a wolf child in reverse: an animal raised by humans, until he escaped.

  - Thus, Mowgli becomes a member of the Seeonee Pack and is inducted into the world of the talking animals, including

Baloo; Bagheera; Akela, the leader of the pack; and Kaa, the giant python.

The End of Shere Khan

- The idea of a human who has all the powers of an animal is thrilling, but Mowgli isn't safe from all dangers. Several of the stories are adventure tales, telling how Mowgli copes with his enemies, especially Shere Khan.

- After Mowgli has been adopted by the wolves in "Mowgli's Brothers," the story skips 10 years. During this time, the wolf pack has deteriorated. The young wolves have started following Shere Khan for scraps, and they are ready to get rid of their old leader, Akela. Shere Khan has taken over at the wolves' council, and once again, he demands Mowgli as his right.

- But Mowgli has been down to the Indian village in the jungle and come back with the Red Flower: fire. With this, he cows Shere Khan and rescues Akela. The story ends with him going down to the village to become a man. In the sequel "Tiger! Tiger!" he's learned human language and has been semi-adopted by a woman who thinks—or hopes—that he may be her son, who was taken by the tiger.

- Mowgli uses the village herd to settle accounts with Shere Khan. He knows that the tiger is waiting for him in a ravine. He splits the village herd, driving the bulls down the ravine, while Akela and his wolf brothers herd the cows and calves up the ravine. The two stampedes collide, with Shere Khan caught and killed between them.

Mowgli and Kaa

- In "Kaa's Hunting," Mowgli, who is mad at Baloo for beating him into learning the Law of the Jungle, makes friends with, and is carried off by, the *bandar-log*, the monkey people. The Law of the Jungle is a main theme for Kipling, projecting a powerful and influential image of how people, especially young people, should behave.

- The *bandar-log* are the only animals who are outside the Law of the Jungle. They squabble, boast, and chatter and never get anything done—all too much like people. They are quite lacking in animal dignity and discipline.

- The *bandar-log* live in large numbers in an old ruined city, which makes it difficult for even Baloo and Bagheera to rescue the man cub. But Mowgli also has a friend in Kaa, a 30-foot rock python, of whom the monkeys are terrified. Kaa rescues Mowgli, and the boy learns a painful lesson from Baloo about obedience.

- Kaa is also vital to Mowgli's tactics in "Red Dog." Here, a giant pack of red dholes (Indian wild dogs) has come up from the south to take over the Seeonee wolf pack's hunting grounds. Coached by Kaa, Mowgli provokes the dholes into chasing him across the nests of killer bees. Half the dhole pack is killed, but Mowgli escapes. The dhole survivors are finished off by the wolf pack.

Kipling's Themes

- Such stories as "Red Dog" and "Kaa's Hunting" are principally adventure stories, stories about solving tactical problems. Yet a major theme of the stories as a whole is Mowgli's oscillation between animals and humans. Another theme is the satirical one, directed against human vices. A third is the educational one, in which the well-behaved and law-abiding animals, especially the wolf pack, are held up as role models for young readers.

- We can see how the last two themes work in another story, "The King's Ankus," a kind of homily on the effect of greed.

- Another story, "How Fear Came," is a kind of animal myth, in which Hathi, an elephant, explains how man brought fear into the jungle. The rather low grade Kipling gives humanity is also the theme of "Letting in the Jungle" and "The Spring Running." These

In "Letting in the Jungle," as penalty for the villagers' superstition, Mowgli calls in the elephants to break down their walls.

stories develop the idea of Mowgli's oscillation between the human and animal worlds.

- Although Mowgli is fairly judgmental about humanity, Kipling is not entirely negative. Indeed, these stories put forward a powerful ideal of what humanity should be and could be. Kipling's satire is easy to grasp, as is his moral: that we, too, should observe the essential precepts of the Law of the Jungle.

- Kipling expresses the meaning of the Law of the Jungle in a poem found at the beginning of one of the stories in *The Jungle Book*. The poem provides good general advice—don't be deceived by flattery, know who your friends are, and so on—but it also covers such issues as welfare and lays down rights and responsibilities. The poem is a kind of constitution—a notably libertarian one. But the main thrust of it is discipline: self-discipline first, then obedience to the law.

- Much of this teaching was taken over by the Boy Scout movement, which teaches a balance between self-reliance and cooperation. We don't know the full effect this movement has had on the Western world in the last 100 years, but it's interesting to note the surprising strength of Western democracies when faced with military challenges. That surely has something to do with their many nongovernmental institutions.

- People often say that Kipling was an imperialist, and he was. But imperialism had many shades. Note that Mowgli is an Indian boy, not an English boy, and there's never the slightest suggestion that this might affect his legendary, heroic, and near-mythical status. Kipling's ideology of self-discipline as a basis for liberty—imperialist in origin or not—proved readily acceptable and capable of transplantation, even into the republican and democratic soil of America.

Continuations of Kipling

- As with so many of the authors we've looked at, Kipling left openings for continuations. These openings led another author, Pamela Jekel, to write *The Third Jungle Book*, which includes two stories based on hints of other adventures Kipling gave in "Red Dog."

- The well-known fantasy writer Neil Gaiman produced a kind of analog of *The Jungle Books* called *The Graveyard Book*. It's about a child who loses his parents and is brought up, not by animals, but by ghosts.

- Much earlier, it's likely that Mowgli provided some inspiration for another feral child hero, Tarzan of the Apes, created by Edgar Rice Burroughs. Tarzan plays on the same human wish to be immensely strong, fearless, and at home in the wilderness.

- In the end, Mowgli learns obedience from Baloo and cooperation from Kaa. He learns to reject greed, cruelty, and superstition. But he also learns that he must move on from the carefree life of the jungle and take on adult responsibilities. As Kaa says, "Man goes to Man at the last, though the Jungle does not cast him out." Gray Brother, the wolf, says, "From now, we follow new trails." Many a Boy and Girl Scout must have taken those words in and silently accepted their truth.

Essential Reading

Kipling, *The Jungle Book*.

———, *The Second Jungle Book*.

Suggested Reading

Jekel, *The Third Jungle Book*.

Montefiore, "Kipling as a Children's Writer and *The Jungle Books*."

Questions to Consider

1. Kipling seems to put great stress on obedience and discipline while telling stories about freedom and independence. Do you think he got the balance right?

2. Do you think Mowgli and the wolves, adopted into the symbolism of the Boy and Girl Scout movement, are suitable role models for the present day?

Mowgli—The Wolf Child
Lecture 18—Transcript

This course is on heroes and legends, and the character I'm talking about this time starts off, at least, as a legend. There's also, as with some of our earlier characters, like Guinevere, a hint of a myth hanging about in the background. Yet this character has also, perhaps more than any other, had an institutional impact on the world, starting a hundred years ago, but continuing right up to now.

The character I mean is Rudyard Kipling's Mowgli, the jungle boy, central character of *The Jungle Book* and then *The Second Jungle Book*. Kipling wrote nine stories about Mowgli, the first of which wasn't in either of the Jungle Books, but appeared in an earlier collection in 1893. Kipling followed it up with *The Jungle Book*, which has three Mowgli stories, in 1894, and *The Second Jungle Book*, which has five stories, in 1895.

The legendary thing about Mowgli, however, is that he is a feral child, a wolf child, a child raised by animals. Legends of such children go back a long way. The obvious case being Romulus and Remus. They are, in legend, the founders of Rome, and in legend also were fed and raised from infancy by a she wolf. These legends are so strong that cases keep being reported in real life, though it's very hard to see how, in reality, a human child, far more helpless for far longer than any animal, could really be protected and fed by any animal mother.

Kipling would deal with this with his usual neatness. But it's not in the first published Mowgli story; that's the one that isn't in the Jungle Books, and it's the last one in terms of the chronology of Mowgli's life. It's called "In the Rukh," R-U-K-H, which means "In the Forest." This story focuses first on a young Englishman called Gisborne, who works for the British Indian government's Department of Woods and Forests. He lives on his own, deep in the jungle of central India in the Seeonee Hills, and there he supervises new plantations, and irrigation, and fire control, and sustainable felling, as well as animal and human welfare.

Another task is dealing with man-eaters. The story starts with a report coming to Gisborne of a forest guard killed by a tiger. A tiger that kills man, he's told, will kill again. "He may be behind us even as we speak." What to do? Suddenly, out of the jungle, comes a man, naked, except for a loincloth and a wreath of white flowers. He knows where the tiger is; he knows the tiger; he knows how many teeth the tiger has. Tigers don't usually turn man-eater until they can't bring down any other prey, but this one still has twelve teeth and no excuse. The strange man offers to drive the tiger down on to Gisborne's gun. When Gisborne doesn't believe he can do it, he guides him to a place where Gisborne has a clear shot.

Who is this person who walks all but naked, unlike even the little Gond aborigines, and who knows everything in the jungle? The person who knows the answer is Gisborne's boss, Muller, who is a German. He is old and wise, and when he sees the jungle man, he asks to see his elbows, knees, and ankles. He finds the scars he knew would be there. For it turns out that this is Mowgli. The ankle scars are bites from his wolf-cub brothers, and the others are from running on knees and elbows when he was little.

What Mowgli is, says Muller, is an anachronism, from before the Iron Age, from before the Stone Age. And here the myth comes in, for Muller has been educated in the classics too. Mowgli is Faunus himself, the Latin woodland deity. Muller admits that only Mowgli, not even Muller himself, will ever know the true inwardness of the forest. And yet, for all Mowgli's feral nature, the story "In the Rukh" describes how Mowgli finds a human mate and takes service with the government as a forest guard. He's accepted into society, if only on its very outmost edge.

So that's the end of the wolf-child's story, but it left Kipling with the problem of describing the start. It's never absolutely clear where Mowgli comes from. Somehow, as a toddler, he escapes from the tiger Shere Khan, who has maybe frightened off his parents. He toddles laughing into a wolf lair inhabited by Father and Mother Wolf and their four newborn cubs. What saves him is that Shere Khan comes after him and demands his prey. This annoys Mother Wolf, who is impressed by the way the man cub has pushed in with her own cubs to be suckled by her. So she faces off the tiger in the narrow mouth of the lair and says that from now on Mowgli is a wolf.

He has to be accepted by the Seeonee Pack, and he needs two non-related sponsors to save him from Shere Khan, who is watching the wolf-pack meeting and demanding his prey. Mowgli's two sponsors are Baloo the bear, who is the wolves' schoolmaster, and Bagheera the Black Panther, who has no right to be there but offers to pay a ransom—a fat bull, newly killed, not half a mile away. Bagheera has a fellow feeling for Mowgli, for he is a wolf child in reverse, an animal raised by humans till he escaped. And so Mowgli becomes a member of the Seeonee Pack and is inducted into the fabulous world of the talking animals—Baloo; Bagheera; Akela, the leader of the pack, Kaa, the giant python, to which list Disney added King Louie, the king of the monkey people, in the Jungle Book movie.

Now all this information about Mowgli's beginnings can be found in "Mowgli's Brothers," which is the first story in Kipling's *Jungle Book*. So now we know something about Mowgli's early life, and we've also glanced at "In the Rukh," the tale of how Mowgli marries and settles down. In between, a major theme is Mowgli's oscillation between being a wolf and being a human. But the first thrill of it all is just the idea of a human who has all the powers of an animal. Fleet as a deer, surefooted as a goat, strong as a leopard, able to swing through the trees like an ape, and safe from many dangers, because he knows the Master Words from Baloo the bear. Mowgli can drop into a cave full of cobras, the Poison People, and tell them, "we be of one ye, thou and I," and they reply, "Even ssso! Down hoods all!" Don't we all wish we could do that?

But Mowgli isn't safe from all dangers, and several of the stories are adventure tales, telling how Mowgli copes with his enemies, first of all, Shere Khan. After Mowgli has been adopted by the wolves in "Mowgli's Brothers," the story skips 10 years. During this time, the wolf-pack has deteriorated. The young wolves have started following Shere Khan for scraps, and they are ready to get rid of the old wolf, their leader Akela. He misses his hold on a kill, and by wolf law is open to challenge. Shere Khan has taken over at the wolves' Council, and once again he demands Mowgli as his right.

But Mowgli has been down to the Indian village in the jungle, and he comes back with the Red Flower—fire. With this, he cows Shere Khan and rescues

Akela. The story ends with him going down to the village to become a man. In the sequel, "Tiger! Tiger!," he's learned human language and been semi-adopted by a woman who thinks, or hopes, that he may be her son Nathoo, who was taken by the tiger and has come back to her. But the rest of the village are suspicious.

Mowgli, though, means to use the village to settle accounts with Shere Khan. He knows that while the tiger will take a cow, or a buffalo, if either strays from the herd, as long as they stay together, the cattle and the buffaloes are irresistible. And so, helped by Akela and his wolf brothers, when he knows Shere Khan is lying up in a ravine waiting for him, Mowgli splits the village herd. He drives down the ravine with the bulls, while the wolves herd the cows and calves up the ravine the other way. And when the two stampedes collide, with Shere Khan between them, that's the end of Shere Khan. Mowgli places the tiger's skin on the wolves' Council Rock.

You could call "Tiger! Tiger!" a tactical story, and there are two others like that. One of these, which forms the main body of the 1967 Disney animated film, is called "Kaa's Hunting." In this, Mowgli, who is in a bad mood with Baloo for beating him into learning the Law of the Jungle, makes friends with and is carried off by the *bandar-log*, the monkey people. Now, it's not only Baloo who teaches the Law of the Jungle, it's a main theme for Kipling as well, projecting an image—a powerful and influential image—of how people should behave, and especially young people, for whom these stories were primarily written. We will see later on the surprising effect this has had, and something of the ideology Kipling was presenting.

In "Kaa's Hunting," however, the *bandar-log* are the only animals who are quite outside the Law of the Jungle. They squabble, and boast, and chatter, and never get anything done. All too much like people, to tell the truth. They are quite lacking in animal dignity and discipline. Just as an aside, I can confirm that I, at least noticed, the satirical element here very young. I knew the story in childhood in India—I must have been about six—and my mother took me out for a treat to Firpo's, the big department store and café in Calcutta. She tells me that I looked round in wonder at all the people, mostly British people, talking and gossiping, and I said, because I didn't speak much English then, "Dekko, ma, *bandar-log*." "Look, Mummy, the monkey people," which was very rude of me, but I'm pretty sure was what Kipling intended.

However, back to the story. Disorganized, though, the *bandar-log* are, since they are arboreal and live in very large numbers in an old ruined city, it's hard for even Baloo and Bagheera to rescue the man cub. But he has another friend, and that is Kaa, the enormous, 30-foot rock python. Kaa is arboreal too, and the monkeys are terrified of him. He rescues Mowgli, and Mowgli learns a painful lesson from Baloo, about obedience, not the last lesson he receives in the Law of the Jungle. Kaa is also vital to Mowgli's main masterstroke of tactics in "Red Dog." Here, a giant pack of red dholes—that's Indian wild dogs—have come up from the south to take over the Seeonee wolf-pack's hunting grounds. Even tigers get out of the way of the dholes. They've even been known, in reality, to take an elephant calf from its furious mother. Everyone in the jungle turns aside for them.

But there's another creature in the jungle from whom everyone turns aside, and that's the wild Indian killer bees, who live in the river ravines. What Mowgli does, coached by Kaa, is provoke the dholes into chasing him across the wild bees' nests. He jumps from the cliff into the river, where Kaa is waiting to catch him. Half the dhole pack is killed by the disturbed bees, but Mowgli escapes, first by being fast, and second, by being rubbed all over with wild garlic, which, for a moment, repels the bees. The dholes' survivors are swept downstream to where the wolves are waiting for them. It's a great battle scene. The story ends by saying that of all that pack of two hundred fighting dholes, not one returned to their home to carry the word of their defeat. It's just like parts of Beowulf. Kipling deliberately challenges comparison with traditional heroism, and his story bears the comparison well, notably the scene of the death of Akela.

Stories like "Red Dog" and "Kaa's Hunting" are principally adventure stories, stories about solving a tactical problem. Yet, as I've said already, a major theme of the stories as a whole is Mowgli's oscillation between the animals, whom he loves, and the humans, whom he does not love, apart from the woman who believes she is his mother. Another theme is the satirical one, directed against human vices. A third is the educational one, in which the well-behaved and law-abiding animals, especially the wolf-pack, are held up as role models for young adult readers.

One can see how the last two themes work in another story, "The King's Ankus." In this, Mowgli is led by Kaa to a lost king's treasure. Mowgli, here, more like a wolf than a human, is not very interested in the gold and the jewels, but he takes a jeweled ankus, or elephant goad, because he likes the way it shines. The old cobra who guards the treasure, tries to kill Mowgli, because the cobra has been humanized and does not know or obey the Master Words of the jungle any more. But when he's thwarted by Mowgli and Kaa, and Mowgli takes the ankus away from him, the cobra tells Mowgli the ankus is Death.

And it is. Mowgli eventually throws it away. A man finds it. He's killed for it by a Gond, one of the little forest hunters who shoot poisoned arrows. The Gond is killed by four woodmen. The woodmen kill one of their number to make their own shares bigger. But before he died, he'd poisoned their food, so they die too. Mowgli and Bagheera trace all this out by following the various trails, and once they have seen its effects, Mowgli returns the ankus to the old cobra, and says he was right. Death it is. The story is a kind of homily on the effect of greed.

There's another story, "How Fear Came," which is a kind of animal myth, Hathi the elephant explains how Man brought into the jungle not Death— it was the first tiger who did that, not Shame—that was the monkey; Man brought Fear. That's why all the animals fear humans, even the tiger, who springs from behind, except on the one night a year when he is released from fear. So, Kipling gives humanity a rather low grade. That's the further theme of a couple of stories, "Letting in the Jungle," and "The Spring Running," which develop this idea of Mowgli's oscillation between the human and animal worlds.

In the first of them, Mowgli finds that his adoptive human mother is accused of being a witch, because she's fostered Mowgli, and he must be some kind of forest demon on good terms with the wolves, capable of dealing on his own with tigers. So the villagers imprison both her and her husband, and they plan to burn them and divide up their money and their cattle. In other words, the villagers are typical humans, motivated by greed and cruelty. Mowgli frees his human mother and sends her and her husband off through the jungle with an escort of wolves. Then he and Bagheera stay behind to teach the village a lesson.

There's a comic scene when Bagheera, who has a strong sense of humor, says, "Let me look after this." He lies down on the bed where the woman had been tied awaiting torture and death. When the excited villagers rush in, what they see is a giant panther, "stretched at full length on the bed, his paws crossed and lightly hung down over one end, black as the pit, and terrible as a demon." Bagheera doesn't move, but there's immediate panic. Mowgli, though, follows through. As penalty for the villagers' superstition and cruelty, he calls down the deer to eat up the crops, the pigs to root up the earth, in the end, the elephants to break down the walls and bring back the jungle.

So Mowgli is pretty judgmental about humanity. But Kipling is not only negative. Indeed, what these stories also do is put forward a powerful ideal of what humanity should be and could be. My childish remark about the customers in Firpo's shows that Kipling's satire was easy to grasp, and so was his moral, which is that we too should observe the essential precepts of the Law of the Jungle. Let's take a look at them. If you don't know the stories already, they won't be what you would expect. In normal usage, now, "law of the jungle" means, and here I quote from a couple of dictionaries, "A system [...] in which the strongest survive, presumably as animals in nature or as human beings whose activity is not regulated by the laws or ethics of civilization." Or if you prefer, "a state of ruthless competition or self-interest."

But Kipling gives the phrase a quite different meaning, expressed discursively in the stories, but also quite directly in a poem. So, built into the story "Tiger! Tiger!," don't be like Shere Khan, who eats, and drinks and sleeps when he should be on his guard, very good general advice. Don't be like the young wolves who follow Shere Khan for scraps. Don't be like Mowgli, who's deceived by the flattery of the *bandar-log*. Know who your friends are and your enemies. Know the Master Words of diplomacy, because anyone, even Chil the kite, may be an ally in times of need, and so on.

But there's a poem at the start or finish of each of the nine stories, and one of them is "The Law of the Jungle," as taught by Baloo. It says things like, "The strength of the Pack is the wolf, and the strength of the wolf is the Pack." It recommends, in verse, all the things I've mentioned already, but it also in a way covers issues like welfare. According to the Law of the Jungle, cubs up to a year old are allowed, from any one of the pack who has made a kill, "full gorge when the killer has eaten: and none may refuse him the same." That is Cub-right, but there's also Lair-right. A nursing mother is allowed to claim from all members of the Pack who are the same age as her, "one haunch of each kill for her litter, and none may deny her the same."

The Law lays down rights, including the right to be judged only in full council, just like our trial by jury, but it also lays down responsibilities. No one is allowed to enter the wolf's lair, not even the Head Wolf or the Council. But if the wolf makes his lair in a place which is too obvious, and so draws attention, then the Council can order him to change, and so on. It's a kind of constitution, and I'd add, a notably libertarian one. But the main thrust of it is discipline. Self-discipline first, but then obedience to the law. Baloo's teaching ends up. "now these are the laws of the jungle, and many and mighty are they; but the head and the hoof of the Law and the haunch and the hump is—Obey!"

Well, as you no doubt know, much of this was taken over pretty solidly by the Boy Scout movement. Young Scouts are still called Wolf Cubs. The head of their pack is called Akela. The whole ethos of the movement teaches a balance between self-reliance and cooperation, "The strength of the Pack is the wolf," that's self-reliance, "and the strength of the wolf is the Pack," that's co-operation. Now, what effect the Boy-Scout movement has had on the Western world in the last hundred years, I cannot tell. I can only note two things, which may not be related.

One is the surprising strength over the last hundred years of Western democracies when faced by all kinds of military challenge. That surely has something to do with their many non-governmental institutions. And the other is this. My endowed Chair at St. Louis University was called after the famous Jesuit Walter Ong. He lived to be very old, and I often talked to him. But although he was a very distinguished man in many ways, what he seemed to be most proud of was the fact that as a boy he had attended one of the first worldwide Boy Scout jamborees, I guess the one in 1929, more than seventy years before.

People say very often that Kipling was an imperialist, and he was. But imperialism had many shades. Note that Mowgli is an Indian boy, not an English boy, and there's never the slightest suggestion that this might affect his legendary and heroic and near-mythical status. We might note, likewise, that Kipling's other famous child hero, Kim, wasn't English either, but Irish—Kimball O'Hara. Kipling was also notably sympathetic to different faiths, Hindu, Muslim, Buddhist, as well as Roman Catholic. So his ideology of self-discipline as a basis for liberty, imperialist in origin or not, proved readily acceptable and capable of transplantation even into the republican, and also the democratic soil of America.

The Jungle Books have remained children's' classics ever since. As with so many of the authors we look at, Kipling left an opening, or even provided an opening, for continuations. At the start of the story "Red Dog," Kipling explains that Mowgli's adventures could make "many many stories," just like all the Sherlock Holmes cases that Dr. Watson mentions but never gets round to recording.

There's the time he met the Mad Elephant of Mandhla, who killed the bullocks pulling carts of new-coined silver to the Government Treasury, and how Mowgli, who has no use for money, "scattered the shiny rupees in the dust." There's the story about how Mowgli fought Jacala the crocodile all one long night and broke his knife on the crocodile's armored back; there's the story about how he got his replacement knife and the price he paid for it; and how he and Hathi the elephant took turns at saving each other from traps.

All these have led another author, Pamela Jekel, to write *The Third Jungle Book*. This came out in 1992 and has ten stories in it, including two based on the hints Kipling gave in "Red Dog." Another author, the very well-known fantasy writer Neil Gaiman, has produced a kind of analog of *The Jungle Books*, called *The Graveyard Book*. It's about a child who loses his parents and is brought up, not by animals, but by ghosts. One of the stories in it is a close analog of "The King's Ankus," and there are other unmistakable similarities. And of course the Disney film of 1967 has made versions of Kipling's characters familiar to almost everyone in the Western world, largely though the music track, with the big hits, King Louie's "I Wanna Be Like You" and Baloo's "The Bear Necessities." Though we have to admit that the film washed out most of Kipling's serious intentions, and it was a strange idea to make King Louie into an orangutan, a creature never found in the hills of Central India.

Much earlier, it's likely that Mowgli provided some inspiration for the other feral child hero we can all recognize, who of course is Tarzan of the Apes. Edgar Rice Burroughs's hero, who first appeared in 1912. Tarzan plays on the same human wish to be immensely strong, fearless, at home in the wilderness. But Tarzan is really all muscle, the Basic Male Hero taken to an extreme. And in Burroughs's original, I have to say, pretty strongly racist. It's strange that Burroughs, an American, makes his hero not only English, but an aristocrat as well. Lord Greystoke, no less!

So, I haven't given Tarzan equal billing with Mowgli. Mowgli ("the frog") is a much humbler, much cleverer, and a much more vulnerable hero. In the end, Kipling's fable about animals is really an analysis and a recommendation about what it is to be truly and successfully human, and truly and successfully grown-up. Mowgli learns obedience from Baloo, cooperation from Kaa. He learns to reject greed and cruelty and superstition. In the end, he learns, also, that he must move on from the carefree life of the jungle and take on adult responsibilities. As Kaa says, "Man goes to Man at the last, though the Jungle does not cast him out." Gray Brother the wolf says, "From now, we follow new trails." Many a Boy and Girl Scout must have taken those words in and silently accepted their truth.

Celie—A Woman Who Wins Through
Lecture 19

O ver the centuries, the trend has been for heroes and heroines to move closer to us in social status. In our course, we've seen this steady decrease in social status, from Thor, a god; to Aeneas, the son of a goddess; to Beowulf, the grandson of a king; and so on. Our first character who appears to be a normal person is the Wife of Bath, but it wasn't until we began looking at Americans that we returned to her level. In this lecture, we move even further into the new American territory with an exploration of Celie, the heroine of Alice Walker's book *The Color Purple*.

Celie's Social Status
- The heroine of *The Color Purple*, Celie, is poor and black in a thoroughly racist society, and she's been told all her life that she's ugly. She's at the bottom of the social ladder, a position that's underscored by the epistolary nature of the novel: Most of it consists of letters written by Celie in nonstandard English.

- Every one of the book's early chapters has yet another terrible revelation in it about Celie. In chapter, 1 the man she thinks is her father rapes her, and she gets pregnant. In chapter 2, her mother dies cursing her, her supposed father takes her baby away, and she thinks he kills it. In chapter 3, he sells their second child, then brings back a new wife.
  - Celie is offered as a wife in place of her younger sister, Nettie, and is taken out of school; on her wedding day, her stepson hits her in the head with a rock.

  - Worst of all, Nettie is sent away, but she promises to write. Celie tells us: "She say, nothing but death can keep me from it. She never write."

- Celie's low status prompts us to ask two questions: What indications of heroic character can someone show from the bottom? More urgently, what's the strategy for getting up and out?

Strategies for Fighting Back
- One strategy for raising oneself from the bottom is to fight, and naturally, people tell Celie to do just that. But does fighting work in *The Color Purple*? As with several of the stories we've looked at, this one operates by pairing and contrasts. We see different women try different strategies.

- Sofia, who marries Harpo, Celie's insolent stepson, is a fighter. In fact, Celie slyly sets Harpo up for a fight. She advises him to beat Sofia, to put her in her place. Soon, he shows up saying that the mule kicked him, he walked into a door, and he shut a window on his hand. Obviously, the decision in that bout went to Sofia. But Harpo is poor and black, too. In the contest between him and his wife, it's just strength and aggression that are the deciding factors.

- Later, the town mayor's white wife asks Sofia if she wants to become her maid, and Sofia replies, "Hell, no." The mayor slaps her for insolence, and Sofia knocks him down. Sofia is beaten unrecognizable, then gets 12 years in jail for assault.

- The traditional strategy of the weak is trickery and cajoling, which Celie and Sofia's relatives try to get Sofia out of the prison laundry.
  - Harpo's new girlfriend, Squeak, reluctantly admits that the prison warden is her uncle. The plan is that Squeak will tell the warden that Sofia is happy in the laundry, but she needs to be punished more, perhaps by being made "some white lady maid." Sofia's boyfriend says, "This sound mighty much like some ole uncle Tomming to me." But Shug, the smart one, says, "Uncle Tom wasn't call Uncle for nothing."

  - And the trick works, to a degree. Although her uncle rapes Squeak, Sofia is let out of the laundry to work for the mayor's wife as a maid. The result is not good, but it's better than what Sofia got from fighting.

- All this time, Celie is learning, especially from Shug, who was once her husband's girlfriend. Shug has gotten along by using her sex and her singing; she makes a living with her music. Shug explains to Celie about sex, and she fixes the worst hurt that has been done to Celie: the fact that she never heard from her sister Nettie. Celie's husband, Albert, has been intercepting and hiding the letters. Celie gets all of Nettie's letters at once and learns from them, as well.

- Nettie has been educated and has broader horizons. She was taken in by a missionary couple, African American themselves, and went to Africa with them. It's Nettie who finds out that Celie's children are alive and have been adopted by the missionary couple. Further, the man she and Celie thought was their father, Fonso, is not their father at all. Their real father was lynched while they were babies for setting up in competition with white traders, and Fonso married the widow to collect her inheritance.

- Celie even learns from Fonso, who gave her away to be married. According to him, the world is all about money. Run the store, as Celie's real father did, but put in a white manager and pay the kickbacks.

Celie and Uncle Tom

- *The Color Purple* and *Uncle Tom's Cabin* have marked similarities. Celie, for instance, suffers the same two temptations that come to Tom: to do violence against her oppressors and to despair.

- At the start of the novel, all of Celie's letters are addressed "Dear God." She writes to God for two reasons: She has no one else to write to, and she takes literally what her abusive supposed father said to her after he raped her: "You better not tell nobody but God. It'd kill your mammy."

- Just like Tom and the slaves on Simon Legree's plantation, Celie begins to think that there is no God or that God has forgotten her.

  o Early on, arguing with Sofia, Celie says that she couldn't be angry with her rapist father because the Bible says to honor your father and your mother. Sofia says that she ought to bash her abusive husband's head open, but Celie says, "This life soon be over. Heaven last all ways."

  o But once Celie starts writing back to Nettie and no longer has only God to write to, her attitude changes. Shug asks her why, and Celie says, "What God do for me?" It's a fair question, and Celie concludes that God is just like all the other men she knows: "Trifling, forgetful, and lowdown."

  o This is a kind of blasphemy that goes beyond anything we heard from Uncle Tom or Legree's slaves. This scene between Shug and Celie, though, rather like Tom's vision of the crown of thorns, turns into the existential heart of the novel. Despite what she says, Celie cares about God; even if he's not there, doing without him is hard.

The Color Purple

- The color purple appears in an important scene between Shug and Celie that Celie reports in a letter to Nettie. Celie tells Shug that she writes to Nettie now, not to God. Shug wants to know why, and Celie tells her she has lost faith in God. But then Shug explains the basis for her own faith.

  o Shug tells Celie that God isn't found in church or even in the Bible. The church God, the Bible God, is a white invention. But the God Shug believes in is inside her and inside everyone else. And this God is also "everything … Everything that is or ever was or ever will be." God is an it, not a him. And the way to serve it is by being happy, enjoying all the things it has created.

  o You are letting God down, says Shug, if you walk past the color purple in a field and don't notice it. Forget the God who looks like an old white man. Appreciate the color purple instead.

- ○ Celie takes Shug to mean that she should notice God's creation instead of trying to locate God. A bush or a tree shows God's goodness, far more than her husband or her stepfather or any of the other men Celie has encountered.

- What Shug is preaching is a kind of pantheism, though neither she nor Celie knows the word, and in her way, she is duplicating the kind of visionary sense we associate with the Romantic poets: Wordsworth and the daffodils or Coleridge's Ancient Mariner. Like the Ancient Mariner, once Celie finds herself able to love creation, she is at least on the way to freedom.

Celie learns to find God in his creation— among trees, stalks of corn, and wildflowers.

- Celie takes up her needle, instead of the razor with which she meant to kill her husband. She soon owns her own clothing business and employs other seamstresses. She inherits from her stepfather, and her sister comes back to her. All, it seems, comes from one revelation. The color purple stands for happiness, for acceptance, for forgiveness. It's a long road from the utter misery of the novel's beginning.

- Part of what makes Celie a heroine is fortitude, as it was with Uncle Tom. Like Frodo Baggins and Sam Gamgee, Celie just keeps plugging along, in spite of discouragement and hostility.

- Also like Tom, Celie puts aside the temptations of violence and, worse than violence, of hatred. She has good reason to hate, but she finds the emotion is self-destructive. Unlike Tom, though, and in different circumstances, she does not become a martyr. She finds her own way out—with the powerful assistance of Shug, Nettie, and some other women. Female solidarity is an important resource throughout the novel.

- This points to a major difference between *The Color Purple* and *Uncle Tom's Cabin*. The enemy in the latter is slavery, but by Celie's time, slavery has been long abolished, though it often doesn't seem so. Nevertheless, Walker's major target has shifted from racism to sexism.
    o Celie's main oppressors are her stepfather, Fonso; her husband, Albert; and until she deals with him, her stepson, Harpo. Male role models, such as Sofia's brother-in-law Jack or Samuel the missionary, are present but peripheral.

    o Nettie's experiences in Africa, which she relates in her letters to Celie, give a telling picture of white colonial exploitation in Africa. And for a while the Olinka people among whom Nettie lives seem a model of cooperation, benevolence, and closeness to nature, yet they, too, believe firmly in male supremacy.

- Perhaps the threat from which the color purple releases us is that of having to play a role insisted on by convention: male or female, submissive or dominant, harsh or gentle. In any of those ways, the role can be a straitjacket.

Essential Reading

Walker, *The Color Purple*.

Suggested Reading

Bates, *Alice Walker*.

Dieke, ed., *Critical Essays on Alice Walker*.

1. Do you agree that appreciating beauty is an adequate substitute for religious faith? Can the two maybe be combined?

2. Would you consider *The Color Purple* to be a feminist work? Remember that many feminists have found it too passive in its recommendations (once again, like *Uncle Tom's Cabin*).

Celie—A Woman Who Wins Through
Lecture 19—Transcript

We are three quarters of the way through this course, and I guess you will by now have noticed something. The heroes and heroines we're looking at are—how shall I put this without seeming disrespectful?—going steadily downscale in social status. I'm not saying they're becoming less heroic, far from it. No, it's just that over the centuries, the trend has been for heroes and heroines to move closer to us, for us to identify with, and perhaps to emulate.

So, just to recap, Thor was a god, though a god with severe limitations and many human qualities. Aeneas is the son of a goddess, Venus. Odysseus is helped by and on speaking terms with the goddess Athena. The Christian author of Beowulf has no time for pagan gods, but, he makes his hero the grandson of a king. Guinevere is a Queen, and Criseyde is at least well up the social ladder, with princes as lovers.

Our first character who appears to be a normal person is the Wife of Bath, heroic because of her feistiness, vulnerability, and merry heart. But we don't find another like her for some time. Robin Hood is only a yeoman of sub-gentry status, but he puts on airs, as does Don Quixote. Even Don Quixote, though, mad as he is, is a hidalgo, short for hijo de algo, son of a somebody. Robinson Crusoe and Elizabeth Bennet are both sort of ordinary people, but Robinson has no competition; he's a loner. And Elizabeth goes up in the world very much by snagging an immensely rich aristocrat as a husband. I admit, by her own efforts and superior qualities.

It's not till the Americans come in that we go back to Wife-of-Bath level, with the Deerslayer, like Robin, except that he doesn't put on airs. And Woodrow, who starts life, and ends it, as a nobody. With Huck Finn and Uncle Tom, we're in different territory. Neither speaks standard English, or standard American. One is a slave; the other is called a pariah, a social outcast, though of course, that's what he likes being. Our British Victorian heroes, Sherlock and Mowgli, moved us in another direction. They're not ordinary people, but it's not because they have some special status, it's because they have some special and peculiar quality, as of course does Dracula.

Well, with the character we're looking at today, another heroine, we are moving even further into the new American territory. She is Celie, the heroine of Alice Walker's book *The Color Purple*, published in 1982, but set in Georgia in the 1930s, which is why we put it here, ahead of the post-World War II heroes, whom we'll discuss in the next two lectures. Again, I don't want to sound disrespectful, but Celie is a character who, initially, has nothing going for her at all. She's poor; she's black, in a thoroughly racist society; her husband's girlfriend looks at her and says, "You sure is ugly."

Celie's been told that all her life. The man she thinks is her father refuses to let a suitor have his other daughter, Celie's sister Nettie, because she's too good looking. He has his own intentions for Nettie. So he tells him to take Celie instead. "She ugly […] She ain't smart, either […] And another thing—She tell lies." He has to throw in a cow to get the man to take her. All that puts Celie pretty much at the bottom of the social ladder. She gets no respect from anyone, except her sister, and if she has any self-esteem left, it's a miracle. And this is rubbed in by the fact that *The Color Purple* is another epistolary novel, like Dracula, and most of it consists of letters written by Celie.

She can write, but it's not standard American at all. On the first page of the book, no more than two hundred words, I count about 25 errors, or deviations from standard. She writes, "don't never" for "didn't ever." She simplifies "a kind word" to "a kine word," and "children" to "chilren." She consistently misses the ending off verbs like "she say" and "he grab." Conversely, she adds an ending to "I feel," so it's "I feels sick." Now, I've got nothing against this. I'm a Professor of English language. I know that much of what we all regard as correct English is historically incorrect and would have been rejected with horror by people in earlier centuries. That s ending is on the way out! Even in England some dialects have dropped it, the ones which are our grammatical bellwethers. Celie says "us" for "we" as well, and later on in the novel someone tells her that's the way country folks talk. Quite right. Where I live, in south-west England, it's very common. Two girls see someone waving to them across the road, and one girl says to the other: "Why be 'er waving at we? Us don't know she."

So, like I say, I'm not going to despise Celie for the way she talks and writes. But it does mark her as uneducated. In fact, she's had very little schooling. Her schoolteacher stopped arguing for her to be allowed to come to school when she realized Celie was fourteen and pregnant as a result of rape. Celie is astonishingly ignorant, even of matters you don't learn in school. She writes, "a girl at church say you git big if you bleed every month. I don't bleed no more." Doesn't she know what's happening?

Anyway, Celie's life is truly awful. Every one of the book's early chapters has another terrible revelation in it. In chapter 1 the man she thinks is her father rapes her, and she gets pregnant. In chapter 2 her mother dies cursing her, and her supposed father takes her baby away, and she thinks he kills it. In chapter 3 he sells their second child. Then he brings back a new wife. He beats Celie. Someone asks to marry her younger sister. Her pa offers him Celie instead. She's taken out of school. She gets married, and on her wedding day her stepson hits her in the head with a rock.

Worst of all, her sister Nettie is sent away, but promises to write. "She say, nothing but death can keep me from it. She never write." Nearly every chapter ends with a flat downer of a line. About her mother, too sick to last long; about her baby, kilt it out there in the woods. Kill this one too if he can; And look what happen to ma; I don't bleed no more; She tell lies; What you setting there laughing like a fool fer? Good question. Celie doesn't have much to laugh about. I guess I made my point. Celie is right down there on the bottom.

Two questions, what indications of heroic character can you show way down there? And more urgent, what's the strategy for getting up and out? That takes us back to Uncle Tom's Cabin. Naturally, people tell Celie she has to fight, fight her husband, Albert, who beats her with his children watching. "Celie, git the belt," he says. People also tell Celie to fight her stepchildren, who are encouraged to be rude to her and won't do any chores.

Now, does fighting work? As with several of the stories we look at, this one operates by pairing and contrasts. We see different women try different strategies. So there's Sofia, who marries Harpo, Celie's insolent stepson. She's a fighter. Celie, in fact, slyly sets her stepson Harpo up for a fight. She advises him to beat Sofia, to teach her her place. Soon he shows up saying the mule kicked him. And he walked into a door. And oh, he shut a window on his hand. So, good, the decision in that bout went to Sofia. But Harpo is poor and black too. In the contest between him and his wife, it's just strength and aggression which decide.

But later, the town mayor's white wife asks Sofia if she wants to become her maid, and Sofia says, "Hell, no." The mayor slaps her for insolence, and Sofia, who doesn't do slaps, knocks him down. Her boyfriend is with her, a prizefighter. He doesn't jump in because, as Celie puts it, "Polices have they guns on him [...] Six of them, you know." Sofia is beaten unrecognizable and then gets twelve years in jail for assault. Strength and aggression didn't help her.

Okay, try another route, just to get Sofia out of the prison laundry. Try the traditional strategy of the weak—trickery and cajoling. You recall what I said about Uncle Tom's Cabin and the racial mixing going on undercover in this overtly racist and segregationist society. It means that most people, black or white, have relations of the other color. So Celie and Sofia's relatives start thinking. Who's the prison warden? Doesn't he have a brother? Anyone know his brother? Squeak, she's Harpo's new girlfriend, reluctantly admits he's her daddy. So the prison warden is her uncle, and the warden knows that.

Off you go, Squeak. The plan is that she will tell the warden Sofia is happy in the laundry, she needs to be punished more. Make her "some white lady maid." The prizefighter, Sofia's boyfriend, says: "This sound mighty much like some ole uncle Tomming to me." But Shug, who's the smart one, she says, "Uncle Tom wasn't call Uncle for nothing." And the trick works, kind of. Her uncle rapes Squeak, saying it's not incest, just ordinary fornication, everyone does that. But they let Sofia out of the laundry to work for the mayor's wife as a maid. Not good, but a better result than Sofia got from fighting.

All this time Celie is learning. She learns from Shug, which I guess is short for sugar, who was once her husband's girlfriend. Shug is a woman who's got on by using her sex, and especially, her voice, music being one of the few ways of social advancement open to African Americans. She sings in juke joints, she earns money, she ends up with a big house in Memphis. She also explains to Celie about sex, which is a kind of liberation for her—in passages which probably account for the frequent censorship of this novel as promoting lesbianism.

Shug also fixes the worst hurt which has been done to Celie, the fact that she never heard from her sister Nettie. But that's not because Nettie never wrote, it's because Celie's husband Albert has been intercepting and hiding her letters. So Celie gets all of Nettie's letters at once, and she learns from them as well. Nettie has been educated; she writes well, she has broader horizons. She's been taken in by a missionary couple, African American themselves, and gone to Africa with them. It's Nettie who finds out that Celie's children are alive and have also been adopted by the missionary couple.

Furthermore, the man she and Celie thought was their father—Fonso—is not their father at all. Their real father was lynched while they were babies for setting up in competition with white traders, and Fonso married the widow to collect her inheritance. Celie even learns from Fonso, who gave her away with the cow. He says, it's all about money. Pay the white folks off. Run the store, like Celie's real father did, but put in a white manager and pay the kickbacks. Now Fonso too has a big house and property, like Shug. Cunning is the resort of the weak. But it's the resort of the brave as well. If you're weak, you need even more courage, or fortitude, as I call it, to be a hero, or a heroine.

So, there's a kind of debate about strategies going on in *The Color Purple*, conducted mostly between the central female characters, Celie, Sofia, and Shug. But that doesn't answer fully the other question I posed a while back, which was about the heroic qualities it's possible to demonstrate way down there at the bottom level of society. Why are we classifying Celie as a heroine? Well, the more I look at *The Color Purple*, the more I see the connection, and the contrast, with *Uncle Tom's Cabin*. The two novels have had very different receptions in the last generation or so. "Uncle Tom" has become a term of disapproval, which is how Sofia's boyfriend the prizefighter sees it, and Stowe's novel is now not much read, except in university courses. *The Color Purple*, by contrast, won a Pulitzer prize in 1983 and was turned into a Broadway musical and a movie directed by Steven Spielberg, with Whoopi Goldberg as Celie and Oprah Winfrey, no less, as Sofia. Fame doesn't get much bigger than that!

Just the same, the two novels have marked similarities. Celie, for instance, suffers the same two temptations which come to Tom. There's the temptation to violence against her oppressors. Cassie told Tom to kill Simon Legree with an axe. When Celie finds out about the way her husband Albert has been hiding Nettie's letters, and after she's retrieved and read them, she wants to kill him with the straight-edge razor he uses for shaving. Shug reminds her of the commandment, Thou Shalt Not Kill, but this doesn't have much effect. Shug reminds her also, and this is very like Uncle Tom, that Christ too suffered on the Cross, without retaliating on his murderers. Slowly this brings Celie round.

But both Celie and Tom feel another temptation, which is to despair. When Celie writes her letters at the start of the novel they're all addressed "Dear God." She has no one else to write to. And she does it because she takes literally what her abusive supposed father said to her after he raped her, "You better not tell nobody but God. It'd kill your mammy." So she tells God what's happened. But the first few words of the novel make clear she is in despair. "Dear God. I am fourteen years old. I am [crossed out] I have always been a good girl. Maybe you can give me a sign." The crossing out means that she thinks she can't be a good girl any more. She's been "spoilt," the word her supposed father uses. She asks for a sign, but she doesn't get one.

So, just like Tom and the slaves on Simon Legree's plantation, Celie starts to think there is no God, or God has forgotten them. This feeling takes a while to build up. Arguing with Sofia early on, Celie says she couldn't even be angry with her rapist father, because the Bible tells you to honor your father and your mother. Sofia more practically says, she ought to bash her abusive husband's head open, but Celie says, "This life soon be over. Heaven last all ways." Traditional resignation.

But once Celie starts writing back to Nettie and no longer has only God to write to, her attitude changes. Shug asks her why, and Celie says, "What God do for me?" It's a fair question. He gave her life and a woman who loves her, says Shug. Yes, says Celie, and a lynched father, a crazy mother, a lowdown dog for a stepfather, and a sister she never sees. She could have added, a husband from hell as well. So, Celie concludes, God is just like all the other men she knows, "Trifling, forgetful, and lowdown." Someone with no time for poor colored women. This is a kind of blasphemy which goes beyond anything we heard from Uncle Tom or Legree's slaves. This scene between Shug and Celie, though, rather like Tom's vision of the Crown of Thorns, turns into the existential heart of the novel. Because whatever she says, Celie cares about God, even if He's not there, doing without Him is hard.

And this is where we come to the mysterious title of the novel. What does "the color purple" mean? Let's try to get at an answer by looking at a few occurrences of the word "purple" in the book.

The first time the color purple appears, Albert's sister Kate, who is trying to get Celie to stand up for herself against her husband and her stepsons, takes her out to buy a dress. What color would she like? Celie says, "Somethin purple, maybe little red in it too." But the store doesn't have anything like that. The choice is brown, maroon, navy blue, and Celie opts for navy. She seems not to have forgotten the disappointment though, because near the end of the novel, when she can choose her own colors for her house, she has everything in her own room purple and red.

The important scene, however, which I've called the existential heart of the novel, is the scene between Shug and Celie, which Celie reports in a letter to Nettie. Celie tells Shug she writes to Nettie now, not to God. Shug wants to know why, and Celie tells her she has lost faith in God, as I said just a minute ago. But then Shug explains the basis for her own faith. She tells Celie, you won't find God in church. You won't find Him even in the Bible. The church God, the Bible God, is a white invention. When you imagine Him, He has blue eyes. That's who you see if you pray in church, and that's why you think He never listens to poor, colored women any more than the mayor and his wife do. That's not her God, says Shug. The God she believes in is inside her and inside everyone else. And this God is also "Everything [...] Everything that is or ever was or ever will be." God is an It, not a Him. And the way you serve It is by being happy, enjoying all the things It has created. You are letting God down, says Shug, if you walk past the color purple in a field and don't notice it. Forget the God who looks like an old, white man. Appreciate the color purple instead.

Another way of putting it, and this is the way Celie takes it, is that she should notice God's creation instead of trying to locate God. A bush or a tree shows God's goodness far more than her husband or her stepfather or any of the other men Celie has encountered. Look at blades of corn. Look at wildflowers. And once again, look at the color purple.

What Shug is preaching is a kind of pantheism, though neither she nor Celie knows the word, and in her way, she is duplicating the kind of visionary sense we associate with the Romantic poets—Wordsworth and the daffodils; or Coleridge's Ancient Mariner blessing the sea-snakes for their brilliant colors, as he stands tied to the mast on a ship with a dead crew, and an albatross tied round his neck to mark his crime. And like the Ancient Mariner, once Celie finds herself able to love Creation, she is at least on the way to freedom.

Her more practical way out is to take up her needle, instead of the razor she meant to kill her husband with. She makes a pair of pants for Sofia's brother in law Jack, who is everything the other men in Celie's life are not. Then other people start wanting pants like his. Turn the page, and Celie has her own business—Folkspants Unlimited, at Sugar Avery Drive, Memphis. A page on, and she is an employer of seamstresses. She inherits from her stepfather, house and dry goods store together. Her sister comes back to her. And she even reaches a kind of forgiveness for her abusive husband Albert. In her own room, in her own house, on the mantelpiece, is a little purple frog carved by Albert. All, it seems, from the one revelation. The color purple stands for happiness, for acceptance, for forgiveness. It's a long road from the utter misery of the novel's beginning.

I asked the question, what makes Celie a heroine, and the first part of the answer must be fortitude, as it was with Uncle Tom. Like Frodo Baggins and Sam Gamgee, Celie just keeps plugging along, in spite of every discouragement and every hostility. Also, like Tom, Celie puts aside the temptations to violence, and worse than violence, to hatred. She has good reason to hate—Remember, "Celie, git the belt"? But she finds the emotion is self-destructive.

Unlike Tom, though, and in different circumstances, she does not become a martyr. She finds her own way out. With, it should be said, the powerful assistance of Shug, first and foremost. But also Nettie, by letter, and some other characters like Sofia's sister and Albert's sisters as well. Female solidarity is an important resource all the way through.

In the bewildering chains of marriage and remarriage and other relationships, one might expect Celie and Shug to be enemies, rivals for Albert, who was not always cruel and embittered, or so Shug says. But they're allies instead. Squeak has also replaced Sofia as Harpo's partner, but she goes to try to rescue Sofia just the same. Shug helps Squeak start her own career as a singer, this time under her own name, Mary Agnes.

The missionary wife, Corinne, becomes jealous of Nettie, for she sees the family resemblance between Nettie and Celie's children, whom they have adopted, and imagines they must be Nettie's children by her husband Stephen. But she too realizes the truth before she dies. This points to a major difference between *The Color Purple* and *Uncle Tom's Cabin*. The enemy in the latter is slavery; no question about that. By Celie's time, slavery has been long abolished, though as someone in the novel says, it doesn't look like that. What are Sofia's twelve years as an unpaid lady's maid, a sentence imposed for the crime of hitting back, if not slavery?

Nevertheless, and not forgetting the casual disrespect shown from time to time by the few white people who appear in the book, Alice Walker's major target has shifted from racism to sexism. Celie's main oppressors are her stepfather Fonso, her husband Albert, and until she deals with him, her stepson Harpo. Male role models, like Sofia's brother-in-law Jack or Samuel the missionary, are present but peripheral.

Nettie's experiences in Africa, which she relates in her letters to Celie, give a telling picture of white colonial exploitation in Africa. And for a while the Olinka people, among whom Nettie lives, seem a model of cooperation, benevolence, closeness to Nature. Yet they too believe firmly in male supremacy. Girls should not be educated; they must have the tribal scars cut into their faces. The African girl whom Celie's son Adam marries even insists on undergoing what is called "female initiation," which means, though Walker doesn't say this straight out, excision of the clitoris, with the aim of making women sexually unresponsive and so not likely to cheat their husbands.

It is not just in Georgia that women are oppressed, and not only by white men. Perhaps, and this takes us back to what I was saying about Huckleberry Finn, the threat from which the color purple releases us, is that of having to play a role insisted on by convention—male or female, submissive or dominant, harsh or gentle. Either way, the role can be a straitjacket. By the end of the novel, even Albert seems to have broken free of his and become a passable human being again.

One final point is that Alice Walker has been accused of sentimentality, but there's one scene which shows her rejecting it firmly. During her twelve-year servitude, Sofia naturally took over child-rearing duties, and one of her taskmistress' daughters remains attached to her. As an adult, this white woman brings her husband and baby to see Sofia and fishes for compliments on her baby. "Don't you just love him?" she asks. She wants Sofia, you might say, to take on the role of Mammy to her own Scarlett O'Hara, as in the nostalgic and determinedly sentimental weepie *Gone with the Wind*. But Sofia refuses. No, she says, I don't. Colored women who say that kind of thing are lying. She doesn't feel hatred, but she doesn't feel love.

And so, despite the happy ending, in which Celie has won through to her sister, and her independence, and her new understanding, there's still a long way to go for the rest of us. But if Celie can overcome all her obstacles and find her own way out, well, we can too. If we have her heart, and her faith.

Winston Smith—The Hero We Never Want to Be
Lecture 20

Winston Smith is the central character of George Orwell's novel *Nineteen Eighty-four*, published in 1949. Unlike Odysseus or Don Quixote, Winston did not give a word to the language, but his creator did. That word is the adjective "Orwellian," and the noun it usually accompanies is "nightmare." Winston himself is at the center of an Orwellian nightmare. Of all the characters in our course, he is the least obviously heroic, and his story ends in cowardice, treachery, and defeat. Still, he is an important hero—the hero anyone of the World War II generation might have become and the hero our descendants might become yet.

Winston as Hero
- Winston Smith is the least obviously heroic of all the characters in our course. He's afraid all the time and never puts up any overt show of resistance to the Orwellian nightmare in which he finds himself. In the end, under torture, he cracks. Of course, Orwell's point is that in the nightmare, everyone cracks. In the end, everyone gets taken to room 101, where we each meet our private nightmare.
  - The Party, which rules Britain, knows our terrors. With Winston, it's rats. In room 101, a cage will be put over his head, and starving rats will be let into the cage to eat his face. He realizes that the only thing that will save him is to betray his lover, Julia, and he does so.

  - Winston cracked under torture, and he remains cracked. At the end of the novel, released from his torturers, though still aware that he will ultimately be executed, he sits listening to the propaganda flowing from the telescreen and tells himself that everything is now all right: "The struggle was finished. He had won the victory over himself. He loved Big Brother."

- Winston's story ends in cowardice and defeat, yet he is an important example of a hero that might have existed if things had gone differently in World War II and might yet exist in the future. The Orwellian nightmare hasn't occurred in the Western world, but we must continue to heed Orwell's warning.

The World of *Nineteen Eighty-four*

- Readers of *Nineteen Eighty-four* can guess some of the basic facts of Winston's lifetime more easily than he can. He was born in 1945. His family name, Smith, is probably the most common family name in English society; calling him Smith is similar to calling him Everyman.
  - The name Winston means something more particular, something obvious now and even more obvious in 1949, when Orwell's book was published. Winston Smith's birth date, 1945, marked the end of World War II, and Winston Churchill was the victorious British leader of that war.

  - But Winston has never heard of Winston Churchill. Nor does he know who won World War II or even who fought it.

- In Orwell's imaginary world, the Party's ideology is known as Ingsoc, short for "English socialism"; note the parallel this has with Nazi, short for Nationalsozialistische Partei, "National Socialist Party."

- Britain is now called Airstrip One, and it's part of Oceania, which probably includes Britain, the United States, Canada, Australia, and New Zealand. Oceania is one of three superpowers, Oceania, Eurasia, and Eastasia, and these three are always at war.
  - This imagined world is not far removed from reality in 1949. At the time, Britain had a socialist government, and for years, it had been an airstrip for British, Canadian, and American bomber fleets.

  - The world division into three superpowers could readily be seen as a development from Britain, the United States, and Western Europe (Oceania) facing off against the Union of Soviet Socialist Republics (Eurasia) and, on the other side of the world, the Communist Party of China, perhaps having taken over Japan, Southeast Asia, and the Indian subcontinent (Eastasia).

- Under Ingsoc, all food is rationed; London is full of unrepaired bomb sites; and the population is highly militarized—all situations that were also reality in Britain in 1949. The basic facts of the Orwellian nightmare were not unfamiliar to a 1949 readership.

- But the Orwellian nightmare was far worse than real life in 1949. In Winston's world, there's a TV in every apartment, called a telescreen, but it's two-way, and it can't be turned off. Everyone is under surveillance all the time. It's a one-party state, and the Party has total control. The agents of the Party's control are the Thought Police.

- Of course, the emblem of the Party is Big Brother, whose face is everywhere. He's modeled on the great dictators of Orwell's recent past: Hitler and Stalin. But Big Brother may not even exist. He has no name and no personality; if he were a real person and he were to die, he could be replaced without anyone noticing. According to O'Brien, Winston's torturer, Big Brother is immortal; he's gone beyond being a dictator or a king and become something like a god.

Ingsoc's Means of Control
- The first stage in the Party's efforts toward total control seems to be making people accept obvious nonsense. The slogans of the Party are: "War is peace. Freedom is slavery. Ignorance is strength."

- The second stage is controlling the language. In Winston's future, the aim is that English will be replaced by Newspeak, which will have a far more limited vocabulary than English. The idea is to prevent even the conception of an unorthodox opinion by eliminating the words people might use to express such an opinion.

- Another means of control is to teach people to use "doublethink," the ability to be completely convinced of two contradictory opinions at the same time, without knowing that they contradict each other.

- The method of control that most affects Winston—and which he cannot stop himself from struggling against—is the idea of controlling the past.
  - Winston works for the Ministry of Truth, which is concerned only with propaganda. His job is to rewrite history. Any statement of fact that contradicts the idea that the Party is always right must be erased.

  - Throughout Oceania, all reliable evidence of events in the past is destroyed. In fact, the only place where any trace of the past remains is inside people's minds—and even there, one wonders. The people have been trained to control their minds and memories.

  - The most extreme example of this collective amnesia occurs during Hate Week, when the people switch their hatred from Eurasia to Eastasia on a moment's notice. As Orwell himself pointed out, much the same thing had occurred among British communists in the 1940s after Hitler invaded Russia.

Inner and Outer Stories in the Novel
- In Book One, the Orwellian nightmare is described in detail. In Book Two, Winston becomes involved with Julia, a younger woman who joins him in resistance to the Party's attempt to completely control sex. The two have an affair but are eventually captured by the Thought Police. Book Three takes place almost entirely in the torture dungeons of the Ministry of Love and consists largely of a conversation between Winston and O'Brien.

- The inner story of *Nineteen Eighty-four*, however, is focused on Winston's attempt to remember the past. The first gesture of resistance he makes is to buy a diary, but he doesn't even know how to write in a diary. Again and again, he writes, "Down with Big Brother."

- As the novel continues, we find Winston trying to make sense of his scattered memories, some of which come to him in dreams. He questions an old prole about life before Ingsoc, but the prole's replies seem random. In the end, Winston gets nowhere in his attempt to recover the past, but he treasures every approach to it. He perseveres in his heroic initiative, but we must admit that it ends in failure.

- *Nineteen Eighty-four* is a science fiction novel of a particular type, often called an enclosed universe novel. Such novels generally feature some kind of disaster in the past and a hero trying to find out what it was, using only degraded information.
  - Most writers have their heroes find a document that explains what has happened. O'Brien, in his capacity as a stool pigeon, gives such a document to Winston—a book, supposedly written by the great enemy of Big Brother, a man called Goldstein. The book explains how Ingsoc came about.

  - Why is the world always at war? It's a way of preserving power for the Party hierarchy. The world populations are too busy fighting each other to rebel against their masters.

  - The new power system creates an oligarchy and stifles any possibility of equality. But what is the motive for all this? Why do people, even in reality, hand themselves over completely to a political system that gives them nothing back?

  - It seems that even Orwell didn't know the answer to that question; he just knew that it happened. The great anti-climax of *Nineteen Eighty-four* occurs when Winston reaches the point in Goldstein's book where the motive is explained, and he puts the book down. He never returns to it because the Thought Police arrive.

- In his conversation with Winston in the torture dungeons of the Ministry of Love, O'Brien says that if Winston wants to have an image of the future of the human race, it's this: a boot stamping on a human face forever. That is what the Party aims to do. But we still don't understand why.

- Winston is trying to probe the great political failures of Orwell's time. This is the reason he deserves to be called a hero.

The Orwellian Nightmare in Our Time

- *Nineteen Eighty-four* has been successful in persuading Westerners about the nature of the Orwellian nightmare. Do we still need to worry about it?

- Newspeak isn't a reality, but the growth of specialist jargons—academic, legal, and political—sometimes makes it difficult to think straight. We're watched by closed-circuit TV cameras, and we

© Ingram Publishing/Thinkstock.

We know that video surveillance, airport searches, and other measures are taken for our own security, but many still fear the ever-increasing power of the state.

know that our governments have the ability to monitor our emails and phone calls. We're told that these intrusions are for our own security, but some people still appeal to Orwell to justify their resistance to encroachments on liberty.

- For example, taking Winston as their cue, many people ask: How far are we prepared to go in granting powers to Homeland Security? Appeals to remember Orwell's warning about the Orwellian nightmare are still current. The fears are still present, and they're not wholly imaginary.

Essential Reading

Orwell (Crick, ed.), *Nineteen Eighty-four*.

Suggested Reading

Crick, *George Orwell: A Life*.

Davison, *George Orwell: A Literary Life*.

Shippey, "Variations on Newspeak."

Questions to Consider

1. Are you satisfied with the current balance between the need for homeland security and the right to a private life, the right not to be interfered with?

2. How satisfied are you that the images you have of the past—say, of World War II or the war in Vietnam—are basically truthful? Do you have any evidence that they are not?

Winston Smith—The Hero We Never Want to Be
Lecture 20—Transcript

Winston Smith is the central character of George Orwell's novel *Nineteen Eighty-four*, which was published in 1949. Unlike Odysseus or Don Quixote, Winston has not given a word to the language, but his creator has. The word is the adjective "Orwellian," and the noun it usually goes with is "nightmare." Winston Smith is the central character in the Orwellian nightmare.

I'll describe the nightmare in a moment, but first let's concentrate on Winston. Can he be called a hero? Well, of all the characters in this course, he is the least obviously heroic. Is a hero big, strong, fearless? Winston is certainly not big and strong. He's 39. He's small and thin. Hobbits are small too, but unlike hobbits, Winston is frail, whereas they are rather tough. He's in poor shape, as we find out when he's rebuked by the physical training instructor who is watching him on the two-way TV. And again, unlike hobbits, he's in poor health. He's undernourished, he has a varicose ulcer on his leg which won't heal. Near the end, O'Brien, his torturer, makes him look in a mirror. He looks like a skeleton, hair falling out, teeth falling out, arms and legs like pipe stems. In fact, he looks like someone from a concentration camp, an image fresh and vivid to Orwell and his audience, in 1949.

All right, enough of the physique. Is Winston fearless? No he isn't. He's afraid all the time, and to tell the truth, he never puts up any overt show of resistance to the Orwellian nightmare. In the end, under torture, he cracks. Of course, Orwell's point is that in the nightmare, everyone cracks. In the end, everyone gets taken to room 101, and in room 101 you meet the worst thing in the world. Every one of us, I guess, has a private terror, and in the nightmare, the Party knows what it is. With Winston, it's rats. They're going to put a cage over his face, and then let starving rats into the cage, who will eat his face alive. O'Brien says to him, "Sometimes they attack the eyes first. Sometimes they burrow through the cheeks and devour the tongue."

Winston, completely terrified, suddenly realizes that there is just one thing he can say which will save him. There is one person in the world he can put between him and the rats, and that is his lover Julia. He screams out, "Do it to Julia! Not me! Julia! I don't care what you do to her. Tear her face off, strip her to the bones. Not me! Julia! Not me!" Winston's act of cowardice and treachery saves him from the rats. Well, he cracks under torture, as according to Orwell everyone would. But Winston stays cracked, because in the Orwellian nightmare, the Party does not want you just to submit. They want you to convert, to have no corner of resistance anywhere in your soul, no matter how concealed.

And Winston doesn't. At the very end of the novel, released from the torturers, though still well aware that it's only a matter of time before he's executed, he sits listening to the propaganda flowing from the telescreen and telling himself that everything is now all right; "The struggle was finished. He had won the victory over himself. He loved Big Brother."

Winston's story, then, ends in cowardice, treachery, failure, final defeat. Yet in spite of all that, I still think we should count Winston as a hero, and a very important hero. He is the hero anyone my age might have had to be if things had gone differently. And he is also the hero our descendants in the future might yet have to be. The Orwellian nightmare didn't happen; 1984 in reality wasn't like 1984 in the novel—or not in the Western world. In other parts of the world, East Germany, say, they were getting there. In places like Cambodia, the Killing Fields, they'd been there. Orwell warned the Western world, and it took notice. But we have to keep repeating the warning, and that's why "Orwellian" has remained an important word in the political vocabulary.

So, what makes Winston a hero (kind of)? It's because he has something in him, something he's never learned, certainly never been taught. It's just something in him that's there spontaneously, like a soul, a little spark of divinity. It shows in the fact that he wants to know. He wants to understand. He wants to know what happened, and why. We, the readers of *Nineteen Eighty-four*, can guess some of the basic facts of Winston's lifetime better than he can. If Winston was 39 in 1984, he was born in 1945, just after I was, so I find it easy to identify with him. The date fits his name. His family name, Smith, is probably the most common family name in English society, so calling him Smith is about the same as calling him Everyman.

Winston means something more particular, something obvious now and even more obvious in 1949, when Orwell's book was published; 1945, Winston's birthdate, marked the end of World War II, and Winston Churchill was the victorious British leader of that war. In 1945 lots of little boys were called Winston, and Winston Smith must have been one of them. But Winston has never heard of Winston Churchill, nor does he know who won World War II, or even who fought it. And now we come to the nightmare.

In Orwell's imaginary 1984, Britain is ruled by the Party. The Party's ideology is known as Ingsoc, obviously short for English Socialism, and note the parallel with Nazi, short for Nationalsozialistische Partei, National Socialist Party. But it's not just Britain. Britain is now called Airstrip One, and it's part of Oceania, which I guess is what we now sometimes call the Anglosphere—Britain, the USA, Canada, Australia, New Zealand. Oceania is one of three superpowers, Oceania, Eurasia, East Asia, and these three are always at war with each other. It seems that at any one time two will be in alliance against the third.

Now this is not so very far removed from reality in 1949. In 1949 Britain really did have a socialist government, though it wasn't called Ingsoc. For years it had been an airstrip for the British, Canadian, and American bomber fleets. As for the world division into three superpowers, this could readily be seen as a development from Britain and the USA and Western Europe, Oceania; faced off against the Union of Soviet Socialist Republics, Eurasia; and on the other side of the world, the other great Communist Party of China, perhaps having taken over Japan and Southeast Asia and the Indian subcontinent, Eastasia.

Going on from there, under Ingsoc things are bad. Everything is in short supply, everything is rationed. Well, I remember, even in the 1950s, having a ration book and taking it with me to the shop to buy chocolate. Under Ingsoc again, London is full of unrepaired bomb sites. As it was in reality in 1949. Under Ingsoc the British population is highly militarized. So were we! At the age of thirteen I was doing rifle drill on the Parade Square, and I didn't go to a military academy. Shortly after that, I had a German schoolboy staying with me as an exchange student, and he was quite amazed by the sight of us all drilling on the square. I could see he thought, "Aren't these guys supposed to have won the war?" Under Ingsoc as well, no one has cars, or fridges, or any kind of domestic appliances, and there's only one channel you can watch on the TV. Once again, that's pretty close to real life in Orwell's own time. So the basic facts of the Orwellian nightmare were not at all unfamiliar to 1949 readership.

But the Orwellian nightmare was far worse even than 1949 real life. In Winston's world there's a TV in every apartment, called a telescreen, but it's two way, and you can't turn it off. You're under surveillance all the time. It's a one-party state, and the Party has total control. I mean ,total. The way O'Brien puts it, Winston's torturer, is this. He says that the Party has gone far beyond all previous forms of total control. The old dictatorships, with which the world has long been familiar, they had gotten as far as being able to say to their slaves, "thou shalt not." Later on, totalitarian states had gotten as far as being able to say to their populations, "thou shalt." The Party has gone a stage beyond even that. They can say to their slave populations, and this includes members of the Party as well, not "thou shalt" but "thou art." The Party has the ambition and the power to control not only the body and outward behavior, but also the mind and the inner thoughts. The agents of their control are not the regular police, but the Thought Police. Under Ingsoc, there's no nonsense about having to commit a crime before you're guilty. You only have to think the wrong thoughts.

And the emblem of the Party is Big Brother, whose face is on every hoarding, on every telescreen. There's a model for Big Brother, of course, in the great dictators of Orwell's very recent past—Hitler, the Leader, and Stalin, whom the Western powers tried to make popular, as long as he was their ally against the Nazis, by calling him "Uncle Joe." Stalin, in his disguise as Uncle Joe, is perhaps the obvious model for Big Brother, but there's one big difference. In the Orwellian nightmare Big Brother may not even exist. He has no name; he has no personality. If he were a real person and he were to die, then he could be replaced without anyone noticing.

O'Brien says that Big Brother is immortal. He's got past being a dictator or a king and turned into something very like a god. The slogan you see everywhere under Ingsoc is "Big Brother is watching you." It might well remind one of the slogan people used to embroider and hang up on 19th-century walls, "thou God seest me." But in the case of Big Brother, it's literally true. He has all those telescreens. The Party, then, is set on total control of minds as well as bodies. It has various ways of doing this.

You might say that the first stage is by making people accept obvious nonsense. The slogans of the Party are: "War is peace. Freedom is slavery. Ignorance is strength." So, stage one is creating nonsense. Stage two is controlling the language. In Winston's future, the aim is that English shall be replaced by Newspeak. This will have a far more limited vocabulary than English. The idea is that it will prevent even the conception of any unorthodox opinion by eliminating all the words that you might use to express such an opinion. There will be no word for science. You just say Ingsoc. There will be no word for religion. You just say Ingsoc. The word "free" will have no political meaning. In Newspeak you could say—for even grammar will be regularized—"All mans are equal," but it would be obvious nonsense, like saying, "All mans are red-haired."

Control the language, yes. Train people to control the brain by teaching them how to use "doublethink," the ability to be completely convinced of two contradictory opinions at the same time, without knowing that they contradict each other. But the method of control which really affects Winston, and which he cannot stop himself struggling against is, the idea of controlling the past. Controlling the past is Winston's job. He works for the Ministry of Truth, which is, of course, the Ministry of Lies, being concerned only with propaganda. His job is to rewrite history. Since the Party is always right, and since the Party is all powerful, any statement of fact which contradicts that must be erased.

Near the start we see Winston at work. It has been reported, in the official Party newspaper, that Big Brother had predicted that the South Indian front would remain quiet, but that the Eurasians would attack in North Africa. In fact, the reverse happened. The Eurasians attacked in South India and not in North Africa. So it's necessary to rewrite Big Brother's speech so that his prediction becomes perfectly true. And even more important, to make certain that there is no trace left of anything to contradict that! What Winston does, in this and other cases, is rewrite the speech and then consign the real speech, the one that was actually made, down the "memory hole" to be destroyed.

This is done on a massive scale throughout the whole of Oceania so that there is never any reliable evidence of what happened in the past at all.

In fact, the past has vanished. The only place where any trace of it remains is inside people's heads. And even there, one wonders. The population has, after all, been trained in controlling its own minds and its own memories. If the chocolate ration is reduced from thirty grams to twenty, immediately there will be joyful demonstrations in the street by people thanking Big Brother for raising the chocolate ration to twenty. The fact that it once was thirty? No evidence for that, no memory of that. Winston asks himself at one point whether he is the only person left in the world who is in possession of a memory.

The most extreme example of this collective amnesia in the book occurs during Hate Week. For months, the population of Airstrip One has been worked into a frenzy of hatred against Eurasia. A speaker is lashing the crowd into an even further frenzy when someone comes up and hands him a piece of paper. The speaker looks at it, and without hesitating, continues his speech, but now it's hatred against Eastasia. The two-against-one Alliance has shifted. Immediately, everyone starts tearing down the posters and the banners which they spent months creating, and hate week continues without a pause. The war against Eurasia has been immediately forgotten. Eurasia is on our side now.

There's no doubt about what made Orwell create this apparently insane scene. As he pointed out himself, much the same thing had happened in the 1940s to everyone who was a committed communist, as many of Orwell's friends were. Up to September 1939, British communists were totally against the Nazis and Hitler. Once Stalin had signed his non-aggression pact with Hitler, suddenly, the Nazis were acceptable, even though they were at war with Britain, because they were on the same side as Stalin. But as soon as such an English communist heard the eight o'clock news on the morning of 22nd of June 1941, which was when Hitler invaded Russia, then once again, Nazism was the enemy and the most hideous evil the world had ever known. So people really could make these total shifts of opinion, apparently without becoming insane. Had they no memory?

Winston is in rebellion against the abolition of the past. That is the inner story of *Nineteen Eighty-four*. It's much more important than the outer story. I'll tell you the outer story briefly. In part one, we have the Orwellian nightmare described in some detail. In part two, Winston falls in love with—no, that's not true. Winston hooks up with Julia, a much younger woman who joins him in resistance to the Party's attempt to completely control sex. They have an affair. They find themselves a little secret apartment among the proles— that's the Orwellian term for the lower classes, below the middle class Outer Party to which Winston and Julia belong, and below the Inner Party who are the real controllers.

Winston and Julia also make contact with an Inner Party member, O'Brien, who claims to represent the secret resistance to the Party. But O'Brien is a stool pigeon. So is the junk dealer who rents them the secret apartment. Winston and Julia are captured by the Thought Police. And part three of *Nineteen Eighty-four* takes place almost entirely in the torture dungeons of the Ministry of Love and consists largely of a conversation between Winston and O'Brien. That's the whole outer story.

The inner story of *Nineteen Eighty-four* is really about Winston's attempt to remember the past. The first gesture of resistance which he makes is to buy a diary, an old diary, because diaries aren't made any more. The purpose of a diary is to help you remember the past, and that's forbidden. Winston, of course, doesn't know how to write in a diary at first, and all he can do is write again and again "Down with Big Brother. Down with Big Brother."

But as the novel continues, we find Winston trying to make sense of his scattered memories, some of which come to him in dreams. He remembers being in an air raid when he was little. He remembers stealing chocolate from his little sister and running away, and coming back to find that his mother and his sister have vanished, presumably taken by the Thought Police. He tries to find out what happened from other sources. At one point he has a conversation with an old prole, someone maybe thirty years older than him, and so born about 1915. He asks him what life was like before Ingsoc. Was it true, as it says in the Party's history books, that everyone was wretchedly poor except the capitalists, who went about wearing top hats? Was it true that the capitalists could do anything they liked and went around with escorts of lackeys? Could they just push you off the street into the gutter?

The old prole just replies with random memories, the day he wore a top hat at a funeral, the day a young drunk pushed him off the pavement. We, Orwell's readers in 1949 or any other date since then, know that the old prole is, in fact, completely contradicting the Party's history. The young drunk may have pushed him off the pavement, but the old prole, back then, was at perfect liberty to push him back and was in fact going to punch him one until... And then the prole's memory wanders off in another direction.

Winston really gets nowhere in his attempt to recover the past, but he treasures every approach to it, even physical objects, like his diary, or the nursery rhyme "Oranges and Lemons," which preserves the names of the old churches of London. Winston perseveres in his heroic initiative, but we have to admit that it ends in total failure—total failure for Winston, not quite for us. I would describe *Nineteen Eighty-four*, as a novel, like this. It's a science fiction novel, as is obvious, but it's a science fiction novel of a particular type, which people often call the "enclosed universe" novel.

I won't try and detail the different kinds of "enclosed universe" plots which writers have invented. What they have in common is some kind of disaster in the past, and a hero trying to find out what it was. But all he has to go on is what we would call "degraded information." The question in such stories is always, is it logically possible to get to the truth of a situation based solely on "degraded information." Logically, the answer is "no." But that spoils the story. So what most writers do is have their hero find a document, which explains what has happened—a logbook, a chronicle, a diary. Now that is what O'Brien, in his capacity as a stool pigeon, gives to Winston. It's a book, supposedly written by the great enemy of Big Brother, a man called Goldstein; his Communist analogue in the real world would be Trotsky. This book explains how Ingsoc came about.

Why is the world always at war? It's a way of preserving power for the Party hierarchy. The world populations are too busy fighting each other to rebel against their masters. It makes no difference anyway, because the three superpowers are all the same. Behind that statement, of course, is another real-life observation, that the Nazis might be right-wing and the communists left-wing, but it didn't really make any difference. What the new power system does is create an oligarchy, another word for which might be the Russian *nomenklatura*, and to stifle any possibility of equality.

But what is the motive even of this? After all, in the Orwellian nightmare, even the Inner Party doesn't have much fun! So why do people, even in reality, hand themselves over completely to a political system which gives them nothing back? I don't think Orwell knew the answer to that; he just knew it happened. The great anti-climax of *Nineteen Eighty-four* is this. Winston has just got to the point in Goldstein's book which says that the original motive which created the whole apparatus of continuous warfare, Thought Police, and all the rest of it, really consists... And then Winston puts the book down, looking forward to reading the rest of it later, which he never does, because the Thought Police arrive. But the real reason for the unfinished explanation is that Orwell didn't know what the original motive was, any more than Winston did. Or, I'd add, any more than Tolkien did. Tolkien created his Ringwraiths, who have lost all their humanity and been eaten up from inside, but we don't know how they got there. Tolkien's friend C. S. Lewis created a very similar image to Orwell's *Nineteen Eighty-four* in his 1945 book, That Hideous Strength. But Lewis didn't know the answer either. He suggested such people might have been possessed by devils. Kurt Vonnegut was just as puzzled, in *Slaughterhouse Five*.

All these authors had lived through the same sort of real-life experiences, and they knew what had happened, and they knew how it had happened, but they were all puzzled as to why it had happened. In his conversation with Winston in the torture dungeons of the Ministry of Love, O'Brien says that if Winston wants to have an image of the future of the human race, it's this, a boot stamping on a human face, for ever. That is what the Party aims to do. But we still don't understand why.

Now this is why I think Winston is so important and why he deserves the name of hero. He's trying to probe the great political failures of Orwell's time, and my own time—your time too. Yes, *Nineteen Eighty-four* has been totally successful in persuading Westerners about the nature of the Orwellian nightmare. But it's all over now, right? Well, perhaps not. Take Newspeak, for instance. It hasn't actually happened, but even in my lifetime I've noticed the growth of specialist jargons which seem to make it difficult to think straight. There's academic jargon; there's legal jargon; there's management jargon; and most of all, there's political jargon. During the Watergate hearings I heard a great deal of stuff which sounded to me as if it had been produced by someone who'd mastered the idea of doublethink.

Or take the idea that Big Brother is watching you. Well, perhaps he is. I'm told that Britain, where I live, has more closed-circuit TV cameras per head of population than anywhere else in the world, and I'm told that the purpose of this is to reduce crime, but it hasn't. I'm sure all of us have had the experience of being pulled out of line at the airport and searched, for, as far as we know, no reason at all. And you can't answer back. It's for security.

We also know that our governments have the ability to monitor our emails and our phones, and we know that's the kind of thing they do, but we don't know how much they do it. Yes, all for our own security, and that may well be true. But there is still the hidden fear of ever-increasing state control, and the ever-increasing power of the state. People take different attitudes to this, but some still appeal to Orwell to justify the resistance to encroachments on liberty.

For example, taking Winston as their cue, many people are asking, how far are we prepared to go in granting powers to Homeland Security? A science fiction writer called Cory Doctorow has written a kind of positive riff on Orwell called *Little Brother*, and he followed it up with one called *Homeland*. So appeals to remember the Orwellian warning about the Orwellian nightmare are still current and felt to be live issues. The fears are still there, and they are not wholly imaginary.

So, to conclude, *Nineteen Eighty-four* and the Orwellian nightmare are just science fiction, that's right. And they'll stay science fiction. But only so long as we all have a bit of Winston in us. He was a hero of his own time, and of Orwell's time. But we need people with that untaught and spontaneous spark of resistance in them in all times—past, present, and future.

James Bond—A Dangerous Protector
Lecture 21

Of all the heroes and legends we discuss in this course, James Bond probably has the greatest global name recognition. The reason for that is that the Bond franchise is probably the most successful in world history. Ian Fleming, who created James Bond, died in 1964, after having published a dozen Bond novels and two collections of Bond short stories. There have since been more than 20 Bond novels written, with permission, by authors other than Fleming, and the original novels and their sequels have been used to create more than 20 movies. In this lecture, we'll ask: What is the secret of this continuing and readily exportable success?

Bond's Success in the 1950s

- One reason the Bond novels were successful when they first came out in the 1950s was the dreary and disappointing atmosphere of Britain in the immediate postwar years. The nation had been among the winners of the war, but it remained poor, cold, regulated, and rationed.

- As we saw in the last lecture, Orwell looked into the future at this time and saw things getting worse. In his vision, the new socialist government would turn into Ingsoc, and the country would be taken over from within by a new tyranny.

- Fleming's response was the exact opposite. He didn't think that the future would be like the present only worse; he thought Britain could return to the past. The country would still have enemies, but they wouldn't be internal ones; they'd be external ones: foreign criminals, Soviet spies and saboteurs. And they'd be dealt with as they had been in the past; the traditional authorities would still be in control.
  - That's the point of being "licensed to kill." It's a kind of reassurance. Obviously, democracies are not supposed to use murder or assassination as a political tool. But if the other

side does and we don't, aren't we inflicting a handicap on ourselves? In *Live and Let Die*, Bond says that the success of Mr. Big "shows how one can push a democracy around." Maybe we need to get tough, too.

o But someone has to control these tools, someone reliable and trustworthy. Bond is a killer but not a vigilante. He operates under some kind of system of democratic control, though we never find out quite what that system is.

- Along with this need for traditional authority, there was also a strong element of nostalgia in the 1950s for the time before World War II. For this reason, Bond starts off his career driving a 1930 Bentley. In his world, the movers and shakers still operate in the gentlemen's clubs of London.
  o Significantly, the first Bond novel, *Casino Royale*, is set in a French seaside town that has decided to get back on its feet by reopening its casino and trying to "regain some of its Victorian renown."

  o This nostalgia for a vanished past merges easily into a luxurious present, though that luxurious present had to be somewhere outside 1950s Britain, notably the United States.

  o Some people have said that the secret of the Bond success is snobbery, but it seems more a response to deprivation and a reassurance. Bond is at home in any company; he always knows the right thing to do, to say, to eat and drink. He's the very incarnation of *savoir faire*.

- Bond's sophistication over minor matters, such as what dishes to order in a restaurant, turns into knowledge about many other things. This became a major element in the movies, in which Q, the quartermaster of the Secret Service, constantly issues gadgets to Bond. Some of this interest in gadgetry comes from the original books. In *From Russia with Love*, for example, Bond has a briefcase with built-in throwing knives.

Bond's Success in Modern Times

- In the rather frightened and deprived context of the 1950s, Bond provided a sense of confidence about the future even as he satisfied readers' nostalgia by taking them back to a better past. In later decades, there's a strong element of wish fulfillment in his success.

- Bond is the kind of man every man wants to be: omni-competent and cool in any circumstances. He's the basic male hero that we've often seen—big, strong, and fearless—but he's never quite unbelievable. He's not unusually big or strong, and he does have moments of fear. More than Odysseus, Beowulf, or Robin Hood, he's versatile.
  - Bond is good at swimming, and he can handle scuba gear, but he has to train for it. He makes an escape on skis in *On Her Majesty's Secret Service*, but he only just gets away from the professionals who are chasing him. He's a good shot but not as good as his instructor.

  - Although it's Fleming's fault, Bond doesn't know much about guns. In the early novels, Bond's preferred weapon was a Beretta .25, but Fleming was told by a gentleman called Boothroyd that this was just a popgun. Accordingly, in *Dr. No*, Fleming introduced a character called Major Boothroyd, who makes Bond shift to a Walther PPK.

- Bond is a masculine fantasy, but of course, he also appeals to women, though he ought to look like bad news.
  - One of the adjectives Fleming repeatedly uses about Bond

Bond is versatile, but his fallibility, such as his inexperience with guns, helps to make the character more plausible.

is "cruel." And he is cruel. He kills nearly 40 people in the adventures described by Fleming.

o Further, in almost every book, he acquires an extremely attractive woman, who disappears or is disposed of before the start of the next one. He seems like a hit-and-run lover or the classic bad boy.

o But there's another side to Bond; he's gallant, even protective in an old-fashioned way. Nearly all the women in Bond's life have been badly treated and are scarred psychologically or even physically. Honeychile in *Dr. No* has been beaten and raped; Tiffany Case in *Diamonds Are Forever* was gang-raped as a teenager; and other female characters have similar histories.

o Tracy and Vesper, the two women Bond marries or means to marry, both have hidden sorrows or secrets: One is rescued from suicide by Bond; the other commits suicide because she has betrayed him.

o In his ninth Bond novel, *The Spy Who Loved Me*, Fleming experimented by telling the story from the viewpoint not of Bond but of the woman he rescues. She is warned off him at the end by a kindly policeman, but he treats her better than any of her former partners did.

• A third reason for Bond's success in the modern era is Fleming's ability to create quite imaginative villains. Perhaps the best of them is Dr. No, with his prosthetic hands, his lethal aquarium, and his desire for artistry in crime.
o Goldfinger has an obsession with physical gold and a habit of painting girls with gold, so that if they're not aerated, they die. Ernst Stavro Blofeld is a running opponent through three novels. His female sidekick, Irma Bunt, follows Rosa Klebb in the list of dangerous hags.

○ Two other awesome figures are the Irish psychopath Red Grant, recruited by the Russians to become chief executioner for SMERSH, and Goldfinger's Korean bodyguard Oddjob, the karate expert, invulnerable to any kind of hand-to-hand assault.

Bond and M

- The relationship between Bond and his boss, M, is a rather odd one. M seems to regard Bond as nothing more than an expendable employee. By contrast, Bond seems excessively loyal to M. In one of the short stories, "From a View to a Kill," Bond goes outside the terms of his "license to kill" to murder people who have murdered old friends of M. But this is private enterprise, not government business, and even Bond knows he shouldn't be doing it. The relationship seems like one between a father and son.

- A similar relationship may apply, in a way, to some of the villain figures, as well. One repeated and rather implausible scene in the whole Bond corpus is the one in which Bond is captured by one of the villains, who then tries to explain his motives before torturing Bond. Kingsley Amis noted that this scene echoes the lecture a child might get before a punishment.

- Although M might appear to be the kindly—rather than frightening—father figure, he isn't kindly, and in fact, Bond actually tries to kill him at the start of *The Man with the Golden Gun*. True, it's because the Russians have brainwashed him, but their success suggests a kind of ambiguity in the relationship between Bond and M.

- If Fleming's novels are full of father figures for Bond, one might expect that, for all his womanizing, Bond might suffer from some form of castration anxiety. He's not been allowed to grow up. We might even say that Bond is not exactly an adult male fantasy but a teenage fantasy, with the teenage dreams of strength, sophistication. and sexual attraction—all to a disproportionate but not-quite-impossible level.

- Still, Bond has a fairly well-developed moral conscience. His duty is to kill villains, and he does, but he hesitates when asked to do so as a private favor by M. He also claims never to have killed anyone in cold blood. He doesn't physically abuse women, and he's capable of falling in love. He shows concern for some of his partners, and although they sometimes dump him, he doesn't dump them.

- We could sum up by saying that Bond never quite becomes a vigilante. He is always operating under license, which means there is some kind of restraint on him. And this is one of the ways in which he has had a continuing influence on popular culture, especially in the movies: He is a lonely imposer of justice. In this, he's been followed by actors who have tended to take the same kind of role, such as Clint Eastwood as Dirty Harry.

- One other thing Fleming's Bond did was give new life to the old genre of spy stories. Len Deighton and John le Carré reacted against Bond by writing what were, in effect, spy procedurals, sordid and unglamorous. Such writers as Tom Clancy took up the technological interest and developed it almost beyond recognition.

- Unlike Frodo Baggins or Harry Potter, Bond does not seem to have deep roots in older myth or legend. He is essentially a new-style hero. Like Winston Smith, he's a product of his time, the old Cold War, which did not end with the fall of the Berlin Wall in 1989. Like so many of the tales we've looked at, Bond's story mutated, and he has gone on to be a lasting success beyond the place and time in which he was created.

Essential Reading

Fleming, *Casino Royale*.

———, *From Russia with Love*.

———, *Dr. No.*

———, *Goldfinger*.

Suggested Reading

Amis, *The Bond Dossier.*

Lycett, *Ian Fleming.*

O'Connell, *Catching Bullets.*

Questions to Consider

1. Do you find it possible to accept the various justifications offered for presenting an assassin as a popular hero, or is there a hidden motive for Bond's continuing popularity?

2. With the end of the Cold War, would you say that the Bond franchise has increasingly become comic in tone, each sequel and movie trying to outdo the others in exaggeration?

James Bond—A Dangerous Protector
Lecture 21—Transcript

Of all the heroes and legends we discuss in this course, the character I'm about to present probably has the greatest global name recognition. His name is James Bond. I think if you went into a village in Central Africa or Central Asia, and said to anyone there, "You know Bond?" Someone would reply, "Bond. James Bond. 007. Licensed to kill. Shaken not stirred," or some other catchphrase from the Bond books and the Bond movies.

The reason for that is that the Bond franchise is probably the most successful in world history. I say franchise deliberately. There are authors who have sold more copies, like Tolkien, who began this course, and J.K. Rowling, who will close it. Movies based on their books have taken more at the box office. However, in both those cases, the Tolkien estate, or Rowling herself, have kept close control over the material and not allowed sequels or spin offs to be produced. This is not the case with the Bond phenomenon.

Ian Fleming, who created James Bond, died in 1964 after having published a dozen Bond novels from 1953 onwards, as well as two collections of Bond short stories. These began to be filmed with *Dr. No* in 1962. On this basis has been built a whole edifice of sequels and further movies. There have been more than 20 Bond novels written, by permission, by authors other than Fleming, and the original novels and their sequels have been used to create more than 20 movies. There's no sign of this process concluding. Indeed, a 2013 TV program, which looked at fifty years of Bond movies and tried to identify the most iconic scenes from them, ended with a producer looking forward to a further 50 years. So, as I often do in these lectures, I ask, what is the secret of this continuing and readily exportable success?

Several people have given answers. One disapproving reviewer said it's just sex, sadism, and snobbery. Or you might say, rather more politely, it's girls, gadgets, and glamour. But these answers are on the whole from the movies, and I don't want to concentrate on them. The seed of success was in the original novels, and the center of that success is just the character of James Bond himself. So, I'll ask my question again. What is the secret of his success? And I'm going to give two answers. One is to say why I think the Bond novels caught on way back then in the 1950s and 1960s. And the other is to say why I think they've achieved a lasting success, even in the different circumstances of the late 20th and early 21st centuries. I'm probably a good person to give these two different answers, because I read the Bond novels pretty much as they came out in the 1950s, and I've re-read them just recently, so I have at least an idea about both.

Why were the Bond novels a success in the 1950s? Well, remember what I said when I discussed Orwell's *Nineteen Eighty-four*, which came out only four years before the first of Ian Fleming's novels? I pointed out how dreary and disappointing Britain was in those immediate post-war years. Sure, Britain had won the war, or been among the winners of the war. But Britain remained, as I well remember, poor, cold, regulated, rationed. No wonder that Orwell looked into the future and saw things just getting worse. In Orwell's vision, the new socialist government would turn into Ingsoc, and the country would be taken over from within by a new tyranny, very similar to the one which the war had been fought to overthrow.

Well, that was one response to the situation. Fleming's was the exact opposite. He thought the future would not be the present, only worse. He thought we could return to the past. We'd get back on our feet again. We'd still have enemies, but they wouldn't be internal ones, they'd be external ones—foreign criminals, Soviet spies and saboteurs, often in alliance with each other. And we'd deal with them as we had done before. The traditional authorities would still be in control. That's the point, really, of being "licensed to kill." It's a kind of reassurance. Obviously, democracies are not supposed to use murder or assassination as a political tool. But if the other side does, aren't we inflicting a handicap on ourselves? Bond says in *Live and Let Die* that the success of Mr. Big "shows how one can push a democracy around." So, maybe we should get tough too. But somebody has to control this, somebody reliable, somebody we can trust. Bond, in fact, or his boss M, or whoever it is that his boss reports to. Bond is a killer, but not a vigilante. He's operating under some kind of system of democratic control, though we never find out quite what this is.

Along with this, back in the 1950s, there was a strong element of nostalgia. For the time before World War II, which must have been fresh in the memories of Fleming and many of his audience, like my parents. What kind of car does Bond drive? He starts off driving a 1930 Bentley. He has his cigarettes specially made for him, by Morlands of Grosvenor Street in London. The movers and shakers in his world still operate in the gentleman's clubs of London, like Blades, where Bond plays the bridge game with Hugo Drax in *Moonraker*.

Bond naturally fits in okay because he is a gentleman, though not quite an insider. His parentage is not English, but Scots and Swiss. He went to the two top schools in England and Scotland, Eton and Fettes respectively, though he was expelled from the former after a hushed-up scandal with a maid. His rank is Commander, Royal Navy, and his only income is his pay as a middle-grade civil servant. Enough, back then, for him to run a London flat with a housekeeper.

Going back to nostalgia, quite significantly, the first Bond novel, *Casino Royale*, is set in a French seaside town, which has decided to get back on its feet by reopening its casino and trying to, and I quote, "regain some of its Victorian renown." Gambling, of course, is another old aristocratic pastime from back when aristocrats were rich, and the Fleming novels have Bond or his enemies playing high-stakes games of baccarat, bridge, golf, and canasta, all very well and knowledgeably described.

This nostalgia for a vanished past merges easily into a luxurious present, though that luxurious present has to be somewhere outside 1950s Britain, notably the USA. I remember one tiny detail which struck me many years ago, and that's in the novel *Diamonds are Forever*. Bond is in New York, and his friend Felix Leiter is taking him out to dinner. He says, "I've ordered you smoked salmon and Brizzola." Now, I didn't know what Brizzola was, and I still don't, but Leiter says it's the best cut of the finest meat in America. "Beef, straight cut across the bone. Roast and then broiled." I can tell you, in a world where meat was rationed and you were lucky to get scrag-end of mutton, this roast and broiled straight-cut Brizzola sounded fantastically good. Bond and his sidekicks are always saying things like that. In *Goldfinger* Bond is in France, wondering what to have for dinner and decides against the local catch because, as he puts it, "The fish of the Loire are inclined to be muddy." So he has sole meunière from Orleans instead.

And Bond is, of course, notoriously knowledgeable about drinks. There's been a long argument online about whether his famous "shaken not stirred" is good advice or not, but there's a scene, again, in *Diamonds are Forever*, where Bond gets his own back on the American Leiter by laying down the law about how to make a martini. That's why people have said that the secret of the Bond success is snobbery, but I don't think so. It's a response to deprivation. It's also a reassurance. Bond is at home in any company; he always knows the right thing to do, the right thing to say, the right thing to eat and drink. He's the very incarnation of *savoir faire*.

The sophistication over these minor matters turns into knowledgeability about many other things. This became a major element in the movies, where Q, the quartermaster of the Secret Service, is always issuing Bond with gadgets. His cars in the movies are fitted with machine guns and ejector seats and turn into submarines when required. He has tracers and trick cigarette cases and goodness knows what else. Some of this does, indeed, come from the original books. In *From Russia with Love* Bond has a briefcase with built-in throwing knives. His enemy Rosa Klebb goes one better with poisoned blades, which click out of her shoes. In *Goldfinger*, the Korean villain Oddjob has the famous bowler hat with a steel brim, which can be flicked like a lethal Frisbee, all surprising and fascinating, with just a little potential also for humor.

But all that was back then. Things have developed a great deal since then, and what was shocking once isn't so any more. Fleming could assume, for instance, that no one had ever heard of karate, first mentioned in *Goldfinger*. We all know about that now. He could also expect us to be impressed by gambling for what now seems rather small amounts of money. In *Goldfinger*, once again, when Bond plays a round of golf against Goldfinger, they're playing for $10,000, and Fleming notes, "There had probably never been such a high singles game in history." Not true any more! Inflation of all kinds has made those original novels look a bit small time. In *The Man with the Golden Gun* a hundredweight of marijuana is reckoned to be a big deal.

Still, all that kind of thing can very readily be updated, and in the movies, it has been. But what is it about James Bond, the hero, that has survived the passage of time? In the rather frightened and deprived context of the 1950s,

Bond provided a sense of confidence about the future, even as he satisfied readers' nostalgia by taking them back to a better past. How, though, has he managed to appeal to readers over the course of later decades? Well, pretty obviously, there is a strong element of wish fulfillment. Is Bond the kind of man that every man wants to be? Well, he's omni-competent. Give him a strange machine, like a marsh buggy or a giant excavator, as happens in *Dr. No*, and he can run them immediately and fight off a giant squid in between, instead of wondering where to find the ignition key, like the most of us.

He always keeps his cool under any kind of circumstances. He can burn himself out of his bonds with a blow torch held in his mouth, as he does in *Goldfinger*. He has the letters R-U-T after his name in his personal file, standing for Reliable Under Torture. And he gets tortured quite a lot, in fact, in six of the first seven books. The torture with the carpet beater in *Casino Royale* is particularly horrible and unexpected, just as bad as Winston Smith's rats.

There's also the circular saw in *Goldfinger*, which the movie updated to become an industrial laser. And a scene which frightened me a lot as a boy, at the end of *Live and Let Die*; there Bond, and his girlfriend Solitaire, are tied to a paravane towed behind a yacht, which is going to drag them on to a sharp coral reef, and then drag their bleeding bodies over the reef to where the sharks and the barracuda will be waiting. Bond decides to use his body to protect Solitaire from the reef, and then, if they're dragged over it, to roll her under him and deliberately drown her before the first shark fins appear. They're saved when the limpet mine, which he had previously attached to the yacht, goes off before they get to the reef, so it's Mr. Big who keeps the appointment with the sharks.

Okay, masculine wish fulfillment, you might say that Bond is the Basic Male Hero which I've often talked about. He's big, strong, and fearless, right. But notice that he's never quite unbelievable. He's not unusually big or unusually strong, and he does have moments of fear. What he really is, more than Odysseus or Beowulf or Robin Hood ever needed to be, is versatile. He's good at swimming, and he can handle scuba gear, but he has to train for it. He knows how to ski, and he makes an escape on skis in *On Her Majesty's Secret Service*, but he only just gets away from the professionals who are chasing him. He's a good shot, but not as good as his instructor. He's good at golf, but plays from a nine handicap. And it's not Bond's fault, it's Fleming's, but he really doesn't know much about guns. In the early novels, Bond's preferred weapon was a Beretta .25. But Fleming was told by a gentleman called Boothroyd that this was just a popgun, which is correct; I had one once, and I wouldn't have trusted it over six feet.

In *Dr. No*, Fleming accordingly introduced a character called Major Boothroyd, who makes Bond shift to a Walther PPK. Fans have pointed out a whole string of mistakes to do with Bond's gunnery, like the trick-draw holster he matches up with the wrong kind of pistol and Fleming's idea of a quick draw, which would not impress the FBI at all. Just the same, Major Boothroyd the Armorer became the model in the movies for Q, the Quartermaster, the man with all the gadgets, and the idea has been imitated. There's an armory scene, for instance, in the Van Helsing movie I mentioned when talking about Dracula.

So, Bond is versatile, but he's also fallible, which helps to make him just about plausible—more so in the books than in the movies. Does this amount to saying he's vulnerable? Is there maybe a hint of something damaged about him? Which raises the further question, he's a masculine fantasy, yes. Does he appeal to women as well? And if so, why? Because you could easily say that from the woman's point of view, he ought to look like bad news. The first question is the easy one. Does he appeal to women as well? Yes, he certainly does. A 2013 survey of female users of audiobooks in Britain found that their favorite fantasy male partner was indeed James Bond. Why he appeals is not so easy.

One of the adjectives Fleming repeatedly uses about him is "cruel." And Bond is cruel. He kills nearly 40 people in his adventures as described by Ian Fleming, one of them by dropping him into a shark tank. And there's no doubt either that in almost every book—*Moonraker* is the only exception—he acquires an extremely attractive woman, who disappears or is disposed of before the start of the next one. He looks like a classic hit-and-run lover, the sort of person we saw in Diomedes when I talked about Cressida. Or, you might say, the classic Bad Boy whom every woman would like to have a fling with, as opposed to the Nice Boy she will eventually settle down with. There's some truth in that.

But there's another side to him, which is that he's gallant in an old-fashioned kind of way, even protective. Nearly all the women in Bond's life have been badly treated and are scarred psychologically or even physically. One of the iconic moments of the movies is Ursula Andress coming out of the water in a white bikini in *Dr. No*. In the book, she doesn't have a bikini, she's naked. But when she realizes someone is watching, her hand flies up, not to cover her breasts, but to cover the broken nose of which she is ashamed. You can see why they had to change that scene for the movie.

So. Honeychile in *Dr. No* has been beaten and raped. Tiffany Case in *Diamonds Are Forever* was gang-raped as a teenager. Pussy Galore in *Goldfinger* was abused even earlier. Other female characters have similar histories. Tracy and Vesper, meanwhile, the two women Bond marries, or means to marry, both have hidden sorrows or hidden secrets; one is rescued from suicide by Bond, the other commits suicide because she has betrayed him. It's a very marked pattern. In Fleming's novels, Bond girls may be fantastically attractive, as they are in the movies, but they are also vulnerable. They're waifs. They respond to Bond because he's kind to them and treats them like human beings.

In his ninth Bond novel, *The Spy who Loved Me*, Fleming experimented by telling the story from the viewpoint, not of Bond, but of the woman he rescues. She is warned off him at the end by a kindly policeman, but not only does Bond rescue her from rape and murder, he treats her better than any of her former partners did. Because he's a gentleman, old-style. So, men want to be Bond, women want to meet Bond. That's two reasons for the saga's continuing success, both in the wish-fulfillment area.

A third reason is Fleming's ability to create really unpleasant and threatening villains. Sometimes the plots they hatch look, from a modern perspective, rather small time. Destroy London with a private-enterprise ICBM in *Moonraker*, that's pretty good; steal atomic bombs and take out Miami in *Thunderball*, that's pretty good. But destabilize the British economy by gold smuggling, or diamond smuggling, or spreading bio diseases to wipe out British agriculture? There are worse threats than that.

Even if the plots can be faulted, however, the villains are really memorable and imaginative. Perhaps the best of them is *Dr. No*, with his prosthetic hands, his lethal aquarium, his obstacle course, which takes you into the tentacles of a giant squid, his flame-throwing marsh buggy disguised as a dragon, and his desire above all for finesse, for artistry in crime. An ambition he shares with Mr. Big, and with Goldfinger. As for Goldfinger, he has his obsession with physical gold and his habit of painting girls all over with gold so that if they're not aerated, they die. Ernst Stavro Blofeld is a running opponent through three novels. The scene in which he assembles his associates and electrocutes one of them without warning during the meeting, has become a classic. His female sidekick Irma Bunt follows Rosa Klebb in the list of dangerous hags.

Two other awesome figures are the Irish psychopath Red Grant, recruited by the Russians to become Chief Executioner for SMERSH, whom Bond kills in a hand-to-hand struggle thanks to the knife concealed in his briefcase. And Goldfinger's Korean bodyguard Oddjob, the karate expert, invulnerable to any kind of hand-to-hand assault. Bond kills him by suddenly breaking a window in the plane they're in so that the pressure differential sucks him through the window while Bond stays safely belted in. Many people have kept their safety belts on throughout a flight just from the memory of that scene. The movies added on Jaws, the giant with the steel teeth, and Nick Nack, the midget, in *The Man with the Golden Gun*.

Well, one could go on from the female partners and the male and female villains to look also at Bond's male partners and associates. But perhaps the last relationship we should look at is that between Bond and his boss, M. It's a rather odd one. M seems to regard Bond as just an employee, and an expendable one at that. By contrast, Bond seems excessively loyal to M, even loving. In one of the short stories, "From a View to a Kill," Bond goes outside the terms of his "license to kill," to murder people who have murdered old friends of M. But this is private enterprise, not government business, and even Bond knows he shouldn't be doing it. It really does look like a father-son relationship.

This may apply, in a way, to some of the villain figures as well as M. One repeated and rather implausible scene in the whole Bond corpus is the one in which Bond is captured by Hugo Drax; or Dr. No; or Goldfinger; or Le Chiffre, the Communist trade union boss in *Casino Royale*, and all of them talk to him, to explain why they're doing what they do, before getting on with the torture. Kingsley Amis pointed out once that this is a very familiar scene from the days when schoolboys were routinely caned, or paddled, or got the strap, from their headmaster or from their father. You're called into the study, or the library, and then you get told what a disappointment you are before the beating starts.

So the villains, in a way, seem like father figures as well as M. And while M might appear to be the kindly rather than the frightening father figure, in the first place, he isn't kindly, and in the second place, Bond does actually try to kill him at the start of *The Man with the Golden Gun*. True, it's because the Russians have brainwashed him, but their success does suggest a kind of ambiguity in the Bond-M relationship to begin with.

I don't usually go for psychological interpretations, but if Fleming's novels are full of father figures for Bond, one might expect that, for all his womanizing, Bond himself might suffer from some form of castration anxiety. He's not been allowed to grow up. In which case, we might go on to say, as many people would, that Bond is not exactly an adult male fantasy, but a teenage fantasy, a fantasy of a male who also hasn't quite grown up, who has the teenage dreams of strength, and sophistication, and savoir faire, and sexual attraction, all to a disproportionate but not quite impossible level.

I think you could make out a case for this, and indeed, I just have, but it leaves out some of the other things which I've mentioned. Bond has a fairly well developed moral conscience. His duty is to kill villains, and he does, but he does hesitate when asked to do it as a private favor by M. He also claims never to have killed anyone in cold blood. In another of the short stories, "The Living Daylights," he deliberately shifts his aim when he realizes that the Russian sniper he is covering is a woman. He doesn't physically abuse women. He falls in love first with Vesper, then with Tracy, and is heartbroken when he loses the latter. Possibly also when he loses the former, though he covers it up. He arranges plastic surgery for Honeychile Rider in *Dr. No*, he shows concern for some of his other partners, and we know they sometimes dump him, he doesn't dump them.

I could sum up by saying that he never quite becomes a vigilante. He is always operating under license, which means there is some kind of restraint upon him. And this is one of the ways in which he has had a continuing influence on popular culture, especially in the movies. He is a lonely imposer of justice. And in this he's been followed, not so much by individual fictional characters, as by actors, who've tended to take the same kind of role, like Clint Eastwood as Dirty Harry, or as Pale Rider; or Arnold Schwarzenegger in a whole string of movies. Both of them have also made a point of the kind of wisecrack or one liner which Sean Connery introduced to the early Bond movies.

One other thing Fleming's Bond did was give new life to the old genre of spy stories. Len Deighton and John le Carré reacted against Bond by writing what were, in effect, spy procedurals, sordid and un glamorous, like *The Spy who Came in from the Cold*. Writers like Tom Clancy have taken up the technological interest and developed it almost beyond recognition.

But the last thing I have to say about Bond is that, unlike Frodo Baggins, say, or Harry Potter, he does not seem to me to have deep roots in older myth or legend. Though interestingly, in the 23rd Bond movie, *Skyfall*, released in 2012, the character M, who in this movie is a woman, quotes the Tennyson lines about Ulysses, which I mentioned at the end of my Odysseus lecture, "To strive, to seek, to find, and not to yield."

Despite that, I still think Bond is essentially a new-style hero. Like Winston Smith, he's a product of his time, of the old Cold War. This did not end with the fall of the Berlin Wall in 1989. Like so many of the tales we've looked at, it mutated. And so, Bond has gone on to be a lasting success beyond the place and time in which he was created.

Fairy-Tale Heroines—New-Style Princesses
Lecture 22

airy tales came up a few times early on in our course. Behind *Beowulf* lurks the fairy tale of the Bear's Son, and Odysseus and the giant Polyphemus also go back to a fairy tale. As we'll see, fairy tales sometimes underlie modern narratives, as well. Fairy tales are very old, older than Homer. They're also tenacious—still circulating and still mutating. We still respond to them, though we don't always know why. In this lecture, we'll look at a composite figure, the fairy-tale heroine. In particular, we'll see how she has changed or has been changed in the last 40 years.

A Single Story Transformed?

- During the 19th century, every nation in Europe felt that it ought to have its own collection of fairy tales in imitation of the Grimms. There was the Norwegian collection of Jørgen Moe and Peter Christen Asbjørnsen, which gave us "The Three Billy Goats Gruff." There was the Russian collection of Alexander Afanasyev, which introduced us to the witch Baba Yaga. There were Scottish, Irish, and English collections and others.

- In the modern world, a rather small group of tales has formed a focus of interest, including "Cinderella," "Snow White and the Seven Dwarfs," "Rapunzel," Rumpelstiltskin," "Beauty and the Beast," "Sleeping Beauty," "Little Red Riding Hood," and "Bluebeard."
  - o The last is the story of a husband who tells his new bride never to open a locked room; what he doesn't explain is that in it are the corpses of all his former brides.

  - o Of course, the bride opens the room, but Bluebeard finds out and plans to kill her. She's saved at the last minute by her brothers.

- This group of eight tales has several common threads. For example, they always have a threatened heroine, and several have useless or unhelpful fathers. Sometimes, one story seems to be an alternative version of the other. "Beauty and the Beast" seems as if it will turn into the same plot as "Bluebeard," but it turns out that the Beast is not a beast after all. Many people have been tempted to say that all the stories are transformations of an underlying story.

Transparent, Suggestive, and Pliable

- Sometime around the 1970s, people began to see that fairy tales were transparent, suggestive, and pliable. Let's consider each of these adjectives in turn.

- Perhaps the most transparent fairy tale of all is "Little Red Riding Hood." For hundreds of years, people have understood that this tale carries two warnings: Girls should be careful about male sexual predators, and don't judge by appearances. "The Frog Prince" also tells us not to judge by appearances, but with the reverse implication: What looks like a frog on the outside may be a handsome prince on the inside.

- Fairy tales are suggestive in that they sometimes make us wonder whether there is something beneath the surface.
  - "Cinderella," for example, is a story about growing up and becoming independent. Cinderella has a wicked stepmother and a fairy godmother—a mean mother and a nice mother—but somehow, she has to get away from both. She also has to get away from her father, who may be useless or dangerous. The glass slipper, which fits only one person in the world, seems to stand for the real Cinderella, the core of her personality, what she wants to be loved for.

  - In "Snow White," many have said that the phrase "Mirror, mirror, on the wall ..." is a projection of the appraising male gaze—something that every woman is aware of and something that the stepmother, a generation older than Snow White, fears.

  - According to Bruno Bettelheim, who wrote one of the first psychological analyses of fairy tales and introduced the idea of transformations, the dwarves—male but not romantic possibilities—represent a stage of arrested adolescent development for Snow White, a sort of safe house.

- ○ The thing that betrays Snow White are the gifts offered by the disguised stepmother, all of which have some connection with sexual attraction: the stay laces, part of a kind of corset; the hair comb, long hair being a kind of premodern advertisement for single status; and the red apple of temptation, Eve's apple.

- ○ Beneath the surface, these tales are about gender and about growing up. Further, Bettelheim insisted that we need these tales, or something like them, to help us grow up.

- Once the idea spread that fairy tales were using suggestion to teach life lessons, feminist authors pointed out that they were teaching the wrong lessons, that is, indoctrinating girls into a patriarchal way of thinking. After the 1960s, there was an outbreak of books with such titles as *Kiss Sleeping Beauty Goodbye: Breaking the Spell of Feminine Myths and Models* or *The Cinderella Complex: Women's Hidden Fear of Independence*.

© iStockphoto/Thinkstock.

The sense that all fairy tales are transformations of a deep underlying story has been very productive, especially for feminist writers.

- This brings us to our third adjective, pliable. Many people, often female authors, began rewriting fairy tales. Key collections included: Angela Carter's *The Bloody Chamber* (1979); Tanith Lee's *Red as Blood, or Tales from the Sisters Grimmer* (1983); and Jack Zipes's *Don't Bet on the Prince* (1986). The main aim of such rewrites is to reject the passivity of the traditional fairy-tale heroine; to refuse to see her in her usual roles as victim, caregiver, or sex object; and to challenge the whole basis of the fairy tale and make it relate to modern life.

Transformations

- The phenomenon of the feminist fairy tale is much assisted by the idea of transformation. Once two or three people have turned a tale inside out, doing it again becomes easier. One retelling seems to feed off another.

- Angela Carter started off the trend. The second story in her *Bloody Chamber* collection is "The Courtship of Mr. Lyon," a rewrite of Charles Perrault's version of "Beauty and the Beast." It follows the original fairly closely, translated into 20th-century England.
    - A man is snowbound, deep in the country, in a broken-down car. He goes for help to a grand house, where he meets no one, except a welcoming spaniel. He finds food and drink, he phones a rescue service, and on his way out, he sees, under the snow, one perfect white rose—just what he promised to bring his daughter.

    - The man picks the rose, but the house owner appears, a great roaring lion, who calls him a thief. In Perrault, a transparent bargain is made. For the white rose he's picked—the traditional emblem of virginity—the father must hand over his virgin daughter. Carter's version softens this: The snowbound motorist must bring his daughter to dinner.

    - The story ends with a vision of happy domesticity: "Mr. and Mrs. Lyon walk in the garden; the old spaniel drowses on the grass, in a drift of fallen petals."

- In the next story in the collection, "The Tiger's Bride," Carter rewrites "Beauty and the Beast" in a different way.
  - The father is much more culpable: He loses Beauty at cards. She is much more dynamic. She plays out a tough bargain with the Beast; he wants to see her naked, but she makes conditions, ignores his presents, and reduces him to tears. Eventually, she agrees to see him naked in his tiger's shape and only then bares herself.

  - At the end, the Beast licks her, his tongue ripping off layers of skin until he reaches the beautiful fur underneath. Beauty doesn't make the Beast human; the Beast turns Beauty into a tiger.

- We find a similar twist in Kathe Koja's "I Shall Do Thee Mischief in the Wood." In Koja's telling, Little Red Riding Hood appears to be a poor waif, trying to sell trinkets in the market. A merchant offers to take her back to her granny in the woods, meaning to take wicked advantage of her. But he's not the wolf; Granny is, and Little Red Riding Hood has delivered her a victim.
  - Red Riding Hood stories seem to be especially popular in this new mode of writing. Tanith Lee's "Wolfland" again has Granny as a werewolf, with the Little Red Riding Hood equivalent set to succeed her in her power and estate.

  - We might ask whether Granny is the guilty party, trying to keep her granddaughter in childhood when she is already a woman. But in Carter's "The Company of Wolves," Little Red Riding Hood jumps cheerfully into bed with the wolf, ignoring the clattering of old bones under the bed.

- The opening story in Jack Zipes's collection *Don't Bet on the Prince* is Jeanne Desy's "The Princess Who Stood on Her Own Two Feet."
  - Here, the princess is taller than the prince arranged for her, rides as well as he does, and is equally intelligent. The prince is resentful, so the princess decides to sacrifice for love, even

giving up her talking dog. The dog dies, saying, "Sometimes one must give up everything for love."

- o But the dog comes back as a prince, ready "to look up to a proud and beautiful lady." In the end, a talking cat tells us: "Sometimes one must refuse to sacrifice."

- The most disturbing story in Zipes's collection is "Bluebeard's Egg" by Margaret Atwood. In this modern story, Sally, a Canadian housewife, is taking a course on fairy tales, taught by a feminist professor. One of her assignments is to write a fairy tale from a different point of view, and she decides to rewrite "Bluebeard."
  - o Sally never writes her assignment because she herself is in the story "Bluebeard." Her husband isn't a serial bride-murderer, but he is a serial husband.

  - o It's possible that Sally is not the bride who marries Bluebeard but the previous bride—one of those whose corpses are hidden away in the locked room. The threat to Sally is divorce, a return to work, and the inability to find a career because she let herself be sidelined by marriage.

  - o The moral here is plainer than the ones we've seen: A woman shouldn't put all her eggs in the one basket of a nice, comfortable marriage.

- There are numerous possible transformations in fairy tales, and just as we saw a new-style Elizabeth Bennett in Bridget Jones, so we see a new composite fairy-tale heroine in, for example, "The Princess Who Stood on Her Own Two Feet." She's a creature not of the Brothers Grimm but, as Tanith Lee puts it, of the Sisters Grimmer.

Essential Reading

Carter, *The Bloody Chamber and Other Stories*.

Datlow and Wildling, eds., *Snow White, Blood Red*.

Lee, *Red as Blood*.

Maitland, *Gossip from the Forest*.

Zipes, ed., *Don't Bet on the Prince*.

Suggested Reading

Bettelheim, *The Uses of Enchantment*.

Hunter, *Princes, Frogs and Ugly Sisters*.

Questions to Consider

1. Do you think that premodern fairy tales, written for premodern conditions, are now irrelevant, as far as life lessons are concerned? Would you say the same about the earlier Disney movies?

2. Can you compile a list of 6 to 10 favorite fairy tales not mentioned in this lecture? Why do you remember them best?

Fairy-Tale Heroines—New-Style Princesses
Lecture 22—Transcript

Fairy tales came up a few times early on in this course. Behind Beowulf there lurks the fairy tale of the Bear's Son. Odysseus and the giant Polyphemus go back to a fairy tale, of which Homer clearly knew two versions, which he conflates. They sometimes underlie modern narratives as well, as I will point out later. Fairy tales are very old, older than Homer. They're also tenacious. They're still circulating, still mutating. We still respond to them, though we don't always know why.

So today I'm going to look at a composite figure, the fairy-tale heroine, and I'm going to look particularly at how she's changed, or been changed, in about the last forty years, well within my own lifetime. Now, there are thousands of fairy tales. During the 19th century every nation in Europe felt it ought to have its own collection, imitating the Grimms. There was the big Norwegian collection of Jørgen Moe and Peter Christen Asbjørnsen, which gave us "The Three Billy-goats Gruff." There was the big Russian collection of Alexander Afanasyev, which introduced us to the witch Baba Yaga and her hut mounted on chicken legs. There were Scottish and Irish and English collections, and Italo Calvino brought out a particularly fine Italian set. And of course, before the Grimms, there was the French vogue for fairy tales, fostered by Charles Perrault and several earlier female collectors.

So, thousands of tales, scores of collections eventually from all over the world. Nevertheless, in the modern world a rather small group of tales has formed a focus of interest. I've only to mention them, and I'm sure you'll know all the stories. There's Cinderella—fairy godmother, Prince Charming, glass slipper; there's Snow White and the Seven Dwarfs—wicked stepmother, magic mirror, poisoned apple, glass coffin; there's Rapunzel, imprisoned in her tower, letting her long hair down for the prince to climb; there's Rumpelstiltskin, the dwarf who knows how to spin straw into gold, whose name the princess has to guess; there's Beauty and the Beast; and Sleeping Beauty, also known as Briar Rose; there's Little Red Riding Hood; and there's Bluebeard, the husband who tells his new bride never to open a locked room, because in it are all the corpses of his former brides. The

369

key she uses is enchanted, so Bluebeard knows she's opened the room; he's going to kill her, but she's saved at the last minute by her brothers.

I'm sure you know the stories, but just remember that sometimes they exist in more than one version, so the story often has an alternative ending. You can see how this group of eight hangs together. They always have a threatened heroine. The threat may come from the stepmother, as in Cinderella and Snow White; or scary or downright abusive husbands, as in Beauty and the Beast and Bluebeard; or from malevolent witches, as in Rapunzel or Sleeping Beauty, or a dwarf, or a wolf.

Common to several of them are useless or unhelpful fathers: Cinderella, Snow White, Rumpelstiltskin, Rapunzel, Beauty and the Beast. I know about them, because in our village pantomime in 2012, I was cast as Cinderella's spectacularly useless, and in our version, drunken father, Baron Hangover. And the threats can mutate into each other. You may have wondered why Cinderella was so determined to sit among the cinders. In the Grimms' version of that story, it's because her father, who is a widower, has sworn not to marry anyone who is not as beautiful as his dead wife. But then he notices that his daughter is just as beautiful as her mother. The daughter heroine has to run away, rub herself with dirt, wear a strange robe made of many furs, in order to disguise her beauty. And sometimes one story seems to be an alternative version of the other. Beauty and the Beast looks very much as if it is going to turn into the same plot as Bluebeard, the abusive husband, but it turns out that the Beast is not a beast after all.

Are these fairy tales really all the same story? To adapt the title of a famous book about myth, are we looking at "the heroine with a thousand faces"? I think it would spoil the stories if they were all the same. But it's very tempting, and many people have been tempted to say that all the stories are transformations of some underlying story. As all English sentences, if you believe Noam Chomsky, are transformations of underlying deep structures.

Well, I'm not going to try to find the deep structure. I'll just say that this sense that there is something deep down there has been very productive in the last couple of generations—the feminist generations. The way I would put it is that somewhere around the 1970s people began to see that fairy tales were transparent, suggestive, and above all, pliable. Let's consider each of those three adjectives in turn.

Transparent, Perhaps the most transparent fairy tale of all is Little Red Riding Hood. Take your granny a present. Do not stray off the path. Wolf persuades her to stray off the path. Gobbles up the granny and lies in wait for the little girl. In the Grimm version, a woodcutter comes along with his axe and saves Little Red Riding Hood. In the Perrault version, the wolf, who has gobbled up the granny, tells Little Red Riding Hood to undress and get into bed with him. Which she does! And then we get the "what big eyes you've got, what big teeth you've got" scene. After which, he gobbles her up.

We all know this is not about wolves, or not the animal kind. In the 1984 movie *The Company of Wolves*, which is based on an Angela Carter rewrite of "Little Red Riding Hood," we're told explicitly, "the worst kind of wolves are hairy on the inside." But Perrault had already got the message back in 1697, when he appended a little moral to his version of the tale. From his tale, he wrote, we see that young girls should not listen to everyone. Wolves are not all of the same sort. Some seem very pleasant and charming. But alas, *qui ne sait que ces loups doucereux / de tous les loups sont les plus dangereux*—"Who does not know that these gentle wolves are of all wolves the most dangerous wolves?"

For hundreds of years people have understood that "Little Red Riding Hood" carries a warning, or two warnings: Girls should be careful about male sexual predators, and don't judge by appearances. By contrast, the story of "The Frog Prince" also tells us not to judge from appearances, but with the reverse implication; what looks like a frog on the outside may be a handsome prince on the inside. How do you find Mr. Right? I'm sure we've all heard young women say, to find a Prince you have to kiss a lot of frogs first. Everyone sees the point of stories like these. They're transparent. They're about the risks and rewards for females, of gender. And what one story says may be transformed, turned inside out, by another one.

That covers "transparent," let's go on to "suggestive." What do fairy tales suggest? Something which may not be quite as transparent as the sort of thing I've just said. Do fairy tales sometimes make us wonder if there's something beneath the surface? Like, what is it with Cinderella? She has a wicked stepmother and a fairy godmother, who appears out of nowhere. Surely these are transformations, again, of the real mother. There's nice mommy, who loves you and looks after you, and there's nasty mommy, who makes you do the chores and won't let you go to all-night raves. But somehow, you have to get away from both. And get away from daddy as well, who may be useless, may be dangerous. This is a story about growing up, about becoming independent.

Yes, but what about the glass slipper? Unyielding; won't stretch; fits only one person in the whole world—the one Prince Charming is looking for. I'd say it stands for "the real me." The core of the personality. What we want to be loved for. To quote the pop song, "Most of all, I love you 'cos you're you." 'Because you're worth it.' Okay, of these clichés, enough already. But it's very easy to do this sort of symbol spotting. "Mirror, Mirror, on the wall …" Feminists would say, and they have said, and I can go for it too, that this is the projection of the appraising male gaze, which every woman is aware of, and which the stepmother, a generation older than Snow White, fears as she sees Snow White growing up.

So, what about the dwarves? Bruno Bettelheim, who wrote one of the first psychological analyses of fairy tales and introduced the whole idea of transformations, said that the dwarves—male, but not romantic possibilities—represent a stage of arrested adolescent development for Snow White, a sort of safe house, a halfway house, just as it is in the Disney movie, right? And what betrays her? They're the gifts the disguised stepmother offers, all of which have some connection with sexual attraction. There's the stay laces. Stays used to function as a kind of corset and also a kind of pre-modern bra, so wearing stays is a sign of growing up. There's the hair comb, long hair, being a kind of pre-modern advertisement for single status. And finally, there's the red apple of temptation, Eve's apple.

And what about the glass coffin? Well, I'll leave you to do that one. This game is easy. The hedge of thorns round Sleeping Beauty—keep off, don't touch me, till I'm ready to be wakened. Rapunzel safe and sound in the tower, but then letting her long hair down for the Prince—I'm ready now. The locked room your husband forbids you to enter—the dangerous memories the new bride does not share. Anyone can do interpretations like these. And they have! These tales are about gender and about growing up—beneath the surface. Bettelheim insisted, furthermore, that not only are these tales about growing up, we need something, or something like them, to help us grow up. To quote the title of a book written by my friend Dr. Allan Hunter, these are *Stories We Need to Know*. He says more about why in his other book, *Frogs, Princes, and Ugly Sisters*.

Okay, we could agree that fairy tales contain life lessons concealed by suggestion. But are they the right life lessons? Once the idea spread that these stories were using suggestion to tell us something, pretty soon feminist authors started saying, sure they're telling us; they're telling adolescent and preadolescent girls the wrong lessons. Indoctrinating them into a patriarchal way of thinking. You can see what they mean. What does Cinderella tell a girl? Hang around, and "one day your prince will come," and then everything will be okay. But prince charmings are thin on the ground.

What does Sleeping Beauty tell a girl? Maybe, put up a hedge of thorns and only Mr. Right will get through it; or Little Red Riding Hood? Just stay on the straight and narrow, little girl, and do what mommy and granny tell you. This was not welcome advice after the 1960s. So we had an outbreak of books with titles like *Kiss Sleeping Beauty Goodbye: Breaking the Spell of Feminine Myths and Models*, or *The Cinderella Complex: Women's Hidden Fear of Independence*.

The early Disney movies, by the way, got a lot of criticism at this point for showing Snow White as a kind of ideal housewife. The criticism has been taken into account by the later scripts, and you might note that most of what I call the core group of fairy tales have been turned into Disney movies— Snow White in 1937; Cinderella in 1950; Sleeping Beauty in 1959; then a gap until Beauty and the Beast, 1991; The Princess and the Frog, 2009; and one year later, Tangled, which is "Rapunzel." And way back in 1922, Little Red Riding Hood.

Now, this is where our third adjective comes in—pliable. People, overwhelmingly, though not absolutely always female authors, started rewriting fairy tales. This is a phenomenon I can't possibly cover in full;

there was so much of it. But vital collections include, and the titles give you a good idea of what we're talking about, *Angela Carter's The Bloody Chamber*, from 1979; Tanith Lee's *Red as Blood or Tales from the Sisters Grimmer*, from 1983; And Jack Zipes' anthology, *Don't Bet on the Prince*, from 1986. In 1993, Ellen Datlow and Terri Windling brought out a collection of rewritten feminist fairy tales called *Snow White, Blood Red*, and it was so successful that it had a whole string of successors with similar titles. Yet another collection of rewrites is Sara Maitland's *Gossip from the Forest*, in 2012. "Gossip," as Ms. Maitland points out, is an old word for the female companion another female will talk to.

I can only give a few examples of such rewrites, and only briefly. Their main aim is to reject the passivity of the traditional fairy-tale heroine, to refuse to see her in her usual roles as victim, or carer, or, to speak frankly, as sex object. Along with that, though, goes a readiness to challenge the whole basis of the fairy tale, to ask it questions, to make it relate much more obviously to modern life.

The phenomenon of the feminist fairy tale, and it's a collective phenomenon created by scores of writers, is much assisted by the idea I've already mentioned of "transformation." In a way, once two or three people have turned a tale inside out, insisted on writing it from someone else's point of view, it becomes easier to do it again. One retelling seems to feed off another. Angela Carter started it off. In *The Bloody Chamber* collection, story number two, after the title story, is "The Courtship of Mr. Lyon." This is a rewrite of Charles Perrault's version of "*Beauty and the Beast*," and it follows the original fairly closely, if translated into 20th-century England.

A man is snowbound, deep in the country, in a broken-down car. He goes for help to a grand house he sees, where he meets no one, except a welcoming spaniel. He finds food and drink, he phones a rescue service, on his way out he sees, under the snow, one perfect white rose, just what he promised to bring his daughter. He picks it, and the house owner appears, a great roaring lion, who calls him "thief." In Perrault, a very transparent bargain is made. For the white rose he's picked—traditional emblem of virginity—the father must hand over his virgin daughter. Angela Carter's version softens this, though it's still pretty suggestive. The forfeit the snowbound motorist must pay is just, "bring your daughter to dinner." After that, it's more like a proper courtship. The Beast helps Beauty's ruined father to win his court cases, recover his fortune, and lets her go back to him in London, where she starts to turn into a familiar type of spoiled beauty, women who are like "pampered, exquisite, expensive cats." What saves her and the Beast—an entirely original addition by Carter—is the spaniel. He drags her back to the Beast, who is transformed into human shape by her tears. Quite like "The Frog Prince." The story ends with a vision of happy domesticity. "Mr. and Mrs. Lyon walk in the garden; the old spaniel drowses on the grass, in a drift of fallen petals."

So far, so traditional, but Carter was quite ready to transform herself as well. In the next story in the collection, "The Tiger's Bride," Carter rewrites "Beauty and the Beast" a different way. The father is much more culpable., He loses Beauty at cards. She is much more dynamic. She plays out a tough bargain with the Beast; he wants to see her naked, but she makes conditions, ignores his presents, reduces him to tears. Eventually she agrees to see him naked in his tiger's shape, and only then bares herself. The deed is done; she can go back to father. But she goes back to the Beast to see if he will, like the wolf in Riding Hood, gobble her up. But he doesn't. He licks her, purring, and his tongue rips off layer after layer of skin till he gets to the beautiful fur underneath. Beauty doesn't make the Beast human. The Beast turns Beauty into a tiger. "The tiger will never lie down with the lamb [...] The lamb must learn to run with the tigers." That moral went down very well with feminist readers.

We find a similar twist in one of the stories collected in *Snow White, Blood Red*, Kathe Koja's "I Shall Do Thee Mischief in the Wood." In Koja's retelling, Little Red Riding Hood appears to be a poor waif trying to sell trinkets in the market. A merchant offers to take her back to her granny in the wood, meaning to take wicked advantage of her. But no, he's not the wolf. Granny is the wolf, and Little Red Riding has delivered her a victim. Seducers don't gobble little girls up; little girls see they get gobbled up. Or is it grannies who do that? Red Riding Hood stories seem to be especially popular in this new mode of writing. Tanith Lee's "Wolfland" again has Granny as a werewolf, and the Little Red Riding Hood equivalent is going to succeed her in her power and her estate.

Okay, but maybe Granny is the guilty party, not the wolf, for trying to hold her granddaughter in childhood when she is already a woman. In Carter's "The Company of Wolves," the story that got made into the 1984 movie, Little Red Riding Hood performs a much more active striptease than Perrault ever suggested. Then she jumps cheerfully into bed with the wolf, ignoring the clattering of the old bones under the bed. In the end, "Sweet and sound she sleeps in granny's bed, between the paws of the tender wolf."

You see what I mean about fairy tales being pliable and about them being open to question. Why does the wicked witch lock Rapunzel up in the tower? Are we so sure she's wicked? Maybe she's trying to protect Rapunzel from something that happened to her, to the witch? You might note the echo of this in Charles Dickens's classic novel Great Expectations, where Miss Havisham, who has been ditched at the altar and still wears her moth-eaten wedding dress, brings up an orphan girl in isolation to act out her own revenge on men. Fairy tales provoke a lot of questions, offer a lot of gaps for later authors to write into.

So, many stories, many transformations. But I'll just pick two more, the ones which frame Jack Zipes's collection, *Don't Bet on the Prince*, at start and finish. The opening story is Jeanne Desy's "The Princess Who Stood on Her Own Two Feet." It's a very propagandist story. Once upon a time there was a Princess "tall and bright as a sunflower." Trouble is, the Prince arranged for her is not as tall as she is, and the Prince can't take it. Nor can he take the fact that she rides as well as he does and also keeps making intelligent remarks. So the Princess decides to sacrifice for love; don't stand tall, don't go riding, don't betray intelligence; and give up her talking dog, who dies saying, "sometimes one must give up everything for love."

But that's too much. She buries the dog, but he comes back as a prince, still several inches shorter than her, but very ready "to look up to a proud and beautiful lady." The wizard in the tale says, echoing the dog, "Sometimes one must sacrifice for love." But the wizard's cat says, "Sometimes one must refuse to sacrifice." That's right. The only deal on offer should be equality and independence. That's the propaganda version, all right. But that, too, can be challenged. The most disturbing story in Zipes's collection—I think it disturbed him as well—is entitled "Bluebeard's Egg," by Margaret Atwood.

This is a very modern story, so modern that the central character is Sally, a Canadian housewife, who is taking a course on fairy tales, taught, of course, by a feminist professor. One of her assignments is to write a fairy tale from a different point of view, and she's decided to rewrite "Bluebeard" from the point of view of Bluebeard's egg, which in the version she knows is the object which tells Bluebeard that his bride has entered the forbidden room.

Sally never writes her assignment version of "Bluebeard," because she herself is in the story of "Bluebeard." No, she can't be. She's a woman in a modern city, with a husband who's a heart surgeon, he can't be a serial bride murderer. No, but he can be a serial husband. He's been married before. Sally sees him canoodling with her best friend Marylynn. What's going to happen next? Bluebeard's egg, one day it will hatch. What will it hatch into? Dr. Zipes says Sally is going to hatch, take the first steps towards liberation. Or maybe Ed the husband is going to hatch. Maybe he'll see the error of his ways and stop saying "femininist" because he doesn't understand the word "feminist," let alone the idea. Maybe Ed will become a modern husband.

But I think the egg isn't going to hatch; it's going to break, because Sally hasn't realized which character she is in this story. She's not the bride who marries Bluebeard; she's the bride before the bride who marries Bluebeard, one of the ones whose corpses are hidden away in the locked room, the "bloody chamber." The real and realistic threat to Sally is divorce, back to work, no great job, no career, because she let herself be side lined by marriage, etcetera.

And if one wants a moral, it's something plainer than the ones we've had before. Something like, a woman shouldn't put all her eggs in the one basket of a nice, comfortable marriage. That's the bargain Bluebeards offer, and it's a bad bargain and a bad egg, which will hatch only disaster. A woman needs a plan B, as well as a plan A. Atwood's story came out in 1983, but it strikes me as very 21st century. Still, as you can see, even from that very brief summary, there are a lot of options here, a lot of possible transformations. Writers have discovered what a lot of scope there is in traditional stories.

Perhaps there always have been. Isn't Pride and Prejudice a concealed Cinderella story? Elizabeth Bennet doesn't have a wicked stepmother, but she does have a silly and embarrassing mother. She also has a careless and unhelpful father. And while she has no ugly stepsisters, she has three silly and embarrassing sisters, one of whom, Mary, is decidedly plain. And Elizabeth has a Prince Charming who has to come looking for her. Has to come twice, in fact. Of course, Jane Austen's novel has all kinds of things you don't find in a fairy tale: money, entails, social snobbery, rounded characters. Okay, but the plot that provides the motor for the whole novel? It's a fairy tale. That goes for a surprising number of classic novels.

Still, the point I want to make is that just as we have a new-style Elizabeth Bennett in Bridget Jones, so we have a new composite fairy-tale heroine in, you might say, "The Princess Who Stood on Her Own Two Feet." A creature not of the Brothers Grimm, but as Tanith Lee puts it, of the Sisters Grimmer. Although the old plots have not gone away, as Margaret Atwood points out, neither have the old fears. The woods are still full of wolves, the cities full of serial Bluebeards.

In the last couple of lectures, on James Bond and *Nineteen Eighty-four*, I looked at heroes who are new style, created by highly contemporary circumstances. This lecture has shown that very old-style heroines can suddenly take on new life and be adapted to contemporary circumstances. As Bilbo Baggins so rightly says, "The old that is strong does not wither, / deep roots are not reached by the frost."

In the next two lectures of this course, we'll be looking, accordingly, at an extremely contemporary heroine, who nevertheless seems to recreate a very old pattern, and at a hero who steps into a world as magical as fairy tale, only to be dogged by entirely contemporary pressures and anxieties.

Lisbeth Salander—Avenging Female Fury
Lecture 23

In this course, we have come across a number of different kinds of continuation and revival: authors writing into a gap, straightforward makeovers, echoes, independent reinvention, and deliberate rewriting. Elements of all these appear in this lecture and in the character who is at the core of it: Lisbeth Salander, the heroine of Stieg Larsson's trilogy of crime novels that began with *The Girl with the Dragon Tattoo*. Although we might think of Lisbeth as strikingly original, in fact, she seems to be a case of reconstruction from an ancient myth—an avenging female Fury.

"A Heroine Whom No One Will Like"
- The three books in Stieg Larsson's Millennium trilogy all focus on the character Lisbeth Salander. She's a very unexpected heroine and, once more, a challenge to the basic male hero stereotype. She seems to be fearless, but she's not big and strong. Although she is 24 at the time of the first novel, she is said to look 14. Salander makes up for her weakness with other characteristics. As one character says of her, "She always gets revenge." She knows no moderation.

- Salander is also said to feel "no emotional involvement." She responds to many kinds of social interaction only with silence or, sometimes, rage. It's safe to say that she is difficult to deal with.

- She displays a horrific ingenuity in the many ways she takes revenge. Consider, for example, the climactic scene of the final book of the trilogy.
  - Salander is looking through an old industrial building that has come to her on the death of her father, a death for which she herself is largely responsible. There, she finds two female corpses, and then she discovers that she has been locked in by her half-brother, whose name is Niedermann. He is a creature out of a fairy tale, an ogre. His German name means something like "Deep Down Man."

o   Niedermann is six feet, six inches tall and weighs more than 300 pounds. He's a mass murderer, and he has congenital analgesia; he can't feel pain. He's bent on killing Salander.

o   The tiny Salander slips away from him and hides underneath a cabinet. From this position, she uses a nail gun to fire seven-inch nails into Niedermann's feet, anchoring him to the floor.

o   Salander has other enemies to take care of, in particular, a biker gang, whose members have their own reasons for turning on Niedermann. She texts the bikers, telling them where they can find Niedermann. She then texts the police to report where the bikers are. The bikers kill Niedermann and are, in turn, caught by the police. Salander's enemies are eliminated in a clean sweep.

A Version of Winston Smith

- Although it may seem surprising, we could say that Salander is a kind of Winston Smith, even though we know that in *Nineteen Eighty-four*, it is Winston who is tortured, and he never gets revenge. The similarity between the two stems from the vastly increased power of the state in the 20th and 21st centuries compared to preceding centuries.

- Both Smith and Salander are victims of governmental institutions. The modern Swedish institutions are benevolent in intention, but Larsson points out that they may not be so in practice. Salander earns her own living, but because she has been declared legally incompetent to handle her own affairs, she cannot have access to the money she earns without the authorization of her court-appointed guardian. And Salander's guardian, Bjurman, is a sexual predator.

- Salander can't turn to the state for help because Bjurman has the authority of the state behind him and because she's been declared incompetent. Further, in Salander's case, this situation has been in place for a long time.

- Salander's father beat her mother to the point that she ended up in a nursing home with permanent brain damage. Lisbeth, aged 12, could not defend her mother physically, but she filled a bottle with petrol, tossed it over her father as he sat in his car, and then set it alight, crippling him for life.

- She was certified as violent and became subject to any treatment her court-appointed psychiatrist deemed reasonable. The treatment her first psychiatrist chose was to have her strapped down on more than 380 occasions.

- Salander's father is Alexsander Zalachenko, a Soviet defector and former officer of the Soviet Secret Service. As such, he is valuable to the Swedish Secret Service, the Säpo, which is more concerned with protecting this valuable defector than the rights of his daughter. We might say that Salander faces a bad James Bond in the form of the state—not glamorous, not protective (except in theory), but above the law.

A Version of Sherlock Holmes
- Salander is also a modern Sherlock Holmes—in effect, a consulting detective—and a super-hacker. She knows how to find information in the modern electronic environment.

- The Millennium trilogy opens with what Sherlockians would call a classic "locked-room mystery."
  - Many years ago, on an island owned by a wealthy family, a 16-year-old girl vanished. The island has only one exit, and the girl's grandfather is sure that someone in his family must have murdered her. Nearing the end of his life, the grandfather is desperate to find an answer to the mystery.

  - The grandfather hires an investigative journalist, Blomkvist, to look into the case. He doesn't hire Salander, but she gets coincidentally involved. Gradually, Blomkvist becomes the Dr. Watson to Salander's Sherlock. He observes and deduces, but she digs up essential information.

- The second volume of the trilogy, *The Girl Who Played with Fire*, switches to Salander's unfinished business with her father, a criminal who is still protected by Säpo and by her half-brother. She is shot by her father and buried alive by her half-brother and, at the end, is digging herself out to take an incomplete revenge.

- In the third volume, *The Girl Who Kicked the Hornet's Nest*, the focus switches to Säpo and its attempts to silence Salander. By this time, her father is seen by Säpo as a liability. The book builds to what we might call a classic Perry Mason or courtroom scene, in which Salander turns the tables on the psychiatrist Teleborian, who is once again contending that she should be released into his care.

For the members of the Hacker Republic, the Internet is a workplace, and they react with violence to any attempt to impair it.

  o Salander is a member of Hacker Republic, an electronic gang with power that rivals that of the state. The hackers can crack any password, unearth any secret, and retrieve documents thought to be safely buried by Säpo.

  o We might think the activities of the Hacker Republic are reprehensible, but Larsson reminds us that the state engages in similar activities, including tapping our phones and reading our emails. The hackers are, in a way, Little Brother set against Big Brother.

Themes of the Millennium Trilogy

- Looking at Larsson's Millennium trilogy as a whole, we can see several important themes: a reaction against the greatly increased power of the modern state, a feminist backlash against "the patriarchy," and a focus on an electronic and a political environment.

- Do these themes lead us to feel sympathy for this fierce, alienated woman? One of her associates says that she is the most judgmental person he's ever met. But she's also completely tolerant of other people's weaknesses or personal habits. Is this a paradox?

- It seems that the basis for her judgmentalism, her personal sense of ethics, is not law—she has no respect for that—and it's certainly not traditional morality. Instead, it seems to be something rather old-fashioned for such a contemporary character: a strong sense of honor. She will not do anything that diminishes her own sense of self-respect, and she will intervene violently to protect or avenge the weak and the vulnerable.

- The end of the trilogy offers a hint that Salander can be rehabilitated.
  - At the end of the first volume, Salander has grown to like and trust Blomkvist, and she hopes to have her first romantic relationship with him. But then she sees him with his long-time lover and realizes that any approach she might make would be an embarrassment.

  - In contrast, at the end of the third volume, Blomkvist calls on Salander, bringing bagels and coffee. He says that he's "just company … a good friend who's visiting a good friend." In an ending that is muted but hopeful, she opens the door and lets him in.

Summing Up Salander and Larsson
- In Greek myth, the Furies are sometimes called to become protectors of Athens and to act for justice, not vengeance. They become the Semnai, "the Venerable Ones," and some call them the Eumenides, "the Kindly Ones." In the case of Salander, remembering the petrol and the nail gun, "venerable" seems to apply.

- As for Larsson, we've suggested that there are echoes in his work of Sherlock Holmes, James Bond, and Winston Smith, as well as mythical figures. But nowadays, if you're writing a detective story, it's hard to avoid some hint of Sherlock, and the "Orwellian nightmare" of *Nineteen Eighty-four* is never far from anyone's mind in contemplating the power of the modern state.
  - These stories, all the heroes and legends we've seen, are part of our mental furniture now. They are the framework of our imaginations, but they don't create the picture inside the frame.

  - In fact, Larsson has credited a totally different heroine as his original inspiration, which is Pippi Longstocking, a little girl in the Swedish children's stories written by Astrid Lindgren. The connection seems to be that both Pippi and Salander are extremely confident females.

- Finally, it's important to note that Lisbeth Salander is not the only case where an old and archetypal pattern has come back to be a smash hit in the modern world. Suzanne Collins's successful Hunger Games trilogy was based, she says, on the Greek myth of Theseus and the Minotaur, the children sent each year as a tribute and sacrifice to the bull god of Crete.
  - *The Hunger Games* has at its heart another ancient female image, what we might call "the virgin with the bow," in this case, Katniss Everdeen.

  - This virgin is a kind of paradox; she pretends to be in love and fakes the *Liebestod* ("lovers' suicide") to manipulate her manipulators.

  - Katniss recaps Theseus and Diana, just the way that Lisbeth Salander recaps the Furies and the Valkyries.

  - The old myths and images can come back, of course, transmuted. But we also add to them all the time. And the new ones are available for transmutation, as well.

Essential Reading

Larsson (Keeland, trans.), *The Girl with the Dragon Tattoo*.

————, *The Girl Who Played with Fire*.

————, *The Girl Who Kicked the Hornet's Nest*.

Suggested Reading

Pettersson, (Geddes, trans.), *Stieg*.

Questions to Consider

1. C. S. Lewis called his last novel, *Till We Have Faces*, "a myth retold." Can you think of other modern examples of myths being retold, openly or covertly?

2. Would you rather have James Bond on your side or Lisbeth Salander? Which do you think is more realistic as a protector of abused women?

Lisbeth Salander—Avenging Female Fury
Lecture 23—Transcript

In this course we have already come across a number of different kinds of continuation and revival. The great tales never end, no, but they mutate, they breed, they even cross fertilize. So we've had Authors writing into the gap, like Virgil, setting his *Aeneid* in the gap left between Homer's two epics; straightforward makeovers, like *Pride and Prejudice* being revived as *Bridget Jones's Diary*; and echoes, like the echoes of the Don and Sancho popping up in *Tom Sawyer* and *Huckleberry Finn*. We've had what may be independent reinvention, similar, but different, circumstances creating similar, but different, heroes, like Robin Hood with his English longbow reappearing as the Deerslayer, with his American long rifle. And as we saw in the last lecture, we've had very deliberate rewriting for a particular purpose, traditional fairytales being revived with a feminist slant.

Elements of all these reappear in this lecture and in the character who is at the core of it. She is Lisbeth Salander, the strikingly original heroine of Stieg Larsson's trilogy of crime novels, which began with *The Girl with the Dragon Tattoo*. I just said "original," but the first thing that struck me about Lisbeth Salander is that, a bit like Guinevere, she seems to be a case of a reconstruction of something from ancient myth. She's an avenging female fury, like the Greek Erinyes or the Latin Dirae, the Furies who avenge crimes which are beyond the scope of normal crime and punishment. Or you might say, given the Scandinavian setting, the Valkyries, the daughters of Odin, the choosers of the slain. Or, and these are repeatedly referred to by Larsson, the Amazons, the female warriors of Greek myth. Whichever the original, and Larsson credits a completely different original, which I'll mention at the end, there is no doubt that Salander is an avenging female fury.

She's also set in the genre of Scandinavian *crime noir*. This is a strange phenomenon in itself. Larsson's homeland of Sweden looks to most of us like a successful example of a socialist welfare state, where there is little poverty, advanced gender equality, and developed democracy, a state where the motives for crime would seem to be about as low as they could ever get. Sweden is also famous for hedonism, sexual freedom and tolerance. And yet, in Scandinavian *crime noir* generally, it's astonishing how often the motive for horrific crimes is a sexual one, old sins coming back to haunt their perpetrators—illegitimacy, incest, child abuse, serial murderers, and psychopathic behavior, all of these mixed in with corporate corruption.

Both the financial corruption and the sexual sins are very much the focus of Larsson's world in his "Millennium" trilogy. The Swedish title of the first book in the trilogy was, in fact, *Men som hätar kvennor*, "men who hate women." That's a good description of what he writes about, but a bad title. The English titles for the three books in Larsson's trilogy are much better: *The Girl with the Dragon Tattoo, The Girl who Played with Fire,* and *The Girl who Kicked the Hornet's Nest*. They all focus not on a general problem, but on the lead character, Lisbeth Salander.

She's a very unexpected heroine, and once more a challenge to the Basic Male Hero stereotype. Big, strong, fearless? Well, she seems to be fearless. But big and strong? No. We're told she only weighs 88 pounds. The physical description of her says that she was born thin, "with slender bones that made her look girlish," so that although she is 24 at the time of the first novel, "she sometimes looked fourteen." One of Larsson's characters, a former professional boxer who describes how she came to his club for training, says that Lisbeth was amazingly quick, but at the start, when she hit him, it was like being flicked with a feather duster.

She makes up for her weakness by other characteristics. The same character says that it was impossible to train her very much, because when she sparred with other girls, "she only had one style, which we called Terminator Mode." Another character says of her, "She always gets revenge." She knows no moderation. In normal life also, she seems to feel "no emotional involvement." She responds to many kinds of social interaction only by silences, or sometimes, by rage. Someone remarks that she has a photographic memory, meaning it as a compliment, and her reaction is "almost explosive." First she looks furious, then her expression changes to despair, and then she turns on her heels and runs away. We could sum up by saying, very moderately, that she is difficult to deal with.

She also displays in her many revenges a horrific ingenuity. Take the climactic scene of the final book of the trilogy. Given what's gone before in all three volumes, it would seem difficult for Larsson to reach a final climax, something which goes beyond all the other scenes he has already described. But near the very end of *The Girl who Kicked the Hornet's Nest*, he pulls it off. Salander is looking through an old industrial building, which has come to her on the death of her father, for which death she herself is largely responsible. There she finds two female corpses in a pool of industrial refuse, and then she discovers that she has been locked in by her half brother, whose name is Niedermann. And he is a creature out of fairy tale. He's an ogre. His German name even means something like "Deep Down Man."

He's two meters tall, that is to say six-foot six. He weighs over three hundred pounds. He's a mass murderer. And just to make him completely invulnerable, he has congenital analgesia. He can't feel pain. And he's bent on killing her in a locked room with no weapons available, except for some old carpenters' tools which are still lying around. But what good can they be? Axe, knife, saw? We've already had a description of a fight between him and the ex-pro boxer Roberto, and Roberto reports that hitting him as hard as ever he could just had no effect at all. So what can eighty-eight pound Lisbeth do against this monster?

Well, naturally, she keeps dodging, and she is very quick. But he only needs to lay hands on her once. So while he's climbing down slowly from a pile of crates, which she has just slipped away from, she hides. He looks round. Is she in the cabinet with sliding doors? He starts sliding the doors open, first one, then another. But she's not in the cabinet. With her tiny frame she's gotten underneath it. As he looks for her, she's under there with the carpenter's nail gun, which fires seven-inch nails.

She reaches out and nails his left foot to the floor. Because he can't feel pain, he doesn't realize immediately, not until he's been anchored by another five seven-inch nails straight through his right foot and his boot sole as well. By the time he realizes what's happening, she's shifted back and put another four nails through his left foot. He's still not hurt, but he can't move. And then Salander comes out and goes behind him, holding the nail gun to his spine. That's horrific, but here's the ingenuity.

Salander has other enemies to clear up, in particular, a biker gang, who have their own reasons for turning on Niedermann. So she texts them, and tells them where he is. And then she texts the police, to tell them where the bikers are. The bikers kill Niedermann. The police turn up and catch the bikers red-handed. All her enemies taken care of—clean sweep. Salander isn't just violent; she thinks ahead. She does total and final revenges. Her half brother is only one of several characters who bear the brunt of her savage ingenuity. There's a couple of scenes I'm not even going to tell you about. If you decide to read the books, or else, see the movies, just brace yourself.

All this may well seem to add up to what Jane Austen said of one of her own characters, who is, of course, about as far removed from Salander as you could possibly imagine, "a heroine whom no one will like." Is it possible to feel any sympathy for this extraordinarily violent and uncontrolled character? Well, I said she is an avenging female Fury. And although this may seem surprising, I could also say she is a kind of Winston Smith, although in Nineteen Eighty-Four, it's Winston who is tortured, and he never gets any revenge at all. So why do I say that she's like Winston?

To explain that, I need to comment yet again on changed cultural values. The main difference between the 20th and 21st centuries, and all those which have gone before, must be the vastly-increased power of the state, by which I mean, national governments. This has kind of snuck up on us, and not everyone's noticed. But it's been a theme in the *Nineteen Eighty-four* lecture, and the James Bond lecture, and it will return in the next and last lecture, about Harry Potter. Just to illustrate that, note how little the government of Queen Victoria impinges on Sherlock Holmes. The state delivers his post, and that's about it. The state also provides police officers for Sherlock to show up, but then Sherlock hands the criminals over to the justice system, in which he has complete faith. So, the similarity between Winston Smith and Lisbeth Salander is that both are victims of state power, governmental institutions. True, the modern Swedish ones are entirely benevolent in intention, but, Stieg Larsson asks, in practice?

What he shows us is Lisbeth Salander, aged 24, and earning her own living. But she cannot have access to the money she has earned herself without the authorization the lawyer who is her court-appointed guardian, because she is a ward of the state, declared legally incompetent to handle her own affairs. And this situation means that the servants of the state can do almost what they like with her. They're her caretakers, the people who watch out for her. But to quote the Latin phrase *quis custodiet ipsos custodes*, "Who keeps watch on the watchers?" It turns out that her caretaker-guardian, a man named Bjurman, is a sexual predator who preys on the vulnerable girls and women who are entrusted to him, Lisbeth included, and very horrifically.

Now, who can Lisbeth turn to, the officials of the state, like the police? The state has put her in Bjurman's hands. He has all the authority of the state behind him. Who's going to believe someone certified as unable to handle her own affairs? Furthermore, in Lisbeth's case, this has been going on for a long time. Salander's father was one of those "men who hate women." He beat her mother, until she ended up in a nursing home with permanent brain damage. Lisbeth, aged twelve, could not defend her physically. So what she did was fill a bottle with petrol, toss it over her father as he sat in his car, and then set light to it, crippling him for life.

That's why she became a ward of the state, certified violent, subject to any treatment her court-appointed psychiatrist deemed reasonable. And the treatment her psychiatrist deemed reasonable—his name is Teleborian, and he becomes prominent in the third volume—was to have her strapped down. From the age of twelve she was subject to strap down, all properly recorded and legally signed off on, on 381 occasions. No wonder she has no respect for the state, or the police, or authority figures in general.

There are even more sinister elements. Her father is Alexsander Zalachenko, a Soviet defector, a former officer of the Soviet Secret Service. As such, he is very valuable to the Swedish Secret Service, known as the Säpo. They are concerned, above all, to protect their valuable defector. In the interests, of course, of guarding the state, much more important than one little girl, who may be crazy anyway. Larsson has a lot of information to back this up. According to him, between 1950 and 1992, the Säpo budget increased by a factor of 130. I don't mean 130 percent. I mean 13,000 percent. His whole story is bound up with genuine Swedish high-level scandals and mysteries, notably the murder of the Swedish prime minister Olof Palme in 1986, a murder which has never been solved and whose motive remains obscure.And here's another echo from one of our former heroes. What Lisbeth is facing, you might say, is James Bond—Bad Bond. Not glamorous, not protective, except in theory, but above the law. In reality, not quite "licensed to kill." But that's not the way some members of Säpo see it.

In one scene one of their senior officers, the counterpart of Ian Fleming's M, says, "We're the ones who don't exist [...] We're the ones nobody will ever thank. We're the ones who have to make the decisions that nobody else wants to make. Least of all the politicians." And as he says these words, his voice "quiver[s] with contempt." These officers of the state think, like Lisbeth's lawyer-guardian Bjurman, that they are above the law. Perhaps I've said enough to explain why we might feel pity for Lisbeth Salander, and even understanding. Does it go as far as sympathy? I'll take a rain check on that question, but I'll say that we cannot help feeling admiration.

Here is yet one more echo from an earlier lecture in this course. Lisbeth is a modern Sherlock, in effect, a consulting detective. But there's been another major change in our lives, not one of cultural values, but of technology—electronics. Lisbeth is also a super hacker. She knows how to find things out in the modern electronic environment. The whole trilogy opens with what Sherlockians would call a classic "locked room mystery." That's a crime which takes place in a totally sealed environment, like a murder in a room with all entry points locked from the inside. Crime fiction fans love them.

In Lisbeth's case, what happened is that many years ago, on an island with only one exit, an island totally owned by a rich family of Swedish industrialists, a 16-year-old girl vanished. Her grandfather is sure one of his family—a brother, a nephew—must have murdered her, but no trace of her has ever been found. Nearing the end of his life the grandfather is desperate to find an answer to the mystery. He hires an investigative journalist called Blomkvist, who has just lost a big libel case, is going to serve time, and is going to be bankrupted, along with the magazine he runs, the magazine which gives the trilogy its collective title, 'Millennium.'

Now, the old man doesn't hire Salander, but she gets coincidentally involved in the case. Gradually the lead investigator Blomkvist becomes, in a way, the Dr. Watson to Salander's Sherlock. Not that her abilities are identical to

Sherlock's, they aren't. He observes and deduces. She digs up information. But as with a Sherlock Holmes mystery, the information is there, and Salander, like Sherlock, has the special skills to find it.

I won't detail the vanished-girl case, as it would spoil the book for those of you who haven't read *The Girl with the Dragon Tattoo*. I can tell you, though, that the breakthrough is a kind of decoding. What everyone thought to be a list of phone numbers in the vanished girl's diary is a list of Bible references. Once Salander has that clue, it leads to a string of sadistic and unsolved rapes and murders. And once she knows that, she can find out a great deal just by googling. This particular novel ends with another horrific scene in a torture dungeon, where many women have been murdered, and another fierce and dramatic intervention by Salander to save Blomkvist.

So the locked-room mystery is solved in volume 1, while simultaneously Salander turns the tables on her abusive state-appointed guardian Bjurman. In volume 2, we switch to Salander's unfinished business with her father, a criminal, still protected by Säpo and by her ogre of a half brother. This one, *The Girl who Played with Fire*, ends with her being shot by her father, buried alive by her half brother, and digging herself out to take what is in volume 2 an incomplete revenge.

In volume 3, *The Girl Who Kicked the Hornet's Nest*, the focus switches to Säpo and its attempts to silence Salander, and by this time, her father, now seen by his former protectors in Säpo as a liability. It builds up to what we might call a classic Perry Mason or courtroom scene, in which Salander turns the tables on the psychiatrist Teleborian, who is once again contending that she should be released into his care. In other words, that she should be permanently institutionalized.

What saves her this time is the electronics. She is a member of Hacker Republic. This is an electronic gang with only 62 members, but it has a power which even rivals that of the state. If they all decided to launch a coordinated cyber attack against an entire country, Larsson tells us, "The country might survive, but not without having serious problems." They use all kinds of strange devices—electronic cuffs on cable links; hostile takeovers with mirrored hard drives. They can crack any kind of password, unearth any kind of secret, retrieve all the documents Säpo thought were safely buried.

Is this reprehensible? In the first place, Hacker Republic is entirely opposed to the kind of person who invents viruses and tries to spread them on the Internet. The Internet is their place of work, and they react violently to any attempt to spoil it. Furthermore, Larsson reminds us that what they do, the state does too, with devices like the Random Frequency Tracking System, developed by the U.S. National Security Agency. The state can tap our phones; it can read our emails; and we have reason to believe that it does so. So the hackers are, so to speak, "Little Brother" set against "Big Brother." They are investigative journalism taken to a higher electronic power.

Looking at Larsson's Millennium trilogy as a whole, we can see several important themes. There's a modern reaction against the greatly increased power of the modern state. There's a feminist backlash against "the patriarchy," which according to Larsson, and I'm not saying he's right about this, but according to him, it turns a relatively blind eye to crimes like sex trafficking and enforced prostitution. And all of this occurs in an electronic and a political environment which Sherlock Holmes could never have imagined.

Still, to go back to the question on which I took a rain check, do these themes lead us to feel sympathy for this fierce, alienated, unfriendly woman, said to be a paranoid schizophrenic, thought even by those who are on her side to perhaps have Asperger's syndrome? Certainly someone who is not socialized, and though not a psychopath, could well be called a sociopath. Can she be rehabilitated, if she doesn't want to be? I'm still not answering my own question, but one of her associates says she is "the most judgmental person" he's ever met. On the other hand, she's completely tolerant of other people's weaknesses or personal habits. Is this a paradox?

Well, this is what I think. And it's an attitude for which I have strong sympathy. It seems to me that the basis for her judgmentalism, her personal sense of ethics, is not law; she has no respect for that, though it does come to her assistance in the end. It's certainly not traditional morality. Among other things, she herself is bisexual and in some ways promiscuous. No, what she has is something rather old fashioned for such a contemporary character. She has a strong sense of honor, and that is what drives her decisions, her judgments, and her revenges. She will not do anything which diminishes her own sense of self respect. Like one of King Arthur's knights, she will also intervene violently to protect, or to avenge the weak and the vulnerable, abused women in particular. So, I do feel sympathy for her, and there is at least a hint that she can be rehabilitated.

The end of the first volume is sad. Lisbeth has grown to like and trust Blomkvist and is hoping for the first time in her life maybe to have a romantic "relationship." She buys him an expensive 1950s-retro Elvis Presley icon, as a present, to give her an excuse to knock on his door. But as she goes to call on him, she sees him coming out with his long-term lover, and she realizes that she would only be an embarrassment. She turns back and throws Elvis away—back on her own again. By contrast, at the end of volume three, Blomkvist calls on her, with bagels and coffee. He gets the usual detached response, her door only just ajar. He says he's "Just company [...] a good friend who's visiting a good friend." No relationship offered or expected. Just a friend. And she opens the door and lets him in. It's a very muted ending, rather like the end of Lord of the Rings, when Sam Gamgee comes home and just says, "Well, I'm back." But it's a hopeful one. A change in her pattern.

I have three final things to say, about Lisbeth, about her creator Larsson, and about where things stand now with the invention of heroes and heroines. About Lisbeth, we might remember that in Greek myth the Furies are sometimes brought on board to become protectors of Athens and to act for justice, not vengeance. They become the "Semnai, the Venerable Ones," and some call them the "Eumenides, the Kindly Ones." In the case of Lisbeth, remembering the petrol and the nail gun, I'll settle for "venerable."

About Larsson, I've suggested that there are echoes in his story of Sherlock, and Bond, and Winston Smith, as well as mythical figures. But that doesn't mean that he started off from them. Nowadays, if you're writing a detective story, it's hard to avoid some hint of Sherlock. And the "Orwellian nightmare" of Nineteen Eighty-four is never far from anyone's mind in contemplating the power of the modern state. These stories, all the heroes and legends I've been talking about, are part of our mental furniture now. In a way, they're what we think with. They're the framework of our imaginations, but they don't create the picture inside the frame. In fact, Larsson has credited a totally different heroine as his original inspiration, which is Pippi Longstocking, a little girl in the Swedish children's stories written by Astrid Lindgren. I'd never have thought of that. Pippi is a nice little girl who certainly has not been abused and who has good friends, human and animal, all quite unlike Lisbeth. She also has superhuman strength. She can lift up a horse one handed, again, quite unlike Lisbeth. The only connection, I guess, is that they're both extremely confident females, who can do anything they set their minds to.

As for my third closing remark about the invention of heroes and heroines in general, Lisbeth Salander is not the only case I can think of where an old and maybe archetypal pattern has come back to be a smash hit in the modern world. Suzanne Collins's very successful Hunger Games trilogy was based, she says, on the old Greek myth of Theseus and the Minotaur, the children sent each year as a tribute and sacrifice to the bull-god of Crete.

The Hunger Games also has at its heart another ancient female image, which I call "the virgin with the bow"—the goddess Diana. Edmund Spenser's heroine Belphoebe, brought back into the modern world the way that Thor was brought back, by the Incomplete Enchanter series. Now she's Katniss Everdeen, a kind of paradox, the virgin who only pretends to be in love, who fakes the *Liebestod*—the lovers' suicide—to manipulate her manipulators. The female whose normal role, in Fenimore Cooper say, would be to be in constant peril in the forest, without male protectors, but who, with her bow and her woodcraft rivals Chingachgook himself as a danger.

Katniss recaps Theseus and Diana just the way that Lisbeth Salander recaps the Furies and the Valkyries. So the old myths and the old images can come back, of course, transmuted. But we're adding to those old myths and images all the time. And those new ones are available for transmutation as well, like Bond and Winston and Sherlock. The Tree of Tales, as Tolkien called it, puts out new leaves all the time, and even the ones that fall create leaf mold to nourish the old roots—the roots of our imagination, the roots of legend.

Harry Potter—Whistle-Blower Hero
Lecture 24

W e started these lectures with Tolkien, the unexpected success of the 20th century, and we will close with the equally unexpected success of the 21st-century: J. K. Rowling's Harry Potter. The Harry Potter story was, if anything, even more unexpected as a success than Tolkien's work. The tale of its creation is a heroic story in itself, with its author, a divorced single mother, writing in a café because she couldn't afford to heat her own room. She has since become one of the richest women on the planet. Returning to our theme of what creates such successes, in this lecture, we'll ask: What can Harry Potter teach us?

A Fairy-Tale Start
- Harry has a strong element of the fairy tale about him, with a Cinderella start. We first meet him in his bedroom, which is the cupboard under the stairs of Number 4, Privet Drive. He's being sheltered, reluctantly, by his aunt and her horrible husband, who neglect and bully him.

- Harry is saved by the half-giant Hagrid, who sweeps him out of the hands of the muggles (ordinary people) and off to the great school for wizards and witches, Hogwarts, with its headmaster, Albus Dumbledore.

- There, Harry finds that he's famous, the only person to have survived the attack of Lord Voldemort. The attack killed his parents but not him, and that failure is thought (wrongly) to have eliminated Voldemort forever.

- One of the charms of the Harry Potter books is the immensely detailed and amusing magical world in which Harry finds himself. And this world shows us how much Rowling has to draw on. She takes ideas from myth, medieval romance, fairy tales, and her own imagination. In addition, the Harry Potter books are a twist on the

In Rowling's world, a magic community exists alongside our real world, but it has enacted a Statute of Secrecy to keep its existence concealed.

high school story. Hogwarts isn't an ordinary school, but in the seven books, Harry advances a grade every year and undergoes the usual teenage trials.

Harry's Success

- For all his fame and importance, Harry is quite normal. What has made him so special to us?
  - As we said, the hobbits, Tolkien's new-style heroes, were created out of the trauma of two World Wars that had severely shaken traditional models of heroism. That trauma is behind us now, but it hasn't quite gone away. Rowling's Dark Lord has been defeated, but he has every intention, like Tolkien's Sauron, of returning.

  - And the threat of the Dark Lord is a recognizable one. The magic users will take over. They will become the master race, overlords over us muggles. Rule will be restricted to those of pure wizard blood. Everyone else will be known as "mudbloods" or "half-bloods." If they're "pure bloods" who sympathize with muggles, they'll be called "blood traitors." We know all about that kind of racist ideology.

- There are also new traumas and anxieties. The truly modern element in Harry is that in his repeated struggles with the Dark Lord, he must fight a war on two fronts.
  o In the fifth book of the series, *Harry Potter and the Order of the Phoenix*, the magic community's government refuses to face up to the fact that the Dark Lord has returned and is rallying his followers. Rather than address the situation, the powers that be prefer to hush it up. This involves discrediting Harry and his mentor, Dumbledore, and taking over Hogwarts.

  o The Ministry of Magic puts a stooge into Hogwarts, Dolores Umbridge, to teach the class called Defense against the Dark Arts. Her approach to her subject is to issue all students a new handbook, the aim of which is, essentially, to do nothing.

  o Harry, who has already formed a kind of unofficial self-help group for learning magical self-defense, protests. He gets put in detention, where he must write out "I must not tell lies" repeatedly. Dumbledore and the other Hogwarts teachers who sympathize with Harry can't protect him because Umbridge has the authority of the state behind her.

- The point here is that Harry is fighting against both the Dark Lord and against the people who also ought to be fighting the Dark Lord. And they fight Harry with modern weapons, such as the media. Harry and his friends fight back with modern methods, as well.

Harry the Whistle-Blower
- This war on two fronts is a contemporary situation. Just like Harry, we face serious threats to our security: terrorism, financial turmoil, climate change, and more. We have to trust the state to protect us from those threats, but do we trust the institutions of the state?

Skepticism about politicians, lobbyists, and bureaucrats is very much a part of the modern mindset.

- For this reason, ever since Watergate, we've had a word for another new kind of hero: the whistle-blower. As a whistle-blower, Harry tries to alert his community to one threat, but he also faces the other threat of the forces that are trying to hush him up.

- Harry is made to query himself and his own deepest attachments. He is devoted to the memory of his dead parents, but when he begins to receive access to other people's memories, he learns that his father was a bully. In fact, James Potter's bullying has led one of the teachers at Hogwarts, Severus Snape, to dislike Harry.

- One other thing that creates self-doubt in Harry is his awareness that he is, in some mysterious way, connected to the Dark Lord. He gets flashes of what the Dark Lord is doing, and like the Dark Lord, he can speak Parseltongue, the language of snakes. He even finds himself inside the body of the Dark Lord's familiar, the giant snake Nagini, as it attacks his friend Ron's father. Can Harry even trust himself?

- All these pressures naturally make Harry increasingly bad-tempered. He has the teenage sense that no one understands him, and he's repeatedly in danger of alienating even the people who are on his side, especially his two closest companions, Ron and Hermione. As we said in the first lecture, the dominant feeling on the modern battlefield is loneliness, and that applies even on the psychic battlefield where Harry fights.

- One more strongly modern and original element is seen in the Dementors. At the start of the series, these are the guards of the wizards' prison, but they change sides later on. They work by sucking the happiness out of their victims, until everything seems utterly depressing and all resistance ceases. Their last act is the "Dementor's kiss," which sucks away the soul. A real-world correlative, perhaps, is the loss of nerve, the reluctance to stand up for themselves and their values that has so often seemed to afflict Western democracies in modern times.

More Changing Values?

- Interestingly, in all seven books of the Harry Potter series, there's not the slightest trace of religious belief, in Christianity or any faith. No one prays or even thinks about the possibility of divine assistance. Magic itself seems to be just a variation of muggle technology—broomsticks and hexes instead of planes and guns—and is only occasionally superior to it.

- Perhaps this is another major shift in cultural values: the erosion or loss of the religious faith that upheld so many of our earlier heroes and heroines. And this loss of faith may explain why the Dark Lord is on a quest for personal immortality. Such a quest is natural in a society that no longer has faith in a life after death; one must abolish death instead.

- The strange thing about Harry, in this world seemingly without faith, is that at the end of his struggle with the Dark Lord, in order to succeed, Harry must die himself, because he had one of the Dark Lord's souls within him. And then he comes back to life because of the blood he shared with the Dark Lord. The symbolism of this is hard to read, but the term "Christ figure" certainly comes to mind.

- This strange blank at the heart of the Rowling universe—this hole where faith used to be—once again makes the point that Harry, his friends, and the whole magic community are on their own. The dangers arise from within themselves, and that's where the solutions will have to come from, as well.

- Still, the moral values of Harry Potter don't seem to have changed dramatically. Tolerance is vital, as is kindliness, concern for the vulnerable, and humility. The overall moral of the series seems to be traditional. Despite the fact that Harry often has the feeling that he stands alone against the world, the real power in Rowling's universe is love. Perhaps modern heroes, such as Harry, are thrown back on themselves in a way that's never been true before, but the answer to loss of faith—to existential loneliness—is love.

The House of Legend

- Tolkien talked about the "Tree of Story," which puts out new leaves all the time, but in at least one way, that metaphor is inaccurate. Trees put out leaves organically, but that's not how stories get written. For our purposes, then, let's use the metaphor of a House of Legend.

- This house has deep foundations and many rooms on many floors. On the top floors are the gods, goddesses, and humans born of goddesses, such as Thor and Aeneas and, perhaps, Guinevere. Lower down are people with extraordinary talents, such as Sherlock Holmes, the Deerslayer, and Robin Hood. On the ground floor are people like us, such as Celie, Elizabeth Bennet, or the Wife of Bath, who nevertheless get the chance to show what they're made of.

- Anyone can a build new room in this House of Legend and decorate and furnish it to his or her liking. But it will always rest on deep, strong foundations that go down to bedrock in the human heart.

- No story, no hero or heroine, comes out of nothing. Even at the dawn of history, the story of Odysseus and Polyphemus was already old. We're fortunate now that the House of Legend has become so large, with unmeasurable amounts of human ingenuity poured into it for everyone to draw on.

- New rooms in the House of Legend are always welcome, and people are building them right now. But they're still building them on the old foundations. The house possesses two resources, one of which is sustainable and the other, always growing.
  - The growing resource is all the heroes and heroines in the House of Legend. The old ones are still present, and we're adding new ones all the time.

o   The other resource—our most sustainable—is what's adding them: human creativity.

Essential Reading

Rowling, *Harry Potter and the Sorcerer's Stone.*

————, *Harry Potter and the Chamber of Secrets.*

————, *Harry Potter and the Prisoner of Azkaban.*

————, *Harry Potter and the Goblet of Fire.*

————, *Harry Potter and the Order of the Phoenix.*

————, *Harry Potter and the Half-Blood Prince.*

————, *Harry Potter and the Deathly Hallows.*

Suggested Reading

Kirk, *J. K. Rowling.*

Saxena, *The Subversive Harry Potter.*

Questions to Consider

1. Can you think of real-world examples where a warning has been given, a whistle blown, but the proper authorities have taken no notice or tried to cover up the threat? What do you think causes such behavior?

2. How important has faith been to any of the heroes we have followed, and what are the alternative sources of inner strength?

Harry Potter—Whistle-Blower Hero
Lecture 24—Transcript

This course has taken us on a long journey, from Homer, 3,000 years ago, right up to now. I started off, however, with Tolkien, the enormous and unexpected success of the 20th century, and I'm going to close with the equally unexpected and enormous success of the 21st century, which is J. K. Rowling's Harry Potter. The Harry Potter story in its seven volumes, from Harry Potter and the Sorcerer's Stone in 1997, to Harry Potter and the Deathly Hallows, ten years later, was, if anything, even more unexpected as a success than Tolkien. The tale of its creation by J. K. Rowling is a heroic story in itself, by now well known.

Joanne Rowling as a divorcee single mother, writing in a café, because she couldn't afford to heat her own room. Her first book, published by a small press, and becoming known just by word of mouth, without the benefit of a giant marketing campaign. Intended as a work for children, but soon so popular with adults that Bloomsbury Press had to start printing her books with special covers, so adults could read them while commuting without feeling embarrassed.

In the first lecture, I mentioned the haughty reviewer of Tolkien, who wrote, "This is not a work that many adults will read right through more than once." He couldn't have been more wrong, but that remark may well have been beaten for wrongness by Rowling's agent, who said to her, "Now remember, Joanne, this is all very well, but it's not going to make your fortune." Ms. Rowling is now one of the richest women on the planet. I'd add that I don't think anybody grudges her her success. She did it all by herself, and she is well known, also, for acts of charity and of personal kindness to her fans. Sometimes the right people get the big rewards. Still, going back to our theme of what creates super successes, I asked in lecture one, "What could Frodo Baggins teach us about heroes?" And now I ask, "What can Harry Potter teach us?"

The first thing to note is that Harry has a strong element of the fairy tale about him. It's a Cinderella start. Cinderella had to sit among the cinders, because her stepmother and the ugly sisters treated her as a domestic slave.

We first meet Harry in his bedroom, which is the cupboard under the stairs of number 4, Privet Drive. He's being sheltered, very reluctantly, by his aunt and a horrible husband, who neglect and bully him. Though he doesn't have an ugly sister, he has an ugly cousin called Dursley, who gets all the pampering that Harry doesn't.

Harry is saved, not by a princess charming, but by the half-giant Hagrid, who sweeps him out of the hands of the "muggles," as we ordinary people are called in Ms. Rowling's universe, and off to the great school for wizards and witches, Hogwarts, with its headmaster Albus Dumbledore. There, Harry immediately finds that he's not a nobody. He's famous, as the only person who has, as a baby, survived the attack of the Dark Lord, Lord Voldemort. The attack killed his parents but not him, and that failure is thought, wrongly, to have got rid of the Dark Lord for ever.

At Hogwarts, Harry finds that he is, and this is a word I haven't used before, he's a "celebrity." I expect that there have always been celebrities, as there have always been wannabes, but modern mass media have made celebrity status much more important, and more dangerous. So, good start, and I have to say that one of the great charms of the Harry Potter books is the immensely detailed and amusing magical world Harry finds himself in. It's a world which is parallel to our own, a magic community which exists alongside our real world, but which has enacted a Statute of Secrecy to keep its existence concealed.

Further reinforcing what I said at the end of the last lecture, about us adding to our stock of myths and legends all the time, Rowling's magic universe shows what a lot she has to draw on. She takes her ideas from everywhere. There are creatures from classical myth and medieval romance, like basilisks and hippogriffs, centaurs and dragons. There are creatures from fairy tales, like goblins and trolls, boggarts and house elves. And there's a great deal which is Rowling's own invention, like the magic community's favorite game of quidditch, a bit like violent basketball with the players flying broomsticks. Harry turns out to be a natural at it.

In addition, the Harry Potter books look like a twist on the high-school story. Hogwarts isn't an ordinary school, true, but in the seven books Harry goes up a grade every year and undergoes the usual teenage trials, like not knowing who to take to the school Christmas dance. For all his fame and importance, then, Harry is very normal indeed. His name, Harry Potter, is by English standards, even more normal than Winston Smith. So what has made Harry so special to us?

Tolkien's new-style heroes, the hobbits, were created, I suggested, out of the trauma of two World Wars, which severely shook traditional models of heroism. Now, unlike Tolkien, Rowling is not a combat veteran. That trauma is behind us. But it hasn't quite gone away. Rowling's Dark Lord has been defeated, yes. But he has every intention, like Tolkien's Sauron, of coming back. And, the threat of the Dark Lord is a very recognizable one. The magic users will take over; they will become the master race, overlords over us "muggles." Rule will be restricted to those of pure wizard blood. Everyone else will be known as "mudbloods," or "half-bloods." Or if they're "pure bloods" who sympathize with us "muggles," "blood traitors." We know all about that kind of racist ideology. We've been there before.

But meanwhile, there are new traumas, new anxieties. The really modern element in Harry, one of the things which have made him such a success, is this. In his repeated struggles with the Dark Lord, who is determined both to come back and to eliminate Harry, Harry has to fight a war on two fronts. I'll pick out one sequence which shows what I mean. As I said about Tolkien's Frodo, The Lord of the Rings is a long book, and everyone would pick out a different pivotal moment in it. The Harry Potter series is even longer, well over 3,000 pages, and so the choice is even greater, but the scene I respond to comes in book 5, Harry Potter and the Order of the Phoenix. It centers on Harry and the character of Dolores Umbridge. What has happened is that in spite of the growing evidence that the Dark Lord is back and is rallying his followers who have only gone underground, in spite of all this, the magic community's government does not want to know.

Admitting the danger exists would be inconvenient. It would say that the government was not in control. It would be career threatening, or even career ending, for the Minister for Magic and the thousands of bureaucrats who work for him. The Minister's name, by the way, is Cornelius Fudge, and fudging solutions is what he does. Anyway, rather than face up to the situation, the powers that be prefer to hush it all up. Deny it's happening. This involves discrediting Harry and his mentor Dumbledore, and also, taking over Hogwarts.

The Ministry puts their stooge into Hogwarts, and she is Dolores Umbridge. Her role is to teach the class called Defense against the Dark Arts. Umbridge puts on a very nice front, in fact, she's aggressively nice. Her crockery and decorations have a motif of pretty kittens gamboling. She has a little-girl hairstyle and a little-girl voice. Since she's such a nice person, she can do anything she likes. Especially to her under-age pupils. We shouldn't ever forget that apart from everything else, Harry is a teenage hero. Younger than Salander, with far more responsibilities than Huck Finn. In that uniquely vulnerable teenage position.

Going back to Dolores Umbridge, her way of teaching her subject is to issue all students with the new handbook, *Defense against the Dark Arts: a Return to Basic Principles*. It is a "carefully structured, theory-centered, Ministry-approved course." And its aims are: "(1) Understanding the principles underlying defensive magic," (2) Learning to recognize situations in which defensive magic can legally be used," and "(3) Placing the use of defensive magic in a context for practical use." In other words, not doing anything. There's no need to do anything. There is no problem.

Harry, who has already formed a kind of unofficial self-help group for learning practical magical self defense, protests. He gets put in detention, and there he has to write out "I must not tell lies." for an hour—with a magic quill which sucks his blood. Every time he writes a line, it carves the words into his hand, which heals again. Until he writes the next line. Dumbledore, and the other Hogwarts teachers who sympathize with Harry, can't protect him. Umbridge has the authority of the state behind her.

This resonates with me, because I spent 28 years teaching in different British universities, all of them state-funded institutions, and saw this kind of classroom control steadily being extended, often by people who were aggressively nice while dodging serious issues. I well remember one very nice professorial colleague saying—ever so nicely—to a student with a genuine complaint, "You don't want to become known as a recalcitrant troublemaker, do you?" So I've seen how the state-backed Umbridges of this world work.

My point about Harry's modernity as a hero is this. As I said, he's fighting a war on two fronts—Against the Dark Lord, yes, but also against the people who ought also to be fighting the Dark Lord, and they fight him with modern weapons. If you can't control the situation, control the media. Harry is, of course, a celebrity in the magic community, which makes him useful. When he won't go along with the official cover up, *The Daily Prophet*, the magic community's official newspaper, starts printing little pieces mocking Harry as deluded, self important. His friends start getting hate mail. Inconvenient witnesses get sent to the wizards' prison of Azkaban.

Harry and his friends fight back with modern methods as well, just as Lisbeth Salander does. Hermione, the cleverest of Harry's friends, blackmails an investigative journalist who normally works for the Ministry into writing a piece putting Harry's point of view, though this can only be published in a journal generally regarded as lunatic fringe—*The Quibbler*. Umbridge, then, makes the mistake, as media controllers do, of trying to ban all Hogwarts students from reading it. Naturally, everyone suddenly wants a copy, and some of them start to see things Harry's way. But note, the Ministry has a carrot, as well as a stick. If Harry goes along with them, he'll be a hero again, in the media, of course, not in reality, just a celebrity-hero.

This war on two fronts, as I've called it, is a very contemporary situation. Just like Harry, we know that we're facing serious threats to our security, not just terrorism—financial turmoil, climate change, the war on drugs, collapsing banks, and disappearing pensions. We have to trust the state to protect us from those threats. But on the other front, do we trust the institutions of the state? We certainly don't know very much about them. Do they, perhaps, have their own agendas? Skepticism about politicians, lobbyists, and bureaucrats is very much part of the modern mindset. How much of what we're told is, to use another modern word, media "spin"?

All this is why, ever since Watergate, we've had yet another new word for yet another new kind of hero, which is "whistle-blower." Harry is a whistle-blower hero. He's trying to alert his community to one threat, but the other threat he faces is all the forces which are trying to hush him up. They do this by casting doubt on everything he says or does. Harry faces continuous threats to his own self esteem. Harry can take Umbridge's torture. He takes the rigged trial at the start of book five; here he's threatened with expulsion from Hogwarts on a charge of improper use of magic. It was self defense, and Harry has a witness, and a kind of defending attorney in the shape of Dumbledore. But the Ministry does its best to defeat that by changing the place and time of trial and making sure Harry's defenders and Harry himself aren't told about it so that he is almost condemned unheard. It's the kind of chicanery whistle blowers are likely to be faced with.

Still, Harry gets off, but he's then deeply hurt because his mentor Dumbledore just walks away and ignores him. Good tactics, maybe, so the two are not too closely identified in future, bad psychology with a teenager. Harry is also made to feel, later on, that he has let Dumbledore down by not trying hard enough to probe secrets for him. He has excuses, other things were happening, how come he has to solve everything. As teenagers so often say, "why does it always have to be me?"

Harry is also made to query his own deepest attachments. He is devoted to the memory of his dead parents. He also hates one of the Hogwarts teachers, Severus Snape, who returns the hatred and appears out to get Harry at all costs. But when Harry starts being let into other people's memories, through the device of the Pensieve, he comes to realize that his father was a bully. It's the humiliating way in which James Potter bullied Snape as a schoolboy that makes Snape dislike Harry Potter, seeing his father in him. So, the Ministry of Magic puts pressure on Harry. Dumbledore puts pressure on Harry. The other kids at Hogwarts put pressure on Harry. Harry puts pressure on himself.

And there's yet one more thing which creates self doubt in Harry, which is his awareness that he is, in some mysterious way, connected to the Dark Lord. He keeps getting flashes of what the Dark Lord is doing. Like the Dark Lord, but unlike nearly everyone else in the magic community, he can speak Parseltongue, which is the language of snakes. This is amusing in the first book, when Harry uses it to talk to a boa constrictor in the zoo. But in the fifth book, he finds himself somehow inside the body of the Dark Lord's familiar, the giant snake Nagini, as it attacks his friend Ron's father. Can Harry trust himself?

All these pressures naturally make Harry increasingly bad tempered. He has that teenage feeling, nobody understands me; no one's on my side. He's repeatedly in danger of alienating even the people who are on his side, especially his two closest companions, Ron and Hermione. In the summer vacations they get to go home, but Harry is returned to number four Privet Drive. Harry feels everyone has forgotten him. They're having a good time, and he doesn't even get mail!

As I said in the first lecture, quoting General Slim, the dominant feeling on the modern battlefield is loneliness, and that applies even on the psychic battlefield where Harry fights. He does have good and loyal companions. But they aren't always there; sometimes they don't quite trust him, and sometimes he doesn't quite trust them. He also has every reason to think that society is not on his side. It's not a crushingly brutalist society, like Ingsoc in *Nineteen Eighty-four*, more a suffocatingly conformist society. Stay on message. Be a team player. Accept the consensus. Don't make waves. I guess we've all felt something like that.

One more strongly modern and original element is the dementors. At the start of the series, these are the guards of the wizards' prison Azkaban, but they change sides later on. The way they work is they suck the happiness out of you. Everything seems utterly depressing; there's no point in going on, all resistance ceases. Their last act is called "the dementor's kiss," which sucks your soul away. It's quite like the Black Breath of Tolkien's Ringwraiths. Their real world, correlative, maybe, is the loss of nerve, the reluctance to stand up for themselves and for their own values, which has so often seemed to afflict western democracies, ever since Munich in 1938. Once you've been persuaded to doubt yourself, where's the motivation to defend what's right?

All this means that, as with Tolkien's hobbits, many of us can recognize something of our own experience in Harry, as I've told you, I did. But my mention of values raises one other strange part of the Rowling universe, and an especially strange part of Harry's own seven-year journey. The strange thing about the universe is this. Hogwarts appears to be firmly modern-world normal in one respect. The students are studiedly multi ethnic, with names like Cho Chang and Parvati Patil, as well as all the Potters and Grangers and Finnegans. But there's a kind of overall Christian background. The holidays of Christmas and Easter are observed. There's a giant Christmas tree and Christmas presents. The students sing "O come, all ye faithful."

Do they mean it, though? I don't think so. In all seven books, there's not the slightest trace of religious belief in Christianity or any faith at all. No one ever prays or even thinks about any possibility of divine assistance. Magic just seems to be an alternative technology, which duplicates "muggle" technology—broomsticks and hexes instead of planes and guns—and only now and then rises superior to it. Maybe we are looking here at another very major shift in cultural values; the erosion, or the outright loss of the religious faith which upheld Uncle Tom in his final agony, and the vampire hunters in Dracula, and in changed form upheld Celie as well.

Perhaps this explains why the Dark Lord is questing for personal immortality and the magical items which will give it to him. That's a natural quest in a society which no longer has religious faith, faith in a life after death. You have to abolish death instead. The strange thing about Harry, though, in this world seemingly without faith, is that the end of his struggle with the Dark Lord, in order to succeed, in order to destroy the last of the Dark Lord's external souls, Harry has to die himself. Because he had one of the Dark Lord's external souls within him. It was what created the connection between the two of them. And then he comes back to life, because of the blood he shared with the Dark Lord. The symbolism of this is hard to read, but the phrase "Christ figure" can't be far away. This strange blank at the heart of the Rowling universe, this hole where faith used to be, once again makes the point that Harry, and his friends, and the whole magic community, are on their own. The dangers arise from within themselves, yes. And that's where the solutions will have to come from as well.

For all its comedy and its "young adult" themes, the world of Harry Potter is a bleaker world than, say, Tolkien's. Dumbledore is not an emissary from a better world the way Gandalf is. All the more need for inner heroism, then. Yet in spite of all that the moral values of Harry Potter don't seem to me have changed. Tolerance is vital—Rowling has disclosed that we should think of

Dumbledore as gay; so is kindliness—genuine not faked; and concern for the vulnerable, like "muggles," people with no magic in them; even humility. In a coda nineteen years on from the conclusion, we see Harry, middle aged and happily married, but there's no sign that he's become a very important person in adult life.

Moreover, the overall moral of the Harry Potter series seems to me to be this, and again, it's a very traditional one. Despite the fact that Harry often has the justifiable feeling that it's him against the world, the real power in Rowling's universe is love. It's Harry's parents' love for him, and in particular, his mother's, which defeated the curse of the Dark Lord when he was a baby. It's that love which keeps him safe in his aunt's house, his mother's sister's house, even if it's only number four Privet Drive. Love is the key even of the mysterious figure of Snape.

Now, I don't know, and nor does anyone else, whether love can conquer death, but we all know loving someone is not terminated by their death. Maybe not by ours. True, in the Harry Potter world, we only meet human love, not divine love. But what do I mean, only? We have to create love, as we create all our own solutions, by ourselves. Maybe modern heroes like Harry are thrown back on themselves in a way that's never been true before. But the answer to loss of faith, to existential loneliness, that's love. And that's what Harry has.

I asked a long way back what Harry has to teach us, and I guess the answer is a double one. He has to learn to trust himself, in a new kind of hostile environment, where so much is stacked against him. He also has to learn not to distrust all those around him, not to give way to hatred, not to become embittered. Yes, us too. That can be hard, even when you're not a teenager any more.

Looking back over the whole of this course, I have to ask again, what is the secret of super success? There's still no single answer. Sometimes new conditions seem to create a new heroic situation, as the New World created Robinson Crusoe, or the Fugitive Slave Act created Uncle Tom. Sometimes new circumstances seem to demand a new kind of hero, as World Wars did with Frodo Baggins, or totalitarianism did with Winston Smith. Sometimes an image from the far past comes back, like Dracula, or Thor reappearing in comic books.

But I would put it like this. Tolkien's metaphor, which I used at the end of the last lecture, was the Tree of Tales, and it's a good metaphor. Only it's inaccurate in one respect. Trees put out leaves organically, as a natural process. But stories don't get written that way. Someone always has to do the work. So I'd suggest a different image, and I'll call my image the House of Legend. This House has deep foundations and many rooms on many floors. Up on the top floors, we might say, are the myths of gods and goddesses and humans born of goddesses, like Thor and Acneas, and maybe Guinevere.

Lower down there are people with extraordinary talents, like Sherlock and the Deerslayer and Robin Hood. On the ground floor, a very well-populated floor, there are people like us, ordinary people like Celie or Elizabeth Bennet or the Wife of Bath, who, nevertheless, get the chance to show what they're made of. And characters don't have to stay on the same floor all the time. Criseyde went down one, Huckleberry Finn went up one. People like Don Quixote and Sancho Panza ought to be on separate floors, but they aren't. There are lots of possibilities.

Now, anyone can build a new room in this House of Legend, and they can decorate and furnish it any way they like. But, it will always rest on those old foundations, the deep ones, the strong ones that go down to bedrock, in the human heart. No story, no hero, no heroine, just comes out of nothing. Even back in the dawn of history, when the House of Legend was just a small one, stories like Odysseus and Polyphemus were already old. We're fortunate now that the House has become such a big one, with uncountable amounts of human ingenuity poured into it for everyone to draw on.

There's nothing to beat a new idea, a new angle, a new response, except, as I said right at the start, a new idea which people have been waiting for without knowing it, a new idea which responds to an existing new situation. New rooms in the House of Legend are always welcome, and people are building them right now.

They're still building them on the old foundations, though. Nothing's ever going to stop that. So we have two resources, and the good news is that one of them is sustainable, and the other is always growing. The growing resource is all the heroes and heroines in the House of Legend. The old ones are still there, and we're adding new ones all the time. The other resource is what's adding them, and that is human creativity—human creativity, finally. That is our most sustainable resource.

Bibliography

Amis, Kingsley. *The Bond Dossier*. London: Jonathan Cape, 1965. An early defense of Fleming's Bond against hostile reviewers, by a famous author with excellent academic credentials.

Anonymous. *Beowulf: A New Translation for Oral Delivery*. Translated by Dick Ringler. Indianapolis: Hackett, 2007. Essential reading for Lecture 7. Many other good or adequate translations exist, including those by Kevin Crossley-Holland (repr. 1999), Michael Alexander, (repr. 2003), and Seamus Heaney (2000), but Ringler's, as it says, is meant to be read aloud or recited, like the original poem.

Anonymous. *A Gest of Robyn Hode*. In *Robin Hood and Other Outlaw Tales*. Edited by Stephen Knight and Thomas H. Ohlgren, pp. 80–168. Kalamazoo, MI: Medieval Institute Publications, 2000. Essential reading for Lecture 9. Text and notes available at http://www.lib.rochester.edu/camelot/teams/gest.htm.

Anonymous. *The Poetic Edda*. Translated by W. H. Auden and P. B. Taylor as *Norse Poems*. London: Athlone, 1981. Essential reading for Lecture 8. Other modern translations include those by Patricia Terry (1969) and Carolyne Larrington (1996), but *Norse Poems* is the work of a great poet in his own right.

Arnold, Martin. *Thor: From Myth to Marvel*. New York: Continuum, 2012. "Marvel" in the title means "Marvel Comics." A wide-ranging and up-to-date survey by a major Norse-Icelandic scholar.

Austen, Jane. *Pride and Prejudice*. 1813. Essential reading for Lecture 12. Available in many reprints.

Baring-Gould, W. S. *Sherlock Holmes of Baker Street: The Life of the World's First Consulting Detective*. New York: C. N. Potter, 1962. The best of many half-serious accounts of the detective as a real person.

Bates, Gerri. *Alice Walker: A Critical Companion*. Westport, CT: Greenwood Press, 2005. A good scholarly account of Walker's works as a whole, including *The Color Purple*.

Bettelheim, Bruno. *The Uses of Enchantment: The Meaning and Importance of Fairy Tales*. London: Thames and Hudson, 1976. A groundbreaking study, by a practicing psychiatrist, of the classic fairy tales, as discussed in Lecture 22. Stresses their therapeutic value.

Bradford, Ernle. *Ulysses Found*. London: Hodder & Stoughton, 1963. An attempt to trace Odysseus's route by an author who is amateur scholar and an experienced small-boat sailor.

Byron, W. *Cervantes: A Biography*. Garden City, NY: Doubleday, 1978. The best account in English of the eventful life of this major author.

Carter, Angela. *The Bloody Chamber and Other Stories*. New York: Penguin, 1990. The most important collection of the five listed as essential reading for Lecture 22.

Cervantes, Miguel de. *Don Quixote*. Translated by John Rutherford, London: Penguin Classics, 2000. Essential reading for Lecture 10. The best and most modern translation.

Chadwick-Joshua, Jocelyn. *The Jim Dilemma: Reading Race in Huckleberry Finn*. Jackson: University of Mississippi Press, 1998. Scholarly study of one aspect of Huck's "odyssey."

Chaucer, Geoffrey. *Troilus and Criseyde*. Edited by Stephen A. Barney. New York: Norton, 2006. Essential reading for Lecture 6. A modernized translation by A. S. Kline is available online at http://www.poetryintranslation.com/ PITBR/English/TroilusandCressidaBkI.htm.

———. *The Wife of Bath's Prologue and Tale*. Edited by Valerie Allen and David Kirkham. Cambridge: Cambridge University Press, 1998. Essential reading for Lecture 5. Also recommended is a lively verse translation of *The*

Canterbury Tales as a whole by Tolkien's friend Nevill Coghill (London and New York, Penguin Classics, 2003).

Chrétien de Troyes. *Arthurian Romances*. Translated by D. D. R. Owen. London: Dent; New Clarendon, VT: Tuttle, 1987. Essential reading for Lecture 4.

Clements, Susannah. *The Vampire Defanged: How the Embodiment of Evil Became a Romantic Hero*. Grand Rapids, MI: Brazos Press, 2011. A good study of the whole "literary vampire" phenomenon.

Colebatch, Hal G. P. *Return of the Heroes: The Lord of the Rings, Star Wars, Harry Potter, and Social Conflict*. Christchurch, New Zealand: Cybereditions, 2003. A combative defense of the value of popular heroic fictions, arguing that they have had a major cultural influence in countering the views of liberal elites.

Cooper, James Fenimore. *The Deerslayer*. 1841. Essential reading for Lecture 13. Available in many reprints.

———. *The Last of the Mohicans*. 1826. Essential reading for Lecture 13. Available in many reprints. The best known of Cooper's works.

———. *The Pathfinder*. 1840. Essential reading for Lecture 13. Available in many reprints.

Crick, Bernard. *George Orwell: A Life*. Boston: Little, Brown, 1980. A detailed but rather defensive account of the creator of *Nineteen Eighty-four*, from a British and left-wing perspective.

Cross, T. P., and W. A. Nitze. *Lancelot and Guenevere: A Study on the Origins of Courtly Love*. New York: Phaeton, 1970. Old-fashioned by academic standards but still a perceptive historical account of one of the Western world's major changes in cultural values.

Datlow, Ellen, and Terri Windling, eds. *Snow White, Blood Red.* New York: Avon, 1993. Listed as essential reading for Lecture 22 but of lesser importance than Carter above and Zipes below if one has to choose.

Davidson, Hilda R. Ellis. *Gods and Myths of Northern Europe.* Harmondsworth: Penguin, 1964. An old but lively account of the Norse gods, including Thor.

Davison, Peter H. *George Orwell: A Literary Life.* New York: St. Martin's, 1996. A tougher account than Crick above, by an independent scholar who nevertheless vastly increased the amount of Orwell material known through indefatigable personal inquiries.

Defoe, Daniel. *Robinson Crusoe.* 1719. Essential reading for Lecture 11. Available in many reprints.

Dekker, George. *James Fenimore Cooper: The American Scott.* New York: Barnes & Noble, 1967. A sound and comprehensive academic study of Cooper's many works.

Dieke, Ikenna, ed. *Critical Essays on Alice Walker.* Westport, CT: Greenwood Press, 1999. A good representative collection of modern views of this author.

Dinshaw, Carolyn. *Chaucer's Sexual Poetics.* Madison, WI: University of Wisconsin Press, 1989. An influential modern academic account of Chaucer's female characters, including the Wife of Bath.

Dobson, R. B., and John Taylor, eds. *Rymes of Robyn Hood.* Pittsburgh: University of Pittsburgh Press, 1976. Brings together much of the early Robin Hood material, with an introduction that did a great deal to set the hero in a real-life place and time.

Doyle, Sir Arthur Conan. *The Complete Adventures of Sherlock Holmes.* Edited by Julian Symons. Nationwide Book Service, 1981. There are many reprints of all the Sherlock Holmes novels and short-story collections, but this is a handy and complete set of the essential reading for Lecture 16.

Ellis, Frank H., ed. *Twentieth-Century Interpretations of Robinson Crusoe*. Englewood Cliffs, NJ: Prentice-Hall, 1969. A useful survey of academic opinions about this work, which aroused much interest in the immediate postcolonial era.

Fehrenbach, T. R. *Comanches: The Destruction of a People*. New York: Knopf, 1974. A fascinating if often horrific account of a great but perhaps inevitable tragedy.

Field, P. J. C. *The Life and Times of Sir Thomas Malory*. Cambridge: Brewer, 1993. This study disentangles the real Sir Thomas from several other possibilities and concludes that the author of *Le Morte Darthur* was, in fact, the notorious criminal. Weighs judiciously the (mostly unproved) charges against him and sets him and his family in the context of civil war.

Finley, M. I. *The World of Odysseus*. New York: Viking, 1951. Excellent study of the social institutions revealed in the poem; sets them in the context of the ancient Greek Heroic Age.

Fleming, Ian. *Casino Royale*. 1953. Essential reading for Lecture 21. The first to be published of Bond's adventures and first in terms of his own life. Available in many reprints.

———. *Dr. No*. 1958. Essential reading for Lecture 21. This, the sixth Bond novel, was possibly the one that gave him mass-market appeal with the release of the 1962 movie.

———. *From Russia with Love*. 1957. Essential reading for Lecture 21. Fifth to be published. One of President Kennedy's favorite novels.

———. *Goldfinger*. 1959. Essential reading for Lecture 21. Another of the best of Fleming's novels, seventh to be published.

Forshaw, Barry. *Death in a Cold Climate: A Guide to Scandinavian Crime Fiction*. New York: Palgrave Macmillan, 2012. A study of the phenomenon, with a chapter on Larsson.

Fox, Robin Lane. *Travelling Heroes: Greeks and Their Myths in the Epic Age of Homer*. London: Penguin, 2008. An up-to-date and scholarly account of what is known of ancient Greek voyaging in the age of Homer. Interesting complement to Bradford above.

Frederickson, George M. *The Black Image in the White Mind: The Debate on Afro-American Character and Destiny, 1817–1914*. New York: HarperCollins, 1972. A study that sets *Uncle Tom's Cabin* in a much wider context.

Fulk, R. D., ed. *Interpretations of Beowulf*. Bloomington and Indianapolis, IN: Indiana University Press, 1981. A wide-ranging collection prepared by the major living *Beowulf* scholar.

Garth, John. *Tolkien and the Great War*. London: HarperCollins, 2003. A close study of Tolkien's life and movements from 1914 to 1918 and of the poetry written in that period, during which his mythology of Middle-earth began to take shape.

Gordon, Ida L. *The Double Sorrow of Troilus*. Oxford: Clarendon, 1970. An almost line-by-line study of the poem. Follows Troilus's movement from sorrow to joy and back again to sorrow.

Gossett, Thomas F. *Uncle Tom's Cabin and American Culture*. Dallas, TX: Southern Methodist University Press, 1985. A scholarly study that sets Harriet Beecher Stowe's work in a wider context.

Graves, Robert. *Homer's Daughter*. Garden City, NY: Doubleday, 1955. An exceptionally fine historical novel by a learned writer, putting forward the view that *The Odyssey*, as we have it, must have been written by a woman.

Griffin, Jasper. *Virgil*. Oxford: Oxford University Press, 1986. A good short study of the life and works of this major author.

Haber, Karen, ed. *Meditations on Middle-Earth*. New York: St. Martin's Press, 2001. This collection brings together informed tributes to Tolkien by many successful professional authors, including Poul Anderson, Ursula Le Guin, George R. R. Martin, Terry Pratchett, and Michael Swanwick.

Hall, Edith. *The Return of Ulysses: A Cultural History of Homer's Odysseus*. Baltimore: Johns Hopkins University Press, 2008. This study covers the long reception of Homer's *Odyssey* and its hero from classical times onward.

Henryson, Robert. *Poems*. Edited by Denton Fox. Oxford: Oxford University Press, 1981. Essential reading for Lecture 6. Contains, besides the *Testament of Cresseid*, a number of other poems, including Henryson's retellings of Aesop's fables and tales of Reynard the fox.

Holt, J. C. *Robin Hood*. 2nd ed. London: Thames & Hudson, 1989. A comprehensive survey of what is known about Robin Hood and his historical context, by a major historian.

Homer. *The Odyssey*. Translated by Robert Fitzgerald. New York: Knopf, 1991. Essential reading for Lecture 2. Famous translations of the past include those by George Chapman (1616) and Alexander Pope (1725). Another good modern translation is Richmond Lattimore's (1965).

Honan, Park. *Jane Austen: Her Life*. New York: St. Martin's Press, 1987. A detailed study of the life of the author.

Hunter, Allan G. *Princes, Frogs and Ugly Sisters: The Healing Power of the Grimm Brothers' Tales*. Forres, Scotland: Findhorn, 2010. Goes on from Bettelheim above with an updated account of the tales' therapeutic value for all of us.

Inge, M. Thomas, ed. *Huck Finn among the Critics: A Centennial Selection*. Frederick, MD: University Publications of America, 1985. A good survey of the way in which Huck has been read and responded to over the century since his story was published.

Irving, E. B., Jr. *A Reading of Beowulf*. New Haven: Yale University Press, 1968. The most accessible full-length study of the poem.

Jekel, Pamela. *The Third Jungle Book*. Niwot, CO: Roberts Rinehart, 1992. Continues and amplifies Kipling's stories by creating an additional 10 stories in the spirit of the originals.

Bibliography

Keen, Maurice. *The Outlaws of Medieval England*. Rev. ed. London and New York: Routledge, 2000. A survey of the medieval outlaw tradition, of which Robin Hood is the most famous part.

Kipling, Rudyard. *The Jungle Book*. 1894. Essential reading for Lecture 18. Available in many reprints.

―――. *The Second Jungle Book*. 1895. Essential reading for Lecture 18. Available in many reprints.

Kirk, Connie Ann. *J. K. Rowling: A Biography*. Westport, CT: Greenwood, 2003. Gives an account of the creation of the Harry Potter books.

Klinger, Leslie S, ed. *The New Annotated Dracula*. New York: W. W. Norton, 2008. Useful backup to the essential reading for Lecture 17.

―――. *The New Annotated Sherlock Holmes*. New York: W. W. Norton, 2005. Useful backup to the essential reading for Lecture 16.

Kyle, Chris. *American Gun: A History of the U.S. in Ten Firearms*. New York: William Morrow, 2013. Two of the firearms discussed are the American long rifle and the early Colt revolver, both mentioned in Lecture 13.

Larsson, Stieg. *The Girl with the Dragon Tattoo*. Translated by Reg Keeland. London: MacLehose Press, 2008. Essential reading for Lecture 23. If you should choose to read only one book in the sequence, this contains all the major themes, though its focus is not initially on Lisbeth Salander.

―――. *The Girl Who Kicked the Hornet's Nest*. Translated by Reg Keeland. London: MacLehose Press, 2009. Essential reading for Lecture 23.

―――. *The Girl Who Played with Fire*. Translated by Reg Keeland. London: MacLehose Press, 2009. Essential reading for Lecture 23.

Lee, Tanith. *Red as Blood: Tales from the Sisters Grimmer*. New York: DAW Books, 1983. Listed as essential reading for Lecture 22 but of lesser importance than Carter above and Zipes below if one has to choose.

Lewis, C. S. "What Chaucer Really Did to *Il Filostrato*." In *Selected Literary Essays*, edited by Walter Hooper, pp. 27–44. Cambridge: Cambridge University Press, 1969. Compares Chaucer's poem with its source, *Il Filostrato* by the Italian poet Boccaccio, and argues that Chaucer made the story and the characters more medieval.

Lycett, Andrew. *Ian Fleming: The Man behind James Bond*. Atlanta: Turner, 1995. Gives an account of the creation of the James Bond books, drawing interesting parallels between the author's life and his fiction.

MacQueen, John. *Robert Henryson: A Study of the Major Narrative Poems*. Oxford: Clarendon, 1967. A very good if purely literary account of *The Testament of Cresseid*.

Maitland, Sara. *Gossip from the Forest: The Tangled Roots of our Forests and Fairytales*. London: Granta, 2012. Considers and rewrites 12 of the Grimm tales, relating each one to a visit to a British forest. Tales and forests exist, she argues, in a symbiotic relationship. Listed as essential reading for Lecture 22 but of lesser importance than Carter above and Zipes below if one has to choose.

Malory, Sir Thomas. *Le Morte Darthur*. Edited by Eugene Vinaver. London: Oxford University Press, 1954. The last two sections of this book, entitled by Vinaver "The Book of Sir Launcelot and Queen Guinevere" and "The Most Piteous Tale of the Morte Arthure," are essential reading for Lecture 4. They amount to some 150 pages. Also recommended is Vinaver's selection from Malory with modernized spelling, *King Arthur and His Knights* (London: Oxford University Press, 1968).

McMurtry, Larry. *Comanche Moon*. New York: Simon and Schuster, 1997. Essential reading for Lecture 13. In terms of the heroes' lives, this book is second in the series of four. If you should choose to read only one of this series, this is probably the one to pick as best describing the pivotal period of history in the American West.

————. *Dead Man's Walk.* New York: Simon and Schuster, 1995. Essential reading for Lecture 13. In terms of the heroes' lives, this book is first in the series of four.

————. *In a Narrow Grave: Essays on Texas.* Albuquerque: University of New Mexico Press, 1968. Historical essays by the author of the Lonesome Dove series.

————. *Lonesome Dove.* New York: Simon and Schuster, 1985. Essential reading for Lecture 13. In terms of the heroes' lives, this book is third in the series of four.

————. *Streets of Laredo.* New York: Simon and Schuster, 1993. Essential reading for Lecture 13. In terms of the heroes' lives, this book is last in the series of four.

Montefiore, Jan. "Kipling as a Children's Writer and *The Jungle Books.*" In *The Cambridge Companion to Rudyard Kipling.* Edited by Howard J. Booth, pp. 95–110. Cambridge: Cambridge University Press, 2011. A focused critical account of the essential reading for Lecture 18.

Niles, John D., ed. *Beowulf and Lejre.* Tempe, AZ: Arizona Center for Medieval and Renaissance Studies, 1997. An extended account of the archaeological excavations at Lejre in Denmark, which have caused a rethink of the traditional view that *Beowulf* is pure fiction, with no historical foundation.

O'Connell, Mark. *Catching Bullets: Memoirs of a Bond Fan.* London: Splendid Books, 2012. An engaging personal account of what the Bond phenomenon, franchise movies included, has meant to one fan.

O'Donoghue, Heather. *From Asgard to Valhalla: The Remarkable History of the Norse Myths.* London: J. B. Tauris, 2007. Discusses the reception and influence of Norse mythology.

Orwell, George. *Nineteen Eighty-four.* London: Secker and Warburg, 1949. Essential reading for Lecture 20. Available in many reprints. The edition by Bernard Crick (Oxford: Clarendon, 1984) can be recommended, though Davison above and Shippey below are useful correctives.

Person, Leland S., ed. *A Historical Guide to James Fenimore Cooper*. New York and London: Oxford University Press, 2007. A collection of essays on the life, works, and historical context of the author.

Pettersson, Jan-Erik. *Stieg: From Activist to Author*. Translated by Tom Geddes. London: Quercus, 2011. An interesting account of Larsson's life and background by a personal friend; does much to explain his dominant themes or obsessions.

Predmore. Richard L. *The World of Don Quixote*, Cambridge, MA: Harvard University Press, 1967. Sets Cervantes and his works in the context of his time.

Quinn, Kenneth. *Virgil's Aeneid: A Critical Description*. Ann Arbor: University of Michigan Press, 1968. A good readable account of the entire work.

Rowling, J. K. *Harry Potter and the Chamber of Secrets*. London: Bloomsbury Press, 1998. Essential reading for Lecture 24. In terms of Harry's life, second in the series of seven.

———. *Harry Potter and the Deathly Hallows*. London: Bloomsbury Press, 2007. Essential reading for Lecture 24. In terms of Harry's life, last in the series of seven.

———. *Harry Potter and the Goblet of Fire*. London: Bloomsbury Press, 2000. Essential reading for Lecture 24. In terms of Harry's life, fourth in the series of seven.

———. *Harry Potter and the Half-Blood Prince*. London: Bloomsbury Press, 2005. Essential reading for Lecture 24. In terms of Harry's life, sixth in the series of seven.

———. *Harry Potter and the Order of the Phoenix*. London: Bloomsbury Press, 2003. Essential reading for Lecture 24. In terms of Harry's life, fifth in the series of seven. If you choose to read only one of the series, this, the longest, is probably the one to pick.

———. *Harry Potter and the Prisoner of Azkaban*. London: Bloomsbury Press, 1999. Essential reading for Lecture 24. In terms of Harry's life, third in the series of seven.

———. *Harry Potter and the Sorcerer's Stone*. London: Bloomsbury Press, 1997. Essential reading for Lecture 24. In terms of Harry's life, first in the series of seven. The original U.K. title was *Harry Potter and the Philosopher's Stone*.

Saler, Michael. *As If: Modern Enchantment and the Literary History of Virtual Reality*. Oxford and New York: Oxford University Press, 2012. Chapter 3, on the Sherlock Holmes phenomenon, is especially valuable as showing perhaps the first literary character to escape from his author and take on a life of his own. Tolkien is also discussed in chapter 5.

Saxena, Vandena. *The Subversive Harry Potter: Adolescent Rebellion and Containment in the J. K. Rowling Novels*. Jefferson, NC: McFarland, 2012. Considers issues in the Harry Potter sequence.

Scheuermann, Mona. *Her Bread to Earn: Women, Money and Society from Defoe to Austen*. Lexington, KY: University Press of Kentucky, 1993. Takes up one of the themes of Lecture 12, with wider reference.

Seidel, Michael. *Robinson Crusoe: Island Myths and the Novel*. Boston: Twayne, 1991. Looks at the "desert island" motif, among others, with a focus on Defoe's story.

Shelley, Mary. *Frankenstein; or, The Modern Prometheus*. 1816. There are many reprints of the 1816 work, but the edition by Maurice Hindle (London: Penguin Classics, 2005) contains Polidori's story "The Vampyre," which is a valuable backup to Lecture 17.

Shippey, Thomas. "Variations on Newspeak: The Open Question of *Nineteen Eighty-Four*." In *Storm Warnings: Science Fiction Confronts the Future*.

Edited by George Slusser, Colin Greenland, and Eric S. Rabkin, pp. 172–193. Carbondale and Edwardsville, IL: Southern Illinois University Press, 1987. Takes up some of the issues discussed in Lecture 20 and shows how they reappear in later fiction.

———. *Beowulf*. London: Edward Arnold, 1976. An introduction to the poem for students, with the merit of being extremely short, some 60 pages.

———. *Tolkien: Author of the Century*. Boston: Houghton Mifflin, 2001. Most accessible account of Tolkien's major works, especially chapters 1 through 4.

Snorri Sturluson. *The Prose Edda*. Translated by Anthony Faulkes. London: Dent; New Clarendon, VT: Tuttle, 1987. Essential reading for Lecture 8. The main source of modern knowledge of tales about the god Thor.

Souhami, Diana. *Selkirk's Island: The True and Strange Adventures of the Real Robinson Crusoe*. New York: Harcourt, 2002. Discusses the real-life original of Defoe's hero, the Scottish sailor Alexander Selkirk.

Spargo, J. E. *Virgil the Necromancer*. Cambridge, MA: Harvard University Press, 1934. An engaging and scholarly, if oddball, account of how Aeneas's visit to the underworld was changed into legends of Virgil's magical powers. These legends in their turn influenced Dante's great poem *La Divina Commedia*.

Stegner, Paige. *Winning the Wild West: The Epic Saga of the American Frontier, 1800–1899*. New York: Free Press, 2002. A serious and up-to-date account of the true history of events described in the second section of Lecture 13.

Steiner, Enit Karafili. *Jane Austen's Civilised Women: Morality, Gender, and the Civilizing Process*. Brookfield, VT: Pickering & Chatto, 2012. A close look at what is most admirable in Austen's heroines, taken together.

Stoker, Bram. *Dracula*, 1897. Essential reading for Lecture 17. Available in many reprints. The edition by Maurice Hindle (London: Penguin Classics, 1993) has a valuable introduction.

Stowe, Harriet Beecher. *Uncle Tom's Cabin*, 1852. Essential reading for Lecture 14. Available in many reprints.

Sutherland, John. *Who Betrays Elizabeth Bennet? Further Puzzles in Classic Fiction*. Oxford and New York: Oxford University Press, 1999. Starts off with a consideration of one unexplained question in the essential reading for Lecture 12: Who alerted Lady Catherine to Elizabeth's developing relationship with her nephew? Other puzzles concern Sherlock, Dracula, Huck, and Jim.

Tolkien, J.R.R. *The Hobbit*. London: George Allen & Unwin, 1937. Essential reading for Lecture 1. Available in many reprints.

———. *The Lord of the Rings*. 3 vols. London: George Allen & Unwin, 1954–1955. Essential reading for Lecture 1. Available in many reprints.

———. *The Monsters and the Critics*. Edited by Christopher Tolkien. London: George Allen & Unwin, 1983. Contains, among other essays, Tolkien on *Beowulf*, said to be the most-cited academic article of all time, and Tolkien on the importance of fairy tales.

Twain, Mark. *The Adventures of Huckleberry Finn*. 1884. Essential reading for Lecture 15. Available in many reprints.

———. *The Adventures of Tom Sawyer*. 1876. Essential reading for Lecture 15. Available in many reprints.

Virgil (Publius Vergilius Maro). *The Aeneid*. Translated by Robert Fitzgerald. New York: Knopf, 1990. Essential reading for Lecture 3. Other translations include John Dryden's of 1697 and three from the 21st century, by Robert Fagles (2006), Fredercik Ahl (2007), and Sarah Ruden (2009).

Walker, Alice. *The Color Purple*. New York: Harcourt Brace Jovanovich, 1983. Essential reading for Lecture 19.

Walters, Lori J., ed. *Lancelot and Guinevere: A Casebook*. New York: Garland, 1996. Collection of essays centered on the relationship and characters discussed in Lecture 4.

Williamson, Edwin. *The Half-Way House of Fiction: Don Quixote and Arthurian Romance*. Oxford: Oxford University Press, 1984. Relates the subjects of Lectures 10 and 4 and points to the sources of Cervantes's work and the origins of Don Quixote's derangement.

Zipes, Jack, ed. *Don't Bet on the Prince: Contemporary Feminist Fairy Tales in North America and England*. New York: Methuen, 1987. The second most important collection of the five listed as essential reading for Lecture 22.

Notes

Notes

Notes

Notes